D1546211

The Conservative Revolution of Antonin Scalia

The Conservative Revolution of Antonin Scalia

Edited by
David A. Schultz and
Howard Schweber

LEXINGTON BOOKS
Lanham • Boulder • New York • London

Published by Lexington Books
An imprint of The Rowman & Littlefield Publishing Group, Inc.
4501 Forbes Boulevard, Suite 200, Lanham, Maryland 20706
www.rowman.com

Unit A, Whitacre Mews, 26-34 Stannary Street, London SE11 4AB

British Library Cataloguing in Publication Information Available

Library of Congress Cataloging-in-Publication Data

Names: Scalia, Antonin, author. | Schultz, David A. (David Andrew), 1958– editor. | Schweber, Howard H., editor.
Title: The conservative revolution of Antonin Scalia / edited by David A. Schultz and Howard Schweber.
Description: Lanham : Lexington Books, [2018] | Includes bibliographical references and index.
Identifiers: LCCN 2018022772 (print) | LCCN 2018031412 (ebook) | ISBN 9781498564496 (Electronic) | ISBN 9781498564489 (cloth : alk. paper) |
Subjects: LCSH: Scalia, Antonin—Criticism and interpretation. | Scalia, Antonin—Political and social views. | Judicial opinions—United States. | Political questions and judicial power—United States. | Conservatism—United States. | Judges—United States. | United States. Supreme Court—Officials and employees—Biography.
Classification: LCC KF8745.S33 (ebook) | LCC KF8745.S33 S33 2018 (print) | DDC 347.73/2634—dc23
LC record available at https://lccn.loc.gov/2018022772

Contents

Introduction   Assessing Antonin Scalia's Place in Supreme
                Court History   vii
                David Schultz and Howard Schweber

1   Scalia, Sissies, and Administrative Law   1
     David Schultz

2   Justice Scalia's Modest Employment Discrimination Law Legacy   19
     Henry L. Chambers Jr.

3   Playing Defense in the "Culture Wars": Justice Scalia on Race,
     Gender, and Sexual Orientation   47
     Mary Welek Atwell

4   Justice Scalia and Criminal Justice: A Mixed Record with
     Conservative Impact   67
     Christopher E. Smith and Charles F. Jacobs

5   Threat and Suspicion: Scalia's Legacy for a Transnational
     Judicial Dialogue   93
     Maureen Stobb

6   The Anti-Madison: Antonin Scalia's Theory of Politics   125
     Howard Schweber

7   Justice Scalia and the Legal Conservative Movement:
     An Exploration of Nino's Neoconservatism   155
     Jesse Merriam

8   Justice Scalia and the Originalist Fallacy   189
     Stephen M. Feldman

9 The Jurisprudence of Justice Scalia: Common-Law Judging
Behind an Originalist Façade   219
Ronald Kahn and Gerard Michael D'Emilio

10 Justice Scalia and Oral Arguments at the Supreme Court   245
Timothy R. Johnson, Ryan C. Black, and Ryan J. Owens

11 Justice Scalia's Concurring Opinion Writing   273
Ryan J. Owens and Christopher J. Krewson

12 Justice Scalia's Confirmation Hearing Legacy   293
Alexander Denison and Justin Wedeking

13 Was Antonin Scalia a "Great" Supreme Court Justice?   315
James Staab

Index   351

About the Contributors   371

Introduction

Assessing Antonin Scalia's
Place in Supreme Court History

David Schultz and Howard Schweber

Upon his death and in the memorials and eulogies, many conservatives lauded Antonin Scalia as one of the greatest justices to ever serve on the Supreme Court (Calabresi and Braga 2015, 796). He was described as the intellectual leader of the conservatives from 1986 to 1996, serving as the fulcrum and force that pushed the Supreme Court into a clearly conservative direction. His influence on the Court included his impact on several substantive areas of the law including the Second Amendment, criminal law, free speech, and administrative law. He was the voice of opposition when it came to gay rights and marriage, abortion, and the death penalty. But Scalia was also renowned for his acerbic, often biting opinions that attacked the other justices. He was as legendary in dominating oral arguments with his battery of questions as Clarence Thomas was for his silence. He was a polarizing figure in terms of how he was assessed.

Scalia's influence extended beyond the bench. He was one of the founders and leaders of the Federalist Society, a powerful and influential coalition of lawyers, law students, and academics, which articulated and moved the law in a conservative direction. There were also his many speeches and television interviews, which practically made him a pop culture celebrity, perhaps rivaling or surpassing the status of the "Notorious RGB" that Ruth Bader Ginsburg had acquired. Given all of that, it is no surprise that some labeled Antonin Scalia the "intellectual leader of the Supreme Court" and who was the "most visible and influential teacher of American law to sit on the U.S. Supreme Court since Justice Joseph Story" (Calabresi and Braga 2015, 796, 803).

Many hoped or feared that Antonin Scalia's appointment to the Supreme Court in 1986 would guarantee a conservative counter-revolution that would reverse the liberal jurisprudence of the Supreme Court under Chief Justice Earl Warren and which was continued to some extent under the Burger

Court through the influence of Justice William Brennan. Yet by the time of his death in 2016 it was unclear to what extent Scalia had affected the legal revolution anticipated. While the Court did move to the right and reverse or modify many Warren-Burger precedents, both acts or events were already occurring before Scalia took the bench, raising questions regarding the depth or scope of his contribution or impact. Early on in his service on the Court William Brennan still dominated, managing to achieve a few more liberal victories perhaps beyond what anyone expected. Moreover, in his early years on the Court, Scalia, much like William Rehnquist, when he was an associate justice on the Burger Court, was often the lone dissenter in cases. But even over time, Scalia was often challenged by others as the leader of the Court. Anthony Kennedy throughout most of his time served as perhaps the most important swing justice, casting the deciding 5–4 vote in many of the most landmark cases since his appointment in 1988. Finally, with his appointment to the Court as chief justice in 2005, John Roberts too has assumed a leadership position that challenges the alleged importance that Antonin Scalia presumably had.

While Scalia's proclivity in oral arguments and sting in his opinions, mostly dissents, may have earned him headlines in the news, they also often guaranteed that he would be alone (or joined by Clarence Thomas) in his views. Unlike Brennan, who was legendary in his ability to win over others and build coalitions, Scalia was not famous for that. His professorial attitude toward others may have cost him influence and majorities.

Overall, Scalia's influence on the Court may have turned out to be far less than it could have been, and his ability to persuade other justices to adopt his legal views—both substantively and methodologically—was perhaps less than many mainstream media accounts recognize. The fact that his death and the controversy surrounding his replacement was so intense speaks to the fragile legacy that Scalia really has had on the Supreme Court after thirty years. Now that Neal Gorsuch has replaced him, there is no guarantee that he will follow in the footsteps of Scalia. Moreover, the retirement and replacement of Anthony Kennedy or Ruth Bader Ginsburg are perhaps far more of a consequential institutional or ideological shift in the Court than what was seen by Scalia. If, as the old adage goes, the Supreme Court follows elections returns, then the 2016, 2018, and perhaps 2020 elections will be more determinative in terms of determining the influence and legacy of Antonin Scalia.

The purpose of this book is to assess Scalia's legacy. It assembles leading legal and judicial scholars who evaluate his views and impact across a range of jurisprudential issues. Certainly, it is not possible to cover all areas of law or all the issues upon which Scalia had a possible impact. It is more selective. It collects a range of scholars' thoughts on the legal, political, and intellectual legacies of the late Supreme Court Justice Antonin Scalia. The approaches in these essays are motivated by a perspective rooted in the methods and intellectual approaches of political science, written by scholars whose studies of courts and judicial opinions goes beyond a review of legal doctrine to consider institutional, political, and intellectual contexts of Justice Scalia's judicial reasoning. While some of the essays focus on the development of constitutional jurisprudence, others ask broader questions about Scalia's ideas and actions as they relate to events and actors outside the courts. Additionally, some of the essays look at institutional issues, such as oral arguments, the confirmation process, judicial review of administrative agencies, or constitutional interpretation. These are topics that address both institutional-political issues as well as questions that explore the interaction of law and politics.

In considering Scalia's legacy for constitutional law, David Schultz focuses on administrative law. While for many, and Scalia even acknowledges this in one of his most famous speeches and articles, administrative law is seen as a dry and unappealing subject, the topic of the relationship between administrative agency interpretation of the law and what type of deference, if any, the courts should give to such interpretations, raises important questions about separation of powers, judicial review, and the respective powers of Congress and the president. It is about institutional power. Prior to Scalia becoming a Supreme Court Justice, he was an administrative law professor, the chair of the American Bar Association's section on administrative law and worked for and counseled administrative agencies at the federal level. He was considered by many to be the leading administrative law expert in the country. If there is any area where Scalia's footprint should be greatest it would be in this subject. In assessing Scalia's legacy Schultz examines how the Justice embraced *Chevron. v. Natural Resources Defense Council*, 468 U.S. 1227 (1984). While this Stevens' majority opinion was decided before Scalia joined the Supreme Court, the latter came to be identified with the opinion and employed it in an effort to imprint the law with his vision of administrative law and separation of powers. Schultz argues that as Justice Scalia had to contend with others in terms of securing institutional support for his views, it is not clear that he prevailed either during his time on the bench or that his views will necessarily survive beyond him.

Henry Chambers looks at Scalia's influence in the area of employment discrimination law. Many of the issues in this important area turn on the interpretation and application of statutes rather the constitutional provisions. True to his principles, Scalia generally adopted a "light touch" in considering these cases where questions of substantive legal rights were concerned. However, Chambers finds that Scalia was far more prescriptive where the issue concerned procedural questions that determined access to courts by individuals or groups trying to assert claims. As a result, Chambers concludes that Scalia's influence on the future development of procedural doctrines is likely to be greater than his contribution to the development of substantive doctrines. More specifically, Scalia consistently crafted rules that would narrow the possibilities of bringing claims to court, both by limiting the terms on which claims can be brought and by strengthening the force of arbitration agreements that prevent judicial determinations of specific disputes.

Mary Welek Atwell contributes an evaluation of Scalia's jurisprudence in the general area of Equal Protection, with a particular focus on his treatment of issues concerning race, gender, and sexual orientation. Atwell finds that Scalia's positions in these areas were consistently "conservative" in the sense of preserving the status quo against potentially transformative equality claims. Specifically, Scalia leaves a doctrinal legacy of limiting gains to race rather than extending protections of gender and, especially, rejecting the idea that there is a compelling interest in preventing discrimination on the basis of sexual orientation. Reviewing these positions, Atwell further finds that Scalia's analyses in case opinions cannot be explained by his avowed principles of interpretation. Instead, Atwell presents a persuasive case that Scalia's views on equal protection questions were powerfully driven by his positions in the politics of American culture wars.

Christopher Smith and Charles Jacobs review Scalia's influence on our understanding of the rights of individuals who become involved in the criminal justice system. One might expect that as a political conservative Justice Scalia would have authored opinions that gave the greatest possible latitude to agents of the government, and in many cases this supposition was confirmed. Scalia sided with individuals in criminal justice cases less than 20 percent of the time. Where the issues before the Court involved the Eighth Amendment's prohibition on cruel and unusual punishment, the application of equal protection principles to the criminal justice system, or the general interpretation of the procedural rights afforded to criminal defendants, Scalia's opinions consistently pushed the Court in the politically conservative direction that one might have expected. On the other hand, where the Fourth Amendment was concerned, Scalia's preferred approach led to a more complex pattern of outcomes. In a number of controversial cases Scalia joined with colleagues usually regarded as liberal to limit the authority of the police, especially with respect to the constitutional limits on police searches. The fact that in this area of jurisprudence Scalia's originalism and textualism led him to "liberal" conclusion has been used to strengthen the claim that those methods of constitutional interpretation are at least potentially politically neutral. Nonetheless, in the authors' view the results in Fourth Amendment cases are more the exception than the rule, as, in general, Scalia's influence and his legacy for criminal justice jurisprudence was to move the Court toward more conservative outcomes.

Another contribution that considers Scalia's legacy for legal doctrine is Maureen Stobb's discussion of Scalia's resistance to the use of foreign law. While there are no cases in which the Supreme Court has relied on foreign law as a source of direct authority, there has been a trend toward increasing discussion of non-American sources in judicial opinions and a possibility (difficult to quantify) that those sources are influential on judicial reasoning. Maureen Stobb also considers Scalia's legacy for legal doctrine, adopting an empirical approach to analyzing the impact of Scalia's resistance to the use of foreign law. The Supreme Court increasingly discusses non-American sources in its opinions, but the influence of this trend on the reasoning of higher and lower court judges has yet to be determined. Stobb assesses the extent to which Scalia succeeded in shaping the use of foreign law, finding that he encouraged citation to English common-law, but failed to dissuade his fellow justices from employing the laws of other nations in interpreting the U.S. Constitution. In addition, her results indicate that, controlling for relevant factors, a reference to foreign law in a Supreme Court opinion is associated with a significant increase in the number of total citations to that precedent before and after Scalia joined the Court. Thus, although Scalia succeeded in drawing attention to the strategic use of foreign sources to achieve policy goals, he failed to remove the incentive to continue the practice.

Two of the chapters presented in this collection examine Scalia's role as a public intellectual and his legacy for American politics both on and off the Court. Howard Schweber considers a largely tacit dimension of Scalia's thinking, his views on the form of democratic politics that the Constitution supports or requires what he calls "constitutionalist politics." Schweber finds that Scalia's approach is fundamentally "anti-Madisonian" in that Scalia rejected Madison's key concerns: the dangers of faction and the need for virtue in political representatives. In Schweber's analysis, Scalia did not merely deny that the Constitution requires attention to such Madisonian concerns, he affirmatively claimed that the virtues of democratic politics inhere in the rejection of Madison's core principles. Schweber finds illustrations of Scalia's normative political standards in a range of areas, particularly cases involving First Amendment claims, laws regulating political practice, and minority protections. Ultimately, Schweber finds that Scalia valorized a form of politics marked by tribalistic competition for domination by local majorities through any means available, a conception of politics that Schweber asserts was inimical to Madison's vision of the system of constitutional government.

Jesse Merriam reviews Scalia's transformative influence on the intellectual underpinnings of American conservatives. Merriam describes Scalia as an intellectual entrepreneur who pursued a deliberate strategy to influence conservative thinking. Specifically, Merriam finds that Scalia's intellectual home was the branch of conservative thought known as neoconservatism, an approach to political ideas that emphasizes a "redemptive" narrative in which wrong elements must be purged from the movement and by extension from the politics that it supports. In Merriam's illuminating reading, this narrative connects Scalia's judicial politics with his political ideology. The influence of Scalia's and others' influence on American conservatism has been profound, and the connections between political neoconservatism and the form of judicial conservatism displayed by current justices including Scalia's successor are deeply entwined with a larger and extrajudicial political narrative.

Two chapters specifically address Scalia's commitment to originalism and textualism as modes of constitutional and statutory interpretation. It may be difficult for modern readers to remember the extent to which Scalia, along with Robert Bork and Edwin Meese, made originalism a prominent—indeed, publicly the best known—mode of constitutional reasoning starting in the early 1980s, and how radical a departure that was from the intellectual fashions of the preceding decades. Through the force of his writing and speeches, his role in creating and promoting the Federalist Society, and his mentoring of individuals who went on to have judicial careers, Scalia was a major influence in this regard. But to what extent was Scalia, himself, truly an originalist, and what did that term mean applied to his particular approach to constitutional reasoning?

Stephen Feldman finds that Scalia's success in this endeavor is essentially "Machiavellian" in that Scalia was successful in persuading judges and the general public despite neither following an originalist approach consistently nor adequately explaining its premises in his own writings. Feldman traced the evolution of originalist theories from original intent to original meaning to a combination of lexicographical textualism and an imagined "reasonable historical actor" standard. Reviewing Scalia's reasoning in a series of cases across a range of doctrinal areas, however, Feldman finds that none of these originalisms characterizes the arguments presented. Instead, Feldman concludes that Scalia's rulings were directly motivated by political ends, leaving a legacy of public rhetoric of originalism that opened the door for a hidden politicization of judicial reasoning.

Ronald Kahn and Gerard Michael D'Emilio focus on the inherent tension between Scalia's two methodological commitments: textualism and originalism. Applying and building on a sophisticated model developed elsewhere, Kahn and D'Emilio find that these two potentially opposing principles existed in a state of "balanced realism" characterized by a "bidirectional" approach in which historical sources and the text mutually informed one another. Among other places, the authors find evidence of this approach in Scalia's controversial opinion finding an individual right to bear arms under the Second Amendment. While that opinion is controversial, however, the authors ultimately conclude that the differences between Scalia's approach and that of other justices was more a difference of degree than a genuine divergence in basic approach. Scalia favored formalistic rules and historical analyses more than some of his colleagues, to be sure, but in the practice of writing judicial opinions Scalia acted as a common law judge applying a complex mixture of principles and sources to the case at hand. In this respect Scalia's legacy for constitutionalism is more an affirmation of the consistency of the intellectual roots of American jurisprudence than any kind of a sharp break.

A third set of contributions focus on Scalia's influence on institutional practices. Tim Johnson, Ryan Black and Ryan Owens study Scalia's influence on the practices of oral argument in the current Court. Johnson uses empirical analysis, coding for frequency of speaking, frequency of interruption of other justices, and use of harsh verbiage during oral arguments. Johnson then studies the conduct of other justices to see whether Scalia's behavior influenced that of others. His conclusions will be reassuring to some readers, perhaps less so to others; the data show that while Scalia's conduct significantly affected that of his colleagues during his tenure there is little evidence of a lasting impact. The institutional norms of polite discourse may be more robust than many observers may have expected.

Ryan Owens and Christopher Krewson focus on Scalia's practices in writing concurring opinions. The practice of writing concurrences is understudied, with the result that there is not a clear understanding of what motivates justices to author concurrences. Using Scalia as a test case, Owens and Krewson find that the late justice was more likely to write concurring opinions when he was ideologically distant from the majority position, when he needed to rebut dissents, in salient cases, and when the Court altered precedent. On the other hand, and contrary to expectations, the clarity or force of the majority opinion had no clear relationship to Scalia's decision to author a concurrence, nor did the point in the term, past patterns of cooperation, or a variety of other variables for which the authors controlled. Finally, Owens and Krewson note that Scalia was an unusually prolific writer of concurrences and that more generally the practice has become more common in recent years. The likelihood, therefore, is that going forward Scalia's legacy will be felt in the form of frequent concurrences by justices who share his ideological commitments. Whether the pattern of motivating factors will be the same for others as it was for Justice Scalia is a question to be determined; this chapter thus ends with an invitation for valuable future research.

Alexander Denison and Justin Wedeking focus on a different kind of institutional element, specifically the process of confirmation hearings in the U.S. Senate. Scalia's own hearing followed the extremely contentious hearings addressing the nomination of Robert Bork. Surprisingly, Scalia's own confirmation hearing was relatively placid, particularly by comparison, despite the fact that Scalia was no less committed to the same judicial conservatism with which Bork was associated. Subsequent hearings, however, have been both contentious and marked by high levels of ideological conflict. Denison and Wedeking conclude that the anomalous event was Scalia's confirmation and that despite the lack of conflict at that hearing both the event and Scalia's own later influence helped usher in an era of highly partisan ideological examinations of judicial candidate, a development of which Scalia himself personally approved.

Finally, James Staab attempts to give a rigorous treatment to the kind of question that is more often treated as the subject of intellectual parlor games: Was Scalia a great justice? To answer this question Staab sets out a set of criteria for greatness, then evaluates Scalia on each dimension. Staab also considers specific aspects of Scalia's work that might prevent him from being assessed as "great," including his tendency to divide himself from other justices and his tendency to side with a position that stood against developing trends in constitutional law. Staab's conclusions invite discussion and perhaps disagreement, but his approach suggests a way to get beyond mere opinion in addressing this favorite question of Supreme Court historians.

Overall, the essays in this volume may not be the final word on Scalia's legacy or place in history. History of course will eventually answer that question. Nor are the essays here exhaustive of all the topics or areas of law from which one can examine the legacy of this justice. However, collectively they do offer a rich perspective and assessment of Antonin Scalia that raise questions regarding whether he was among the greatest justices ever on the Supreme Court, or even its intellectual leader.

REFERENCES

Calabresi, Steven G., and Justin Braga. (2015). "The Jurisprudence of Justice Antonin Scalia." *New York University Journal of Law & Liberty* 9: 793–849.

Chapter 1

Scalia, Sissies, and Administrative Law

David Schultz

Was Antonin Scalia a sissy when it came to administrative law? Among the numerous quotes attributed to him, perhaps one of the most famous is from a 1989 *Duke Law Journal* article of his where Justice Scalia declared that "Administrative law is not for sissies" (Scalia 1989, 511). He warned his audience (the article was based on a lecture he gave) to "lean back, clutch the sides of your chairs, and steel yourselves for a pretty dull lecture" (511). If anything, Scalia's tenure on the Supreme Court was anything but dull. Instead, depending on whom one spoke to, the assessment of his influence and role ran the gamut, often along ideological lines.

Scalia's impact on the Supreme Court is part fact, part fiction, or perhaps a contrast in fact versus fiction. To many Republicans or conservatives, he ranks among the greatest justices ever, the intellectual leader of the Supreme Court for nearly thirty years, To Democrats and liberals, he will be remembered for his assault on reproductive, gay, and civil rights, in general, and his role in *Bush v. Gore*, 531 U.S. 98 (2000), which halted the Florida 2000 presidential recount, will forever be remembered as him and his Republican colleagues putting George Bush in the White House. Apart from an occasional liberal outcome in criminal due process (offset by his support for the death penalty), he was the kind of conservative appointment expected from President Ronald Reagan. He was a reliable vote for conservative causes, including in administrative law. Proof of that was that one of his very last votes on the bench before he died was in *West Virginia, et al. v. EPA*, 577 U.S. (2016), halting Obama executive orders regulating emissions from power plants. Scalia's legacy may well be summed up by Murphy (2014) who saw him as a "court of one," suggesting that his effort to dominate the Supreme Court and other justices resulted in him alienating his colleagues, rendering him less influential than he could have been.

What impact Scalia made on the Supreme and lower federal courts, and his legacy lasting beyond his life, are very much contested, as evidenced by other chapters in this volume. But if there was one area where his legacy and impact was certain and greatest, one would think it would be in administrative law. Scalia's administrative law bio is impressive. As stated by Richard Pierce in a memorial tribute:

> Justice Antonin Scalia contributed more to the development of administrative law than any other Justice in history. His contributions began long before his three decades of service on the Supreme Court. He was Chairman of the Administrative Conference of the United States—the government think tank that conducts studies of the administrative process and recommends best practices to agencies, Congress, and reviewing courts. He taught administrative law at University of Chicago and University of Virginia, where he made path-breaking contributions to administrative law scholarship. Before he was elevated to the Supreme Court, he served as a member of the Court of Appeals for the District of Columbia Circuit—the court that decides far more administrative law cases than any other. (2016, 66)

Scalia, too, fancied himself an administrative law expert (1987; 1989a), and beyond he and Pierce, others contend that this is the area of law where the justice's impact was greatest. But was it?

In many ways, Scalia's reputation as the administrative law justice is connected to an important case decided in1984, two years before his ascent to the Supreme Court. The case is *National Resources Defense Council v. Chevron,* 467 U.S. 837 (1984). *Chevron*, authored by Justice Stevens, is a legendary case, described by Cass Sunstein as the "counter Marbury," because of the rule it articulated regarding judicial deference to administrative agency construction of unclear congressional statute (Sunstein 2006a: 2589). The connection of Scalia to *Chevron* is supposedly about how he and the case redefined the role of the Supreme Court vis-à-vis administrative agencies, the executive branch, and Congress.

This chapter examines Scalia's impact and legacy in the field of administrative law. To do that, the approach will be to use the justice's connection to *Chevron* as a means of evaluating both his impact and legacy. The use of the *Chevron* case is shorthand or proxy for looking at three components in terms of how to assess Scalia in terms of whether he was the reputed leader in the field of administrative law. The argument will be that: (1) Scalia did not prevail in terms of direction of how the Supreme Court moved doctrinally in administrative law; (2) the *Chevron* method that he proposed was not a neutral interpretive tool; and (3) *Chevron*'s waning influence, both while Scalia was on the Court and perhaps since his departure, questions the legacy of him in administrative law.

CHEVRON AND JUDICIAL REVIEW OF ADMINISTRATIVE AGENCIES

Four characteristics have often defined Scalia's jurisprudential vision (Schultz and Smith 1996). They are his commitment to separation of powers, statutory textualism, constitutional originalism, and his questioning of New Deal legal theory.

In cases such as *Synar v. United States*, 626 F.Supp. 1374 (D.D.C 1986) (while still serving on the D.C. Court of Appeals), *Morrison v. Olson*, 487 U.S. 654 (1988), and *Mistretta v. United States*, 488 U.S. 361 (1989), Scalia carved out for himself a role as someone who strictly interpreted or ruled on matters supporting separation of powers as a major constitutional principle. That adherence to separation of powers continued late into his Supreme Court career in cases such as *Blakely v. Washington*, 542 U.S. 296 (2004) (Scalia majority opinion), and *United States v. Booker*, 543 U.S. 220 (2005). Scalia defined himself as a textualist when it came to statutory interpretation, eschewing searches for congressional intent:

> And to tell the truth, the quest for the "genuine" legislative intent is probably a wild-goose chase anyway. In the vast majority of cases I expect that Congress neither (1) intended a single result, nor (2) meant to confer discretion upon the agency, but rather (3) didn't think about the matter at all. (Scalia 1989a, 517)

Scalia also defined himself as a constitutional originalist, although a "faint-hearted" one (Scalia 1989b). Finally, his commitment to these principles came together in terms of how his jurisprudence questioned the role administrative agencies and decisions since the New Deal fit into a constitutional originalism.

One of the defining tasks for the Supreme Court since the New Deal has been reconciling administrative decision making with the Constitution. Constitutional law courses and books tell the story of the First and Second New Deal where in cases such as initially in *Schechter Poultry v. United States*, 295 U.S. 495 *(*1935), the Supreme Court invalidated parts of Roosevelt's first New Deal legislation on both delegation and separation of powers grounds. Whereas in later cases such as the *National Labor Relations Board v. Jones and McLaughlin*, 301 U.S. 1 (1937), the Court upheld the Second New Deal legislation, turning back the delegation and separation of powers issues in an almost identical fact patterns to *Schechter* and other earlier Second New Deal cases.

The point here is that one of the challenges for the judiciary in the New Deal administrative state era is how judges should address the issue of congressional delegation of rulemaking to administrative agencies and, with that, how to determine whether agencies were correctly construing congressional laws when crafting the rules. Put simply, when administrative agencies were interpreting laws of Congress, what type of deference, if at all, should the courts give to agency construction?

One early answer was supplied by the Supreme Court in *Skidmore v. Swift & Company*, 323 U.S. 134 (1944). In that case the Court declared that the level of deference given to an administrative agency's interpretation of a law would be decided case by case. Specifically, the Court said that: "The weight of such a judgment in a particular case will depend upon the thoroughness evident in its consideration, the validity of its reasoning, its consistency with earlier and later pronouncements, and all those factors which give it power to persuade, if lacking power to control" (144). The *Skidmore* persuasiveness test was the standard used for nearly forty years, but it was flawed, failing to provide guidance regarding the actual factors that would be considered and used to decide what constituted persuasiveness. The problems with that test led the Court to another articulated in *Chevron U.S.A. Inc.* v. *Natural Resources Defense Council, Inc.*, 467 U.S. 837 (1984).

Chevron involved an interpretation of the Clean Air Act Amendments of 1977, specifically regarding the creation of a permit program regulating "new or modified major stationary sources" of pollution. The issue in the case centered on an EPA interpretation of a "stationary source" and whether the EPA's decision to allow states to treat all of the pollution-emitting devices within the same industrial grouping as though they were encased within a single "bubble" is based on a reasonable construction of the statutory term "stationary source" under the amendments (839). Writing for the Court, Justice Stevens argued that the Court had long given agencies broad deference to interpret statutes and that reason was grounded in the expertise that agencies had.

> Judges are not experts in the field, and are not part of either political branch of the Government. Courts must, in some cases, reconcile competing political interests, but not on the basis of the judges' personal policy preferences. In contrast, an agency to which Congress has delegated policy-making responsibilities may, within the limits of that delegation, properly rely upon the incumbent administration's views of wise policy to inform its judgments. While agencies are not directly accountable to the people, the Chief Executive is, and it is entirely appropriate for this political branch of the Government to make such policy choices—resolving the competing interests which Congress itself either inadvertently did not resolve, or intentionally left to be resolved by the agency charged with the administration of the statute in light of everyday realities. (865–66)

Separation of powers and deference to administrative agencies that have expertise, which are accountable to the political branches, and which are better suited to address political and policy tradeoffs, should be the ones who are given deference to interpret federal laws when they are ambiguous. As formulated by Stevens, the *Chevron* test thus was:

> When a court reviews an agency's construction of the statute which it administers, it is confronted with two questions. First, always, is the question whether Congress has directly spoken to the precise question at issue. If the intent of Congress is clear, that is the end of the matter; for the court, as well as the agency, must give effect to the unambiguously expressed intent of Congress. If, however, the court determines Congress has not directly addressed the precise question at issue, the court does not simply impose its own construction on the statute, as would be necessary in the absence of an administrative interpretation. Rather, if the statute is silent or ambiguous with respect to the specific issue, the question for the court is whether the agency's answer is based on a permissible construction of the statute. (842–43)

The *Chevron* test was thus a two-step process. If the law is clear, then the Court will interpret the statute. If unclear or ambiguous, then judicial deference to a permissible agency construction of the law.

While *Chevron* did not explicitly overrule *Skidmore*, it articulated a new standard or rule of deference that was more generalizable than the old one. It was also a rule of deference compatible with textualism and separation of powers. Therefore, Scalia liked the *Chevron* rule. As noted above, Scalia argued that the search for legislative intent is often a futile process, and the courts should adopt the rule that Congress intended for an administrative agency to make the interpretative choice.

Scalia described *Chevron* as one of the most important administrative law cases ever (Scalia 1989a, 512). He sees the justification for the rule as first located in "the constitutional principle of separation of powers" (515). By that, when Congress, according to Scalia, leaves some policy questions unanswered or open and leaves it to the executive branch to resolve, then the judiciary, out of respect to the policy branches, should defer to administrative agency construction of ambiguous laws, so long as their interpretation is reasonable (515). Second, for *Chevron* deference to make sense there must be ambiguity in congressional intent. Given Scalia's skepticism regarding ascertaining legislative intent, *Chevron* makes sense. By that, if one is a plain language devotee or textualist when it comes to reading statutes (because it is hard to determine legislative intent) then deferring to administrative agencies to construe statutes when their plain language meaning is indeterminate is a consistent strategy.

In sum, Scalia's affinity for the *Chevron* doctrine lies in his skepticism toward the politics that has undermined Congress and the legislative process and in his preference for an efficient means to address statutory silence or ambiguity. Given what he views as the fragmented nature of policy-making, searching for a unified intent is impossible, especially if that search involves an appeal to legislative history, including recourse to committee reports, and statements of representatives, among other things. *Chevron* makes sense for Scalia because of his skepticism of determining the intent of Congress as well as his belief in separation of powers, congressional delegation, and textualism. According to Scalia, the *Chevron* precedent offers a consistent approach that the judiciary ought to apply when seeking the meaning of federal statutes.

Even though *Chevron* was not Scalia's decision, he embraced it and it became inextricably identified with his administrative law jurisprudence. But did Scalia "own" *Chevron*? By that, was his interpretation or use of the principle the one that prevailed? No. Instead, Scalia battled with other members of the Court, including Justice Breyer, for what *Chevron* meant and how it would be applied (Clayton 2015, 9).

Prior to his appointment to the Court, Justice Stephen Breyer, in a 1986 article on *Chevron*, argued that there were two ways to read this decision. One approach, which he labeled the more complex reading, suggests that a "range of relevant factors," perhaps even the statute's legislative history, may be considered when seeking to determine if Congress delegated interpretative power to administrative agencies. There is also a simpler approach to reading *Chevron*, which Breyer connected to the Court of Appeals for the District of Columbia Circuit where Scalia sat as judge.

> Yet the language may also be read as embodying a considerably simpler approach, namely, first decide whether the statute is "silent or ambiguous with respect to the specific issue" and, if so, accept the agency's interpretation if (in light of statutory purposes) it is "reasonable." (Breyer 1986, 373)

Scalia has adopted what Breyer has characterized as the simpler reading of *Chevron*. What *Chevron* means to Scalia is that if the plain meaning of a statute is not clear, reasonable executive determinations of the statute ought to be applied and preferred over alternative interpretations. For example, in both *INS v. Cardoza Fonseca*, 480 U.S. 421 (1987) and *Sullivan v. Everhart*, 494 U.S. 83 (1990), among other decisions, Scalia cites *Chevron* to support his claims that the plain meaning advanced by Congress in its statutory language should guide judicial interpretations unless the law is ambiguous, then deference to administrative agencies should prevail—if such administrative interpretations exist.

Scalia argues that the virtue of *Chevron* does not lie solely in its respect for separation of powers (Scalia 1989a, 515–16). According to Scalia, prior to *Chevron*, the court engaged in resolving ambiguity by assuming one of two things:

> Congress intended a particular result, but was not clear about it, or (2) Congress had no particular intent on the subject, but meant to leave its resolution to an agency. . . . *Chevron*, however, if it is to be believed, replaced this statute-by-statute evaluation (which was assuredly a font of uncertainty and litigation) with an across-the-board presumption that, in the case of ambiguity, agency discretion is meant. (Scalia 1989a, 516)

Thus, part of the appeal of *Chevron* lies in its across-the-board utility, as opposed to a pick and choose case-by-case application of deference as was the situation in *Skidmore* deference.

While Scalia acknowledges that the *Chevron* rule is not perfect, it is for him an improvement over previous judicial practices that sought to understand legislative intent on a case-by-case basis. Scalia makes a blanket and perhaps not-unfounded claim that statutory ambiguity was intended to give agencies some discretion to interpret the law. However, it is equally possible that statutory ambiguity or silence is not necessarily intended, yet results from political compromises, unforeseen situations, or the inability to resolve policy issues (Breyer 1986, 376). Alternatively, as Scalia notes, a statute's level of clarity or ambiguity may be disputed, raising questions about how definitive the *Chevron* rule is in resolving statutory meaning (Scalia 1989: 520–21). Given these options, Scalia opted to view *Chevron* as a bright-line rule of judicial deference to administrative agency interpretation of rules when it came to statutory ambiguity.

Applying *Chevron*

Did the Supreme Court adopt Scalia's reading of *Chevron* or was it out of gas from the start? To a large extent Scalia did not prevail in his reading and by the end of his time on the Court he too seemed to retreat from his broader earlier pronouncements regarding how *Chevron* deference should be applied.

Consider first *Christensen v. Harris County*, 529 U.S. 576 (2000), where at issue was the question of whether the Federal Labor Standards Act which governs overtime and pay for states and their political subdivisions prevents them from requiring employees to take comp time off to avoid overtime pay. Writing for the majority Justice Thomas held no. In reaching that decision he indicated that the Department of Labor argued that *Chevron* deference should be given to an opinion letter of theirs where they had argued that such comp time could only be mandated if the employee had agreed to such a practice in advance (586–87). Thomas rejected that, arguing that such deference was warranted only in cases where rules were promulgated by notice and comment or formal adjudication (587), and this opinion letter was not the product of either. For the Court, not every decision of an agency deserves *Chevron* deference: interpretations such as those in opinion letters—like interpretations contained in policy statements, agency manuals, and enforcement guidelines, all of which lack the force of law—do not warrant *Chevron*-style deference (587), but instead would receive *Skidmore* deference.

In a partial concurrence and dissent, Scalia, while agreeing with the holding, dissents from the reasoning, specifically disagreeing with the use of *Skidmore* deference (590–91). He reads *Chevron* as applying "to authoritative agency positions set forth in a variety of other formats," and not those just confined to the situations the majority holds (590). In dissent, Breyer agrees with Scalia that *Skidmore* may be an anachronism (596), but he did not see *Chevron* as a significant break from the past as Scalia. Instead:

> It simply focused upon an additional, separate legal reason for deferring to certain agency determinations, namely, that Congress had delegated to the agency the legal authority to make those determinations. See Chevron, supra, at 843–844, 104 S.Ct. 2778. And, to the extent there may be circumstances in which *Chevron*-type deference is inapplicable—e.g., where one has doubt that Congress actually intended to delegate interpretive authority to the agency (an "ambiguity" that *Chevron* does not presumptively leave to agency resolution)— I believe that *Skidmore* nonetheless retains legal vitality. If statutes are to serve the human purposes that called them into being, courts will have to continue to pay particular attention in appropriate cases to the experience-based views of expert agencies.

Thus, Scalia was alone in his reading of *Chevron.* He was sandwiched between a majority and a dissent that both agreed that there had to be evidence of congressional delegation to resolve ambiguities, whereas Scalia alone seemed to argue for an automatic belief in letting the executive department perform this task. For the majority and dissenters, all *Chevron* did was create a new middle step requiring proof of congressional delegation, for Scalia no such proof was needed, it was presumed that executives would be given the authority to resolve ambiguity.

Scalia again proved to be the lone dissenter in how to read *Chevron* in *United States v. Mead Corp.,* 533 U.S. 218, 229 (2001). Here Justice Souter, writing for the majority, declared that not all opinions or interpretations by administrative agencies deserve *Chevron* deference. Specifically, the majority said that: "When Congress has 'explicitly left a gap for an agency to fill, there is an express delegation of authority to the agency to elucidate a specific provision of the statute by regulation'" (227). But Souter noted also that the delegation can be implicit (228–29). In reviewing the cases that the Court, since 1984, had granted *Chevron* deference, Souter indicates that they were circumstances where rules were the product of notice and comment or formal rulemaking. Citing Breyer in *Christensen*, Souter concludes that not all interpretations are deserving of *Chevron* deference, only those where it was clear that Congress had meant to give the agency to do so, as evidenced by rulemaking or notice and comment authority, would receive such deference. In cases where *Chevron* did not apply, *Skidmore* deference would.

Scalia was the lone dissenter, reacting harshly to the majority:

> Today's opinion makes an avulsive change in judicial review of federal administrative action. Whereas previously a reasonable agency application of an ambiguous statutory provision had to be sustained so long as it represented the agency's authoritative interpretation, henceforth such an application can be set aside unless "it appears that Congress delegated authority to the agency generally to make rules carrying the force of law," as by giving an agency "power to engage in adjudication or notice-and-comment rulemaking, or . . . some other [procedure] indicat[ing] comparable congressional intent," and "the agency interpretation claiming deference was promulgated in the exercise of that authority." What was previously a general presumption of authority in agencies to resolve ambiguity in the statutes they have been authorized to enforce has been changed to a presumption of no such authority, which must be overcome by affirmative legislative intent to the contrary. (*United States v. Mead Corp.* 2001, 238)

Scalia sees the majority here returning to the *Skidmore* test, which lacked the consistency, predictability, and consistency that litigants want, and which would have forced the Court to follow its own rules (241). Scalia states in his dissent that the *Chevron* doctrine as an across the board rule is rooted in the concept that statutory ambiguity should be left to the "reasonable resolution by the executive" (243) and that the rule the majority was proposing is neither sound in principle nor practice (241). The principle is separation of powers and the idea that congressional ambiguity is best left to the agency to clarify, consistent with the process and assumptions articulated in the Administrative Procedures Act. In practice, he sees the majority opinion leading to more confusion, informal rulemaking, and statutory ossification (246–47). *Chevron* encouraged an agency dialogue with the courts and perhaps Congress to promote statutory clarification, whereas Scalia sees the majority position as discouraging that. In fact, Scalia asserted the *Christensen* opinion would result in a situation where now "I know of no case, in the entire history of the federal courts, in which we have allowed a judicial interpretation of a statute to be set aside by an agency—or have allowed a lower court to render an interpretation of a statute subject to correction by an agency" (248–49).

Finally, now consider *National Cable & Telecommunications Ass'n v. Brand X Internet Services,* 545 U.S. 967 (2005). At issue was whether a Federal Communications Commission's (FCC) declaratory ruling that cable companies providing broadband internet access did not provide "telecommunications service," as defined under Title II of Communications Act. Writing for the Court, Justice Thomas applied the *Chevron* rule and upheld the FCC ruling. In doing so, the Thomas majority stated first that Congress had in fact delegated to the FCC the authority to "'execute and enforce' the Communications Act, § 151, and to 'prescribe such rules and regulations as may be necessary in the public interest to carry out the provisions'" (980). Thus, the conditions specified under *Christensen* were met.

Second, the Court ruled that *Chevron* deference should apply instead of using the standard invoked by the Court of Appeals. The Court of Appeals had used a standard found in *AT&T Corp. v. Portland*, 216 F.3d 871 (C.A.9 2000), which had previously determined that a cable company providing broadband access was a "telecommunications service." The Court of Appeals believed that an administrative agency's construction of an ambiguous statute should not be able to trump a judicial precedent. The Thomas majority did not share this concern.

> A court's prior judicial construction of a statute trumps an agency construction otherwise entitled to Chevron deference only if the prior court decision holds that its construction follows from the unambiguous terms of the statute and thus leaves no room for agency discretion. This principle follows from Chevron itself. Chevron established a "presumption that Congress, when it left ambiguity in a statute meant for implementation by an agency, understood that the ambiguity would be resolved, first and foremost, by the agency, and desired the agency (rather than the courts) to possess whatever degree of discretion the ambiguity allows." Yet allowing a judicial precedent to foreclose an agency from interpreting an ambiguous statute, as the Court of Appeals assumed it could, would allow a court's interpretation to override an agency's. Chevron's premise is that it is for agencies, not courts, to fill statutory gaps. The better rule is to hold judicial interpretations contained in precedents to the same demanding Chevron step one standard that applies if the court is reviewing the agency's construction on a blank slate: Only a judicial precedent holding that the statute unambiguously forecloses the agency's interpretation, and therefore contains no gap for the agency to fill, displaces a conflicting agency construction. (982; citations omitted)

For the Thomas majority, *Chevron* deference should apply because it is the task of agencies and not the courts to fill in statutory gaps when there is ambiguity. Therefore, even if there is judicial precedent, and unless the court has ruled there is no ambiguity, reasonable agency interpretation should be given deference.

Scalia, dissented. In part his dissent was premised by what he saw as an unreasonable interpretation of the statute in question. But second, he objected to the majority position that allows for an agency construction of a statute to override a judicial decision (1015–66). Reiterating his objection that he raised in *Christensen* that the majority there had already carved an exception to the across-the-board *Chevron* rule, he sees them now making another exception to it, one that he thinks unconstitutional in letting an executive agency override a reading by the courts. He declares that the correct rule and application of *Chevron* is that once a court had rendered an interpretation it is precedent and binding on the administrative agency.

Thus, in *Mead, Christensen*, and *National Cable* Scalia was on the losing side of how to apply *Chevron*. Of course, he was not always a loser. In *Arlington v. Federal Communications Commission*, 569 U.S. 290 (2013), Scalia wrote the majority opinion holding that *Chevron* required deference to an agency's interpretation of a statutory ambiguity regarding the scope of its jurisdiction. In holding that an agency had this power Scalia rejected the idea that there were two classes of questions regarding agency decisions, "big, important ones, presumably—define the agency's "jurisdiction. Others—humdrum, run-of-the-mill stuff" (297). That was the wrong question instead, there is a

> misconception that there are, for *Chevron* purposes, separate "jurisdictional" questions on which no deference is due derives, perhaps, from a reflexive extension to agencies of the very real division between the jurisdictional and non-jurisdictional that is applicable to courts. In the judicial context, there is a meaningful line: Whether the court decided correctly is a question that has different consequences from the question whether it had the power to decide at all. (297)

For *Chevron* deference the only real issue is whether Congress has given the agency the authority to act, and if so, then in cases of ambiguity is it up to the executive branch (agencies) and not the courts to resolve the ambiguity. Scalia's opinion in *Arlington* appeared to represent the justice's all-or-nothing application of a broad application of *Chevron,* unqualified by the type of decision being made by the agency.

While Scalia prevailed in *Arlington*, there was vigorous disagreement with his position. Justice Breyer's concurrence, for example, rejects the across-the-board assertion that simply congressional delegation is enough to resolve the matter: "I say that the existence of statutory ambiguity is sometimes not enough to warrant the conclusion that Congress has left a deference-warranting gap for the agency to fill because our cases make clear that other, sometimes context-specific, factors will on occasion prove relevant" (308–9). This is Breyer again making the case for a flexible *Chevron* test (Breyer 2005, 103;

2010, 117). Similarly, Chief Justice Roberts in a dissent joined by Kennedy and Alito declared that *Chevron* deference was not due until the agency was determined by the Court to have been given the authority to address ambiguities, and it must be a court that determines whether that authority exists, and not the agency itself (312).

In many other cases Scalia also prevailed when it came to matters of application or administrative law, but such opinions did not always involve the broad application of *Chevron* deference that the justice was advocating and as advocating a more nuanced reading of it (Tarrien 2016, 245). For example, in *Utility Air Group v. the EPA* ___ U.S. ___, 134 S.Ct. 2427 (2014), this issue was whether the EPA's decision to require best available control technology for greenhouse gases emitted by sources otherwise subject to PSD (Prevention of Significant Deterioration) review is, as a general matter, a permissible interpretation of the statute under *Chevron*. The Court ruled that the EPA's interpretation of applicable law was reasonable, but that it had exceeded its authority in interpreting the law to require stationary sources to be subject to PSD permitting requirements. In doing this, Scalia refused to apply the *Arlington* broad deference to the facts here.

In *Perez v. Mortgage Bankers Association*, U.S. 135 S.Ct.1199 (2015), Scalia questioned how far he was willing to let the Administrative Procedures Act exemption of interpretative rules from notice and comment eventually let agencies construct substantive rules to bind the public. For Scalia: "An agency may use interpretive rules to advise the public by explaining its interpretation of the law. But an agency may not use interpretive rules to bind the public by making law, because it remains the responsibility of the court to decide whether the law means what the agency says it means" (1211). In *Michigan v. EPA,* U.S. 135 S.Ct. 2699 (2015), Scalia wrote for the majority rejecting *Chevron* deference being given to the Environmental Protection Agency when it interpreted the Clean Air Act. Specifically, Scalia did not think that the EPA interpretation was reasonable when it decided to exclude cost as a consideration when deciding under the statute's language, that it had the authority to regulate power plants when it considered to be "appropriate and necessary." Thus, in *Michigan* Scalia again seemed to move away from the broad *Chevron* deference he earlier had articulated. For Tarrien (2016, 245), these opinions suggested that Scalia was even backing off from his broader *Chevron* deference rule, adopting perhaps a position more nuanced, perhaps maybe even closer to that of Breyer or that held by other justices.

But in addition to Scalia not always prevailing in convincing other justices to share his reading of *Chevron*, and what also appears to be his inconsistent or weakening application or deployment of his version of this deference rule, there are questions too regarding whether the Court was even committed to it. By that, Sunstein (2006b) has argued that the Court has augmented the two-step process in *Chevron* with a "step zero," asking whether this deference even applies (191). Consider two major cases. First, in *Food and Drug Admin. v. Brown & Williamson Tobacco Corp.*, 529 U.S. 120 (2000), Justice O'Connor, in writing for the Court (where Scalia joined her opinion), declared that the FDA lacked the authority to regulate tobacco products. This was the case because: "In extraordinary cases, however, there may be reason to hesitate before concluding that Congress has intended such an implicit delegation" (159). In supporting her argument, O'Connor cites to Breyer (1986) as authority for this new step zero.

In *Halbig v. Sebelius*, F. 3d. (D.C. Cir. 2014) and *King v. Burwell*, F. 3d. (4th Cir. 2014), there were split circuit decisions regarding the construction of the Affordable Care Act. The ACA required all individuals to have health insurance and if not, they will be taxed. If they do not currently have health insurance and cannot afford it individuals may be eligible for subsidies to assist in paying for it. In describing who is eligible for the subsidies the ACA indicates that it is, among other factors, for those who have purchased insurance "through an Exchange established by the State." The question here is whether this language limits eligibility simply to those purchasing insurance through a state-run exchange or whether it also includes those purchasing it via a federally-run one. The IRS had interpreted the language to include anyone who purchased via a state or federal exchange. The DC Circuit struck down the subsidies or tax credits for individuals under the Affordable Care Act while the Fourth Circuit upheld it two hours later. The basis of the decision came down to *Chevron* deference and whether the courts should defer to agency construction of a federal law. One court said the law was not clear and therefore the IRS has reasonably construed the law to allow for subsidies to be provided to health care exchanges run by the federal government whereas the other circuit (DC) ruled that congressional intent and language was clear and therefore they did not have to defer to the IRS rule or interpretation.

The Supreme Court refused to apply *Chevron*. For the Roberts' majority (which excluded Scalia): "The ACA is ambiguous and the word "exchange" is used in different ways in the law. Normally when a statute is unclear the courts, following *Chevron*, will defer to reasonable agency construction. Here it is not clear that Congress would have intended the IRS to make this determination. Instead the Court will directly seek to interpret the law." Thus, there is evidence that the Court in major cases would decide not only not to apply broad *Chevron* deference, but also decide not even to use *Chevron* at all.

Eskridge and Baer (2008) reinforce this point about the perhaps mercurial application of *Chevron*, comparing this use of deference to several others on the Court. What they found were several things. First, *Chevron* is only one of

several types of deference it can employ when it comes to agency interpretation of laws and that it is not clear when which test is used and by whom. In
fact, "*Chevron* deference was applied only in eight point three percent 8.3%
of Supreme Court cases evaluating agency statutory interpretations" between
1984 and 2006 (1090). Second, even when *Chevron* deference is applied, its
win rate (court defers to agency construction) is "in the 414 cases where the
Court found the statutory text at least somewhat ambiguous, the agency prevailed 69.1% of the time—virtually the same as the agency win rate of 68.7%
when the Court found the statute had a plain meaning" (1151). *Chevron* deference did not seem to matter. Third, ideology matters. By that, in examining
the justices when approaching an administrative agency's interpretation of
a statute, their political ideology or orientation matters. For Scalia, he was
overall the fifth least deferential justice to agency construction of statutes
during the time frame from when *Chevron* was first decided in 1984 though
Hamdan v. Rumsfeld, 548 U.S. 557 (2006) (1154). Thus, not only has Scalia
not prevailed in convincing his colleagues to support his broad reading of
Chevron, but he also has not convinced them to apply it in an all-or-nothing
fashion and he himself, when applying it, has not used it in such a way that it
is a neutral tool of deference—his ideology has compromised its use.

CONCLUSION: SCALIA, *CHEVRON*, AND
THE FUTURE OF ADMINISTRATIVE LAW

It is difficult to conclude that Scalia has been the Court's intellectual leader
when it comes to administrative law jurisprudence, if application of *Chevron*
deference is a measure of such influence. Certainly, Scalia has prevailed in
many administrative law cases and interpretations, but it is far from clear that
he was the most influential justice, with a good case being made that either
Stevens (author of the *Chevron* opinion) or Breyer were at least equal rivals.
The Supreme Court has not adopted the broad "all or nothing" use of *Chevron* deference that Scalia advocated. *Chevron* has been narrowed from what
Scalia advocated, it is not always invoked, and when it is, it is not clear that
its use really seems to be affecting the Court's review of agency construction
of the law. *Chevron* was not consistently used by the Court, and even Scalia
himself seemed to be inconsistent in its use. Even if all of this does not suggest that Scalia was a sissy when it came to administrative law, it is enough
to question his claims, as the preeminent administrative law justice.

So, what now? With Scalia gone and now replaced by Justice Neil Gorsuch, what might one say about the former's legacy in administrative law?
The initial tempting answer is to say it is too soon to tell. However, Gorsuch

is a different type of conservative when compared to Scalia, and there is a possibility he will approach *Chevron* and administrative law differently. Ezell and Marshall (2017) point to Gorsuch's comment in *Gutierrez-Brizuela v. Lynch* that "We managed to live with the administrative state before *Chevron*," he wrote. "We could do it again" (834 F.3d 1142, 1158 [10th Cir. 2016] (Gorsuch J., concurring). While one should be cautious about reading too much into *Gutierrez-Brizuela*, Bazelon and Posner (2017) along with Feder (2016) and Klein (2017) argue that this opinion suggests a broader assault by Gorsuch and other conservatives against the New Deal administrative state. They note how Gorsuch sees *Chevron* as having swallowed "huge amounts of core judicial and legislative power and concentrate federal power in a way that seems more than a little difficult to square with the Constitution of the framers' design" (834 F.3d. at 1149). In his reading of the Constitution and separation of powers, Gorsuch takes a perspective that appears even more formal and rigid than Scalia, raising questions regarding whether the latter's views on administrative law are shared by the new justice. Early into his tenure on the Supreme Court, Gorsuch in *Scenic America, Inc., v. Department of Transportation*, U.S. (2017), 2017 WL 4581902 (October 16, 2017), in denial of certiorari, already seemed prepared to narrow *Chevron*, stating:

> Of course, courts sometimes defer to an agency's interpretations of statutory law under *Chevron U.S.A., Inc. v. Natural Resources Defense Council, Inc.*, 467 U.S. 837, 866, 104 S.Ct. 2778, 81 L.Ed.2d 694 (1984), and its progeny. But whatever one thinks of that practice in statutory interpretation cases, it seems quite another thing to suggest that the doctrine (or something like it) should displace the traditional rules of contract interpretation too.

If this comment is a harbinger of what is to come, both *Chevron* and Scalia's administrative law legacy may be short and not very deep.

REFERENCES

Breyer, Stephen. 2005. *Active Liberty: Interpreting Our Democratic Constitution.* New York: Alfred A. Knopf.
———. 1986. "Judicial Review of Questions of Law and Policy." *Administrative Law Review* 38(4): 363–98.
———. 2010. *Making Our Democracy Work: A Judge's View.* New York: Alfred A. Knopf.
Bazelon, Emily and Eric Posner. 2017. "The Government Gorsuch Wants to Undo." *New York Times* (April 1) at SR 1. https://www.nytimes.com/2017/04/01/sunday-review/the-government-gorsuch-wants-to-undo.html?_r=1. Clayton, Scott Allen.

2015. *Judicial Review of Administrative Discretion: How Justice Scalia and Breyer Regulate the Regulators.* El Paso, TX: LFB Scholarly Publishing.

Eskridge, William N. and Lauren E. Baer. 2008. "The Continuum of Deference: Supreme Court Treatment of Agency Statutory Interpretations from Chevron to Hamdan." *Georgetown Law Journal* 96: 1083.

Ezell, Trevor W. and Lloyd Marshall. 2017. "If Goliath Falls: Judge Gorsuch and the Administrative State." *Stanford Law Review* 69: 171.

Feder, David. 2016. "The Administrative Law Originalism of Neil Gorsuch." *Yale Journal on Regulation* (21 Nov. 2016), http://yalejreg.com/nc/the-administrative -law-originalism-of-neil-gorsuch.

Klein, Diane. 2017. "Gorsuch, Gutierrez-Brizuela, and Goodbye, Chevron. *Dorf on Law* (1 Feb. 2017), http://www.dorfonlaw.org/2017/02/gorsuch-gutierrez-brizuela -and-goodbye.html.

Leacock, Stephen J. 2014. "Chevron's Legacy, Justice Scalia's Two Enigmatic Dissents, and His Return to the Fold in City of Arlington, Tex. v. FCC." *Catholic University Law Review* 64: 133.

Murphy, Bruce Allen. 2014. *Scalia: A Court of One.* New York: Simon & Schuster.

O'Quinn, John C. 2016. "A Tribute to Justice Scalia," *Administrative & Regulatory Law News* 41: 10.

Pierce, Richard J. 2016. "Justice Scalia's Unparalleled Contributions to Administrative Law." *Minnesota Law Review* 101: 66.

Scalia, Antonin. 1989a. "Judicial Deference to Administrative Interpretations of Law." *Duke Law Journal* 3: 511–21.

———. 1989b. "Originalism: The Lesser Evil." *Cincinnati Law Review* 57: 849–65.

———. 1987. "Responsibilities of Regulatory Agencies under Environmental Laws." *Houston Law Review* 24: 97–109.

Schultz, David A. and Christopher E. Smith. 1996. *The Jurisprudential Vision of Justice Antonin Scalia.* Lanham, MD: Rowman & Littlefield.

Sunstein, Cass R. 2006a. "Beyond *Marbury*: The Executive Power to Say What the Law Is." *Yale Law Review* 115: 2580.

———. 2006b. "Chevron Step Zero." 92 Va. L. Rev. 187.

Tarrien, David. 2016. "The Legacy of Justice Scalia." *Texas Tech Administrative Law Journal* 17: 233.

TABLE OF CASES

Arlington v. Federal Communications Commission, 569 U.S. 290 (2013).

AT&T Corp. v. Portland, 216 F.3d 871 (C.A.9 2000).

Blakely v. Washington, 542 U.S. 296 (2004).

Bush v. Gore, 531 U.S. 98 (2000).

Chevron U.S.A., Inc. v. Natural Resources Defense Council, Inc., 467 U.S. 837 (1984).

Christensen v. Harris County, 529 U.S. 576 (2000).

Food and Drug Admin. v. Brown & Williamson Tobacco Corp., 529 U.S. 120 (2000).

Gutierrez-Brizuela v. Lynch, 834 F.3d 1142, (10th Cir. 2016).

Halbig v. Sebelius, F.3d. (D.C. Cir. , 2014).

Hamdan v. Rumsfeld, 548 U.S. 557 (2006).

INS v. Cardoza Fonseca, 480 U.S. 421 (1987).

King v. Burwell, F.3d. (4th Cir. 2014).

Michigan v. EPA, U.S. 135 S.Ct. 2699 (2015).

Mistretta v. United States, 488 U.S. 361 (1989).

Morrison v. Olson, 487 U.S. 654 (1988).

National Labor Relations Board v. Jones and McLaughlin, 301 U.S. 1 (1937).

National Resources Defense Council v. Chevron, 467 U.S. 837 (1984).

Perez v. Mortgage Bankers Association, 135 S.Ct.1199 (2015).

Scenic America, Inc., v. Department of Transportation, U.S. (2017), 2017 WL 4581902 (October 16, 2017).

Schechter Poultry v. United States, 295 U.S. 495 (1935).

Skidmore v. Swift & Company, 323 U.S. 134, 140 (1944).

Sullivan v. Everhart, 494 U.S. 83 (1990).

National Cable & Telecommunications Ass'n v. Brand X Internet Services, 545 U.S. 967 (2005).

Synar v. United States, 626 F.Supp. 1374 (D.D.C 1986).

United States v. Mead Corp., 533 U.S. 218, 229 (2001).

United States v. Booker, 543 U.S. 220 (2005).

Utility Air Group v. the EPA ___U.S. ___, 134 S.Ct. 2427 (2014).

West Virginia, et al. v. EPA, 577 U.S. (2016).

Chapter 2

Justice Scalia's Modest Employment Discrimination Law Legacy

Henry L. Chambers Jr.

Justice Antonin Scalia cast a long shadow on many areas of the law during his thirty-year tenure on the U.S. Supreme Court. For example, his original-ism—whether faint-hearted as he claimed (Scalia 1989, 864) or more robust as others might suggest (Barrett 2017; Ramsey 2017)—informs how lawyers and others think about constitutional interpretation, even if the Supreme Court uses originalism sparingly when deciding cases (Barrett 2017; Greene 2009). However, his effect on employment discrimination law has been and will likely be uneven. Though Justice Scalia authored important employ-ment discrimination decisions, he did not alter employment discrimination doctrine significantly. Conversely, his effect on employment discrimination cases may be somewhat more significant because his opinions on arbitration and class actions may limit how and whether those cases may be brought in the future.

Justice Scalia's comparatively small doctrinal footprint may result primarily from his judicial approach. He tended to read statutory text relatively simply and resolve only the issues he deemed necessary to decide the case at hand, leaving other legal questions for future courts to resolve. He also tended to provide those courts scant guidance to resolve the unresolved questions. For example, in *Oncale v. Sundowner Offshore Services, Inc.* (1998), he deemed same-sex sexual harassment cognizable under Title VII, but did not discuss and provided no guidance regarding important related issues such as whether sexual orientation discrimination might be actionable under Title VII.

However, when considering issues not addressed directly by statutory text, Justice Scalia tended to issue legally conservative opinions, often limiting the reach of discrimination statutes. For example, his decision in *St. Mary's Honor Center v. Hicks* (1993) narrowed the path for successful Title VII plaintiffs by restructuring the three-part test from *McDonnell Douglas v. Green* (1973) for proving intentional discrimination through circumstantial proof (Chambers 1996). In cases like *Hicks*, Justice Scalia's analysis often depended on his worldview rather than on the relevant statute's purpose. Those decisions may have limited effect if Justice Scalia's worldview is eventually deemed an inappropriate basis for decision.

Though Justice Scalia's direct effect on employment discrimination doctrine may be modest, his decisions limiting class actions and expanding arbitration may have a significant effect on employment discrimination cases, particularly because some of those decisions involved employment discrimination claims. His opinions in *Wal-Mart Stores, Inc. v. Dukes* (2011), narrowing the scope of systemic employment discrimination class actions, and in *Rent-A-Center v. Jackson* (2010), broadening the employment discrimination claims that must be arbitrated, will functionally limit employment discrimination claims (Greenberger 2017, 76–77; Harper 2015). However, how much they limit future cases is unclear.

This chapter is not a comprehensive review of Justice Scalia's opinions. Rather, it considers his most important majority decisions and explores the lasting effects the opinions may have on employment discrimination doctrine and law. It first considers Justice Scalia's contributions to employment discrimination doctrine. It then considers the effect his class action and arbitration decisions may have on broader employment discrimination law.

JUSTICE SCALIA AND EMPLOYMENT DISCRIMINATION DOCTRINE

Proving Intentional Discrimination

Justice Scalia's approach to employment discrimination doctrine was clear in his opinions that addressed how employment discrimination plaintiffs prove intentional discrimination. He focused on statutory text when he found it relevant, relied on his beliefs and worldview to inform his decision making when text did not appear to provide a clear resolution, and left important questions open for future courts to decide. He helped shape doctrine generally, but not foundationally. His contributions are important but are functionally overshadowed by the courts that have decided cases in his wake.

The McDonnell Douglas Test

Promulgated in *McDonnell Douglas v. Green* (1973), the three-part *McDonnell Douglas* test is the standard vehicle by which employment discrimination plaintiffs prove intentional discrimination through circumstantial evidence.[1] Though developed in a Title VII case, the test's usefulness led to its importation into cases involving other employment discrimination statutes, such as the Americans with Disabilities Act (ADA) and the Age Discrimination in Employment Act (ADEA) (Corbett 2009, 97). The test's first part is the prima facie case (PFC). Though the PFC is defined as any set of facts from which a fact finder can infer intentional discrimination (Chambers 2004, 85), some courts have treated it as a formulaic set of facts that must be proven. A PFC triggers a rebuttable presumption of intentional discrimination that shifts the burden of production to the employer to produce evidence that rebuts the presumption. If the defendant declines to rebut the PFC, the plaintiff prevails. The second part of the test allows the defendant to meet its burden of production by articulating one or more legitimate, non-discriminatory reasons (LNRs) for the adverse job action. The third part of the test—the pretext stage—allows the plaintiff to prove that the defendant's LNRs are pretext for unlawful discrimination either by proving that the LNRs are false or that intentional discrimination is a better explanation for the job action than the LNRs. The three-part test is designed to provide a factual basis from which a fact finder may determine whether intentional discrimination caused the adverse job action (Chambers 1996, 10).

Courts have had difficulty applying the *McDonnell Douglas* test. Determining the quantum of evidence necessary to prove a PFC or to win at the pretext stage has been particularly tricky. Justice Scalia addressed those issues and attempted to simplify the test in two majority opinions: *O'Connor v. Consolidated Coin Caterers Corp.* (1996) and *St. Mary's Honor Center v. Hicks* (1993). In both cases, he left important proof issues unresolved, leaving trial and appellate courts to resolve those issues (Harper 2010) and requiring the Supreme Court to address some of those issues in later cases (Chambers 2005, 118–21). In addition, his skepticism of the continued prevalence of employment discrimination affected his decision in *Hicks*.

O'Connor v. Consolidated Coin Caterers Corporation

In *O'Connor v. Consolidated Coin Caterers Corporation* (1996), an ADEA case, Justice Scalia considered how much evidence is necessary to support an ADEA PFC. The ADEA protects employees forty years old and older from age discrimination.[2] In *O'Connor*, the plaintiff, a fifty-six-year-old employee, was replaced by a forty-year-old employee. The plaintiff's case was dismissed because he did not prove a formulaic PFC that required, in part, that he show he was replaced by someone outside of the class protected under the ADEA, as the Fourth Circuit required to prove an ADEA PFC. Justice Scalia rejected the Fourth Circuit's rule, noting that the ADEA focuses on whether age discrimination occurred rather than solely on who replaced the plaintiff. Age discrimination may occur when a younger employee replaces an older employee, regardless of whether the younger employee is inside the protected class. A fifty-six-year-old employee who has been replaced by a forty-year-old employee may be just as likely to have been subject to age discrimination as a fifty-six-year-old employee who has been replaced by a thirty-nine-year-old employee (*O'Connor v. Consolidated Coin Caterers Corporation* 1996, 312). Rather than focus on requiring a formulaic PFC, Justice Scalia required that courts focus directly on whether the plaintiff has presented a set of facts that supports an inference of discrimination (312).

Justice Scalia's ruling simplifies the definition of a PFC, but may allow judges to require more evidence than should be necessary to prove a PFC. *O'Connor* should be read as a departure from PFCs that require proof of particular irrelevant facts and toward PFCs that simply support an inference of discrimination. However, it can be read to suggest a move away from formulaic PFCs altogether and toward allowing judges to require the proof they deem necessary to support an inference of discrimination. That is unfortunate because formulaic PFCs can be useful. They guarantee that plaintiffs know how much evidence will trigger the rebuttable presumption of discrimination that requires that the employer present a substantive defense.[3] Indeed, concerns that judges would require more evidence than necessary in employment discrimination cases animated the *McDonnell Douglas* case and triggered the three-part test (Chambers 1996). Justice Scalia could have suggested a better formulaic PFC that would have supported an inference of age discrimination. Instead, the opinion appears to allow judges to consider seriatim whether a particular set of facts is sufficient to support an inference of discrimination.

The opinion inadvertently provides trial courts latitude to require as much evidence as a court thinks appropriate to support a PFC, rather than the modest amount of evidence that should be sufficient to support a PFC. Trial judges now may determine how much evidence is required to support a prima facie case, with some requiring far more evidence than should be necessary. Some courts require that a plaintiff provide comparator evidence—evidence that similarly-situated employees were treated differently than the plaintiff—to support her prima facie case (Lidge 2002). In a comparator case involving a claim of sex discrimination, a court might require that a plaintiff prove that she was treated differently than a similarly situated man. Comparator evidence is strong circumstantial evidence that is supposed to be one avenue to support a prima facie case and prove discrimination circumstantially (Sullivan 2009, 193). However, some courts now treat it as necessary to support an inference of discrimination and a prima facie case (Goldberg 2011, 812). That is problematic given how difficult comparator evidence may be to produce, and ironic given that the prima facie case is supposed to be easy to prove (Goldberg 2011). This important development may not have been Justice Scalia's plan, but it is an unsurprising result given that Justice Scalia's opinion fairly clearly allows the result.

St. Mary's Honor Center v. Hicks

In *St. Mary's Honor Center v. Hicks* (1993), Justice Scalia attempted to simplify the *McDonnell Douglas* test by clarifying the role of the test's pretext stage. He simplified the test, but muddled its importance by insufficiently analyzing pretext. That left trial and appellate courts free to determine how pretext should be defined and allowed them to interpret pretext inconsistent with *McDonnell Douglas's* original purpose. Eventually, the Court was compelled to address unresolved aspects of pretext in *Reeves v. Sanderson Plumbing Products Inc.* (2000) (Chambers 2005).

In *Hicks*, plaintiff Hicks was fired after an altercation with his supervisor. Hicks sued, arguing that the altercation was manufactured by his supervisor and that his termination was racially discriminatory. St. Mary's responded that Hicks was terminated for an increasingly serious set of rules violations. Hicks offered evidence that St. Mary's LNRs were false. The judge—the fact finder in the bench trial—agreed that the LNRs were false, but also found that Hicks had not met his burden to prove that intentional discrimination caused the termination, and granted judgment to St. Mary's (*St. Mary's Honor Center v. Hicks* 1993, 508).

Before *Hicks*, courts disagreed about what effect an employer's proof that LNRs were false should have on a verdict. Some courts found that proof of falsity left no reason other than intentional discrimination to explain the underlying job action, deeming proof of falsity sufficient to direct judgment in plaintiff's favor. Other courts ruled that proof of falsity provided evidence from which a fact finder could infer, but need not infer, intentional discrimination. Still other courts deemed bare proof of falsity insufficient to support an inference that intentional discrimination more likely than not caused the underlying adverse job action, thus requiring a directed verdict for the defendant-employer (Chambers 1996).

Justice Scalia endorsed the middle approach. He stated that the *McDonnell Douglas* test is merely a procedural device used to force both parties to present evidence from which a fact finder can determine whether intentional discrimination occurred (*St. Mary's Honor Center v. Hicks* 1993, 510).[4] After the plaintiff has presented evidence of pretext, all that remains is evidence from both parties on the key issue of intentional discrimination. Proof that the LNRs are false can usually help prove that intentional discrimination caused the adverse job action, but does not prove that the LNRs are pretext for intentional discrimination. Proof of falsity generally yields a case to be submitted to the fact finder (511).

Justice Scalia's attempt to refocus the *McDonnell Douglas* test solely on whether intentional discrimination had occurred was defensible, but created problems. His solution was somewhat inconsistent with the nature of the *McDonnell Douglas* test, and his commentary on the relevant strength or weakness of proof of falsity was taken by trial courts as an opportunity to rid their dockets of weak, but winnable, discrimination cases (Chambers 2005). The *McDonnell Douglas* test suggests that an unadorned PFC supports an inference of discrimination and that once no LNRs exist to support defendant's defense, intentional discrimination more likely than not caused the adverse job action (Chambers 1996). Justice Scalia reversed the test's thrust, suggesting that a PFC coupled with proof of falsity is not always strong proof of intentional discrimination (*St. Mary's Honor Center v. Hicks* 1993, 514–15).

Just after stating that proof of falsity should generally be sufficient to send the case to the fact finder, Justice Scalia provided trial judges a path to determine that proof of falsity might not be sufficient to support a verdict for plaintiff, and might not be sufficient to allow a plaintiff to avoid summary judgment. That allowed trial and appellate judges to reason that proof of falsity may be insufficient to support a verdict for plaintiff. This was problematic because a fact finder should always be allowed to determine that intentional discrimination is a better explanation for the adverse job action than the LNRs when the LNRs have been proven false (Chambers 1996). When trial courts responded to *Hicks* by granting summary judgment motions in the face of proof of LNR falsity, the Court was required to reiterate in *Reeves v. Sanderson Plumbing Products, Inc.* (2000), that proof of falsity would usually be sufficient to support a disparate treatment verdict (Chambers 2005, 120–21). However, even in the wake of *Reeves*, courts have continued to grant summary judgment in more cases than appropriate (Beiner 2014).

Justice Scalia's attempt to simplify and deemphasize the *McDonnell Douglas* test largely succeeded. In the process, he deemed strong evidence—proof of falsity—to be not particularly strong (Chambers 1996, 32), and allowed relatively strong cases to be disposed of on summary judgment. He may have done so because he may not have believed in the continued prevalence of employment discrimination (McCormick 2013, 418). Whatever his reasoning, his views regarding the strength and weakness of evidence of discrimination have given trial judges the discretion to grant summary judgment in cases in which the plaintiff could reasonably prevail. His opinion allows judges to decide cases on summary judgment that ought to be left to fact finders. That may leave a significant legacy, though not one that is consistent with the *McDonnell Douglas* test's original purpose or Title VII's purposes, and not one that is consistent with a justice who merely interprets the law.

Religious Discrimination

Justice Scalia's straightforward statutory interpretation approach was evident in his decision in *EEOC v. Abercrombie & Fitch* (2015), a religious discrimination case. Title VII bars employers from discriminating against an employee because of the employee's religion and requires employers to reasonably accommodate an employee's religious practices, unless doing so would trigger an undue hardship on the employer's business.[5] An employer that refuses to hire an applicant to avoid accommodating the applicant's religious practices has violated Title VII, and will be liable if it cannot prove that it would have made the same decision had it not considered the plaintiff's religion.[6] The issue in *EEOC v. Abercrombie & Fitch* (2015) was whether an applicant must inform an employer about the need for accommodation before the refusal to hire based on the employer's desire to avoid a possible accommodation can be deemed discriminatory.

In *Abercrombie & Fitch*, plaintiff Samantha Elauf performed well enough in a job interview with Abercrombie & Fitch (Abercrombie) to be hired. However, she was not hired after her interviewer. The store's assistant manager asked Abercrombie's district manager whether Elauf's headscarf—which Elauf wore in the interview and for religious reasons—might violate Abercombie's Look Policy. The district manager stated that the Look Policy barred employees from wearing any headwear—whether religious or not—and told the assistant manager to not hire Elauf (*EEOC v. Abercrombie & Fitch* 2015, 2031).

The justices offered very different analyses on whether Abercrombie discriminated against Elauf. Justice Scalia—writing for the majority—ruled that if Abercrombie suspected that Elauf wore the headscarf for a religious reason, its refusal to hire her was motivated by her religion and was unlawful under Title VII. He treated Abercrombie's decision as a preemptive refusal to reasonably accommodate a religious practice. Justice Alito argued that Abercrombie's application of the Look Policy would not be actionable unless it knew that Elauf wore the headscarf for a religious reason (2035), but found the evidence sufficient to support such a finding. Justice Thomas argued that the application of the Look Policy may trigger disparate impact (unintentional) discrimination, but did not constitute disparate treatment (intentional) discrimination (2038).[7]

Justice Scalia's opinion was clearer and more straightforward than Justice Alito's or Justice Thomas's. Justices Alito and Thomas focused on the Look Policy. Conversely, Justice Scalia realized that Abercrombie's assumption regarding Elauf's response to the application of the Look Policy triggered Abercrombie's refusal to hire Elauf rather than the Look Policy. Abercrombie never applied the Look Policy—an employee dress code—because Elauf was never hired. Had Elauf been hired, she presumably would have either complied with the Look Policy by removing her headscarf or requested an accommodation. Only if she wore the headscarf in the face of a denial of a requested accommodation and been fired would the Look Policy have caused the termination. The discussion would then have turned to whether Abercrombie could have reasonably accommodated Elauf consistent with the Look Policy. None of that occurred because Elauf was not hired. Rather, Abercrombie believed Elauf wore the scarf for religious reasons, and declined to hire her because it did not want to consider whether to accommodate her religious practice. That is religious discrimination under any interpretation of Title VII's text, and Justice Scalia's approach may endure.[8]

Same-Sex Sexual Harassment

Justice Scalia's preference for simple statutory analysis was apparent when he addressed whether same-sex discrimination is cognizable under Title VII, as was his penchant for leaving important questions related to the core question unanswered. Prior to Justice Scalia's opinion in *Oncale v. Sundowner Offshore Services, Inc.* (1998), courts had not reached a consensus on whether same-sex sexual harassment was cognizable under Title VII. Some appellate courts found same-sex hostile work environment (HWE) sexual harassment not cognizable, while others found same-sex HWE sexual harassment cognizable if the harasser was homosexual and the harassment was based on sex or sexual desire. A third group of courts found any sexual harassment, including same-sex HWE sexual harassment, actionable if the harassment was based on the victim's sex (*Oncale v. Sundowner Offshore Services, Inc.* 1998, 79).

In *Oncale*, plaintiff Joseph Oncale asserted that he was constantly harassed, "physically assaulted in a sexual manner," and threatened with sexual violence by male coworkers while working on an oil platform in the Gulf of Mexico (76). After being told by Sundowner's human resources manager that the situation would not be remedied, Oncale quit and requested that Sundowner indicate that he left because he had been sexual harassed and verbally abused. He sued Sundowner for HWE harassment, but his case was dismissed by the trial and appellate courts which ruled same-sex sexual harassment not actionable under Title VII (77).

Justice Scalia decided the issue simply, determining that any behavior—including same-sex sexual harassment—that constitutes discrimination because of sex is actionable under Title VII.[9] The ruling was little more than a restatement of Title VII's text.[10] Justice Scalia's simple reading of the statute's text resolved the narrow legal question at issue, but did not address a broader and lurking question: What styles of behavior constitute discrimination because of sex in a context like *Oncale*? That left courts free (or adrift) to define what harassing conduct constitutes discrimination because of sex based on their own broad or narrow vision of sex discrimination, even though they had been unable to reach a consensus on that issue before the *Oncale* decision.

After broadening Title VII's reach, Justice Scalia allowed courts to narrow same-sex HWE claims by reiterating that HWE harassment requires severe or pervasive harassment, lest Title VII become "a general civility code" (*Oncale v. Sundowner Offshore Services, Inc.* 1998, 81). He did not elaborate on the nature of the severe-or-pervasive inquiry, leaving courts to use "common sense" to resolve the issue (82), and leaving the scope of insufficiently severe and legally acceptable workplace harassment troublingly unclear (McGinley 2007).[11] That has given trial and appellate courts significant power to craft the contours of sexual harassment, and may have functionally narrowed the HWE cause of action (Frank 2002, 440–41) and same-sex sexual harassment cause of action.

In addition, Justice Scalia left sexual orientation and gender identity discrimination issues unexplored. Whether sexual orientation discrimination is sex discrimination might seem a very different issue than whether same-sex sexual harassment is actionable, but the issues are related. Same-sex sexual harassment that is not based on sexual attraction is presumably triggered by the perception that the victim is the "wrong kind" of man or woman. Such conduct is similar to sex stereotyping found potentially actionable in *Price Waterhouse v. Hopkins* (1989), but also is similar to sexual orientation discrimination that the Court has yet to find cognizable. Commentary on the nature of same-sex sexual harassment may have helped inform the discussion surrounding whether sexual orientation discrimination is or can be a form of sex discrimination; none was forthcoming. Why some conduct appears to be actionable sex discrimination, but other similar conduct may be deemed nonactionable sexual orientation discrimination, is not clear (Chambers 2001, 562–64). Not surprisingly, courts continue to struggle with whether sexual orientation discrimination is sex discrimination (Clarke 2017).

Justice Scalia's *Oncale* opinion exemplifies his employment discrimination jurisprudence. He answered the narrow legal question at issue—whether same-sex HWE sexual harassment is cognizable—through simple statutory interpretation but left other important questions unanswered, and limited the effective reach of the decision by declining to discuss what other types of similar sex-related or gender-related behavior might constitute sex discrimination. Ultimately, the opinion leaves courts free to determine what constitutes sexual harassment based on their "common sense" of the severity and nature of the harassment alleged. In response, some courts have aggressively winnowed harassment cases by issuing summary judgment in cases that should be decided by juries (Beiner 2002; Chambers 2005).

Retaliation and Aggrieved Persons

Justice Scalia's approach of interpreting statutes simply and leaving open questions to be answered by future courts extends to his decisions regarding employer retaliation. Title VII bars employer retaliation against those who have informally opposed an employer's unlawful employment practice (UEP) or formally participated in a Title VII proceeding against an employer.[12] Whether third-party retaliation—retaliation against someone other than the employee who engaged in the protected conduct—is actionable was unclear before Justice Scalia's majority opinion in *Thompson v. North American Stainless* (2011).[13] His opinion deemed third-party retaliation actionable, but left its scope undefined by declining to specify which third parties can sue for retaliation. The opinion may get overshadowed by future analyses of which third parties can recover and the circumstances under which they can sue.

An employer's conduct is actionable when, in response to an employee's protected conduct, it takes action that would dissuade a reasonable worker from engaging in the protected conduct (*Burlington Northern & Santa Fe Railway Co. v. White* 2006). In *Thompson*, the plaintiff alleged that he was fired because his fiancée/coworker filed a sex discrimination charge with the EEOC against their common employer. The employer's behavior in *Thompson* was retaliatory because a reasonable employee would be dissuaded from filing a charge against her employer if she knew that her fiancé would be fired because she filed the charge. Having found the employer's conduct retaliatory, Justice Scalia declined to consider where the line should be drawn between actions that would dissuade a reasonable employee and those that would not.[14] The employer had retaliated against plaintiff's fiancée, but whether Thompson, the third-party plaintiff, could recover remained an issue.

Title VII allows persons aggrieved by a UEP, including retaliation, to sue.[15] However, only those within the statute's scope of protection or "zone of interests" are aggrieved persons who can sue under Title VII. Justice Scalia found plaintiff Thompson to be inside of Title VII's zone of interests, as he was explicitly harmed when the employer fired him, and ruled that he could sue (*Thompson v. North American Stainless* 2011, 178). Having determined that the plaintiff was within Title VII's zone of interests, Justice Scalia declined to analyze where the statute's zone of interests might end.[16] Given that he had decided *Director, Office of Workers' Compensation Programs, Dep't of*

Labor (the Director) v. Newport News Shipbuilding and Dry Dock Company (1995), another zone-of-interests case in the employment law area, a decade before *Thompson*, his silence on the issue was particularly unfortunate.[17] Nonetheless, he declined to consider how that case and the *Thompson* case might help illuminate the contours of a statute's zone of interests and provide guidance to third-party retaliation victims and the courts that will decide their cases.

Justice Scalia's *Thompson* decision was a simple exercise in statutory interpretation—first determine whether plaintiff's fiancé would have been dissuaded by the employer's actions, then determine whether plaintiff was aggrieved. Unfortunately, the scope of retaliation and third-party retaliation recovery remain left open for interpretation. *Thompson* was an easy case; the dissuasion standard was easily met, and the plaintiff was clearly an aggrieved person. More difficult issues will arise when an employer's actions are less egregious, or the third-party plaintiff is not the employer's employee. If future courts narrow the content of retaliation claims, as they could, based on the specific questions Justice Scalia left open, *Thompson* may be treated as a relatively unimportant decision that says little about the general run of retaliation cases.

Cat's Paw Liability and Intentional Discrimination

Justice Scalia's approach to cat's paw liability provides a glimpse of how he analyzes employment discrimination when statutory text is not clear. An employer tends to be liable under employment discrimination laws when its decision maker is motivated by discriminatory animus. Cat's paw liability exists when an employer is liable for intentional discrimination even though its decision maker was not motivated by discriminatory animus (Sullivan 2012, 1435).[18] Justice Scalia endorsed cat's paw liability in his opinion in *Staub v. Proctor Hospital* (2011). However, his approach to cat's paw liability may not survive future Court decisions because it rests liability on the role supervisors play in decision making, rather than on the role animus plays in the decision making.

In *Staub*, plaintiff Staub was an angiography technician who served concurrently in the United States Army Reserves. He claimed that his direct supervisor and her supervisor engineered his termination because they were hostile to his military service and the office dislocation it caused. Staub sued under the Uniformed Services Employment and Reemployment Rights Act (USERRA), which prohibits discriminatory employment actions that are motivated by an employee's membership in the military unless those actions would have been taken had the employee not been a member of the military (*Staub v. Proctor Hospital* 2011, 416–17). He claimed that his termination was unlawful, arguing that though the ultimate decision maker (the hospital's vice president of human resources) may not have been motivated by antimilitary bias, the statements of his supervisor and her supervisor that triggered the termination were infected with antimilitary animus and motivated the ultimate decision to terminate him. Proctor Hospital (Proctor) argued that liability should not exist because the ultimate decision maker was not motivated by antimilitary animus.

Rather than focus directly on the ultimate decision maker's motivation, Justice Scalia focused on when the employer should be liable. He suggested that an employer's responsibility depends on whether the employer is responsible for those who caused antimilitary animus to infect the final decision. The employer's supervisors who have input into employment decisions are agents in whom the employer has placed the power to reward, punish, or dismiss employees. Consequently, the employer is responsible when a supervisor gives information to the ultimate decision maker with the intent to bring about an employee's dismissal and the information is a proximate cause of the resulting termination (422).[19]

Justice Alito disagreed with Justice Scalia's analysis. He argued that liability should exist when discrimination motivates the ultimate decision to terminate the employee either if the ultimate decision maker rubberstamps the animus-infected suggestions of others or if the ultimate decision maker is aware that information from others may be based on animus and does not conduct an independent investigation before making the decision. If the ultimate decision maker conducts a serious independent investigation, the ultimate decision maker is the real decision maker whose motivation should matter (425).

The difference in approach between Justices Scalia and Alito is important. It relates to the nature of employer liability. Justice Scalia's focus on supervisors tends to narrow liability because it narrows the group of people whose actions are the employer's responsibility. Justice Alito broadens potential liability by deeming the employer responsible for all employment decisions that may have been infected with discriminatory animus. The distinction may matter if coworkers, in whom no supervisory authority has been placed, provide information that leads a decision maker to take an adverse employment decision. Justice Alito may not care that the information flowed from plaintiff's coworker; Justice Scalia's opinion suggests that he would care because the coworker is not the employer's agent for disciplinary purposes. USERRA's text focuses on whether the employer's decision is motivated by antimilitary animus, not on who provided input into the decision. Though Justice Scalia's explanation of the basis for cat's paw liability is not clearly incorrect, Justice Alito's vision of employer liability may ultimately prevail, in part, because it appears more true to text of the relevant statute.

Accrual of Claims and Statutes of Limitations

Title VII has a short statute of limitations, 180 or 300 days depending on the circumstances, so decisions regarding the accrual of claims are critical.[20] Justice Scalia authored two important opinions—*Lorance v. AT&T Technologies, Inc.* (1989) and *Lewis v. City of Chicago* (2010)—regarding the accrual of employment discrimination claims and statutes of limitations. Though the cases appear to be decided differently, both rest on the principle that a statute of limitations begins to run each time a discriminatory act occurs, but does not restart each time an employee is harmed by the lingering effects of a discriminatory act. Justice Scalia would almost certainly argue that the straightforward application of that principle simply led to different results in different contexts. Nonetheless, the opinions have been received very differently, with Congress legislatively overruling *Lorance* in the 1991 Civil Rights Act.

In *Lorance*, the company and union altered the seniority system in their collective bargaining agreement (CBA). Plaintiff-employees sued after they were demoted in 1982, three years after the new seniority system became effective, alleging intentional discrimination and arguing that the seniority changes intentionally protected male employees from female employees who had just begun to migrate into certain formerly all-male jobs at the company when the seniority system was altered (*Lorance v. AT&T Technologies* 1989, 902). Justice Scalia ruled that plaintiffs should have challenged the CBA when it was altered in 1979. Unless the seniority rules were applied in an intentionally discriminatory manner in 1982, the 1982 demotions were merely the unfortunate effects of the discriminatory 1979 change, and the plaintiffs' 1982 challenge to 1979 discrimination was untimely (Sullivan 2010, 512). In the wake of *Lorance*, Congress passed the 1991 Civil Rights Act which, in part, triggers a new limitations period each time the discriminatory effect of a seniority system harms a plaintiff's employment.[21]

Justice Scalia revisited Title VII's statute of limitations in *Lewis v. City of Chicago* (2010). In *Lewis*, the City of Chicago tested aspiring firefighters who were separated by score into groups deemed well-qualified, qualified, and not qualified (*Lewis v. City of Chicago* 2010, 208–9). The city used the groupings multiple times over the ensuing several years, randomly choosing firefighters from among those in the well-qualified group. Plaintiff, who was in the "qualified" pool, sued, arguing that the practice of choosing only from among those in the "well-qualified" group yielded a separate disparate impact based on race each time the City used the list to select firefighters (209). If each use of the groupings started a new limitations period, the plaintiff's claim would be timely; if not, plaintiff's claim would be time-barred. Justice Scalia agreed with the plaintiffs, allowing them to sue.

The *Lorance* and *Lewis* decisions may seem inconsistent, but they may not be. Justice Scalia ruled that a statute of limitations begins anew each time a new discriminatory act occurs. In *Lorance*, plaintiffs claimed intentional discrimination, but the only intentionally discriminatory act was the initial installation of the seniority rules. In *Lewis*, plaintiff claimed unintentional discrimination, and every use of the rule was an unintentionally discriminatory act. *Lewis* arguably was a simple application of the *Lorance* principle.

Conversely, the two cases may simply be inconsistent. In both cases, the plaintiffs knew that that the employer's rules—AT&T's seniority system and the City of Chicago's groupings—were discriminatory when they were instituted. In *Lewis*, the harm from the rule's implementation occurred the first time the rule was used and with each subsequent use; in *Lorance*, the potential harm from the new seniority system was clear, but might never come. Ironically, the claims in *Lorance* were deemed untimely because plaintiffs did not sue until harm from the discriminatory act materialized, while the *Lewis* plaintiffs were allowed to sue well after the initial harm was visited on them because each subsequent use of the rule harmed plaintiffs anew. To be clear, the equities would seem to have been in favor of allowing the plaintiffs in both cases to sue. However, Justice Scalia decided that the cases should be resolved differently. That may say less about the law than it says about Justice Scalia's opinion regarding what the law should be. Justice Scalia's approach may endure, but more likely because it is more permissive than because it is consistent.

Attorney's Fees and Incumbent Employees

When simple statutory interpretation cannot resolve a case, Justice Scalia injects his personal opinion and worldview into his decisions. His approach to attorney's fees in employment discrimination cases is an example. Like many civil rights statutes, Title VII authorizes courts to award attorney's fees to the prevailing party in a discrimination suit.[22] Fee shifting incentivizes lawyers to bring winning cases that might not otherwise be brought because plaintiffs could not afford the fees necessary to bring the cases (Schwartz 2011, 113). In addition, it validates the notion that prevailing plaintiffs should not have to pay attorney's fees to enforce their civil rights. Though Title VII does not distinguish between prevailing plaintiffs and prevailing defendants, the Supreme Court has. Prevailing plaintiffs will usually be entitled to fees (*Christiansburg Garment Co. v. EEOC* 1978, 417). Prevailing defendants recover fees only if the plaintiff's suit was "frivolous, unreasonable, or without foundation, or the plaintiff continued to litigate after it clearly became so" (422). The Court's ruling ostensibly balanced the statute's dual purposes to allow meritorious suits to be brought by poor plaintiffs and to deter plaintiffs from bringing meritless suits (420). Against that history, Justice Scalia decided *Independent Federation of Flight Attendants v. Zipes* (1989), in which he decided when a court can exercise its discretion to award fees against intervenors.[23]

The *Zipes* litigation initially centered on a discriminatory rule that required that female flight attendants be terminated when they "became mothers" (*Independent Federation of Flight Attendants v. Zipes*, 1989 755). The parties agreed to settle, with plaintiffs receiving back pay, competitive seniority, and attorney's fees. After the settlement had been reached, the intervenor intervened, representing incumbent employees and arguing that the grant of competitive seniority harmed their union members, and should be rescinded. When the intervenor lost, the plaintiffs requested attorney's fees from the intervenor, arguing that they should not have to pay attorney's fees to protect their settlement. The intervenor argued that it should not be required to pay plaintiff's attorney fees because it lost while trying to protect its members' seniority rights, unlike an employer who pays attorney's fees after unsuccessfully defending its unlawful employment practice.

Justice Scalia agreed with the intervenor, deciding that a plaintiff could recover attorney's fees against the intervenor only when an intervenor's "action was frivolous, unreasonable, or without foundation" (*Independent Federation of Flight Attendants v. Zipes* 1989, 761). He suggested that the intervenor's members are innocent bystanders whose attempt to protect their contractual rights was more akin to a plaintiff's attempt to protect her civil rights under Title VII than an employer's attempt to avoid liability in the face of a Title VII violation. Justice Scalia focused rather narrowly on the intervenor's innocence, not fully considering that the grant of competitive seniority merely takes away what the intervenor's members would not have had but for the unlawful discrimination against the plaintiffs.[24] Though the intervenors did not discriminate, their legal action fought to keep their gains stemming from the employer's unlawful discrimination against plaintiffs.

Justice Scalia's solution leaving plaintiffs responsible for their attorney's fees was problematic. The concurring justices suggested an alternative, that the defendant could be required to pay the attorney's fees that plaintiffs had to expend to protect its recovery from the intervenor given that the attorney's fees ultimately stemmed from the defendant's actions (767–68). The dissenters argued that the fee-shifting provision was meant to incentivize plaintiffs who had a good case, but no money, to secure a lawyer who would sue to vindicate their rights. Allowing intervenors to avoid fee shifting may disincentivize plaintiffs from suing or pushing for the most generous settlement because the more generous the settlement, the more likely some of the recovery would be expended to protect it (Brand 1990, 358). Other commentators have argued that defendants would also be incentivized to ignore the interests of intervenors when settling suits because the intervenors can sue to protect their own interests while the defendant will not be responsible for the attorney's fees that a plaintiff spends to defend its judgment against intervenors (Tobias 1992, 807).

Justice Scalia's solicitousness toward intervenors is not surprising. The sentiment favoring incumbent employees that underlies Justice Scalia's *Zipes* opinion tracks his more strident views on incumbent employees evidenced in his dissent in *Johnson v. Transportation Agency, Santa Clara County* (1987), an affirmative action case in which the majority determined that an affirmative action plan that considered sex as a small factor in promoting a qualified female employee over a relatively similarly-qualified male into a job classification in which 0 of 238 workers were women was acceptable. Justice Scalia dissented, deeming the affirmative action policy serious intentional discrimination against men and ending the opinion with the assertion that the real losers in cases like those are well-qualified men who are subject to discrimination.[25] Justice Scalia's dissent confirms his worldview regarding the nature of discrimination, which he suggests may be most keenly felt by incumbent employees who must litigate for their rights. That also helps explain Justice Scalia's concurrence in *Ricci v. DeStefano* (2009) in which he argues that attempts to remedy potential disparate impact discrimination against minorities may violate the Fourteenth Amendment's Equal Protection Clause, a position that was not new for Justice Scalia (Wiecek and Hamilton 2014, 1142).

Justice Scalia's approach to attorney's fee shifting in Title VII cases typifies his approach to employment discrimination law. When an employment discrimination statute's text does not require a particular result, Justice Scalia tends to interpret it consistent with his worldview and vision of fairness, even if that interpretation might limit the statute's effect or ignore the fundamental reasons underlying its passage. His views regarding the equities of Title VII fee shifting appear to track the sympathy he has for incumbent employees who may be negatively affected by the victories of employment discrimination plaintiffs. He views employees who may be unable to keep their benefits that have flowed from the employer's discrimination against plaintiffs as innocent bystanders rather than as unworthy beneficiaries of discriminatory conduct. If that view continues to be shared by a majority of the Supreme Court, his opinions that track that worldview may continue to be influential. If courts reject his worldview, those opinions will likely be rejected.

JUSTICE SCALIA AND EMPLOYMENT DISCRIMINATION LAW GENERALLY

Justice Scalia's indirect effect on employment discrimination law, in general, may be as important as his effect on employment discrimination doctrine. His decisions related to class actions and arbitration may have a longer lasting effect on limiting how and whether employment discrimination cases can be brought than his doctrinal opinions have on how those cases are decided.

Employment Class Actions

Justice Scalia's effect on employment class actions may be significant, but may not be as significant as some believe. Some commentators have argued that his decision in *Wal-Mart Stores, Inc. v. Dukes* (2011) crippled employment class actions (Greenberger 2017, 77). However, the most dire predictions may be overblown (Harper 2015, 1101). Though *Dukes* may affect employment discrimination class actions, the case is as much about class action doctrine as it is about employment discrimination doctrine. In addition, the case addresses private class actions. Public employment discrimination class actions—pattern or practice cases—may not be significantly affected by *Dukes*.

In *Dukes*, plaintiffs claimed that Wal-Mart's employment policies, which gave great discretion to Wal-Mart managers regarding pay and promotions, were systemically discriminatory. Plaintiffs claimed that the policies had a disparate impact on female Wal-Mart employees, and that Wal-Mart's refusal to address the disparate impact constituted disparate treatment. Consequently, the class action involved a certified class of more than 1.5 million people consisting of "all women employed at any Wal-Mart domestic retail store at any time since December 26, 1998, who may have been or may be subjected to Wal-Mart's challenged pay and management track promotions policies and practices" (*Wal-Mart Stores, Inc. v. Dukes* 2011, 346). Whether the class should remain certified was the central legal question in *Dukes*.

Class actions are governed by Federal Rule of Civil Procedure 23. The rule, in part, requires commonality of class members' claims.[26] If sufficient issues, common to the class's claims, bind the class together, the class should be certified and claims should be tried together; if insufficient common issues exist, the class should not be certified, leaving plaintiffs to try their claims individually or in smaller classes. When class members' claims are identical, such as when a contract has been violated in precisely the same way with respect to all class members, commonality is easily met. When class claims appear to rely on various legal theories or involve multiple factual contexts, commonality is more difficult to demonstrate.

Justice Scalia was skeptical of the commonality of the class claims in *Dukes* because the claims relied on the discretion given to and exercised by individual managers. He argued that a policy that allows discretion—as opposed to a policy of discrimination—would tend not to lead to uniform discriminatory decisions.[27] He suggested that "left to their own devices most managers in any corporation—and surely most managers in a corporation that forbids sex discrimination—would select sex-neutral, performance-based criteria for hiring and promotion that produce no actionable disparity at all" (*Wal-Mart Stores, Inc. v. Dukes* 2011, 355). Consequently, Justice Scalia sought proof that individual discretionary supervisor decisions stemmed from a single source or reflected Wal-Mart policy.[28] Justice Scalia found the class's proof—statistical evidence regarding the promotion rates for women and other statistics, about 120 affidavits of anecdotal reports of discrimination, and expert testimony of a sociologist that Wal-Mart's culture left it vulnerable to gender discrimination (Hart and Secunda 2009)—insufficient (Greenberger 2017, 92; Paetzold and Rholes 2017, 118). Consequently, he decertified the class (*Wal-Mart Stores, Inc. v. Dukes* 2011, 367).

Some commentators have suggested that Justice Scalia misunderstood the nature of employment class actions (Paetzold and Rholes 2017, 118). They argue that employment class actions do not merely aggregate discrete and identical individual discrimination claims (116) and Justice Scalia applied incorrect doctrine. In addition, some of Justice Scalia's fellow justices disagreed with him, arguing that employment class actions focus on whether discrimination was standard operating procedure for the employer, even if the standard operating procedure creates multiple styles of claims (*Wal-Mart Stores, Inc. v. Dukes* 2011, 370–72). They asserted that if Wal-Mart operated under a general discriminatory policy, individual employment decisions have a single source and are tied together closely enough for class certification (375). Justice Scalia may have rejected his fellow justices' approach or may have simply required more evidence than the *Dukes* plaintiffs could marshal.

If the quantum of evidence that Justice Scalia required in *Dukes* is so large because he was uniquely skeptical of the kind of argument that the class made in the case, *Dukes* may be an evidentiary case whose effect may be modest. If the evidence required is simply more than the *Dukes* class could produce, private employment class actions may still be viable. Conversely, if the decision reflects a legal conclusion that employment decisions driven by supervisor discretion made in different workplaces in the same company tend to be so dissimilar that the evidence required to prove commonality is almost impossible to provide, the opinion severely limits private employment class actions. If the latter is true, *Dukes* may require more discriminatory intent or animus at the upper levels of the corporation than has been required or reasonably should be required.[29] The opinion is not clear on that point (Green 2011, 397).

Dukes may primarily be an evidentiary decision in a case that involved a gigantic class of more than 1.5 million members that needed to be cut to a more manageable size. That may make *Dukes* a one-of-a-kind case (Greenberger 2017, 112). Of course, if the evidentiary barriers Justice Scalia erected in the case are effectively insurmountable even in much smaller employment discrimination class actions, the *Dukes* decision will be very important. However, regardless of how it may apply to private employment class actions, *Dukes* may not significantly affect the EEOC's ability to bring public employment class actions, that is, the pattern-or-practice claims (Harper 2015, 1135; Morrison 2013). [30]

Arbitration

Justice Scalia has authored several important arbitration decisions (Stone 2017, 192). Though few have involved employment discrimination arbitration agreements, the decisions may indirectly affect employment arbitration agreements and cases significantly (Stone 2017). Through much of the twentieth century, the Court was skeptical of arbitration, particularly the arbitration of civil rights claims.[31] Over time, the Court's chilliness regarding arbitration thawed (Greenberger 2017, 77–78). By the time the Court decided *Gilmer v. Interstate/Johnson Lane* (1991), where the Court—with Justice Scalia joining the majority opinion—deemed ADEA claims arbitrable, the chill was gone. Since then, the Court has reaffirmed *Gilmer* and fully adopted the arbitration of all types of claims.[32] The Court's march in favor of arbitration, including the arbitration of employment claims, has been steady, with Justice Scalia leading the charge (Stone 2017, 191–92). Justice Scalia's guiding principle appears to be to allow arbitration whenever the parties have formally agreed to arbitrate.

Though Justice Scalia has been very amenable to arbitration, he has limited attempts to force arbitration when he believed that the plaintiff had not agreed to arbitrate the claims at issue. In *Wright v. Universal Maritime Service Corp.* (1998), he ruled that the plaintiff could adjudicate his ADA claim rather than be forced to arbitrate the claim when the CBA governing his employability did not contain a waiver of his right to sue. The ADA claim the plaintiff sought to pursue could not be forced to arbitration unless a clear and unmistakable waiver of the right to sue was embedded in the arbitration agreement. No such clear waiver existed, so the plaintiff could not be barred from suing

(82). However, Justice Scalia has made clear that he was willing to enforce arbitration agreements that would lead to the arbitration of civil rights claims.

Justice Scalia's decision in *Rent-A-Center, West, Inc. v. Jackson* (2010) reflects his solicitousness of arbitration. In *Rent-A-Center*, plaintiff Jackson filed an employment discrimination suit against his employer Rent-A-Center, claiming that the arbitration agreement he signed as a condition of employment was unconscionable and invalid under Nevada law. The arbitration agreement contained two key clauses. The first stated that all claims arising between the parties were subject to arbitration. The second—the delegation clause—stated that the arbitrator had exclusive authority to resolve any dispute relating to the agreement's enforceability, including a claim that the arbitration agreement or any part of it was voidable or void. The delegation clause may be challenged in court. If the delegation clause is valid, the arbitrator determines if the contract as a whole is valid.[33] Justice Scalia ruled the plaintiff's claim subject to arbitration because he challenged the validity of the entire contract rather than the validity of the delegation clause (*Rent-A-Center v. Jackson* 2010, 72). The dissent balked at the narrowness of Justice Scalia's decision, noting that plaintiff's claim that the contract is unconscionable is a challenge to the validity of every clause in the contract, including the delegation clause, and suggesting that such an unconscionability claim usually ought to be decided by a court, even if the agreement to arbitrate is embedded in a contract that covers many topics other than arbitration (80).

Rent-A-Center may have been controversial, but Justice Scalia's opinion was more a continuation of the Court's trend toward greater arbitrability. Nonetheless, Justice Scalia's effect on the arbitration of employment discrimination claims may be considered somewhat significant. He was a reliable vote for decisions that broadened the scope of arbitration, as well as a supporter of eliminating any remaining reluctance the Court may have had to allow civil rights claims to be subject to arbitration. He continued to support arbitration as broadly as possible.[34] However, his eventual effect may be quite significant if one considers how his work limiting employment class actions, allowing employers to force employees to waive class claims in arbitration, and expanding arbitration, in general, could combine to limit an employee's effective opportunity to vindicate her employment discrimination rights (Greenberger 2017). His *AT&T Mobility LLC v. Concepcion* (2011) opinion barred states from requiring class arbitration in circumstances where individual arbitration was so economically infeasible that arbitration would almost never occur. If an employee is required to arbitrate a small and costly employment claim and cannot form a class to arbitrate the claim (even when class arbitration would be sensible), the combination of class action and arbitration decisions would work substantial damage to some of the gains employment discrimination plaintiffs made through the 1991 Civil Rights Act (Harper 2015, 1100). However, the breadth of those effects will not be clear for years.

CONCLUSION

This chapter is not a comprehensive review of all of Justice Scalia's employment discrimination opinions. Rather, it has explored some of Justice Scalia's most important employment discrimination opinions and sought to consider his effect on employment discrimination law over his three decades on the Court. Justice Scalia's employment discrimination jurisprudence is not easy to characterize without caricaturing. However, some strains run through much of that jurisprudence. Justice Scalia appeared to attempt to judge with what he thought was a light touch. He was somewhat successful when addressing substantive employment discrimination issues, but was somewhat less successful when addressing procedural issues.

When addressing substantive employment discrimination doctrine, Justice Scalia tended to adhere to statutory text, even when it led to somewhat surprising results. For example, he recognized the same-sex sexual harassment and third-party retaliation causes of action, though he did not explicitly make them broad. In addition, he recognized cat's paw liability and defined religious discrimination relatively broadly. In most of those areas, he left unresolved questions to be addressed by future courts, risking that his opinions will be quickly superseded and his legacy diminished. However, that would not necessarily surprise those who viewed him as a judge who merely decided cases with no intent to change the law (Thomas 2017, 1601).

However, Justice Scalia could judge with a heavy hand when deciding cases where he was not bound by text. In procedural cases and even in some substantive cases, Justice Scalia's personal opinions and worldviews drove his decisions. The *Zipes* case reflects his personal views on the innocence of civil rights intervenors who sought to keep benefits that were only gained because of the employer's discrimination against others. His *Hicks* decision was driven by his concern about how easily a plaintiff could win an employment case in which the employer was disbelieved. Such decisions may endure, but are less likely to endure if judges without Justice Scalia's views populate the courts in the future. The same may be true of Justice Scalia's indirect effects on employment discrimination cases through his structural class action and arbitration decisions, though whether those effects will be modest or large is unclear.

In sum, Justice Scalia authored some important employment discrimination decisions that may leave a mark on the employment discrimination field. However, he has not left an indelible mark on substantive employment discrimination doctrine. That may be by design. Over time, his effect on employment discrimination law through his procedural decisions and through his work on class actions and arbitration may be more significant. That also may be by design.

NOTES

1. Though some courts have suggested that the test is obsolete, plaintiffs may still use the test to prove their circumstantial evidence cases (*Young v. United Parcel Service, Inc.* 2015).

2. See 29 U.S.C. 631(a).

3. For example, the prima facie case in *McDonnell Douglas* was: "(i) that he belongs to a racial minority; (ii) that he applied and was qualified for a job for which the employer was seeking applicants; (iii) that, despite his qualifications, he was rejected; and (iv) that, after his rejection, the position remained open and the employer continued to seek applicants from persons of complainant's qualifications" (*McDonnell Douglas v. Green* 1973, 802). Prima facie cases are not completely formulaic. The *McDonnell Douglas* Court noted that the content of a prima facie case would be somewhat different in different cases.

4. Indeed, *Reeves v. Sanderson Plumbing Products Inc.* (2000) suggests that the *McDonnell Douglas* framework is irrelevant once both parties have presented their evidence.

5. See 42 U.S.C. §2000e(j): "The term religion includes all aspects of religious observance and practice, as well as belief, unless an employer demonstrates that he is unable to reasonably accommodate to an employee's or prospective employee's religious observance or practice without undue hardship on the conduct of the employer's business."

6. See 42 U.S.C. §2000e-5(g).

7. An employer engages in disparate impact discrimination when it uses a rule that has a disproportionate impact on a particular group based on a trait protected from discrimination under Title VII, if the rule is not prompted by business necessity or could be substituted for another rule that provides the same value to the employer but has less of a discriminatory effect (42 U.S.C. §2000e-2[k]). Though disparate impact is thought to address unintentional discrimination, depending on how it is proven it can be considered a form of disparate treatment. For example, if an employer rejects an alternative rule that is equally effective as the one the employer has chosen and has a lessened discriminatory impact, the employer's refusal to adopt the alternative rule can be thought to be intentionally discriminatory.

8. The opinion addresses a relatively narrow slice of Title VII religious discrimination doctrine, but may be influential in years to come as it indirectly helps to clarify how to address cases in which an employer misperceives an applicant's or an employee's religion (Flake 2016).

9. Justice Scalia noted the wrongheadedness of any assumption that a group member would not discriminate against another group member. Courts reject the assumption that people of the same race will not discriminate on the basis of race against others of the same race or that people of the same sex will not discriminate on the basis of sex against others of the same sex (*Oncale v. Sundowner Offshore Services, Inc.* 1998, 78).

10. See 42 U.S.C. §2000e-2(a) ("It shall be an unlawful employment practice for an employer to . . . discharge any individual, or otherwise to discriminate against any individual with respect to his compensation, terms, conditions, or privileges of employment, because of such individual's . . . sex[.]").

11. That is unsurprising to readers of Justice Scalia's concurrence in *Harris v. Forklift Systems, Inc.* (1993), where he noted that the standard for an abusive workplace was so devoid of specificity that juries were left to decide cases without guidance.

12. See 42 U.S.C. §2000e-3(a): "It shall be an unlawful employment practice for an employer to discriminate against any of his employees . . . because he has opposed any practice made an unlawful employment practice by this subchapter, or because he has made a charge, testified, assisted, or participated in any manner in an investigation, proceeding, or hearing under this subchapter."

13. The Supreme Court has been solicitous of retaliation claims. Indeed, the Court has been willing to infer the existence of retaliation claims in discrimination statutes when the statutory text does not mention a retaliation claim (*Gomez-Perez v. Potter* 2008; *CBOCS West, Inc. v. Humphries* 2008; *Jackson v. Birmingham Board of Education* 2005).

14. He noted: "We expect that firing a close family member will almost always meet the [dissuasion] standard, and inflicting a milder reprisal on a mere acquaintance will almost never do so, but beyond that we are reluctant to generalize" (*Thompson v. North American Stainless* LP 2011, 175).

15. See 42 U.S.C. §2000e-5(b).

16. Justice Scalia has not always been particularly solicitous of retaliation claims. He dissented from the Court's decision in *Kasten v. Saint-Gobain Performance Plastics, Inc.* (2011) that ruled that an oral complaint to an employer may be sufficient to trigger the Fair Labor Standards Act (FLSA) retaliation provision. The FLSA bars an employer from retaliating against an employee "because such employee has *filed any complaint* or instituted or caused to be instituted any proceeding under or related to [the Act], or has testified or is about to testify in such proceeding" (*Kasten v. Saint-Gobain Performance Plastics, Inc.* 2011, 4) Justice Scalia argued that no complaint to an employer—oral or written—triggers the FLSA retaliation provision because only complaints to a judicial or administrative body trigger retaliation protection. Justice Scalia's approach was unsurprising given that he believed that the FLSA gave a clear text-based answer to the legal question at issue. However, given how solicitous the Court has been of retaliation claims, barring a sea change on the Court, the ideas underlying Justice Scalia's dissent are not likely to become law soon.

17. In that case, the Director argued that she was "a person adversely affected or aggrieved" by a poor decision by the Benefits Review Board (Board) because as the

Department of Labor official tasked with administering the statute under which the award was made, the poor decision undermined her ability to properly administer the statute. Justice Scalia rejected the argument, deciding that the Director was outside of the statute's zone of interests (*Director, Office of Workers' Compensation Programs, Dep't of Labor (the Director) v. Newport News Shipbuilding and Dry Dock Company* 1995, 136).

18. The term "cat's paw" emanates from an Aesop's fable in which a monkey convinces a cat to reach into a fire and risk injury to get chestnuts the monkey will then take (*Staub v. Proctor Hospital* 2011, 415).

19. Future courts will need to analyze when proximate cause has been proven, as proximate cause is a notoriously difficult concept to apply (Corbett 2013; Sullivan 2012).

20. 42 U.S.C. §2000e-5(e)(1). The short limitations period can be particularly problematic for employees when an employer's discrimination is not obvious. (Brake and Grossman 2008).

21. See 42 U.S.C. §2000e-5(b)(2): "For purposes of this section, an unlawful employment practice occurs, with respect to a seniority system that has been adopted for an intentionally discriminatory purpose in violation of this subchapter (whether or not that discriminatory purpose is apparent on the face of the seniority provision), when the seniority system is adopted, when an individual becomes subject to the seniority system, or when a person aggrieved is injured by the application of the seniority system or provision of the system."

22. See 42 U.S.C. §2000e-5(k): "In any action or proceeding under this subchapter the court, in its discretion, may allow the prevailing party, other than the Commission or the United States, a reasonable attorney's fee (including expert fees) as part of the costs, and the Commission and the United States shall be liable for costs the same as a private person."

23. The discretionary nature of fee shifting arguably provided Justice Scalia latitude to craft his opinion, but the opinion was not required by the statute's text or intent (Brand 1990, 351).

24. The focus is no surprise given Justice Scalia's professorial writings in which he extols the innocence of those who may have benefited from discrimination (Scalia 1979).

25. He notes: "In fact, the only losers in the process are the Johnsons of the country, for whom Title VII has been not merely repealed, but actually inverted" (*Johnson v. Transportation Agency, Santa Clara County* 1987, 677). Of course, Title VII may be used by anyone, even in an untraditional fashion, if that employee has a viable claim (Sullivan 2004).

26. Federal Rule of Civil Procedure 23(a)(2).

27. That opinion regarding how workplaces operate may be incorrect (Wexler 2011).

28. He suggested that the class needs proof of "a common mode of exercising discretion that pervades the entire company" (*Wal-Mart Stores, Inc.* 2011, 356).

29. Such evidence was not required in early systemic disparate treatment cases, which relied heavily on statistical evidence (Paetzold and Rholes 2017, 116).

30. See 42 U.S.C. §2000e-6 (describing class-based pattern or practice cases brought by the EEOC). Pattern or practice claims, such as those in International Brotherhood of Teamsters v. United States (1977) and *Hazelwood School District v. United States* (1977), resemble the claims in *Dukes*.

31. Indeed, in *Alexander v. Gardner-Denver Co*. (1974), the Court determined that Title VII plaintiffs did not lose the right to adjudicate their Title VII claims in court after they arbitrated those claims.

32. Justice Scalia was part of a bare majority that deemed employment contracts arbitrable despite language in the Federal Arbitration Act excluding "contracts of employment" from coverage. See *Circuit City Stores, Inc. v. Adams* (2001) (holding Federal Arbitration Act to exclude only the employment contracts of transportation workers from arbitration).

33. *Nitro-Lift Technologies, LLC v. Howard* 2012, 20.

34. For example, he wrote the majority opinion in *AT&T Mobility LLC v. Concepcion*, 563 U.S. 333 (2011), holding that a company cannot be forced to arbitrate class claims if the arbitration agreement bars class arbitration claims. Plaintiffs had argued that the limitation on class claims was unconscionable. He also joined the majority or per curiam opinions in various cases supporting the expansion of arbitration and joined the dissent in cases restricting arbitration. See *Nitro-Lift Technologies, LLC v. Howard* (2012; per curiam); *14 Penn Plaza v. Pyett, LLC* (2009; majority); *EEOC v. Waffle House, Inc*. (2002; dissenting).

REFERENCES

Barrett, Amy Coney. 2017. "Originalism and Stare Decisis." *Notre Dame Law Review* 92: 1921–43.

Beiner, Theresa M. 2002. "Let the Jury Decide: The Gap between What Judges and Reasonable People Believe Is Sexually Harassing." *Southern California Law Review* 75: 791–846.

———. 2014. "The Trouble with Torgerson: The Latest Effort to Summarily Adjudicate Employment Discrimination Cases." *Nevada Law Journal* 14: 673–704.

Brake, Deborah L. and Joanna L. Grossman. 2008. "The Failure of Title VII as a Rights-Claiming System." *North Carolina Law Review* 86: 859–935.

Brand, Jeffrey S. 1990. "The Second Front in the Fight for Civil Rights: The Supreme Court, Congress, and Statutory Fees." *Texas Law Review* 69: 291–382.

Chambers, Jr., Henry L. 2005. "Recapturing Summary Adjudication Principles in Disparate Treatment Cases." *SMU Law Review* 58: 103–35.

Chambers, Jr., Henry L. 2004. "The Effect of Eliminating Distinctions Among Title VII Disparate Treatment Cases." *SMU Law Review* 57: 83–103.

———. 2001. "Discrimination, Plain and Simple." *Tulsa Law Journal* 36: 557–82.

———. 2000. "A Unifying Theory of Sex Discrimination." *Georgia Law Review* 34: 1591–643.

Chambers, Henry L. Jr. 1996. "Getting It Right: Uncertainty and Error in the New Disparate Treatment Paradigm." *Albany Law Review* 60: 1–59.

Clarke, Jessica A. 2017. "Frontiers of Sex Discrimination Law." *Michigan Law Review* 115: 809–37.

Corbett, William R. 2013. "Unmasking a Pretext for Res Ipsa Loquitur: A Proposal to Let Employment Discrimination Speak for Itself." *American University Law Review* 62: 447–511.

Corbett, William R. 2009. "Fixing Employment Discrimination Law." *SMU Law Review* 62: 81–116.

Flake, Dallan F. 2016. "Religious Discrimination Based on Employer Misperception." *Wisconsin Law Review* 2016: 87–132.

Frank, Michael J. 2002. "The Social Context Variable in Hostile Environment Litigation." *Notre Dame Law Review* 77: 437–532.

Goldberg, Suzanne B. 2011. "Discrimination by Comparison." *Yale Law Journal* 120: 728–812.

Green, Tristin K. 2011. "The Future of Systemic Disparate Treatment Law." *Berkeley Journal of Employment and Labor Law* 32: 395–454.

Greenberger, Steven. 2017. "Justice Scalia and the Demise of the Employment Class Action." *Employee Rights and Employment Policy Journal* 21: 75–113.

Greene, Jamal. 2009. "Selling Originalism." *Georgetown Law Journal* 97: 657–721.

Harper, Michael C. 2010. "The Causation Standard in Federal Employment Law: Gross v. FBL Financial Services, Inc., and the Unfulfilled Promise of the Civil Rights Act of 1991." *Buffalo Law Review* 58: 69–145.

———. 2015. "Class-Based Adjudication of Title VII Claims in the Age of the Roberts Court." *Boston University Law Review* 95: 1099–131.

Hart, Melissa and Paul M. Secunda. 2009. "A Matter of Context: Social Framework Evidence in Employment Discrimination Class Actions." *Fordham Law Review* 78: 37–70.

Lidge III, Ernest F. 2002. "The Courts' Misuse of the Similarly Situated Concept in Employment Discrimination Law." *Missouri Law Review* 67: 831–82.

McCormick, Marcia L. 2013. "Constitutional Limitations on Closing the Gender Gap in Employment." *FIU Law Review* 8: 405–22.

McGinley, Ann C. 2007. "Harassing 'Girls' at the Hard Rock: Masculinities in Sexualized Environments." *University of Illinois Law Review* 2007: 1229–77.

Morrison, Angela D. 2013. "Duke-ing Out Pattern or Practice After Wal-Mart: The EEOC as Fist." *American University Law Review* 63: 87–155.

Paetzold, Ramona L. and W. Steven Rholes. 2017. "Wal-Mart v. Dukes: Justice Scalia and Systemic Disparate Treatment Theory." *Employee Rights and Employment Policy Journal* 21: 115–62.

Ramsey, Michael D. 2017 "Beyond the Text: Justice Scalia's Originalism in Practice." *Notre Dame Law Review* 92: 1945–75.

Scalia, Antonin. 1989. "Originalism: The Lesser Evil." *University of Cincinnati Law Review* 57: 849–65.

———. 1979. "The Disease as Cure: 'In Order to Get Beyond Racism, We Must First Take Account of Race.'" *Washington University Law Quarterly* 1979: 147–57.

Schwartz, Martin A. 2011. "Attorney's Fees in Civil Rights Cases—October 2009 Term." *Touro Law Review* 27: 113–23.

Stone, Katherine V. W. 2017. "The Bold Ambition of Justice Scalia's Arbitration Jurisprudence: Keep Workers and Consumers out of Court." *Employee Rights and Employment Policy Journal* 21: 189–220.

Sullivan, Charles A. 2012. "Tortifying Employment Discrimination." *Boston University Law Review* 92: 1431–183.

———. 2004. "The World Turned Upside Down?: Disparate Impact Claims by White Males." *Northwestern University Law Review* 98: 1505–65.

———. 2009. "The Phoenix from the Ash: Proving Discrimination by Comparators." *Alabama Law Review* 60: 191–239.

———. 2010. "Raising the Dead?: The Lilly Ledbetter Fair Pay Act." *Tulane Law Review* 84: 499–563.

———. 2011. "Plausibly Pleading Employment Discrimination." *William and Mary Law Review* 52: 1613–77.

Thomas, Justice Clarence. 2017. "A Tribute to Justice Antonin Scalia." *Yale Law Journal* 126: 1600–604.

Tobias, Carl. 1992. "Civil Rights Procedural Problems." *Washington University Law Quarterly* 70: 801–19.

Wexler, Leslie. 2011. "Wal-Mart Matters." *Wake Forest Law Review* 46: 95–121.

Wiecek, William M. and Judy L. Hamilton. 2014. "Beyond the Civil Rights Act of 1964: Confronting Structural Racism in the Workplace." *Louisiana Law Review* 74: 1095–160.

TABLE OF CASES

14 Penn Plaza LLC v. Pyett, 556 U.S. 247 (2009).

Alexander v. Gardner-Denver Co., 415 U.S. 36 (1974).

AT&T Mobility LLC v. Concepcion, 563 U.S. 333 (2011).

Burlington Industries, Inc. v. Ellerth, 524 U.S. 742 (1998).

Burlington Northern & Sante Fe Railway Co. v. White, 548 U.S. 53 (2006).

CBOCS West, Inc. v. Humphries, 553 U.S. 442 (2008).

Christiansburg Garment Co. v. Equal Employment Opportunity Commission (EEOC), 434 U.S. 412 (1978).

Circuit City Stores, Inc. v. Adams, 532 U.S. 105 (2001).

Director, Office of Workers' Compensation Programs, Dep't of Labor v. Newport News Shipbuilding and Dry Dock Company, 514 U.S. 122 (1995).

EEOC v. Abercrombie & Fitch Stores, Inc., 135 S.Ct. 2028 (2015).

EEOC v. Waffle House, Inc., 534 U.S. 279 (2002).

Faragher v. City of Boca Raton, 524 U.S. 775 (1998).

Gilmer v. Interstate/Johnson Lane Corp., 500 U.S. 20 (1991).

Gomez-Perez v. Potter, 553 U.S. 474 (2008).

Griggs v. Duke Power Co., 401 U.S. 424 (1971).
Harris v. Forklift Systems, Inc., 510 U.S. 17 (1993).
Hazelwood School District v. United States, 433 U.S. 299 (1977).
International Brotherhood of Teamsters v. United States, 431 U.S. 324 (1977).
Independent Federation of Flight Attendants v. Zipes, 491 U.S. 754 (1989).
Jackson v. Birmingham Board of Education, 544 U.S. 167 (2005).
Johnson v. Transportation Agency, Santa Clara County, 480 U.S. 616 (1987).
Kasten v. Saint-Gobain Performance Plastics Corp., 563 U.S. 1 (2011).
Lewis v. City of Chicago, 560 U.S. 205 (2010).
Lorance v. AT&T Technologies, Inc., 490 U.S. 900 (1989).
McDonnell Douglas Corp. v. Green, 411 U.S. 792 (1973).
Nitro-Lift Technologies v. Howard, 568 U.S. 17 (2012).
O'Connor v. Consolidated Coin Caterers Corp., 517 U.S. 308 (1996).
Oncale v. Sundowner Offshore Services, Inc., 523 U.S. 75 (1998).
Reeves v. Sanderson Plumbing Products, Inc., 530 U.S. 133 (2000).
Rent-A-Center, West, Inc. v. Jackson, 561 U.S. 63 (2010).
Ricci v. DeStegano, 557 U.S. 557 (2009).
St. Mary's Honor Center v. Hicks, 509 U.S. 502 (1993).
Staub v. Proctor Hospital, 562 U.S. 411 (2011).
Thompson v. North American Stainless, LP, 562 U.S. 170 (2011).
Vance v. Ball State University, 133 S.Ct. 2434 (2013).
Wal-Mart Stores, Inc. v. Dukes, 564 U.S. 338 (2011).
Waterhouse v. Hopkins, 490 U.S. 228 (1989).
Wright v. Universal Maritime Service Corp., 525 U.S. 70 (1998).
Young v. United Parcel Service, Inc., 135 S.Ct. 1338 (2015).

Chapter 3

Playing Defense in the "Culture Wars"

Justice Scalia on Race, Gender, and Sexual Orientation

Mary Welek Atwell

While to many jurists, legal scholars, and political activists, the Fourteenth Amendment's promise of equal protection is a doorway to greater rights for groups who have been excluded, to Justice Antonin Scalia it was more often a fortress defending the status quo. Scalia tended to reject the prevailing constitutional framework laid out in the 1938 *Carolene Products* case (*United States v. Carolene Products* 1938). He replaced that model with a much less expansive interpretation of the Fourteenth Amendment. Using the *Carolene Products* paradigm, courts would generally defer to legislatures on economic subjects, working from the assumption that economic regulations were probably constitutional if they had been properly adopted. On the other hand, courts, including the Supreme Court, would exercise greater scrutiny in reviewing laws that limited minority access to the political process or those that might reflect prejudice against "discrete and insular minorities" (1938). But unlike those who subscribed to the *Carolene* model, Scalia argued that the Supreme Court should show great deference to expressions of majority sentiment regarding race, gender, and sexual orientation. As Schultz and Smith (1996) assert, with respect to the Equal Protection Clause, Scalia "advanced a different hierarchy of values or pattern of assumptions" (Schultz and Smith 1996, xxii). His opinions reexamined which rights and which persons were to be protected and seemed to conclude that whites, men, and heterosexuals were in need of safeguards to ensure their interests.

Justice Scalia was a self-described "textualist" who claimed to interpret the Constitution by following the meaning "fairly ascribed" to the words of the text when it was written (Smith 1993, 34). Regarding the Fourteenth Amendment, Ring (2016) explains that, despite the broad sweep of the term "equal protection of the law," Scalia maintained that if an "asserted individual liberty had been restricted or eliminated by the states throughout history, the claim for constitutional protection should fail" (2). With such a reading, any group not envisioned as deserving constitutional protection when the amendment was adopted in 1868 was out of luck in making claims in the twentieth century. But Roosevelt does not find that the text of the amendment compels this interpretation. He asks whether the words "equal protection" mean that "no state shall make any distinction based on race, but discrimination based on sexual orientation is okay?" (Roosevelt 2005, 31). The words of the amendment do not resolve this question. Some theory is called for. The *Carolene Products* theory would hold that the Constitution protects the weaker citizens from the majority, that it was intended to prevent invidious discrimination meant to harm any group (Roosevelt 2005). Scalia would disagree. His version would change the Equal Protection Clause from a general statement that safeguards minorities to a narrow one that only prohibits all classification by race no matter who benefits. Through his constricted reading of the Equal Protection Clause, he "takes the side of the majority and protects them from being asked to make any sacrifice" (33). But, as Roosevelt states, neither Scalia's version nor the *Carolene* reading is compelled by the text. Each constitutes a value choice. Scalia chose the interpretation that maintained existing privilege.

According to Rossum (2006), Scalia was "the Court's most outspoken, intelligent, interesting, high profile, and colorful member" (1). He was eloquent in defense of textualism, arguing that judges must confine themselves to applying the text of the Constitution if its meaning is clear and to employing the contemporary sense of the provision if its language is more general. Rossum maintains that Scalia believed the framers did not intend to have the judiciary resolve evolving modern rights issues by interpreting their own preferences to overrule the majority. Rather, the Constitution created "two conflicting systems of rights," majority rule and the protection of individuals from the tyranny of the majority (28). Scalia's version of which of those should prevail was selective.

Scalia wrote and spoke often about constitutional interpretation. He contrasted those, like himself, who looked for the original meaning with those who believed in the "living Constitution." The latter group, in his view, imposed new constraints upon administrative, judicial, and legal action by substituting their views of social change for the decisions of the majority (Scalia 1997). As for the Equal Protection Clause, Scalia trivialized the concerns of those who argued for its broader meaning. According to the justice, the Fourteenth Amendment did not prohibit discrimination on the basis of age, property, sex, "sexual orientation, blue eyes, or nose rings" (148). Requiring separate toilets for men and women or excluding women from combat did not constitute a denial of equal protection. (No one was really arguing this point.) He advised his colleagues to look at the meaning of equal protection at the time the amendment was adopted in 1868. If the framers' intentions were insufficient, any additional guarantees of rights could be adopted by legislatures (Scalia 1997). Scalia expressed suspicion of his colleagues for "inventing" rights "through abstract legal tests that erode traditional values and practices." He was critical of "elite" judges and the "law professor culture" that supported a "liberal agenda of secular humanism, abortion rights, affirmative action, opposition to the death penalty, and homosexual rights" and tried to impose those values on the majority (Staab 2006, 207). His claims to be a textualist rested on the contrast between his assertion that he read the words of the Fourteenth Amendment as its informed contemporaries would have read them, while the judges he criticized interjected their own modern values.

Epps (2011) writes that Scalia's "easy, simple meaning" of constitutional language "usually coincides" with policies advocated by twentieth-century judicial conservatives. He claims that Scalia's textualism was an intellectual weapon developed to obscure the text of the constitution and its application to present circumstances from ordinary citizens (Epps 2011). Textualism, then, can be merely a device to advance the argument that one meaning of the Fourteenth Amendment—the most narrow and conservative meaning—is inherent in the words of the Amendment.

Bassham (2006/2007) argues against the description of Scalia as a textualist. He asserts that the words of the Equal Protection Clause are not "clear in context" but that the language is "broad and expansive" (147). He cites many arguments by historians regarding the provision's original meaning and is puzzled how Scalia could believe that the text compels a reading that the Amendment prohibits *only* state sponsored racial discrimination. Why did Scalia maintain that the purpose of the Constitution is to "nail down current rights not aspire to future ones"? Scalia claimed it was to prevent activist judges from adding their own list of rights to those protected by the Constitution. But, Bassham maintains, by deciding that the broad language of the Fourteenth Amendment is "deficient," and trying to restrict its meaning, Scalia was, in fact, appealing to the general purpose of the framers and to the spirit of the Constitution. This is not textualism, but equitable interpretation (Bassham 2006/2007).

Dworkin (1997) makes a related point—either the words of the Constitution can have only their literal meaning at the time of writing or they set out abstract principles. He contends that respected jurists would agree that even if the framers did not envision the twentieth century version of equal protection, they did not distinguish forms of discrimination. Rather the Fourteenth Amendment was meant to enact moral principles, not be limited to a single narrow meaning.

The remainder of this chapter will follow this argument—Justice Scalia protests that the Court has read too much into the Fourteenth Amendment by extending it to groups not envisioned when it was adopted in 1868. His colleagues on the other side tend to apply the *Carolene Products* framework and argue for greater scrutiny when majorities have restricted the rights of protected classes including women and same-sex couples. In examining cases dealing with race, gender, and sexual orientation, the chapter will note how Scalia's skepticism about equal protection often coincided with mainstream and traditional views in the culture wars. He saw himself playing defense by speaking for the conservative majority, and opposing the "legal elites" and their ideas of social change.

RACE

During Scalia's tenure on the Court, he had several opportunities to articulate his position on the meaning of the Fourteenth Amendment as it applied to race and especially to the use of affirmative action as a means of addressing previous racial discrimination. According to Rossum (2006), Scalia saw neither ambiguity nor any need to consider tradition in understanding the meaning of "equal protection." He was certain that combined with the Thirteenth Amendment's "prohibition of slavery and the badges of slavery," equal protection meant that any law treating people differently on the basis of race was invalid. Like Justice John Marshall Harlan, Scalia frequently noted that the Constitution was color-blind (*Plessy v. Ferguson* 1896). Given this sweeping ban on any consideration of race, it was not surprising that Scalia made the argument that the government could not endorse racial inequity for any reason—not to make up for past discrimination or to promote diversity. In his view, there was no state interest compelling enough to justify treating racial groups differently (Rossum 2006). Ring (2016) notes that Scalia found no such thing as "benign" racial classification. To him, any racial classification must be subjected to strict scrutiny and consequently, none could stand. He further maintained that the Equal Protection Clause applied to individuals, not to groups. It was unthinkable that the government could burden one individual to provide an advantage to another. To consider that members of a racial group who had suffered historical discrimination might in the present be given an extra advantage for a job or a place in college meant that some other worthy applicant would be disadvantaged on account of *his* (white) race.

Prior to Scalia's tenure, the Supreme Court had ruled on the *Bakke* case. There Justice Lewis Powell wrote that in order to promote diversity, government entities might consider race as a factor in college admissions when all other factors were equal (*Regents of the University of California v. Bakke* 1978). Many believed that such programs were necessary and desirable as a means of rectifying past inequities. But even before he became a member of the Court, Scalia had been arguing that such "racial preferences" were, in fact, a form of racism (Murphy 2014, 91–92).

In *Richmond v. J.A. Croson Co.* (1989), the Court considered the constitutionality of a Richmond, Virginia program designed to assist minority-owned businesses by requiring contractors on city projects to allocate at least 30 percent of their subcontracts to minority-owned businesses. The purpose was to address past discrimination against such companies. The Court, in a 6–3 decision written by Justice Sandra Day O'Connor, applied strict scrutiny in evaluating the affirmative action program. They found the minority set-aside unconstitutional. O'Connor wrote that although the city had a compelling interest in remedying past discrimination, in this case they had not proven that the set-aside program was necessary to address the history of discrimination. Justice Scalia agreed that the Richmond program was unconstitutional but wrote a concurring opinion in which he took issue with O'Connor's contention that race-based programs could ever by justified or that such attempts to rectify past injustices could ever be benign. He quoted Alexander Bickel who wrote that "the lesson of the great decisions of the Supreme Court and the lesson of contemporary history have been the same for at least a generation: discrimination on the basis of race is illegal, immoral, unconstitutional, inherently wrong, and destructive of democratic society" (*Richmond v. J.A. Croson Co.* 1989). He differed from some of his colleagues in defining any consideration of race as a form of discrimination, no matter how benevolent or malignant the purpose. Any classification of people by race could be a source of injustice. To Scalia, the relevant proposition regarding discrimination was not which groups had suffered disadvantages but which individual men and women. He went on to warn that racial discrimination finds "more ready expression at the state and local level than at the federal level" (1989). In a rather remarkable statement about a program developed in the former capital of the Confederacy, he was speaking of discrimination against the white majority when he wrote that not all discrimination was directed against blacks and not all of it occurred in the Old South. Scalia went further in warning against "reverse discrimination" that would victimize white citizens. He called for an "acute awareness of the heightened danger of oppression from political factions in small, rather than large political units [that] dates from the very beginnings of our national history" (*Richmond v. J.A. Croson Co.* 1989). In other words, he was pointing out that the Richmond plan benefitted the city's "dominant" political and racial group—African Americans. Despite the troubled racial history of Virginia, Scalia felt the need to issue a warning that the set-aside program constituted an example of oppression by the local black majority. He acknowledged that blacks had "often been on the receiving end of injustice." Nonetheless, "where injustice is the game, turnabout is not fair play" (1989).

He sounded a theme that would permeate many of his opinions on racial discrimination. It was important to him to admit that even the most well intentioned racial quotas have individual victims who, through no fault of their own are being disadvantaged because of their race. Any attempt to compensate for past injustices, to "even the score," reinforces the tendency of Americans to continue to think of people on the basis of their race. "The relevant proposition is not that it was blacks, or Jews, or Irish who were discriminated against, but that it was individual men and women, 'created equal,' who were discriminated against. And the relevant resolve is that it should never happen again" (1989).

The Court revisited the issue of affirmative action in the 1995 case, *Adarand Constructors, Inc. v. Pena* where they considered a federal program that provided financial incentives to government contractors who hired small businesses controlled by "socially and economically disadvantaged individuals" (*Adarand Constructors, Inc. v. Pena* 1995). The latter term was generally held to mean racial and ethnic minorities and women. Scalia concurred in the decision that applied the standard of strict scrutiny to federal affirmative action programs. This meant that programs involving a racial classification must meet the highest standard of review—they must be narrowly tailored to meet a compelling government interest. Although the Court did not define what constitutes a compelling interest, Justices Scalia and Thomas expressed the view that there can never be a compelling interest for any "racial preference." The remedy for discrimination should be targeted at individuals who had been wronged, not at groups. "Under our Constitution there can be no such thing as either a creditor or a debtor race. That concept is alien to the Constitution's focus upon the individual" (*Adarand Constructors, Inc. v. Pena* 1995). In his view, everyone stood alone before the Constitution, not as part of a group. Scalia wrote "To pursue the concept of racial entitlement—even for the most admirable and benign of purposes—is to reinforce and preserve for future mischief the way of thinking that produced race slavery, race privilege, and race hatred. In the eyes of government, we are just one race here. It is American" (1995). He seemed to be conflating any recognition that racial minorities *because of their race* had been historically disadvantaged with awarding them some sort of "entitlement." From that recognition he found it a slippery slope to slavery and hatred, although it is not clear who would be doing the hating and enslaving.

Greene (2016) wrote that Scalia's insistence on strict scrutiny in affirmative action cases "constitutionalizes a status quo of disparate racial access while subjecting the government's interest in substantive equality to a presumption of unconstitutionality" (171). In other words, the government's hands would be tied; preventing any effort to address the burdens of centuries of racial injustice for fear that recognizing those injustices would represent a form of racism. It was a position that disarmed the Equal Protection Clause as a weapon against racial discrimination.

Affirmative action in higher education was the subject of *Grutter v. Bollinger* (2003) where the Court considered whether the University of Michigan Law School's admission policy was unconstitutional. A white applicant claimed reverse discrimination, arguing that she had been denied admission while less qualified minority students had been accepted. The Court upheld the program that considered race—along with many other factors in assessing applicants—as fulfilling a compelling state interest in achieving a diverse student body. Justice O'Connor's opinion for the Court held that the educational benefits derived from diversity justified a consideration of race and that the means of achieving that goal were narrowly tailored to achieve it (*Grutter v. Bollinger* 2003).

Scalia, joined by Justice Clarence Thomas, dissented from the decision. In an opinion laced with sarcasm, he questioned the benefits of diversity as a compelling state interest. He doubted that a diverse academic environment was a factor in teaching good citizenship. But if consideration of race were necessary to achieve diversity and consideration of race was identical to racial discrimination, then surely private employers should be praised for racial discrimination in hiring as a means of teaching good citizenship to their employees. "The nonminority individuals who are deprived of a legal education, a civil service job, or any job at all by reason of their skin color will surely understand" (2003).

In other non-affirmative action cases, Justice Scalia made a number of comments that raised the question of whether he believed racial discrimination even existed or if it did, whether it mattered. For example, he addressed Justice Thurgood Marshall's dissent in *McCleskey v. Kemp* (1987), a case dealing with racial bias in the administration of the death penalty. Biskupic (2009) quotes Scalia describing Marshall "The dissent rolls out the ultimate weapon, insensitivity to racial discrimination—which will lose its intimidating effect if it continues to be fired so randomly" (155). Was it possible that Scalia thought Marshall's allegation of racial discrimination in the justice system was a mere rhetorical device meant to intimidate? He trivialized the claim that race was a significant factor in determining who got sentenced to death. "What if statistics showed that the shifty-eyed were more likely to get the death penalty?" (Biskupic 2009, 151). Perhaps those statements are merely examples of what Tushnet (2006) calls Scalia's "sound bite style that reduces complex issues to simple—and often misleading—phrases" (150–51). Or perhaps they are indicative of a refusal to admit the reality of racism in the American legal system.

It seems clear that Scalia saw many racial issues, including affirmative action, through the eyes of those who felt they had lost out to racial minorities for jobs or educational opportunities. After the Bakke decision, Scalia often criticized "the Lewis Powells of the world who made it tough for the sons of the working class" (Biskupic 2009, 181). Staab (2006) quotes Scalia's rather defensive resistance to the notion of compensating for past racial injustices. The justice began by denying that his family had ever benefitted from slavery. "Many white ethnic groups—Italians, Jews, Irish, Poles—took no part in and deprived no profit from the major historical suppression of the currently acknowledged minority groups but were, in fact, themselves the object of discrimination by the dominant Anglo-Saxon majority" (2). One might contrast Scalia's perspective on affirmative action with Justice Thomas's position. The latter viewed such programs from the point of view of the intended beneficiaries and often complained that affirmative action was demeaning to African Americans. Scalia, on the other hand believed "racial preferences" were bad for the "Polish factory worker's kid" (Biskupic 2009, 174).

It is a challenge to find that Scalia's narrow reading of the Equal Protection Clause to prohibit any consideration of race, no matter the purpose, is compelled by the text itself. Nor is such an interpretation required by his deference to the majority as the legitimate source of expanding the rights protected by the Constitution. Two examples may be illustrative. The Richmond, Virginia, program he found unacceptable was adopted by the local city council. Yet he faulted it for benefitting the majority, the dominant political group, African Americans. Likewise in *Shelby County v. Holder* (2013), which found sections of the 1965 Voting Rights Act unconstitutional, Scalia voted with the Court majority to nullify an act recently reaffirmed by the majority in Congress, agreeing implicitly with Chief Justice Roberts that racial discrimination is a relic of the past. During oral arguments in that case, he even referred to guarantees of voting access for African Americans as a "perpetuation of racial entitlement" (Murphy 2014, 483).

As Schultz and Smith (1996) point out, Scalia's belief in the efficacy of the political process to legislate regarding matters of race and affirmative action was selective. His faith in the majority seemed to depend on the policy area, as the following discussion of gender and sexual orientation will illustrate.

GENDER

Although there is debate about how the Equal Protection Clause of the Fourteenth Amendment should be applied to distinctions based on race, no one would deny that it is intended to prohibit some types of racial discrimination. There are those, including apparently Justice Scalia, who would limit the amendment's efficacy to issues of race and find no reason to apply it to any other type of discrimination, including that based on gender. In a speech in 2010, Scalia stated that "Nobody thought it [the Equal Protection Clause] was directed against sex discrimination." He further argued that the idea of prohibiting bias against women was "a modern invention" (Murphy 2014, 424). He reiterated the point in an article published the next year in *California Lawyer*. "Nobody ever voted for that [a constitutional prohibition of sex discrimination]. If the current society wants to outlaw discrimination by sex, hey we have things called legislatures, and they enact things called laws" (Murphy 2014, 425. The statement is further evidence that Scalia rejected the *Carolene* framework. That perspective would hold that because the ordinary political processes might not protect minorities (if not a numerical minority, women are often considered analogous to a minority based on their historical exclusion from political power), the courts must exercise a higher level of scrutiny to ensure their protection.

Scalia revealed his reluctance to apply the Equal Protection Clause and expand safeguards against gender discrimination in a number of cases, including *J.E.B. v. Alabama* (1994) and especially *United States v. Virginia* (1996). *J.E.B.* concerned the use of peremptory strikes in jury selection. Could a prosecutor excuse potential jurors on the basis of sex or were such strikes an example of unacceptable discrimination prohibited by the Fourteenth Amendment? The Court found that the Equal Protection Clause forbids intentional discrimination on the basis of sex, just as it forbids intentional discrimination on the basis of race. The biased use of peremptory challenges by state actors (prosecutors) "perpetuates invidious, archaic, and overbroad stereotypes about the relative abilities of men and women" (*J.E.B. v. Alabama* 1996). The opinion compared exclusions based on race to the history of prejudice against women and found both unconstitutional. Justice Scalia in his dissent offered both sarcasm and skepticism. He referred to the opinion as "an inspiring demonstration of how thoroughly up-to-date and right-thinking" the justices were, although he also found most of it irrelevant to the case. Among the "irrelevant" ideas was the discussion of women's historical exclusion from both juries and the practice of law. To Scalia, the only thing those examples have in common is that they both involve "going to the courthouse a lot." He also found the discussion of whether gender is related to jurors' attitudes "utterly irrelevant." He stated that the legal reasoning in the case was "largely obscured by anti-male chauvinist oratory." He wondered whether, when the Court referred to "impermissible stereotypes," it found some stereotypes permissible. He expected to learn in the future "which stereotypes the Constitution frowns upon and which it does not." The whole ruling, in Scalia's mind, did not "eliminate any real denial of equal protection but simply [pays] conspicuous obeisance to the equality of the sexes" (*J.E.B. v. Alabama* 1994). It is the tone of this dissenting opinion that trivializes and diminishes the seriousness of gender discrimination. It is possible that Scalia believed that equality between men and women is just a "modern invention" or a fashionable trend that swept through the Court. It is possible that he did not appreciate the significance of women's historical marginalization from political power. But it is also possible that he chose to resist the expansion of equal protection as a way to fend off social change or perhaps because he actually doubted that women *were* equal to men.

In 1996, the Court ruled in *United States v. Virginia* that Virginia Military Institute (VMI), an all-male state university, must admit women to be in compliance with the Constitution. Justice Ruth Bader Ginsburg wrote the 7–1 opinion. Justice Thomas had recused himself as his son was a VMI student. Scalia was the only dissenter.

Ginsburg had long been a major contributor to the development of constitutional arguments to promote gender equality. As a litigator, she had argued and won several cases before the Supreme Court that extended Fourteenth Amendment protections to women. Now as a member of the Court, she had the opportunity in the VMI case to solidify that progress through a clear statement of equal protection. Ginsburg's strategy had been to draw comparisons between race discrimination and gender discrimination and to show that there was no rational basis for differential treatment based on sex. Such treatment tended to reflect archaic generalizations. Prior to *United States v. Virginia* the Court had ruled in *Craig v. Boren* (1976) that any legal distinctions on the basis of sex must serve important government objectives and must be substantially related to achieving those objectives (Tushnet 2006). This was not strict scrutiny, but "intermediate scrutiny." It was a high standard of review but not as rigorous as the scrutiny given to distinctions based on race.

Justice Scalia could not tolerate the Court's expansion of equal protection to women. In dismissing their refinement of the levels of scrutiny, he charged that his judicial colleagues thought they were free to "evaluate everything under the sun by applying one of three tests." Those "made-up tests cannot displace longstanding traditions as the primary determinant of what the Constitution means" (Rossum 2006, 163). Scalia's dissent in the VMI case is a lengthy, discursive harangue against the damage to the law and to tradition that would be wrought by a decision to admit women to the school. The ruling, according to Scalia, "sweeps aside the precedents of this Court and ignores the history of our people." He was outraged that it deprecated "the closed mindedness of our forebears regarding women's education" and the treatment of women. It was full of "smug assurances" about "current preferences" (*United States v. Virginia* 1996). One can only read his language as a claim that the tradition of regarding women as second class citizens with a truncated version of human rights was a tradition worth preserving. In fact, Scalia wrote that it was the function of the Court "to *preserve* our society's values, not to *revise* them; to prevent backsliding" (*United States v. Virginia* 1996). He seems to be suggesting that the judiciary has no role in recognizing that rights have been denied or in rectifying such denials. It seems a contradiction of the notion of equal protection when Scalia argues that the Fourteenth Amendment cannot supersede "constant and unbroken national traditions" of "open, widespread, and unchallenged use." Surely some such traditions grew out of prejudice and bigotry. Should they be preserved because they are unbroken and widespread? Apparently, in Scalia's view, only a majority could legislate a change to these fixed principles. Judges should preserve, not update, the values of the founding generation (Staab 2006, 217). The Court should not "create" new rights. In doing so, they would deprive the "people" of their "most important right, self-government in a democracy" (Rossum 2006, 164–65).

As for the particulars of the VMI case, Scalia disputed a number of arguments accepted by the Court majority. Unlike his colleagues, he was willing to accept that findings of the lower courts that emphasized the differences between men and women. He rejected the notion that *some* women would flourish at VMI. "There is simply no support in our cases for the notion that a sex-based classification is invalid unless it related to characteristics that hold true in every instance" (*United States v. Virginia* 1996). In other words, sex-based classifications are acceptable if they reflect a general fact about the group. He also accepted VMI's rationale that the school contributed "diversity" to higher education in Virginia as it was the only state-sponsored, single-sex military institute. He rejected the notion that its refusal to admit women reflected antifeminism or misogyny. Finally, Scalia predicted that, as a result of the decision, single-sex education in the United States would be dead and VMI would face destruction. But in the last analysis, he maintained, even the Court could not deprive the school of its honor. "No court opinion can do that." Scalia ended his dissent with a lengthy quotation from a booklet called "The Code of a Gentleman," given to all new VMI students. It spoke of defending the defenseless and treating ladies with respect, of paying debts, and showing good manners in the ballroom. It cautioned against slapping strangers on the back or laying a finger on a lady. Justice Scalia mourned the loss of those values with the end of VMI as an all-male institution.[1]

If interpretation of the Constitution had been left solely in the hands of Justice Scalia, women would not enjoy the protections included in decisions such as *United States v. Virginia.* Classifications based on sex would enjoy little or no scrutiny. Remedies for inequities would be left to the good will of the majority. Greene (2016) accuses Scalia of "chronic insensitivity to cultural out groups," of "dog whistling" (sending coded messages that convey biased views). There are a few dog whistles in his VMI dissent when he proclaims that the Court must preserve rather than "revise" values, and when he predicts that VMI will lose its "manly honor" (Greene 2016, 181).

LGBT ISSUES

Justice Scalia interpreted the Equal Protection Clause quite narrowly when it came to addressing racial justice issues. He denied that the Fourteenth Amendment was intended to address gender discrimination. With respect to Lesbian, Gay, Bisexual, and Transgendered (LGBT) persons, Scalia could not or would not see sexual orientation as an immutable condition. He never developed the perspective of Justice Blackmun who wrote that *Bowers v. Hardwick* (1986) was not about a right to commit sodomy but about the right to choose intimate relationships, about personal autonomy, and about the right to be left alone (Murphy 2014, 148). Scalia persisted in talking about people who "engaged in homosexual behavior," or about the "right to engage in homosexual conduct," rather than about people with an orientation or an identity. This failure to understand LGBT people meant that he never took their claims to equal protection seriously. Instead, he fumed at his colleagues for imposing their "homosexual agenda" on the American public.

The first case of Scalia's Supreme Court career dealing with issues of sexual orientation and constitutional rights was *Romer v. Evans* (1996). The Court found that a Colorado law forbidding protection from discrimination for homosexuals was unconstitutional. Justice Anthony Kennedy wrote for a six-member majority that there was no rational basis for such a law, that it reflected an unacceptable animosity toward a politically unpopular group. Justice Scalia wrote the dissent which was joined by Chief Justice Rehnquist and Justice Thomas. He found a rational basis for the law in the "state's desire to protect traditional sexual mores." He did not see the law as depriving gay people of protection but rather as forbidding special privileges. To Scalia, homosexuals could be compared to polygamists—both engaged in sexual conduct outside the norm and both types of conduct could be prohibited.

However, he also saw homosexuals as powerful, well-financed activists. He argued that the Equal Protection Clause did not prohibit non-racial discrimination if it was consistent with tradition (an argument he also made about gender discrimination in *United States v. Virginia*). Gay rights were not mentioned in the Constitution. Colorado voters were well within their rights in trying to preserve traditional sexual values "against the efforts of a politically powerful minority." Those considerations led him to accuse his colleagues on the Court of "terminal silliness" (Murphy 2014, 234–35). In *Romer*, as in all the cases concerning sexual orientation, Scalia framed the issue as a struggle between a majority who subscribed to traditional moral values and a dangerous minority, supported by elite members of the legal community. These cases were the clearest example of Scalia the Populist who spoke for those who equated "homosexual conduct" with bigamy, bestiality, and murder. In a speech a year after *Romer*, he characterized the decision. "My Court struck it [the Colorado law] down as unconstitutional under, I don't know, the Homosexual Clause of the Bill of Rights. Or whatever it is" (Biskupic 2009, 221).

In *Lawrence v. Texas* (2003) Justice Kennedy wrote the opinion finding a Texas law that banned consensual sodomy between adults unconstitutional. The decision effectively overruled *Bowers v. Hardwick* (1986). Kennedy made the argument that the majority could not "use the power of the State to enforce these views on the whole society through the operation of the criminal law. Our obligation is to define the liberty of all, not to mandate our own moral code" (*Lawrence v. Texas* 2003). Scalia could not have disagreed more as became apparent when he read his dissent from the bench. First of all, he contended that the state's interest in protecting traditional morality provided a rational basis for the law. If protecting morality did not provide a constitutional reason for a law, then why prohibit bigamy, bestiality, prostitution, masturbation, fornication, or incest? All such laws, he argued, were restrictions on liberty, just like anti-sodomy laws. The liberties protected by the Constitution were *fundamental* liberties, "deeply rooted in the nation's history and traditions." "Homosexual sodomy" was not such a fundamental liberty. Such a claim was "at best facetious" (*Lawrence v. Texas* 2003). He also complained that the Court's finding that majority support for the law was an insufficient reason for prohibiting the practice, "effectively decrees an end to all morals legislation." The opinion was the product of a "law profession culture." Elite lawyers had signed on to a "homosexual agenda promoted by homosexual activists to eliminate the moral opprobrium that has traditionally attached to homosexual conduct." The Court had "taken sides in the culture war, departing from its role as a neutral observer, that the democratic rules of engagement are observed." Apparently the side Scalia felt the Court had taken isolated it from the many Americans who want to protect themselves and their families "from a lifestyle they believe to be immoral and destructive" (*Lawrence v. Texas* 2003).

To Justice Scalia, the issue was all about a troublesome group of privileged, dissatisfied people who enlisted the support of elite members of the legal community to win recognition of their right to engage in the sexual conduct of their choice. The majority of right thinking citizens wanted to insist that others abide by their long-standing moral values and avoid all such unorthodox sexual conduct. Thus he was equally opposed to the reasoning in Justice O'Connor's concurrence where she made an equal protection argument. She wrote, "Moral disapproval of a group, like a bare desire to harm a group, is an interest that is insufficient to satisfy rational basis review under the Equal Protection Clause" (*Lawrence v. Texas* 2003). He refused to accept her characterization that the Texas law was directed at "gay persons as a class." All laws, he claimed, are directed at people as a class. Laws against public nudity are directed against "public nudists." His insistence upon treating sexual orientation as "sexual proclivity" meant he would never admit to O'Connor's argument about invidious discrimination.

Writing in *Slate* about Scalia's *Lawrence* dissent and his public speeches attacking Justice Kennedy for the ruling, Dahlia Lithwick noted that he "appears anything but impartial." She wondered why he would decide "to play the role of benighted public intellectual and knight gallant in the culture wars?" (Murphy 2014, 296). It is puzzling why Scalia was becoming more public in his comments on his colleagues and on issues before the Court. Perhaps he loved the adulation of people who agreed with him about threats to traditional values more than he respected the expectation that judges should remain impartial and above the fray.

Although *United States v. Windsor* (2013), concerning the federal Defense of Marriage Act (DOMA), was a Fifth Amendment rather than a Fourteenth Amendment case, the ruling once again brought a stinging dissent from Scalia. DOMA had specified that only marriages between a man and a woman would be recognized under federal law. This meant that someone like Edith Windsor, whose marriage to Thea Spyer had been recognized by the state of New York, was not considered a "spouse" for federal tax purposes. Same-sex couples complained that they were treated differently from heterosexual couples under federal law and that distinction amounted to a deprivation of liberty prohibited by the Fifth Amendment. The Supreme Court, in an opinion written by Justice Anthony Kennedy, invalidated DOMA, saying it served no legitimate purpose and disparaged and injured same-sex couples. Justice Scalia, who described Kennedy's opinion as "a disappointing trail of legalistic argle-bargle" (Murphy 2014, 489), had several major objections to the decision. For one thing, he believed that the Court had no need to rule. Windsor had won the judgment in the lower courts, so the Supreme Court could have chosen not to hear the case. If they had refused to issue a decision, Scalia believed that the Court would have "covered ourselves with honor." The justices might have assured the sides they could settle the debate themselves. "We might have let the People decide" (*United States v. Windsor* 2013). Instead, he saw the ruling as an "assertion of judicial supremacy over the peoples' representatives in Congress and the Executive." He considered *Windsor* an act of judicial activism after DOMA was passed by a democratic legislature.[2]

Scalia's second objection to the decision was the majority's argument that there was no rational basis for distinguishing same-sex marriage from traditional marriage. To Scalia, the purpose was to "defend marriage" as the act's title stated, and he found that basis quite rational. The ruling suggested that Congress had been motivated by a desire to harm gay couples when it passed DOMA. Scalia thought Kennedy's opinion portrayed the act's supporters as an "unhinged lynch mob" who acted out of malice, as enemies of the human race. He went on to predict that the Court would soon invalidate state laws against same-sex marriage. "By formally declaring anyone opposed to same-sex marriage an enemy of human decency, the majority arms well every challenger to a state law restricting marriage to its traditional definition" (*United States v. Windsor* 2013).

He was correct in that prediction. Ironically, proponents of same-sex marriage frequently cited Scalia's *Windsor* dissent in their arguments. Two years later, in *Obergefell v. Hodges* (2015), the Court found that state prohibitions of same-sex marriage were unconstitutional under the Fourteenth Amendment Due Process and Equal Protection Clauses. Scalia joined the dissent written by Chief Justice John Roberts, but he wrote a separate dissent joined by Justice Thomas. He justified his separate statement as a response to "call attention to the Court's threat to American democracy" (*Obergefell v. Hodges* 2015). He described the opinion as the furthest possible extension of the Court's "claimed power to create 'liberties' that the Constitution and its Amendments fail to mention." He argued that when the Fourteenth Amendment was adopted, every state defined marriage as a union between one man and one woman. The current justices had "no basis for striking down a practice not specifically prohibited by the Amendment's text," and endorsed and upheld since its ratification. The Court had discovered a "fundamental right overlooked by every person alive at the time of ratification and almost everyone else in the time since" (*Obergefell v. Hodges* 2015). Not confining himself to opposing the substance of the decision, Scalia also attacked the style. He found that the opinion lacked "even a thin veneer of law," but was composed of "mummeries and striving-to-be-memorable passages." In his view, the style was "as pretentious as the content was egotistic," made up of "showy profundities" that were "profoundly incoherent" (*Obergefell v. Hodges* 2015). And he attacked the Court itself as "a select, patrician, highly unrepresentative panel of nine," who had attended elite law schools, lived on the east and west coast, and did not include a single Evangelical Christian. Those nine judges were willing "to violate a principle even more fundamental than no taxation without representation: no social transformation without representation" (*Obergefell v. Hodges* 2015).

As one reads Scalia's dissents in the gay rights and same-sex marriage cases, one cannot ignore the disrespect and the vociferous anger he expresses. The disrespect is directed at both the petitioners who seek to defend their sexual orientation and at his colleagues who find them worthy of constitutional protections. If he did not intend to sound like a bigot, that was certainly the result of his intemperate statements. An example from a session at Princeton University in 2012 is illustrative. A gay student asked Scalia whether he ever regretted comparing gays to murderers or to those who engage in bestiality. He wondered if such insults were necessary to make the point that the Constitution did not (in Scalia's opinion) protect gay rights. The justice replied that it was not necessary but it was effective. It was an example of a reductio ad absurdum argument. "I don't apologize" (Murphy 2014, 476–77). Either Scalia never understood or he pretended not to understand sexual orientation as an immutable condition. He persisted in talking about a "right to commit homosexual acts" or a "right of sexual preference," as if sexual orientation was something one simply chose, the way one might choose to drive a car or pick a favorite color. Perhaps this perspective was inseparable from his religious beliefs or perhaps he was just temperamentally inflexible.

One of his more liberal former clerks was willing to set aside some of Scalia's more offensive comments and positions on the subject because of the justice's contribution to the way "judges do their work." Samuel (2016) claims that as with all great judges, Scalia's contributions transcend whether he was right or wrong in a particular case or about a particular issue. Greene (2016) on the other hand, cites Scalia's "chronic insensitivity to cultural out groups" (180). Scalia represented the interests of conservatives anxious about social change and spoke of the constitutional past as something worth returning to despite the implications for the millions who would be denied equality. His admirers may have hoped that Justice Scalia would "make the Constitution great again."

CONCLUSION

When Justice Antonin Scalia died in 2016 commentators in all branches of the media described his intellect, his contributions to jurisprudence through his advocacy of originalism and textualism, his devotion to his church and family, his memorable comments and opinions. Among the latter were some that seemed intended to turn back the clock to a time when the nation was less committed to equality. This chapter has made the argument that with respect to the Fourteenth Amendment's guarantee of equal protection of the law, Scalia was a voice for regression, certainly not a voice of progress and tolerance toward racial minorities, women, or LGBT persons.

Scalia was a Roman Catholic of the most traditional sort. After the Second Vatican Council encouraged that the Mass be offered in English, he chose to seek out churches where he could attend Mass in Latin. Murphy (2014) suggests that Scalia became more rigid in his Catholicism after Vatican II encouraged the updating and modernization of the Church to better reflect the spirit of the time. Scalia was comfortable with the patriarchal, hierarchical church of his youth, one that was exclusive in its membership and absolutist in its values. Changes that opened doors to more participation by the laity were both threatening and heretical. He would levy similar charges against those who argued that the meaning of the Fourteenth Amendment should evolve and expand.

Schultz and Smith (1996) wrote that Scalia "rerouted the logic of Equal Protection," not to defend minorities, affirmative action, women, or homosexuals but to support whites, corporations, and property owners. They found a "selective application of judicial protections" along with a "broader deference to majoritarianism" (207). He rejected the role of the courts as protectors of minorities. He repudiated the *Carolene Products* framework that had shaped Fourteenth Amendment jurisprudence, often expressing impatience with his colleagues who advocated extending strict scrutiny to laws that disadvantaged people on the basis of gender or sexual orientation. Instead, he would leave the fate of cultural and socially disadvantaged groups to the mercies of the majority, which would usually mean preserving the status quo. But Scalia's willingness to defer to legislatures as the voice of the majority was selective. He was willing to accept decisions of the majority dealing with the death penalty, or restrictions on abortion, or on gay rights. He was less willing to defer to the majority when they restricted gun ownership or enacted affirmative action policies (Biskupic 2009).

Tushnet (2006) writes that Scalia was not as smart as he thought he was because his intelligence was not always matched with good judgment. For example, his famous pungent style, marked by catchy phrases and memorable examples, often included casting aspersions on his opponents' honesty, intelligence, or even their rationality. He had no problem criticizing his colleagues on the Court in personal terms, calling them out for their elitism, their willingness (in his view) to impose their values on the citizens through "judicially created rights" that threatened democracy (Staab 2006, 311). He condemned his fellow judges in the strongest terms when he envisioned himself as the authentic populist, alone in a sea of privilege. Biskupic (2009) quotes Mary Talbot in *The New Yorker*: "Cases in which Scalia believes elite judges or professors are trying to dismantle the moral positions of 'the people' bring out a particular vituperativeness . . . and leave the unavoidable impression that he is speaking not only for originalism but for his own selective notion of the vox populi" (227). For reasons not entirely clear, Scalia did seem to relish identifying with those he thought were being ignored by the more privileged. His chosen "populi" included "the Polish factory worker's son" disadvantaged by affirmative action, the "gentlemen" of VMI whose sanctuary would be invaded by women students, and the moralizing citizens who did not want to associate with homosexuals. In other words, he sympathized more with those who were trying to hold on to their privilege by excluding others than with those who sought to be included. And he was willing to use judicial power to achieve those conservative goals.

Scalia's interpretation of the Fourteenth Amendment may reach beyond his lifetime. Chief Justice Roberts who has written, "The best way to stop discrimination on the basis of race is to stop discriminating on the basis of race," echoes the view that even benign efforts to equalize opportunity are unconstitutional if they involve any consideration of race (*Parents Involved in Community Schools v. Seattle School District No. 1* 2007). This position was an underpinning of the decisions not only in the *Seattle* case but also in *Shelby County v. Holder*, (2013) and *Schuette v. Coalition to Defend Affirmative Action by Any Means Necessary* (2014).

It seems unlikely that the Court will decide that gender discrimination is not prohibited by the Equal Protection Clause. However, Justice Alito sounded an ominous note in the *Hobby Lobby* case which permitted corporations to raise religious objections to providing contraception to employees (*Burwell v. Hobby Lobby Stores* 2014). In response to Justice Ginsburg's dissent expressing concern that employers could argue that their religion required them to pay women less than men, Alito wrote, "The government has a compelling interest in providing an equal opportunity to participate in the workforce without regard to race and prohibitions on racial discrimination are precisely tailored to achieve that critical goal" (*Burwell v. Hobby Lobby Stores* 2014). Ginsburg had raised a question about sex discrimination. Alito sidestepped that concern. His words could have flowed from the pen of Antonin Scalia.

As for the rights of LGBT persons, freedom to marry seems a settled issue, one where Scalia was definitively on the losing side. However, the fate of religious freedom cases where those who agree with Scalia's characterization of the "homosexual agenda" claim a First Amendment right to deny service to LGBT persons, remains to be seen.

Greene (2016) writes that in an environment where previously excluded groups are challenging social institutions, "the status quo is itself a constituency, seeking to make claims on constitutional law to strive (quixotically) to preserve it as consistent, predictable, and settled." He sees Scalia's symbolic purpose as speaking "for the law's intolerance of social change," a chronic resistance to novelty (148). Scalia provided theory (originalism, textualism) and a reliable vote for a conservative agenda that involved "defending" the Equal Protection Clause of the Fourteenth Amendment from those who would expand its reach.

NOTES

1. VMI flourishes today with a student body approximately 10 percent women.

2. It is impossible to ignore the inconsistency in Scalia's position about judicial activism and democratic legislation when one realizes that this decision was handed down a single day after *Shelby County v. Holder*. There Scalia agreed with the majority that the Voting Rights Act, also passed and reaffirmed by Congress, was unconstitutional.

REFERENCES

Bassham, Gregory. 2006–2007. "Justice Scalia's Equitable Constitution." *Journal of College and University Law* 33: 143–60.

Biskupic, Joan. 2009. *American Original: The Life and Constitution of Supreme Court Justice Antonin Scalia*. New York: Farrar, Strauss, and Giroux.

Dworkin, Ronald. 1997. "Comment." In *A Matter of Interpretation: Federal Courts and the Law*, ed. Amy Gutman, 115–27. Princeton, NJ: Princeton University Press.

Epps, Garrett. 2014. *American Justice 2014: Nine Clashing Visions on the Supreme Court.* Philadelphia, PA: University of Pennsylvania Press.

———. (2011) "Stealing the Constitution: Inside the Right's Campaign to Hijack the Country's Founding Text—and How to Fight Back." www.The nation.com/article/stealing—constitution October 23, 2017.

Greene, Jamal. 2016. "The Age of Scalia." *Harvard Law Journal* 130: 144–86.

Griffin, Stephen M. 2016. "Justice Scalia: Affirmative or Negative?" *Minnesota Law Review* 101: 52–67.

Maskowitz, Seymour. 2015–2016. "Justice Scalia: Class Warrior." *Valparaiso University Law Review* 50: 623–70.

Murphy, Bruce Allen. 2014. *Scalia: A Court of One*. New York: Simon & Schuster, 2014.

Ring, Kevin S., ed. 2016. *Scalia's Court: A Legacy of Landmark Opinions and Dissents*. Washington, DC: Regnary Publishing.

Roosevelt, Kermit. 2005. "Justice Scalia's Constitution—And Ours." *Journal of Law and Social Change* 8: 27–38.

Rossum, Ralph A. 2006. *Antonin Scalia's Jurisprudence: Text and Tradition.* Lawrence, KS: University Press of Kansas.

Samuel, Ian. 2016. "The Counter Clerks of Justice Scalia." *New York University Journal of Law and Liberty* 10: 1–17.

Scalia, Antonin. 1997. *A Matter of Interpretation: Federal Courts and the Law.* Princeton, NJ: Princeton University Press.

Schultz, David A. and Christopher E. Smith. 1996. *The Jurisprudential Vision of Justice Antonin Scalia.* Lanham, MD: Rowman & Littlefield.

Shorter, Jane S. 2003–2004. "Lawrence v. Texas and the Fourteenth Amendment's Democratic Aspirations."

Smith, Christopher E. 1993. *Justice Antonin Scalia and the Supreme Court's Conservative Moment.* Westport, CT: Praeger.

Staab, James B. 2006. *The Political Thought of Justice Antonin Scalia: A Hamiltonian on the Supreme Court.* Lanham, MD: Rowman & Littlefield.

Tushnet, Mark. 2006. *A Court Divided: The Rehnquist Court and the Future of Constitutional Law.* New York: W. W. Norton.

TABLE OF CASES

Adarand Constructors, Inc. v. Pena, 515 U.S. 200 (1995).

Bowers v. Hardwick, 478 U.S. 186 (1986).

Burwell v. Hobby Lobby Stores, 573 U.S. _____ (2014).

Craig v. Bowen, 429 U.S. 190 (1976).

Gratz v. Bollinger, 539 U.S. 244 (2003).

Grutter v. Bollinger, 539 U.S. 306 (2003).

J.E.B. v. Alabama, 511 U.S. 127 (1994).

Lawrence v. Texas, 539 U.S. 548 (2003).

McCleskey v. Kemp, 481 U.S. 279 (1987).

Obergefell v. Hodges, 576 U.S. _____ (2015).

Parents Involved in Community Schools v. Seattle School District No. 1, 551 U.S. 701 (2007).

Plessy v. Ferguson, 165 U.S. 537 (1896).

Regents of the University of California v. Bakke, 438 U.S. 265 (1978).

Richmond v. J.A. Croson Co., 488 U.S. 469 (1989).

Romer v. Evans, 517 U.S. 620 (1996).

Schuette v. Coalition to Defend Affirmative Action by Any Means Necessary, 572 U.S. _____ (2014).

Shelby County v. Holder, 570 U.S. 2 (2013).

United States v. Carolene Products, 304 U.S. 144 (1938).

United States v. Virginia, 518 U.S. 515 (1996).

United States v. Windsor, 570 U.S. 12 (2013).

Chapter 4

Justice Scalia and Criminal Justice

A Mixed Record with Conservative Impact

Christopher E. Smith and Charles F. Jacobs

During his nearly thirty-year career on the U.S. Supreme Court, Justice Antonin Scalia established himself as a consistently conservative jurist in criminal justice cases, albeit with several notable instances in which he supported the claims of individuals (Smith and McCall 2011). According to the Supreme Court Judicial Database (2017), Scalia defended the rights of individuals in less than 18 percent of the 619 cases classified as concerning "criminal procedure" issues during his career on the high court. This category does not capture all of the cases that were related to criminal justice, as there were, for example, small numbers of decisions in separate categories such as prisoners' rights. However, it provides a useful snapshot of the overall application of Scalia's conservative judicial values to the realm of criminal justice. In addition, among the 171 criminal procedure cases in which he voted to support the rights of the criminally accused, seventy-eight cases were unanimous and thereby reflected consensus agreements drawing the support of both liberal and conservative justices. Thus it was in fewer than one hundred cases in this category over the course of nearly three decades that he supported the claims of individuals in opposition to the views of one or more of his colleagues (Supreme Court Judicial Database 2017). He was one of the most consistently conservative justices in the realm of criminal justice, although less conservative than either Justices Clarence Thomas or Samuel Alito during this period (Smith, C.E., McCall, and McCall 2015).

Justice Scalia was an especially outspoken advocate for a variant of the originalist approach to constitutional interpretation known as textualism. Scalia argued that "Textualism, in its purest form, begins and ends with what the text says and fairly implies" (Scalia and Garner 2012, 16). Determining what the text says, and its implications, often involves straying beyond the four-corners of the document to seek insight into the meaning of the words at the time they were drafted. This, Scalia argued, was the only interpretive approach that guaranteed that the meaning of the law remained unchanged and the norms of democratic lawmaking avoided being usurped by meddling judges who impose their own meaning or intent upon a legal text. Yet, when Scalia's opinions used the language of originalist reasoning, they often invited questions about the accuracy of his use of history. Like other originalists, he faced criticisms that his selective use of history, employed to uncover the meaning of the text, was intended to mask his advancement of conservative policy outcomes (Cross 2013). Yet unlike in some other areas of law, Scalia could point to specific criminal justice decisions in which his use of originalism led him to join forces with liberal colleagues to support rights claims by suspects and defendants (Biskupic 2009, 291). Thus, criminal justice cases provided Scalia with ammunition to counter critics' claims that his originalist orientation was merely a pretext to justify his conservative policy preferences. Textualism, he forcefully maintained, is not an interpretive method that is "well designed to achieve ideological ends (Scalia and Garner 2012, 16). Scalia's judicial record regarding the protection of criminal justice rights, one that produced a mix of both conservative and liberal votes and opinions, provides examples his supporters could cite as evidence to bolster the argument that textualism is an ideologically agnostic approach to interpreting the law.

FINDING HIS ORIGINALIST
FOOTING IN CRIMINAL JUSTICE

Justice Scalia took his seat on the Supreme Court in 1986 with a reputation as one of nation's leading advocates of originalist interpretation. He looked for opportunities to advance his argument that only originalist interpretation provided the proper guidance and restraint for judges who would otherwise impose their own personal and political values into constitutional interpretation. In a law review article published in the *University of Cincinnati Law Review* in 1989, Scalia conceded that there might be factual circumstances in certain criminal justice cases that could prove him to be a "faint-hearted originalist" who was unwilling to show complete fidelity to his own interpretive approach (Scalia 1989, 864). He specifically cited the Eighth Amendment prohibition on "cruel and unusual punishments" as a source of discomfort. Under his purported approach, any punishment in use at the time of the Eighth Amendment's ratification in 1792 should be constitutionally permissible. However, he recognized that he was unlikely to approve the eighteenth-century punishment of flogging with a "cat o' nine tails" if a state attempted to introduce such a painful sanction for crimes in contemporary times (Scalia 1989, 864).

In his first five years on the Court, he cast decisive votes and wrote an especially important opinion concerning prisoners' rights. In the Court's hugely-influential decision in *Turner v. Safley* (1987), Scalia provided one of the five votes that endorsed Justice Sandra Day O'Connor's test for prisoners' assertions of First Amendment rights. When prisoners filed lawsuits alleging that laws or policies violated these rights, O'Connor instructed judges to consider whether the law or policy was rationally-related to a legitimate objective of the prison. Judges also were to consider whether there were alternative means to exercise the right, such as writing letters and making collect calls to family members even though prison officials barred letters between non-relative prisoners in different correctional institutions. The other factors to consider were the potential impact on other prisoners and prison staff from a prisoner's exercise of the right as well as the question of whether there existed a simple way to permit the right without diminishing the legitimate goals of prison officials (Smith 2016a, 117).

The *Turner* case concerned a prisoner's asserted right to marry while in prison as well as a claimed right to write to a prisoner in another correctional facility. Initially, O'Connor was joined by the four most liberal justices—William Brennan, Thurgood Marshall, Harry Blackmun, and John Paul Stevens—in concluding that restricting an inmate's ability to marry while in prison violated the prisoner's right to association. On the second issue, O'Connor was joined by the four most conservative justices—William Rehnquist, Byron White, Lewis Powell, and Scalia—in rejecting the claimed right to correspond with other prisoners. According to files in the Harry Blackmun Papers (2003) in the Library of Congress, behind-the-scenes memos written during the circulation of draft opinions in the case demonstrate that the four conservatives were pleased about the potential for O'Connor's test to provide a basis for rejecting a wide array of prisoners' rights claims. One-by-one these justices switched their votes on the marriage issue, as if to reward O'Connor for creating a pleasing test despite their actual disagreement with its application to the marriage issue. Justice Scalia was among those who switched his vote to make the Court's recognition of the right to marry receive unanimous approval from the justices. Yet nowhere in this decision did he raise any issue of the original meaning attached to prisoners' rights by the framers. His votes on the two issues and his decision to avoid authoring any concurring or dissenting opinion made his judicial behavior—and silence—identical to that of the three non-originalist conservatives. Unlike his colleague Justice Thomas, who joined the Court after the announcement of the holding in this case, Scalia did not always seize opportunities to write explanatory concurring and dissenting opinions designed to advocate and explicate textualist perspective (Smith 2016a, 112–14).

In his fifth term on the Supreme Court, Scalia wrote an influential prisoners' rights opinion that made it substantially more difficult for prisoners to claim that conditions inside prisons violated the Eighth Amendment protection against cruel and unusual punishments. In *Wilson v. Seiter* (1991), prisoners claimed that various aspect of prison conditions, including food, ventilation, overcrowding, and other issues, had created unconstitutional conditions of confinement. For a five-member majority, Scalia borrowed a concept from an earlier rights-expanding opinion by Justice Marshall in order to reject the prisoners' claim and establish a new test that would block other conditions of confinement cases in the future. In *Estelle v. Gamble* (1976), Marshall had written that Eighth Amendment violations occur when prison officials are "deliberately indifferent" to prisoners' serious medical needs, thus establishing a limited right to medical care in prisons (*Estelle v. Gamble* 1976, 106). In *Wilson*, Scalia took the test created specifically for medical care claims and applied it to all claims about conditions of confinement. He professed to be following precedent in imposing this subjective test for Eighth Amendment violations in prisons while conveniently ignoring the fact the Court's actual precedents concerning conditions of confinement did not use a subjective test. The opinion appeared to be a clever and effective re-characterization of precedent in order to achieve a conservative result, namely forcing prisoners to achieve the near-impossible task of proving what thoughts prison officials had in their minds as substandard living conditions developed. As Justice White noted in his concurring opinion, in order to avoid any finding of a rights violation, corrections officials merely needed to claim that they cared about the substandard conditions but did not have enough resources to fix them (Smith 2001).

A key aspect of the majority opinion was Scalia's failure to make any mention of originalism in asserting the existence of his test. Soon afterward, Scalia joined opinions by Thomas asserting that an originalist understand of the Eighth Amendment leads to the conclusion that the framers never intended for prisoners to have any constitutional protections concerning conditions of confinement or medical care. However, if Scalia had made such an originalist assertion in *Wilson*, he would not have been assigned the majority opinion by Chief Justice Rehnquist because the four conservative justices who joined his majority opinion did not share that originalist view. Indeed, all four of those justices had joined Justice Marshall's 1976 opinion establishing a limited right to medical care for prisoners under the Eighth Amendment. By contrast, years later, Scalia revealed that he believed that no such constitutional right existed under an originalist interpretive approach. As a result, Scalia is open to criticism that he willingly dispensed with his claimed adherence to originalism if he needed to use a different approach in order to advance a preferred rights-limiting outcome. In response to such criticism, Scalia was likely to say that, unlike his fellow originalist Thomas, he was willing to follow precedent for certain issues. Yet, in this case, his selective utilization and re-characterization of precedent made clear that he was determined to enunciate a test that would curtail litigation regarding conditions of confinement for the incarcerated.

According to a behind-the-scenes description of events by lawyer-journalist Jan Crawford Greenburg (2007) concerning Justice Thomas's first weeks on the Supreme Court in 1991, the new justice's outspoken advocacy for originalism spurred Scalia to more-frequently adopt originalist claims and reasoning in judicial opinions. When the justices expressed their individual viewpoints and votes in the case of *Hudson v. McMillian* (1992), they spoke in order of seniority, as is the traditional practice for this starting point of deliberations. After eight justices expressed support for the finding of an Eighth Amendment rights violation when corrections officers beat a shackled prisoner and caused minor injuries, such as bruises and a broken tooth, the newcomer Thomas spoke last and expressed disagreement. In Thomas's originalist view, the framers did not intend to protect prisoners inside correctional institutions. He saw the Eighth Amendment protection against cruel and unusual punishments applying only to the moment in court that a judge announced a sentence. The Constitution prohibits a judge from imposing a sentence that is too torturous. However, in Thomas's view, if the announced sentence is not torturous, then any implementation of a punishment during confinement, such as corrections officers beating prisoners sentenced to a term of years inside a prison, should be handled by personal injury lawsuits rather than by the recognition of federal constitutional rights claims. According to Greenburg (2007, 120), Scalia changed his vote after listening to Thomas and he joined Thomas's dissent that presented these arguments. Thereafter Scalia seemed to assert originalist viewpoints more consistently in his opinions.

Like Justice Thomas, Scalia sought to limit the recognition of rights for convicted offenders under the U.S. Constitution. This reflected their very narrow view of the legal protection for prisoners as well as their objection to permitting federal judges to intervene into the operation of state prisons in order to identify rights violations and order remedies. Thus, Justice Scalia continued to join Thomas's originalist opinions in conditions of confinement cases, including the case in which Thomas shifted his use of history. Without either Thomas or Scalia admitting error, they changed their originalist claims in *Overton v. Bazzetta* (2003) by arguing prisoners retain whatever rights in prison that states permit them to retain. In effect, they sought to have prisoners' rights defined as a matter of state law, under the control of states, and beyond the authority of interventionist federal judges. Thomas's opinion noted that the framers of the U.S. Constitution's Bill of Rights could not have had any intentions about the Eighth Amendment's applicability to prison conditions since the concept of prisons used for long-term incarceration had not yet developed at the time of the Amendment's ratification. Scholars had criticized Thomas's opinions, beginning with his dissent in *Hudson*, for misunderstanding the history of corrections (Smith and Baugh 2000, 91–92). At the time that they abruptly announced their new approach in *Overton*, neither Thomas nor Scalia acknowledged that they had been wrong for the preceding decade in articulating the previous version of their originalist concept of the Eighth Amendment's applicability to prison conditions cases. By focusing on states' intentions for the retention or eradication of specific rights inside prisons, Thomas and Scalia could claim fidelity to a history-based approach to legal interpretation. At the same time, they could rely on the presumption that this approach, like their previous misreading of Eighth Amendment history, would both limit the existence of rights and curtail the involvement of federal courts in prisoners' rights litigation about conditions of confinement.

Did Thomas's arrival on the Court prick Scalia's conscience about his failure to follow the originalist approach that he espoused? Did Scalia need an ally to shore up his willingness to stand up for originalism? Given Scalia's penchant for outspokenness in a wide variety of cases, it seems more likely to be the former than the latter. Yet by re-committing himself—to some extent anyway—to the originalist approach, Scalia risked limiting his own effectiveness because so few justices adhered to that approach. The fact that Thomas rarely wrote majority opinions in major cases provided evidence that the originalist approach was not typically a vehicle for influence over case outcomes. Yet there were occasions when Justice Scalia was able to use originalist reasoning in other majority opinions for criminal justice decisions that won the approval of liberal and conservative justices alike. For example, in *Blakely v. Washington* (2004), Justice Scalia's opinion for the majority was joined by the Court's more liberal justices (Stevens, Ruth Bader Ginsburg, and David Souter) as well as his fellow originalist Justice Thomas. The majority found a violation of the Sixth Amendment right to trial by jury when a judge used his own factual determination about the defendant's "deliberate cruelty" to lengthen the prison sentence under state sentencing guidelines. According to Justice Scalia's opinion, the jury must be the fact finder that determines the existence of facts that define the sentence. He cited the ideas of John Adams and Thomas Jefferson to support his conclusion. Moreover, he said specifically that his conception of the jury's key fact-finding role for sentencing purposes "ensur[es] that the judge's authority to sentence derives wholly from the jury's verdict. Without that restriction, the jury would not exercise the control that the Framers intended" (*Blakely v. Washington* 2004, 306). Thus originalist reasoning was employed, with the support of the Court's most liberal justices, to expand the conception of the right to trial by jury in the Sixth Amendment. It should be noted that the Court's liberals were not opposed to using originalist evidence in support of judicial reasoning. They simply disagreed with Scalia's claim that it is the *only* approach to constitutional interpretation that is legitimate.

In other cases, Justice Scalia's majority opinions pointed to old English legal traditions, the precursor to principles in the Constitution, as his means to justify his decisions through the use of history as it was presumably understood by the framers. For example, in *Coy v. Iowa* (1988), writing for the majority within a divided Court, Justice Scalia found a violation of the Sixth Amendment's Confrontation Clause when a large screen was placed in the courtroom so that child victims would not have to see the defendant as they testified against him. In concluding that the clause guaranteed to the defendant a right of face-to-face confrontation with accusers and witnesses, Scalia presented a brief, but ancient, genealogy regarding the origins of the right, noting that it dates "to the beginning of Western legal culture" and presented evidence that "the right of confrontation was recognized in England well before the right to jury trial" (*Coy v. Iowa* 1988, 1015). And in his comprehensive citation of precedent related to the question raised in the case, he discovered an originalist fellow-traveler in Justice John Harlan who previously argued in *California v. Green* (1970) that the right guaranteed by the Confrontation Clause to meet an accuser face-to-face could be understood "simply as a matter of English" (*Coy v. Iowa* 1988, 1016). The decision, which attracted the support of five of the seven remaining justices who participated, demonstrated the capacity of originalism to support the rights of the criminally accused while drawing the support of ideologically diverse members of the Court.

A MIXED RECORD ON THE FOURTH AMENDMENT

As illustrated by the foregoing examples, Justice Scalia was noted for parting company with his usual conservative allies for a specific set of issues in criminal justice, especially the right to confrontation and the right to fact-finding by the jury for the sentencing process. In the area of Fourth Amendment search and seizure, Scalia had a more mixed record that included a number of cases in which he joined the liberal justices in order to support rights claims by individuals.

According to the Supreme Court Judicial Database, Justice Scalia supported the claims of individuals in twenty-two out of the ninety-four Fourth

Amendment decisions in which he participated on the Supreme Court. The most striking aspect of these liberal decisions is the fact that eight of these twenty-two rights-supporting votes were cast near the end of his three-decade career on the Supreme Court. Thus questions arise about whether something had changed in these later years, such as his approach to decision making on these issues, the nature and frequency of Fourth Amendment cases accepted for decision by the Supreme Court, or some other factor.

Among Scalia's twenty-two rights-supporting votes in Fourth Amendment cases, nine came in unanimous decisions with strong agreement among the Court's liberals and conservatives that a rights violation occurred. Two additional cases had near-consensus votes of 8-to-1 and 7-to-2 in support of Fourth Amendment rights claims. Because Justice Scalia joined with conservative allies in supporting rights claims in each of these cases, they do not provide evidence that his vote was motived by changing views that pulled him away from his usual allies.

Another piece of evidence indicating that Scalia may not have changed his views in later years was the recognition that Scalia split from his usual conservative allies on occasions early in his career. During his very first term on the Supreme Court, Scalia wrote a majority opinion in *Arizona v. Hicks* (1987) on behalf of his liberal colleagues. It was a 5-to-4 decision that rejected a warrantless search in favor of preserving a rule that would be workable for police officers and judges. This rationale expressed in 1987 foreshadowed a similar, continuing concern for the preservation of workable rules in one of the later Fourth Amendment cases. Similarly, in his third term on the Court, in a dissent endorsed by liberal Justices Brennan and Marshall and joined by Justice Stevens in *National Treasury Employees Union v. Von Raab* (1989), Scalia vociferously objected to suspicionless urinalysis drug testing of U.S. Customs Service Employees. Using his typically strident language, Scalia labeled such searches as "particularly destructive of privacy and offensive to personal dignity" (*National Treasury Employees Union v. Von Raab* 1989, 680), as well as "a kind of immolation of privacy and human dignity in symbolic opposition to drug use" (*National Treasury Employees Union v. Von Raab* 1989, 681). This early example of Justice Scalia sharing the liberals' view that a specific type of search clearly violated the Fourth Amendment may have foreshadowed his later, similarly-outspoken opposition to DNA testing of arrestees in *Maryland v. King* (2013) and to reliance on anonymous phone tips as a basis for traffic stops *Navarette v. California* (2014). These connections support the possibility that contemporary times brought to the Court a flurry of issues in later years that simply triggered more frequently the same rights-protective viewpoints about the Fourth Amendment that Scalia previously expressed early in his career.

Among the more notable opinions drafted by Scalia interpreting the Fourth Amendment came in 2001 in *Kyllo v. United States*. The case produced a somewhat unusual grouping of justices in the 5-to-4 decision when Scalia and his originalist colleague Justice Thomas were joined by the more moderate Justices Stephen Breyer and Souter and one of the Court's most outspoken liberals Justice Ginsburg. The opinion crafted by Scalia grappled with the application and accommodation of new technology in the realm of criminal investigations when the petitioner questioned the constitutionality of a search conducted by officers who aimed a thermal-imaging device at a house in which the occupants were suspected of using hot lights for a marijuana-growing operation.

This case, like those involving the Eighth Amendment, revealed some of the challenges of employing the originalist method when faced with the evolving techniques employed by law enforcement agencies in contemporary America. The question for Scalia and the majority concerned "what limits there are upon th[e] power of technology to shrink the realm of guaranteed privacy" (*Kyllo v. United States* 2001, 34). This demanded that the majority explore how and when government may actually intrude into a home and the extent to which that intrusion violates the privacy insulated from erosion by the Bill of Rights. While Scalia did not dedicate an enormous amount of effort into a review of the historical record that would have buttressed an original reading of the Amendment, his analysis was a clear attempt to overlay an eighteenth-century reading of the Fourth Amendment onto the utilization of modern investigatory tools. Scalia's opinion argued:

> We think that obtaining by sense-enhancing technology any information regarding the interior of the home that could not otherwise have been obtained with physical "intrusion into a constitutionally protected area," constitutes a "search"—at least where (as here) the technology in question is not in general public use. This assures preservation of that degree of privacy against government that existed when the Fourth Amendment was adopted. (*Kyllo v. United States* 2001, 34–35)

The argument made clear that the Court sought to preserve the privacy that existed when the Fourth Amendment was adopted and did so by reinforcing what the majority believed were clear standards that protected the interior of any home from the prying eyes of the police. While recognizing that technological advancements often may necessitate the reshaping of Fourth Amendment doctrine to the detriment of the criminally accused (citing both aerial viewing of the property of individuals and businesses and the use of dialed number recorders to obtain information of phone use), Scalia carved out private residences as the untouchable, in essence the most original, protected class of private space entitled to the full protection of the Amendment. Citing *Carroll v. United States* (1925) Scalia affirmed that "The Fourth Amendment is to be construed in the light of what was deemed an unreasonable search and seizure when it was adopted, and in a manner which will conserve public interests as well as the interests and rights of the individual citizens" (*Kyllo v. United States* 2001, 40). Through the application of an originalist approach, Scalia offered a rights-protecting holding that again attracted the votes of conservative and liberal justices and kept technological advancement from undermining the application of the text of the Bill of Rights.

More than a decade later, Justice Scalia's majority opinion in the case of *United States v. Jones* (2012) provided the precursor for a set of rights-protecting opinions concerning Fourth Amendment jurisprudence in which Scalia joined the Court's most liberal justices rather than his usual conservative allies. His majority opinion in *Jones* (2012) drew from his sense of originalist definitions. Writing for the majority, he concluded that the warrantless installation of a GPS tracking device on a suspected drug dealer's vehicle constituted a "search" under the Fourth Amendment. Justice Scalia employed his originalist approach to constitutional interpretation as he cited the 1765 English case *Entick v. Carrington* declaring that "[w]e have no doubt that such a physical intrusion [on the suspect's automobile] would have been considered a search within the meaning of the Fourth Amendment when it was adopted" (*United States v. Jones* 2012, 949). His justification for that position was based upon common-law conceptions of trespass that preceded the drafting of the Constitution rather than on more contemporary conceptions of a reasonable expectation of privacy. Thus the decision favored the individual's claim that the government lacked the discretionary authority to impose this form of technological surveillance on his vehicle and daily travels. That support, although rights supportive, was clearly wedded to a textual interpretive approach. It should be noted that Scalia's reliance on trespass was not completely satisfactory to one member of the liberal wing of the Court. Justice Sotomayor included a concurring opinion in *Jones* that argued that the majority should rely more on constitutional rights found in the Fourth Amendment rather than merely common-law trespass.

In *Florida v. Jardines* (2013), the Supreme Court revisited a police practice—the use of dogs trained to detect illegal substances—that the Court had previously examined years earlier in different contexts. For example, in *Illinois v. Cabelles* (2005), the Court determined that the exposure of a trained police dog's nose to the exterior of an automobile's closed trunk during a traffic stop was not a search and therefore permissible without a warrant and without any basis for reasonable suspicion. In the *Jardines* case, two detectives approached Jardines's front door with a drug-sniffing dog via the walkway leading to the porch. After several passes, the dog sat directly in front of the entry, an indication that the animal had located the spot with the strongest scent of drugs. Justice Scalia penned the majority opinion for the closely-divided Court declaring that the use of the trained dog at a home constituted a "search" under the Fourth Amendment, thereby requiring a warrant or a recognized justification for warrantless searches. He was joined by Justices Thomas, Ginsburg, Sonya Sotomayor, and Elena Kagan. The holding in favor of Jardines echoed the approach Scalia employed in the *Jones* decision with an admixture of case law from modern holdings and historically-based common law and constitutional doctrines.

Justice Scalia's majority opinion examined what might best be described as the social and legal etiquette for entering a stranger's property and the necessary conditions for lingering more than just a few moments. He concluded that the Fourth Amendment, and its central purpose of protecting the home from government intrusion, would be toothless if it only prohibited law enforcement from crossing a building's threshold without a valid warrant while permitting officers free range on a building's appendages or about the property. The police did not approach the house and its front door with the intention of seeking permission to stay and engage the occupant in a conversation. The sole purpose was to investigate and search, and as such is proscribed by the Fourth Amendment when done without a warrant or recognized warrant-less-search justification. The outcome here was again rights-protective but couched in old-world common-law language and precedent related to trespass that preserved the rights attached to hearth and home.

Justice Scalia contributed a rights-protective dissenting opinion, joined by his most liberal colleagues, in a case that deeply-divided the justices about a form of search unknown to the Constitution's framers that is increasingly important for law enforcement investigations. *Maryland v. King* (2013) involved a conviction for rape based upon DNA evidence collected from a suspect during his intake processing for an arrest for an unrelated assault crime. A Maryland statute authorized law enforcement personnel to collect DNA samples from anyone charged with a violent crime as defined under the law. When he was arrested for assault, a DNA sample was taken from King by a swab of his inner cheek and subsequently tested and matched to a sample in a database containing evidence from unsolved crimes. Writing for the five-member majority, Justice Anthony Kennedy acknowledged that the collection of a DNA sample unquestionably constitutes a search under the Fourth Amendment. In concluding that the search did not violate King's Fourth Amendment rights, the majority opinion analyzed the reasonableness of the warrantless cheek-swab search through a balancing test that weighed the necessity of the search against the intrusion experienced by the individual.

The legitimate government interest recognized by Justice Kennedy's majority opinion was the necessity for proper identification of suspects who have been taken into custody. Justice Kennedy's opinion described the taking of DNA samples as no different than the traditional taking of fingerprint samples from arrestees and described these procedures as essential means for police officers to discover the identity and criminal history of suspects. In the Fourth Amendment balancing analysis, Kennedy declared that "By comparison to this substantial government interest and the unique effectiveness of DNA identification, the intrusion of a cheek swab to obtain a DNA sample is a minimal one" (*Maryland v. King* 2013, 1977).

In his dissenting opinion, Justice Scalia argued that "[w]henever this Court has allowed a suspicionless search, it has insisted upon a justifying motive apart from the investigation of crime" (*Maryland v. King* 2013, 1980). Scalia sarcastically asserted that it "taxes the credulity of the credulous" for the majority to claim that the DNA sample was taken merely to identify those in custody and not to solve crimes, as Maryland did by running King's sample through the database of unsolved crimes (*Maryland v. King* 2013, 1980). Justice Scalia concluded his dissenting opinion with a strong declaration about the need to protect the Fourth Amendment's fundamental purpose, even when that means resisting the temptation to support socially-beneficial crime-control practices. In Scalia's words, "Solving unsolved crimes is a noble objective, but it occupies a lower place in the American pantheon of noble objectives than the protection of our people from suspicionless law-enforcement searches. The Fourth Amendment must prevail" (*Maryland v. King*, 2013, 1989). And Scalia argued it should prevail based upon the historical record. He used the dissent to offer a review of American animus toward the British at the time of the founding, provided a synopsis or early state constitutions supporting freedom from this practice, and quoted from prominent Anti-Federalists and James Madison to hammer home his position that all searches need to be individualized in nature.

Scalia's rights-protective position continued in *Bailey v. United States* (2013) in which the Court considered the legality of the seizure of Churon Bailey during a police investigation and search of his home. Police conducted surveillance on an apartment just prior to the execution of a search warrant. Immediately prior to the initiation of the search, police observed Bailey and a companion exit the apartment and drive away from the scene. At the same time that their colleagues conducted the search of the apartment, officers followed the pair for approximately one mile before stopping the car. During the stop, the police removed Bailey and his acquaintance from the car, discovered a set of keys during a pat-down search, and questioned them regarding their destination. After being driven back to the apartment, police arrested Bailey as a result of drugs and a gun found during the search.

Justice Kennedy wrote the opinion of the Court on behalf of a six-member majority that included Chief Justice John Roberts and Justices Scalia, Ginsburg, Sotomayor and Kagan. In ruling in favor of Bailey's claim, the majority concluded that its precedent on the issue limited the justification for detentions that occurred in conjunction with the execution of search warrants to warrantless seizures of individuals in the immediate vicinity of the premises who might pose dangers or otherwise interfere with the search. Justice Scalia's noteworthy position in the case emerged when he wrote a concurring opinion on behalf of himself and two of the Court's most liberal members, Justices Ginsburg and Kagan that specifically refuted the dissenters, who included his usual conservative allies Justices Thomas and Alito. Justice Scalia argued that his colleagues in dissent were wrong to apply a balancing test, suggesting that precedent made the outcome clear: if a person is in the vicinity of the place to be searched, then he or she may be detained. In this case, Bailey was seized a mile away and therefore the police officers acted improperly. His review of the history of the Fourth Amendment in this instance was less a textual exegesis—the more typical method employed by Scalia—and much more an investigation into the likely opinion the founders might hold about current law enforcement practices. At times, he took pains to refresh the reader's memory regarding the invasion of privacy through the use of general warrants by the British. This fragment of history served as a touchstone for Scalia. The framers, he argued, would not tolerate obvious and blatant assaults by the government on hearth, home, or person—a position he also took in his *King* dissent. If a valid warrant (or exception to the warrant requirement) does not exist, neither does the power of government. There is little or no grey area in the analysis. He supported an uncomplicated and straightforward reading of the Fourth Amendment as a bulwark against creeping government incursions into the private sphere. In effect, Scalia argued for adherence to a governing precedent that established a clear "bright-line rule" that could be readily remembered and applied by officers in the field.

A starker divergence between Scalia and his usual conservative allies emerged in *Navarette v. California* (2014), a 5-to-4 Fourth Amendment decision concerning the justification for traffic stops in which the Court's other self-proclaimed originalist, Justice Thomas, wrote the majority opinion. Justice Scalia crafted the dissent on behalf of the three most liberal justices. The case concerned the reliance by police on an anonymous phone call about a vehicle being driven dangerously and erratically. After following the vehicle for five minutes without observing any traffic violations or erratic driving, the officers stopped the vehicle and found it to be transporting marijuana.

On behalf of the majority, Thomas concluded that officers could consider the anonymous call to be reliable because the caller identified the vehicle, its license number, and its location on the highway.

In systematically refuting Thomas's analysis and conclusions, Scalia began with a reference to originalism, the approach to constitutional interpretation that both justices claimed to share, yet was notably absent in Thomas's majority opinion. In Scalia's words "So long as the caller identifies where the car is, anonymous claims of a single instance of possibly careless or reckless driving, called in to 911, will support a traffic stop. This is not my concept, and I am sure would not be the Framers', of a people secure from unreasonable searches and seizures" (*Navarette v. California* 2014, 1692).

Justice Scalia expressed grave concern about the risk by the Court's new rule that people can anonymously control the enjoyment of Fourth Amendment rights by others simply by claiming that a single instance of careless driving had occurred. Moreover, this could happen without police officers even knowing if the call is being made from within the county where alleged misconduct is reportedly taking place. In expressing strong disagreement with Thomas's majority opinion, Scalia offered a stark assessment of the risks created for the freedom of drivers on American roads:

> Drunken driving is a serious matter, but so is the loss of our freedom to come and go as we please without police interference. . . . After today's opinion all of us on the road, and not just drug dealers, are at risk of having our freedom of movement curtailed on suspicion of drunkenness, based upon a phone tip, true or false, of a single instance of careless driving. (*Navarette v. California* 2014, 1696)

The debate over the original meaning in this case was not as stark as in other Fourth Amendment cases. As Judge William Pryor (2017) noted, "not every originalist debate concerns the particulars of a historical record. Sometimes, the debate concerns the application of an agreed-upon general rule to a modern problem" (179). Pryor argued that *Navarette* was just such an occasion as Thomas and Scalia eschewed a debate over history and instead squabbled over the interpretation of an established doctrine. The result, however, was the same. Scalia's position mirrored that of the rights-protecting stance typical to the liberal arm of the Court based upon a more limited interpretation of the Fourth Amendment.

Do these late-career opinions provide evidence that Scalia's view about Fourth Amendment rights had changed over the course of his career on the Supreme Court? One intriguing factor was the possibility that life experiences and personal knowledge may have affected Scalia's understanding of certain issues. Other justices, such as O'Connor and Stevens, acknowledged that life experience affected their judicial decision making for various issues (Smith 2016b). Although Scalia claimed to follow a principled approach to judicial decision making, he was not immune to showing that his decisions and reasoning were affected by his perceptions of human situations and consequences. Two of the final Fourth Amendment cases in which Scalia parted company with his usual conservative allies concerned police authority in investigating drunk drivers: the *Navarette* case and *Missouri v. McNeeley* (2013), in which Scalia joined Justice Sotomayor's opinion declaring that police must usually get a warrant to order a blood alcohol test. Justice Scalia cast his rights-protective votes in both cases and wrote his strong dissent in one of them (*Naverette*) *after* one of his adult daughters was arrested for drunk driving (Rozas 2007). The human experiences within justices' own families present the possibility of the highest court's decision makers seeing governmental authority and rights in a new light.

DEFINING THE SECOND AMENDMENT

Policy debates about the Second Amendment typically involve arguments about criminal justice. Advocates of gun regulation assert that a major impact of stricter controls over sales of guns and the types of weapons available to the public would be a reduction in criminal violence, including mass shootings. On the other side of the argument, advocates of a broad definition of individuals' constitutional right to purchase, own, and carry firearms typically argue that an armed citizenry is an especially strong deterrent against criminal behavior. In addition, law enforcement officers often assert themselves into debates about law and policy affecting guns because they are placed at risk when people can easily obtain and carry firearms. While there are other policy consideration concerning firearms, such as the problem of firearm suicides, discussions of guns rights often place criminal justice considerations at the center of the debate. Indeed, when Justice Scalia wrote his groundbreaking opinion that first recognized constitutional right of individuals to own firearms, he used language about self-defense against criminal behavior as a central element of his legal holding.

Justice Scalia's most notable success in using originalist interpretation to shape constitutional law came in *District of Columbia v. Heller* (2008), the Court's blockbuster decision concerning the Second Amendment. The Second Amendment's meaning provides a source of significant debate in both the legal and political realms of American society. Many people are familiar with the Amendment's final words, "the right of the people to keep and bear arms shall not be infringed." Fewer people are aware of the precise wording of the Amendment's first clause: "A well-regulated Militia being necessary for the security of a free State." Moreover, the two clauses in the Amendment's single sentence are not stand-alone independent clauses. Honest evaluation of the Amendment's wording requires acknowledgment that this single sentence is written to make the two clauses read together. The challenge for judges is to determine the proper substantive meaning of the sentence as a whole in light of its two constituent clauses.

Prior to the *Heller* case, the Supreme Court had given scant attention to the Second Amendment. In *United States v. Miller* (1939), a man was charged with a federal crime under the National Firearms Act of 1934 for transporting an unregistered shotgun across state lines. He claimed that the law violated his Second Amendment right to keep and bear arms. The unanimous Supreme Court said the Second Amendment concerned the ability of members of the "militia" to keep firearms. It rejected Miller's claim and noted that his shotgun was not a weapon that was recognized as useful for military purposes by a Militia member. According to the majority opinion, "the obvious purpose" of the Second Amendment was "to assure the continuation and render possible the effectiveness of such [citizen-based Militia] forces" (*United States v. Miller* 1939, 178). Thus, the *Miller* precedent was understood to say that the Second Amendment served to protect states' ability to have an armed Militia. Moreover, many people assumed that in contemporary times, this meant that the federal government could not disarm a state's National Guard, because the Revolutionary Era's concept of all able-bodied men being considered part of the local militia had ceased to be a practical reality.

In the decades that followed the *Miller* decision, the Second Amendment's purpose for arming state militias was treated as settled law. When gun-rights interest groups began to argue for an individual-rights interpretation of the Second Amendment beginning in the 1970s, the Supreme Court declined to accept cases to reconsider its interpretation. The situation changed when the Court accepted the *Heller* case for hearing (Tushnet 2013). The case concerned the District of Columbia's law that barred private ownership of handguns except for law enforcement officers or others who were approved for permits. Dick Heller was a security officer at a federal building who claimed that his Second Amendment rights were violated by the District's prohibition on his keeping a handgun in his own for self-defense purposes. In a narrow 5-to-4 decision, the Supreme Court decided that the Second Amendment actually provides a personal right for individuals. Justice Scalia wrote the majority opinion in originalist terms as he redefined the Amendment's meaning. In his dissenting opinion, Justice Stevens answered Scalia's originalist reasoning with his own reliance upon and interpretation of historical sources. Thus, the cases provided the sharpest focus on originalism of perhaps any case in history, with attendant illumination of originalism's problems involving selective use of sources, historians' disagreements about historical meanings, and indeterminacy concerning the framers' actual intentions (Cross 2013).

The originalist basis of Scalia's conclusions about the Second Amendment was strongly challenged by historians and legal scholars. He was criticized for undue reliance on historical sources concerning documents and events from eras other than the time in which the Amendment was drafted and ratified. He was also challenged about the originalist basis for his stated conclusions concerning permissible governmental authority to regulate firearms sales, ownership by convicted felons and those with mental illnesses, and other matters (Cross 2013). In addition, Scalia dismissively rejected arguments asserting that any originalism-based recognition of an individual right should be limited to musket-type, single-shot firearms known to the framers when they wrote the Second Amendment. This could be regarded as a tacit admission that Scalia's version of originalism did not strictly restrain judges as he claimed, but actually invited them to impose their own values and judges in making originalist intentions apply to contemporary circumstances. In what may be a *post hoc* justification for straying in this manner, Scalia later suggested in a treatise on interpretation that the textual method requires obeisance to original language "with the understanding that general terms may embrace later technological innovations" (Scalia and Garner 2012, 16).

Yet there are times when Scalia had difficulty accommodating his originalist approach to the issue of modernity and the law. As with his lack of clarity regarding the application of the Second Amendment to regulation of advanced weaponry, he struggled too with the adaptation of the Constitution to surveillance tools that enhanced the ability of law enforcement to track and investigate suspects and invade their privacy. While Scalia certainly addressed the evolution of doctrine in the area of the Fourth Amendment, his ultimate interpretative approach was often reductionist, returning time and time again to the early common-law definition of trespass. In recent cases such as *Jones* and *Jardines*, Scalia stripped away much of the contemporary constitutional doctrinal development to instead apply basic principles of the common law, reinforcing his belief that the Court should keep easy cases easy. That often compelled his colleagues on the bench to offer complementary analyses in concurring opinions that provided more contemporary interpretations of constitutional provisions that Scalia seems content to leave in the dim past. In *Jones*, Sotomayor notes that "In cases of electronic or other novel modes of surveillance that do not depend upon physical invasion on property, the majority opinion's trespassory test may provide little guidance" (*United States v. Jones* 2012, 415). She noted that electronic eavesdropping by police often avoids actual physical trespass making Scalia's reliance on common-law ideals limited and problematic. Justice Kagan made similar observations in *Jardines* when she noted that the "formal protections" of property law safeguard the rights of individuals from government intrusions, but so too does the concept of privacy developed in more recent cases such as *Katz v. United States* (1967). Scalia's colleagues encouraged him to recognize the need and utility of shedding some of his historical formality, as Kagan suggested "make an 'easy cas[e] easy' twice over" (*Flordia v. Jardines* 2013, 5), reminding him that he had made that leap in *Kyllo*. While trespass doctrine served as a touchstone in that case, it did not overshadow his attempt to recognize that technology, and its possible invasion of rights, must be addressed by the law. While Scalia may have believed that textualism could incorporate technological change, his opinions demonstrate at least some methodological confusion about how that occurs.

Despite the controversy over the accuracy and fidelity of Scalia's use of history, he unquestionably succeeded in using a version of originalist evidence and reasoning in defining the meaning of a constitutional amendment. After starting his career as the Court's lone advocate of originalism, he saw his preferred approach gain recognition, discussion, and legitimacy among legal scholars and judges. Moreover, he gained support from a majority of justices for an originalist majority opinion that broke new ground for a contentious issue that provided the source of significant public debate and political conflict. Justice Scalia did not, however, see his vision of the Second Amendment define law and policy in his lifetime. Based on the facts of the case, his holding in the *Heller* decision limited the individual right to one that protects ownership and possession of a handgun in the home for the purpose of self-defense. The Court later declined to hear challenges to restrictions by cities of ownership of assault rifles as well as rules mandating safe-storage of handguns. In these cases, Scalia joined Thomas's dissents from denial of certiorari. These two justices claimed the Court needed to recognize broader gun rights for individuals in order to fulfill the purposes of the Second Amendment (*Friedman v. City of Highland Park* 2015; *Jackson v. City and County of San Francisco* 2015).

RESISTANCE TO REFORMS ADDRESSING DISCRIMINATION AND INJUSTICE

Throughout the past seven decades, the Supreme Court faced cases concerning the criminal justice system's alleged deficiencies with respect to the ideal inscribed in stone at the top of the Court's own building: Equal Justice Under Law. The aspirational statement implies that the system will both treat people fairly and produce appropriate outcomes. Yet, the system continues to face issues concerning unequal treatment of minorities and the poor, as well disagreements about which outcomes and punishments are appropriate. In cases that addressed these issues, Scalia was often a defender of the status quo and provided arguments against judicial interventions to reform the criminal justice system (Schultz and Smith 1996; Smith 1993).

With respect to race, for example, *Holland v. Illinois* (1990) concerned a claim by a white defendant that his Sixth Amendment right to trial by jury was violated through the exclusion of potential jurors who were African American. Justice Scalia wrote the majority opinion for a divided Court that rejected that claim and asserted that "[r]ace as such has nothing to do with the legal issue in this case" (*Holland v. Illinois* 1990, 486). In actuality, social science research findings must lead us to fear that prosecutors' use of challenges to construct all-white juries may produce more conviction-prone juries than if juries are more diverse with respect to race (Vidmar and Hans, 2007). In response, Justice Marshall's dissent asserted that the majority was permitting racial bias to affect decision making in the justice system. Justice Scalia's majority opinion addressed Marshall's dissent in a blistering way: "Justice Marshall's dissent rolls out the ultimate weapon, the accusation of insensitivity to racial discrimination—which will lose its intimidating effect if it continues to be fired so randomly" (*Holland v. Illinois* 1990, 486).

In the foregoing sentence, Scalia uses sarcasm to dismiss an issue of tremendous importance to society. Moreover, in speaking of the purportedly "intimidating effect" of raising racial issues, he indicates quite clearly that he believes issues of race are raised in illegitimate ways by those who point to problems of racial discrimination.

When the Supreme Court considered the case of *McCleskey v. Kemp* (1987) in which statistical evidence demonstrated that racial discrimination existed in Georgia's system for imposing the death penalty, Scalia provided one of the decisive five votes to reject the Equal Protection claim. In a dissenting opinion, Justice Stevens pointedly accused member of the majority of ignoring racial discrimination solely because they wanted to preserve capital punishment:

> The Court's decision appears to be based on a fear that the acceptance of McCleskey's claim would sound the death knell for capital punishment in Georgia. If society were indeed forced to choose between a racially discriminatory death penalty (one that provides heightened protection against murder "for whites only") and no death penalty at all, the choice mandated by the Constitution would be plain. (*McCleskey v. Kemp* 1987, 367)

Several years later, when internal memos from the Court became available in the Harry Blackmun Papers in the Library of Congress, additional evidence emerged about Scalia's insensitivity to race. While the author of the majority opinion, Justice Powell, later admitted that he did not understand the statistical evidence presented in the case and there is doubt whether several other justices understood this proof of discrimination, Scalia claimed he did. In a memo that circulated internally among the justices' chambers with no thought it could ever be revealed in their lifetimes, Scalia wrote:

> I disagree with the argument that the inferences that can be drawn from the Baldus [statistical] study are weakened by the fact that each jury and trial is unique, or by the large number of variables at issue. And I do not share the view, implicit in [Powell's draft opinion], that an effect of racial factors upon sentencing, if it could be shown by sufficiently strong statistical evidence, would require reversal. Since it is my view that the unconscious operation of irrational sympathies and antipathies, including racial, upon jury decisions and (hence) prosecutorial [ones] is real, acknowledged by the [cases] of this court and ineradicable, I cannot honestly say that all I need is more proof. I expect to write separately on these points, but not until I see the dissent. (Dorin 1994, 1077)

This memo made clear that Scalia understood that the statistical evidence demonstrated the existence of racial discrimination in Georgia's death penalty system. Yet, Scalia asserted that proof of racial discrimination would not be enough to necessarily lead him to find an equal protection violation that might put a halt to the death penalty. Indeed, he regarded racial prejudice and discrimination in the justice system as inevitable (Dorin 1994). Sadly, unlike other justices, he seemed to use this perception as an excuse for doing nothing to stop racial discrimination, even when given a clear opportunity to do so in a particularly stark context: the selection of those defendants who would be put to death by the state for the commission of a murder. In sum, the memo made clear that Scalia was willing to tolerate racial discrimination against African Americans in capital punishment decisions in order to make sure that the option of imposing the death penalty remained available as a criminal sanction.

With respect to wrongful convictions, Justice Scalia took a hard line against expanding post-conviction reviews. He was notable for emphasizing that newly-discovered evidence of innocence did not provide a basis for a legal right to have post-conviction review of that evidence. In *Herrera v. Collins* (1993) Scalia wrote, "There is no basis in text, tradition, or even in contemporary practice (if that were enough), for finding in the Constitution a right to demand judicial consideration of newly discovered evidence of innocence brought forward after conviction" (427–28). In the subsequent case of *In re Davis* (2009), Scalia wrote, "This Court has *never* held that the Constitution forbids the execution of a convicted defendant who has had a full and fair trial but is later able to convince a habeas court that he is 'actually' innocent" (3). In effect, Scalia focused on the absence of an explicit constitutional provision that would prohibit punishment, including execution, of the wrongfully convicted. In his view, if you received your right to a fair trial, an attorney, and the other trial rights, and then the trial simply produced the wrong result—too bad for you. Fundamentally, he simply assumed that the justice system would make errors and that was simply unfortunate for the person wrongly punished, not a basis for judges to intervene to do whatever could be done to ensure a just result. Undoubtedly, other justices would look to the vague right to "due process" in the Fourteenth and Fifth Amendments or to the Eighth Amendment protection against cruel and unusual punishments as providing a basis to examine cases and prevent the punishment of the innocent. More than most justices, Scalia seemed interested in emphasizing the finality of convictions without regard to the likelihood that some of those convictions would be based on errors.

In the case of *Connick v. Thompson* (2011), a man in Louisiana was convicted of murder and sentenced to death after an assistant prosecutor, in an act known to at least one other assistant prosecutor, removed and destroyed evidence that would have assisted in demonstrating his innocence. He served eighteen years in prison and came within weeks of being executed before an investigator for his defense attorney accidently discovered files that demonstrated prosecutorial misconduct that prosecutors had intended to keep hidden. After gaining his freedom from prison, Thompson sued the prosecutor's office and a jury awarded him $14 million in damages for the harms that he suffered from the prosecutorial misconduct. In a majority opinion written by Justice Thomas, the slim Supreme Court majority overturned the jury's decision, took the money away, and declared that Thompson could not successfully sue the prosecutor for failing to train assistant prosecutors properly. Justice Scalia wrote a concurring opinion to support the majority result and chastise the dissenters for arguing that there was a basis for liability in the unethical and illegal conduct of the assistant prosecutor.

Commentators were outraged when Scalia cited in his concurring opinion penned for *Arizona v. Youngblood* (1988), in which the Court had absolved police of responsibility for failing to properly preserve evidence since Youngblood could not prove that the police acted in bad faith. In the *Youngblood* case, a man went to prison on a rape charge while the police failed to preserve biological evidence which, if saved, could have provided a basis to use later-developed DNA tests to prove his innocence. Yet, further development of DNA led to better-refined testing of evidence and led to tests in 2000 that showed Youngblood was innocent all along. Justice Scalia used a case in which a man was shown to be innocent in order to prevent others who might be innocent from making claims about police and prosecutorial misconduct. The rule established in the 1988 *Youngblood* case presumed that he was guilty based on his conviction. When Scalia cited the case in *Connick* in 2011, he knew better yet used the case as if lacking knowledge about the 2000 exoneration. Scalia's emphasis on finality in cases accepted that such finality could come at the cost of those whose lives were destroyed by misidentifications or prosecutorial misconduct leading to erroneous convictions.

CONCLUSION

Over the course of thirty years on the Supreme Court during which time he participated in hundreds of criminal justice-related cases, Justice Scalia cast decisive votes and wrote influential opinions concerning an array of issues. As previously discussed, important examples include his seminal majority opinion re-characterizing the Second Amendment as expressing a constitutional right for individuals to own handguns (*District of Columbia v. Heller* 2008) and his opinion imposing a difficult-to-prove subjective test for Eighth Amendment violations in prison-conditions cases (*Wilson v. Seiter* 1991). Both of these majority opinions were of monumental importance in shaping and constraining the legal arguments, judicial decisions, and policy debates that followed concerning gun rights and conditions of confinement in prison, respectively. With respect to issues at the center of debates about the capacity of the American system to produce just outcomes, including cases concerning racial discrimination, capital punishment, and wrongful convictions, Scalia was outspoken in defending the finality of decisions and presenting arguments to resist change. In these contexts, Scalia's many opinions provided reasoning for judges elsewhere in the judicial system who shared Scalia's skepticism about the extent of discrimination and its susceptibility to correction through judicial decisions. Similarly, his resistance to reducing the application of capital punishment and correcting wrongful convictions provided ammunition for other judges who emphasize finality as a key goal of the justice system, even when that goal collides with efforts to make proceedings accurate, fair, and correctable.

By contrast, in Fourth Amendment cases and Sixth Amendment Confrontation Clause cases, there are many examples of Scalia applying his originalist orientation to argue that the government had violated the rights of individuals. His arguments for a strong definition of the Confrontation Clause right were evident throughout his career. For unknown reasons, his arguments for the recognition of Fourth Amendment violations became more frequent in cases decided by the Supreme Court in the later years of his career. Scholars have concluded that certain justices changed their viewpoints over their course of their careers. It is unclear if this was the case with Scalia and the Fourth Amendment because it is also possible that the nature of search and seizure issues faced by the Court changed over the time and that these new issues, such as the use technological devices for searches, simply elicited the same protective analysis that Scalia would have applied if such issues had arisen early in his career.

While his record in criminal justice cases certainly displays Scalia's conservative bona fides, the review provided here provides evidence that textualism, as Scalia himself often pronounced, was not necessarily an instrumental tool to achieve particular results (Scalia 1997; Scalia and Garner 2012). While his record is substantially conservative in this area of the law, in nearly 1 in 6 decisions, Scalia cast his vote in support of criminal rights. And when looking more narrowly at the outcome in Fourth Amendment cases, that number jumps to nearly 1 of 4 cases. Both in the majority and dissenting opinions concerning the Fourth Amendment, there are numerous instances in which Scalia employed the historical record to arrive at a result favored by his liberal colleagues.

Justice Scalia influenced constitutional law in the area of criminal justice by casting decisive votes in close cases, writing influential opinions that shaped important issues, and expressing skepticism about efforts to reduce discrimination and correct wrongful convictions. His application of that approach led him to support defendants' claims in cases concerning specific issues, particularly those involving the Fourth Amendment and the Sixth Amendment. In this respect, his record was more mixed—with a combination of conservative and liberal decisions—in the area of criminal justice than in some other areas of laws. Yet, his overall record and his impact in major cases generally advanced outcomes preferred by political conservatives. As a result, Scalia's doctrinal record and jurisprudential approach exist today as a yardstick by which future nominees to the high court are measured. President Donald Trump specifically promised during his campaign that Antonin Scalia would serve as a judicial Rosetta Stone that would guide his selection of individuals to fill open seats on the federal bench. True to his word, his first selection to the Supreme Court, Neil Gorsuch, certainly appeared to accomplish the president's pledge. An analysis produced in the weeks prior to the nomination of Gorsuch suggests that the newest justice will likely be even more conservative that Scalia (Epstein, Martin, and Quinn 2016). Yet in at least one early case regarding issues of the Fourth Amendment and unreasonable searches, *Carpenter v. United States* argued in the fall of 2017, Gorsuch revealed sympathy for the rights of the criminally accused that was strikingly similar to that of Scalia. The case, which involves the collection and use of cell phone tower data to track the movements of a suspect without a warrant, sparked Gorsuch to remark during oral argument that the data might be considered the property of the user mirroring the common law sensibilities often employed by his predecessor. While it is too early to offer a clear assessment of the impact of Justice Gorsuch placement on the bench, it may be that in attempting to find Scalia's judicial *doppelganger*, President Trump has appointed a justice that will perpetuate the mixed conservative record of Scalia on issues of criminal justice well into the future, a result that may have pleased the former justice.

REFERENCES

Biskupic, J. 2009. *American Original: The Life and Constitution of Supreme Court Justice Antonin Scalia.* New York, NY: Sarah Crichton Books.

Cross, F. B. 2013. *The Failed Promise of Originalism.* Stanford, CA: Stanford University Press.

Dorin, D. 1994. "Far Right of the Mainstream: Racism, Rights, and Remedies from the Perspective of Justice Antonin Scalia's McCleskey Memorandum." *Mercer Law Review* 45: 1035–88.

Epstein, Lee, Andrew D. Martin, and Kevin Quinn. 2016. "President-Elect Trump and His Possible Justices." http://pdfserver.amlaw.com/nlj/PresNominees2.pdf. Accessed December 14, 2017.

Greenburg, J. C. 2007. *Supreme Conflict.* New York, NY: Penguin.

Harry A. Blackmun Papers. 2003. Library of Congress, Washington, DC, Box 472.

Pryor, William H. Jr. 2017. "Justice Thomas, Criminal Justice, and Originalism's Legitimacy." *The Yale Journal Forum* 127: 173–81.

Rozas, A. 2007. "Daughter of Supreme Court Justice Accused of DUI." *Chicago Tribune,* Feb. 14, 3.

Scalia, A. 1989. "Originalism: The Lesser Evil." *University of Cincinnati Law Review* 57: 849–65.

———. 1997. *A Matter of Interpretation: Federal Courts and the Law.* Princeton, NJ: Princeton University Press.

Scalia, A., and B. A. Garner. 2012. *Reading Law: The Interpretation of Legal Texts.* St. Paul, MN: West.

Schultz, D. A. and C. E. Smith, 1996. *The Jurisprudential Vision of Justice Antonin Scalia.* Lanham, MD: Rowman & Littlefield.

Smith, C. E. 2016a. *The Supreme Court and the Development of Law: Through the Prism of Prisoners' Rights.* New York, NY: Palgrave Macmillan.

———. 2016b. "What If?: Human Experience and Supreme Court Decision Making on Criminal Justice." *Marquette Law Review* 99: 813–39.

———. 2001. "The Malleability of Constitutional Doctrine and Its Ironic Impact on Prisoners' Rights." *Boston University Public Interest Law Journal* 11: 73–96.

———. 1993. *Justice Antonin Scalia and the Supreme Court's Conservative Moment.* Westport, CT: Praeger.

Smith, C. E. and J. A. Baugh. 2000. *The Real Clarence Thomas: Confirmation Veracity Meets Performance Reality.* New York, NY: Peter Lang.

Smith, C. E. and M. M. McCall, 2011. "Antonin Scalia: Outspoken and Influential Originalist." In C. E. Smith, C. DeJong, and M. A. McCall, *The Rehnquist Court and Criminal Justice.* 169–88. Lanham, MD: Lexington Books.

Smith, C. E., M. M. McCall, and M. A. McCall, 2015. "The Roberts Court and Criminal Justice: An Empirical Assessment." *American Journal of Criminal Justice* 40: 416–40.

Sorkin, A. D. 2013. "In Voting Rights, Scalia Sees a 'Racial Entitlement.'" *The New Yorker*, February 28.

Supreme Court Judicial Database. 2017. http://scdb.wustl.edu/.

Tushnet, M. 2013. *In the Balance: Law and Politics on the Roberts Court.* New York, NY: W. W. Norton.

Vidmar, N. and V. P. Hans, 2007. *American Juries: The Verdict.* Amherst, NY: Prometheus Books.

TABLE OF CASES

Arizona v. Hicks, 480 U.S. 321 (1987).

Arizona v. Youngblood, 488 U.S. 51 (1988).

Bailey v. United States, 133 S.Ct. 1031 (2013).

Blakely v. Washington, 542 U.S. 296 (2004).

California v. Green, 399 U.S. 149 (1970).

Carpenter v. United States, U.S. Supreme Court Docket No. 16–402, Argued Nov. 29, (2017).

Carroll v. United States, 267 U.S. 132 (1925).

Connick v. Thompson, 131 S.Ct. 1350 (2011).

Coy v. Iowa, 487 U.S. 1012 (1988).

District of Columbia v. Heller, 554 U.S. 570 (2008).

Entick v. Carrington, EWHC KB J98 (1765).

Estelle v. Gamble, 429 U.S. 97 (1976).

Florida v. Jardines, 133 S.Ct. 1409 (2013).

Friedman v. City of Highland Park, 136 S.Ct. 447 (2015).

Herrera v. Collins, 506 U.S. 390 (1993).

Holland v. Illinois, 494 U.S. 474 (1990).

Hudson v. McMillian, 503 U.S. 1 (1992).

Illinois v. Cabelles, 543 U.S. 405 (2005).

In re Davis, 130 S.Ct. 1 (2009).

Jackson v. City and County of San Francisco, 135 S.Ct. 2799 (2015).
Katz v. United States, 389 U.S. 347 (1967).
Kyllo v. United States, 533 U.S. 27 (2001).
Maryland v. King, 133 S.Ct. 1958 (2013).
McCleskey v. Kemp, 481 U.S. 279 (1987).
Missouri v. NcNeeley, 569 U.S. ___ (2013).
National Treasury Employees Union v. Von Raab, 489 U.S. 656 (1989).
Navarette v. California, 134 S.Ct. 1683 (2014).
Overton v. Bazzetta, 539 U.S. 126 (2003).
Shelby County v. Holder, 570 U.S. 2 (2013).
Turner v. Safley, 482 U.S. 78 (1987).
United States v. Jones, 132 S.Ct. 945 (2012).
United States v. Miller, 307 U.S. 174 (1939).
Wilson v. Seiter, 501 U.S. 294 (1991).

Chapter 5

Threat and Suspicion

Scalia's Legacy for a Transnational Judicial Dialogue

Maureen Stobb

Justice Scalia has been described as the "Unrelenting Provoker" who "by forcing his ideological adversaries to engage with his ideas . . . reshaped and enriched legal discourse," and "won the war even when he lost his hardest-fought battles" (Tribe 2016). One of these hard-fought battles was against the use of foreign law[1] in constitutional interpretation. He appointed himself as the spokesperson for those that condemn such citations.[2] At the center of Scalia's argument is his perception of this international dialogue as a threat to American democracy. Judges can too easily manipulate citation to foreign sources to impose their morality on the American public. Some of his fellow justices, including Breyer and Ginsburg, disagree. They, along with numerous scholars, argue that citation to foreign law is part of a dialogue with judges in other countries that not only improves the Supreme Court's reputation abroad, but provides insight into the common human experience that should guide interpretation of rights protected under our Constitution (Farber 2007; Young 2005; Slaughter 1994).[3] Those in favor of this transnational dialogue argue that Scalia's approach is perceived abroad as an extreme form of provincialism, which ultimately undermines the global legitimacy of the U.S. Constitution (Parish 2007). Scalia's response was to characterize such justifications as mere excuses, or covers for ideological decision making.

Scalia placed himself at the front of a long-standing, contentious debate that recently has received a great deal of attention, inside the court hierarchy and beyond (Gray 2007).[4] Lower court judges have also criticized citation to foreign law as a sign of ideologically motivated decision making that undermines the courts' legitimacy with the American public and within the judiciary (Wilkinson 2004). The issue is considered "one of the hottest topics in legal scholarship" (Bryant 2011, 1006), as many in the legal academy contend that activist justices look abroad for consensus when it does not exist in the United States (Parish 2007). In doing so, they give foreign practices authoritative weight without engaging in the reasoning underlying them (Parish 2007; Young 2005). Congressmen continue to question Supreme Court nominees on the subject, and have proposed legislation that prohibits federal court reliance upon foreign law in constitutional interpretation unless it is a source that provides insight into the Constitution's original meaning, such as English common law.[5] Members of the American public also have strong views on the subject. Passionate critics sent death threats to judges favoring citation to foreign law (Parish 2007), and in 2010, voters amended the Oklahoma Constitution to state: "courts shall not look to the legal precepts of other nations or cultures" (Bryant 2011, 1006). The media publicizes the heated debate, stoking the fire (Curry and Miller 2008).

In this chapter, I examine Scalia's attempt to provide clear criteria for appropriate citation to foreign law. He encouraged his colleagues on the Court to embrace his standards, and attempted to alter the perception of the practice among members of the legal community and the public. Ultimately, Scalia sought to dissuade the strategic use of foreign law to prop-up controversial decisions. I contend that he both succeeded and failed in this endeavor, in part because he was not consistent with this approach in his own decision making. Scalia successfully strengthened the Court's commitment to considering the decisions' of treaty partners' courts when interpreting international agreements. He also effectively stimulated an increase in references to English common law by both liberals and conservatives in constitutional interpretation. However, Scalia failed to defeat the strategic use of foreign law in constitutional interpretation to demonstrate consensus about the meaning of guaranteed rights. He also did not provide clear guidelines in his jurisprudence for when judges should look to foreign practices to learn new approaches. Despite his vocal criticisms of certain uses of foreign law, his inconsistencies undermined his ability to affect the manner in which these citations are perceived by members of the judiciary, and therefore to eliminate the incentive to manipulate such references for policy gain. I conclude that judges will continue to employ foreign law when they feel the need to bolster a decision for which they lack adequate domestic support, because they obtain increased influence by employing this tactic. At the same time, Scalia succeeded in leaving a legacy of suspicion that casts a light upon the reality that Supreme Court justices act strategically when writing opinions, a fact that scholars have attested to for years.

This chapter proceeds as follows. First, I examine Scalia's jurisprudence on the use of foreign law, explaining the four principles he developed concerning the practice, and highlighting his contention that the practice undermines American democracy because judges can selectively choose foreign sources to justify imposing their preferred policy position upon the American people. After presenting his arguments, I examine the extent to which the current Court has embraced his guidelines. I then investigate Scalia's impact on the perception of the practice within the judiciary, conducting an empirical analysis of the degree to which citation to foreign law increases the influence of an opinion. I conclude by exploring the implications of my findings for Scalia's legacy.

SCALIA'S PRINCIPLES FOR
CITATION TO FOREIGN LAW

Scalia's suspicion of reliance on foreign law stems from his textualist approach to interpreting legal texts. As Scalia explained it, he "look[ed] for meaning in the governing text, ascribe[d] to that text the meaning that it has born from its inception, and reject[ed] judicial speculation about both the drafters' extratextually derived purposes and the desirability of the fair reading's anticipated consequences" (Scalia and Garner 2012, xxvi). The context and convention of the text convey a particular idea that can be obtained through a fair reading, which focuses on the limited range of meanings attributable to words and does not go beyond that range (Scalia 1997). Applying this approach to constitutional interpretation, judges should look to the original meaning of the text and figure out the practical implications of those original meanings in modern contexts (Scalia 1997, 38–39). Although Scalia admitted textualism does not always produce consistent results, he argued that its value lies in the fact that it sets boundaries on the range of acceptable decision making and argumentation, and can "curb—even reverse—the tendency of judges to imbue authoritative texts with their own policy preferences" (Scalia and Gardner 2012, xxviii). The integrity of our democratic system and the rule of law depends upon the commitment of judges to such limits (Scalia and Gardner 2012). Scalia issued a caveat, however, admitting that opinions he has written or joined will not always be consistent with his textualist position because he has adhered to precedent, been persuaded by counsel, or "wisdom [came] too late" (xxx).

Scalia enshrined his principles of textualism in his jurisprudence on citation to foreign law. His approach can be summarized in four main principles. First, reliance on foreign law may be necessary to understand the meaning of words in an international agreement, in statutes referencing international law, or in statutes derived from foreign practices. Second, English common law is relevant to interpreting the Constitution because it gives us a sense of the meaning of the words at the time they were written. Modern English law can be referenced when no guidance is found in old English law or American law, if the more recent British practices shed light on the historical meaning. At times, justices may consider the practices of countries with a common heritage or adhering to similar ideals, when those references support already established American practices. Third, foreign law is not relevant to establishing a consensus in areas of constitutional law where such agreement is an important element, as when understanding the Eighth Amendment's prohibition against cruel and unusual punishment. References to practices abroad may be tolerated, however, if they only add to clearly established evidence of consensus among the American people. Foreign law is also irrelevant to determining protected liberty interests that are rooted in our nation's traditions. Fourth, Scalia accepts references to foreign law that add to a discussion of whether certain interpretations of a text have disastrous consequences. This last principle seems inconsistent with a pure textualist approach, as it appears to rely on consequentialist reasoning. Although Scalia does not always act according to his stated commitment to textualism, he is unswerving in his contention that justices' use of foreign law may be strategic. Throughout his jurisprudence, he repeatedly plants the seeds of suspicion. Below, I elaborate on these principles.

In numerous cases involving international treaties, Scalia focused on foreign constructions of the terms to derive the common understanding of the parties (Dorsen 2005). The use of foreign law for this purpose predates Scalia's time on the Court (see, for example, *Air France v. Saks* 1985). For example, Scalia joined the opinion in *Eastern Airlines, Inc. v. Floyd* (1991), in which the majority relied on foreign legal sources to determine that airline passengers could not recover for purely emotional distress under Article 17 of the Warsaw Convention (1929). Scalia used his skill at writing withering dissents to underscore the importance of this approach. In his dissent in *Olympic Airways v. Husain* (2004), Scalia argued that this use of foreign law is appropriate because clear criterion exists to determine which foreign sources are relevant in these cases, as the treaty signatories' decisions are evidence of the original shared understanding of the text's meaning (Scalia, J., dissenting).[6] Interpreting the Warsaw Convention in *Olympic Airways,* the majority determined that the "accident" condition precedent to air carrier liability was met by a flight attendant's refusal to move a passenger's seat, and that refusal led to the passenger's death from an allergic reaction to cigarette smoke. Scalia expressed his frustration that Thomas (the opinion writer) did not include any reference to sister signatories' court decisions on the meaning of accident, particularly given the fact that the Court so readily cites foreign courts when interpreting the U.S. Constitution, a document these nations had no part in crafting. Citing English and Australian decisions, he argued that the Court's reasoning was at odds with the holdings of treaty partners, and that the court should cite these opinions to show our sister signatories "the courtesy of respectful consideration" (*Olympic Airways v. Husain* 2004, Scalia, J., dissenting, 661).

Scalia also generally did not object to the use of foreign law to interpret domestic legislation when Congress specifically referenced international law in the statute. Therefore, judges can discuss norms of international law when applying the Alien Tort Statute, in which Congress granted U.S. courts jurisdiction over noncitizens' civil tort claims for violations "of the law of nations or a treaty of the United States" (*Kiobel v. Royal Dutch Petroleum* 2013). Foreign law may also be relevant if the unique history of the statute derives from other nations' practices, such as a Tennessee statute patterned on election reform efforts in foreign countries (*Burson v. Attorney General* 1992) and Louisiana legal practices based on the French civil law tradition (*Boggs v. Boggs* 1997).

Scalia's approach accorded a high status to English common law in constitutional interpretation. Because he tried to read the Constitution for what it meant when it was written, he found old English law to be an important tool for determining the meaning of "phrases like 'due process' and right of confrontation' . . . taken from English law" (Dorsen 2005, 525). For example, Scalia was a staunch defender of the use of the historical test to determine if parties are entitled to a jury trial. Judges employing this method ascertain whether the rights and remedies in the case are legal in character by comparing the action to eighteenth-century English cases tried in courts of law and those tried in courts of equity (*Tull v. United States* 1987). Scalia objected to any departure from this test, arguing that although it "require[s] us to enter into a domain becoming less familiar with time . . . our whole constitutional experience teaches that history must inform the judicial inquiry" (*Chauffeurs, Teamsters and Helpers, Local No. 391 v. Terry et al.* 1990, 546). He emphasized that judges must put their own views aside. Indeed, Scalia's reliance on English legal tradition sometimes led him to "liberal" outcomes, particularly with regard to the rights of criminal defendants. He dissented from a holding allowing additional jail time for a repeat offender of immigration law because his interpretation of the double jeopardy clause's history led him to doubt the sentence enhancement's constitutionality (*Almendarez-Torres v. United States* 1998). He also felt compelled by English common law to strengthen criminal defendants' right to confront witnesses at trial (*Coy v. Iowa* 1988). Consistent with his stipulation that textualism will not produce uniform results (Scalia and Gardner 2012), Scalia argued with his colleagues about English legal practices and the proper interpretation of words drawn from this tradition on numerous occasions (*Gasperini v. Center for Humanities* 1996; *Immigration and Naturalization Service v. St. Cyr* 2001; *Rasul v. Bush* 2004; *Boumediene v. Bush* 2008).

Scalia also found references to modern British practices to be appropriate if they added to our understanding of English common law. In *United States v. Gaudlin* (1995), Scalia relied primarily on English common law to conclude that, at the time the Bill of Rights was adopted, a clear practice did not exist concerning judicial determination of the materiality of a false statement in perjury prosecutions. He therefore looked to mid-nineteenth century British practices for guidance.[7] He also accepted appeals to foreign law—not only British rules—that strengthen a claim concerning early English practice (*Eastern Enterprise v. Apfel* 1998). He tolerated references to the practices of nations with a common history, including Australia, Canada, and New Zealand, or other Western democracies, if such citations build on a firm foundation in early English or American practices (*Browning Ferris v. Kelco* 1989; *Washington v. Glucksberg* 1997).

When Scalia found, according to this textualist approach, that foreign law was not relevant to understanding the meaning of the words of a statute or the Constitution, or did not add to an established foundation in our nation's history, he argued the Court used these sources selectively to strategically prop up opinions that have no basis in American traditions. As he put it, "when it agrees with what the justices want the case to say, we use the foreign law, and when it doesn't we don't use it" (Dorsen 2005, 521). In these cases, a judge who cites foreign law to grasp our Constitution's meaning is motivated by the desire to find "the best answer to this social question in [his or her] judgment as an intelligent person" (526). He labelled this approach consequentialist because proponents argue that legal texts should be interpreted to achieve desirable results (Scalia and Gardner 2012, 22). Scalia warned, "there is an uncanny correspondence between the consequentialist's own policy views and his judicial decisions" (Scalia and Gardner 2012, 22). Similarly, looking behind the words of the text to determine the author's intent (purposivism), can lead to the substitution of the judge's views for those of the American people (Scalia and Gardner 2012, 19). In short, Scalia argued such uses of foreign law allow unelected justices to impose the manners and morals of other countries, because they agree with them, on the American people (Waters 2005). This practice, he contended, "invites manipulation" and undermines democracy (Dorsen 2005, 531).

According to Scalia's approach, British law is not always relevant, and there are limits to the use of foreign law even when interpreting a statute in which Congress has referenced it. Scalia joined Thomas in objecting to the majority's resort to a twentieth-century British law to find the meaning of a term in the Securities Act (1933) (*Gustafson v. Alloyd Company, Inc.* 1995, Thomas, J., dissenting). Their dissent argues that Congress supplied the definition in the statute, and accuses the majority of being motivated by its policy preferences in its analysis. Similarly, in his concurrence in *Sosa v. Alvarez-Machain* (2004), Scalia criticized the majority's reservation of a discretionary judicial power to create causes of action for the enforcement of international-law based norms. He argued that the Constitution did not give the Court this power, a fair reading of the Alien Tort Statute only granted the court's jurisdiction and did not create a cause of action, and congressional authorization was required to grasp such a substantive lawmaking power (*Sosa v. Alvarez-Machain* 2004, Scalia, J., dissenting). Scalia also rejected scholars' arguments that the framers intended to incorporate international standards because they repeatedly appealed to them to gain global legitimacy (Koh 2004). He labelled such notions as the "20th-century invention of internationalist law professors and human rights advocates," and stated that the framers would have been "appalled by the proposition that, for example, the American peoples' democratic adoption of the death penalty . . . could be judicially nullified because of the disapproving views of foreigners" (*Sosa v. Alvarez-Machain* 2004, 750, 765). Although at the time the Constitution was ratified Americans believed in natural law, Scalia determined these standards were not incorporated because he found no textual basis for concluding that they were (Gray 2007, 1262).

Given his adherence to this textualist philosophy, Scalia's most well-known criticisms of the use of foreign law are predictable. Scalia objected to references to foreign law in several cases interpreting the Eighth Amendment's prohibition on cruel and unusual punishment. In *Thompson v. Oklahoma* (1988), the plurality cited to the views of "other nations that share our Anglo-American heritage, and by the leading members of the Western European community" to support its decision that imposing the death sentence for an act committed at age fifteen "would offend civilized standards of decency" (715–26).[8] In his dissent, Scalia reframed the question in the case as to whether there was a *national* consensus that individuals under sixteen cannot be executed, arguing that the best measure of "evolving standards of decency" would be the legislation enacted by the representatives of the American people (*Thompson v. Oklahoma* 1988, Scalia, J., dissenting, 859, 865). He repeatedly labelled the majority's approach as a strategy to achieve its policy objectives. He contended it was "all too easy to believe that evolution has culminated in one's own views" (*Thompson v. Oklahoma* 1988, Scalia, J., dissenting, 866). In a strongly worded footnote, he chided the plurality for citing the practices of other nations, stating that "where there is not first a settled consensus among our own people, the views of other nations, however enlightened the justices of this Court may think them to be, cannot be imposed upon Americans through the Constitution" (*Thompson v. Oklahoma* 1988, Scalia, J., dissenting, 869, footnote 4). Scalia accused the plurality of relying only on the feelings and intuition of judges (*Thompson v. Oklahoma* 1988, Scalia, J., dissenting, 873).

Scalia also objected to the majority's citation to foreign law to support its determination of an American consensus against imposing the death penalty on the mentally retarded (*Atkins v. Virginia* 2002). Recognizing that such sources were not dispositive, the Court argued, in a footnote, that the decision was consistent with the views of the world community. Scalia directly attacked the decision as "rest[ing] so obviously upon nothing but the personal views" of the majority (*Atkins v. Virginia* 2002, Scalia, J., dissenting, 338). He contended that too few American states agreed with the Court to find a national agreement on the issue, and characterized the Court as "thrashing about for evidence of 'consensus'" (*Atkins v. Virginia* 2002, Scalia, J., dissenting, 347). Scalia awarded the "Prize for the Court's Most Feeble Effort to fabricate national consensus . . . to its appeal to . . . members of the so called 'world community'. . . whose notions of justice are (thankfully) not always those of our people" (*Atkins v. Virginia* 2002, Scalia, J., dissenting, 347). His criticisms in *Roper v. Simmons* (2005) echoed this argument. The majority cited foreign law as confirmation of its finding that imposition of the death penalty on juveniles is a violation of the Eighth Amendment's prohibition on cruel and unusual punishment (*Roper v. Simmons* 2005, 575–77).[9] Scalia contended that "the Court thus proclaim[ed] itself sole arbiter of our Nation's moral standards—and ... purport[ed] to take guidance from the views of foreign courts and legislatures" (*Roper v. Simmons* 2005, 608). Arguing that the justices selectively chose only favorable foreign law, he discussed at length the laws of other countries differing in important respects from American law (*Roper v. Simmons* 2005, 624–25). He summed up his criticisms by stating that "[t]o invoke alien law when it agrees with one's own thinking, and ignore it otherwise, is not reasoned decision making, but sophistry" (*Roper v. Simmons* 2005, 627). Scalia made a similar accusation of error by omission in *Lawrence v. Texas* (2003), in which the Court relied upon decisions from the European Court of Human Rights and the actions of select nations to find a protected right for homosexual adults to engage in intimate, consensual conduct, but ignored the prohibition of sodomy in numerous countries (*Lawrence v. Texas* 2003, 576–77). These examples illustrate the most consistent aspects of Scalia's jurisprudence of suspicion.

At the same time, Scalia's admission that he has behaved in a manner that contradicts his textualist approach bears a ring of truth, as he has both objected to and accepted foreign law references addressing the consequences of a legal policy. For example, in *Printz v. United States* (1997), Scalia strongly criticized Breyer's reference, in his dissent, to the positive experiences of other nations with federal systems in allowing the assignment of federal duties to state officials. Yet, in Scalia's dissent in *McIntyre v. Ohio Elections Commission* (1995), he cited the practices of foreign legislatures (including Australia, Canada, and England) to argue that requiring identification of campaign literature's source does not improve the quality of campaigns. These two stances may be reconcilable, however, because he argued that the countries Breyer cited had federal systems that are very different from our own, while Scalia cited legislatures with a shared English common-law ancestry (*McIntyre v. Ohio Elections Commission* 1995, 381). However, under other circumstances, Scalia tolerated discussions of the consequences of policy choices made by foreign states. In *Washington v. Glucksberg* (1997), Scalia joined a dissent by Rehnquist that discussed the difficulty Dutch policy makers experienced in regulating legalized euthanasia. He also joined an opinion referencing the copyright laws of other nations to address the contention that increasing protections of freelancers' work will have terrible consequences (*New York Times Co. v. Tasini* 2001). Finally, in *Planned Parenthood v. Casey* (1992), he accepted Rehnquist's reference to West German and Canadian case law to accentuate the point that *Roe v. Wade* (1973) resulted in confusion, and should therefore be overruled.

Although Scalia was not entirely consistent in his jurisprudence concerning foreign law, he did loudly voice one clear message. We must be suspicious of justices' resort to the policies and practices of other nations, particularly when such references are made to support decisions not grounded in American history or precedents, or to consider the consequences of a policy. Scalia believed textualism was the best weapon against the propensity for such reasoning to affirm the policy preferences of the justices. The evidence suggests that even Scalia, perhaps unwittingly, fell victim to this tendency. In the next section, I explore the extent to Scalia's four principles are reflected in current judicial practice, noting both his successes and failures.

SCALIA'S FOUR PRINCIPLES IN CURRENT JUDICIAL PRACTICE

If Scalia's goal had been to eliminate all references to foreign law, then he would certainly have failed. Citation to foreign law is firmly embedded in American law. The use of foreign law dates back to 1820 and, although the practice is limited at all levels of the courts (Zaring 2006; O'Brien 2006; Calabresi and Zimdahl 2005), researchers conclude that the Supreme Court references foreign sources now more than in the past, particularly when it invalidates a law (Farber 2007; Black et. al. 2014a; 2014b). Indeed, scholars detect a clear upward movement in the use of foreign law at numerous levels of the judicial hierarchy, although the rate of growth for the lower courts has been much more gradual and constant across time than the Supreme Court's, which appears to have increased dramatically around 1980 (Black and Epstein 2007). Employing Black et al's (2014a; 2014b) data (obtained by searching all Supreme Court decisions from 1953 to 2008) and model, I found that Supreme Court justices were significantly more likely to cite foreign law after Scalia joined the Court. The substantive impact is small, however, as the predicted probability of a positive reference to any foreign law or practice increased approximately 2 percent (from 4 to 6 percent) after Scalia joined the Court.[10]

To investigate the trend during the length of Scalia's time on the Court, I extended Black et al.'s (2014a; 2014b) data through 2016, reviewing all of the Courts decisions during this period to identify and examine opinions in which the Supreme Court positively cited foreign law.[11] The graph below demonstrates that the growth in such citations continued through the remaining time that Scalia was on the Court. In fact, the rate of increase seems to have become more dramatic (figure 5.1).[12]

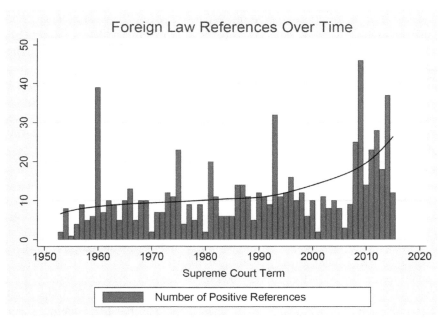

Figure 5.1.   Foreign Law References Over Time

Furthermore, evidence indicates that, as Scalia suspected, judges positively reference foreign law selectively to support controversial rulings (Black et. al. 2014a; 2014b). Justices are more likely to positively reference foreign law when they invalidate laws, overturn precedent, and render ideologically motivated decisions. Liberals and conservatives are equally likely to engage in the practice (Black et al. 2014a; 2014b). Unable to find needed justifications domestically, justices look abroad to reinforce the logic of their arguments, portraying their opponents as dissenting from international consensus, in the hopes of improving the reception of the decision (Black et al. 2014a; 2014b). These findings are consistent with prior research indicating that judges tactically select rhetorical sources to cite, including English common law (Hume 2006; Corley et al. 2005). Justices act strategically, carefully crafting the language of their opinions to be as persuasive as possible, looking to increase the decision's legitimacy, and the reputation of both the opinion and its author (Corley and Wedeking 2014; Hume 2006; Baum 2006; Epstein and Knight 1998). They tend to cite countries they expect will be considered legitimate sources, such as democratic, wealthy, English speaking countries and American allies (Black et al. 2014a; 2014b).

Although it is clear that the use of foreign law is increasing, to truly understand Scalia's legacy, I must examine the manner in which justices employed foreign law. Scalia did not aim to remove all references to foreign law from the Court's jurisprudence, he sought to guide the decision of which foreign sources to employ and when, and to encourage recourse to early English sources. Therefore, next I identify Scalia's successes and failures by examining the degree to which the current Court follows each of Scalia's guidelines.

Scalia's Success in Focusing Treaty Interpretation on the Intent of the Parties

The current Court seems to agree with Scalia that citations to foreign legal practices are appropriate when interpreting the intent of parties to a treaty. In several cases, the majority opinion writer included such references. Kennedy looked to courts and other legal authorities in England, Israel, Austria, South Africa, Germany, Australia, and Scotland, and noted an "emerging international consensus" when interpreting the Hague Convention on the Civil Aspects of International Child Abduction, as applied in U.S. law through the International Child Abduction Remedies Act (*Abbott v. Abbott* 2010, 16–19). Scalia joined the majority. Although Thomas and Breyer joined Stevens' dissent rejecting the holdings of these foreign courts, they did not dispute the relevance of decisions of sister signatories in general. Rather, the dissent contended that "we should not substitute the judgment of other courts for our own," and that international consensus on the matter was lacking (*Abbott v. Abbott* 2010, Stevens, J., dissenting, 43). Thomas embraced such references in a later opinion. Writing for a majority including Scalia, he referenced the decisions of sister signatories when interpreting another provision of the Hague Convention (*Lozano v. Alvarez* 2014). The concurrence by Alito, with Breyer and Sotomayor, did the same (*Lozano v. Alvarez* 2014, Alito, J., concurring). Kennedy also referenced the decisions of foreign courts when interpreting a provision of the United Nations Convention Relating to the Status of Refugees, and its protocol, barring asylum for those who have committed specific crimes (*Negusie v. Holder* 2009). He cited to Canadian, British, and Australian decisions finding that the exclusion is limited to culpable conduct (*Negusie v. Holder* 2009, 517). Scalia solidified the Court's commitment to a method of treaty interpretation that is consistent with his textualist approach. Thus, the evidence indicates that citation to decisions of treaty signatories is likely to be a common practice on the current Court.

Scalia's Success in Emphasizing the Importance of English Legal Practices

Scalia's fondness for citing English common law is apparent to anyone who has read his opinions. Although such references have always been accepted by the Court, Scalia's textualist and originalist principles brought greater attention to these sources. Scalia's presence on the Court is associated with a statistically significant increase in citation to English common law. The substantive impact is greater than that associated with citations to foreign law in general, with the likelihood of a citation to these English sources increasing approximately 11 percent (from 2 to 13 percent).[13] Indeed, employing the data I collected on Scalia's full term, I find that the increase in such citations is dramatic, as demonstrated by the graph below (figure 5.2).

The sharp increase is not due only to citations in opinions written by Scalia. Other justices on the Court, regardless of judicial philosophy, cited to English common law. Thomas, of course, very frequently draws on the source (see, for example, *Safford Unified School District v. Redding* [2009], for his discussion of the English common-law doctrine concerning delegation of parental authority to school officials). Roberts has looked to English legal history to support his interpretation of the boundaries of religious freedom (*Hosanna-Tabor Evangelical Lutheran Church and School v. Equal Employment Opportunity Commission* 2012), his conclusion that individuals can be criminally punished for the unintended consequences of their unlawful acts (*Dean v. United States* 2009), and his arguments concerning the free speech rights of corporations (*Citizens United v. Federal Elections Commission*

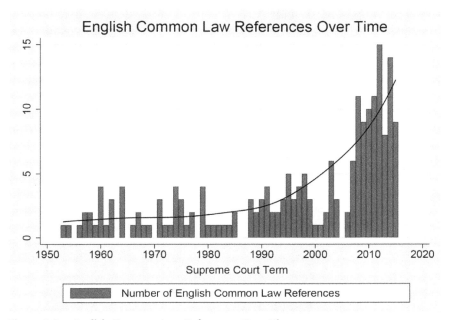

Figure 5.2.   **English Common-Law References Over Time**

2010, Roberts, J., concurring). Similarly, Alito drew on old English law to define the long held tradition of the right of self-defense in *McDonald v. Chicago* (2010), applying the Second Amendment's protection of the right to bear arms to the states. Kennedy, though seen by some scholars as a proponent of a modified version of the "living constitution" approach (Bartl 2014, 2), also draws upon old English cases and doctrines to interpret provisions of the Constitution. For example, concurring in *Stop the Beach Renourishment, Inc. v. Florida Department of Environmental Protection* (2010), Kennedy cited English common law to support his interpretation of the Takings Clause. He also references English legal history in the controversial case *Obergefell v. Hodges* (2015), finding that same-sex couples have a fundamental right to marry under the Due Process and Equal Protection Clauses of the Fourteenth Amendment. He employs these sources to argue that the institution of marriage has evolved over time, abandoning the English doctrine of coverture, under which married men and women were viewed as "a single, male dominated legal entity" (*Obergefell v. Hodges* 2015, 2595).

Justices viewed as liberal have also relied on English common law to boost their arguments. Breyer, known for his references to foreign law in controversial decisions, has looked to English legal history for support. For example, in *Williams v. Illinois* (2012), Breyer cited English common law when concurring with the Court's holding that the Confrontation Clause did not bar the testimony of an expert testifying about lab test results. Breyer cited *Blackstone's Commentary on the Laws of England* to explain that the Confrontation Clause was directed at preventing the practice of denying defendants the ability to confront their accusers, not to prevent the introduction of statements by accredited laboratory employees written in technical reports. Justice Ginsburg relied on past and present English practices to find that the imposition of consecutive sentences based on facts found by the judge (instead of the jury) did not violate the constitutional right to a jury trial (*Oregon v. Ice* 2009). Similarly, Justice Sotomayor cited English common law to interpret the Constitution's patent clause (*Pepper v. Unites States* 2011). Justice Kagan has also looked to English legal practices (*Match-E-Be-Nash-She-Wish Band of Pottawatomi Indians v. Patchak* 2012); however, this case concerned the interpretation of a statute. Citations to English legal practices continue in Scalia's absence. For example, Ginsburg cited English legal history to explain the roots of the right to a speedy trial (*Betterman v. Montana* 2016). Scalia's commitment to studying British practices to understand the original meaning of the Constitution will likely have a long-term impact.

Scalia's Failure to Prevent the Use of Foreign Law for Establishing Consensus

Scalia failed in halting references that conflict with his third principle, that foreign law is irrelevant in establishing consensus when no evidence of American consensus exists. Evidence suggests that justices have increasingly relied on foreign law to increase the legitimacy of their decisions in this manner, and that they look to foreign practices to support overturning American precedents on the basis of changing societal values without engaging with the reasoning underlying foreign law (Simon 2013). I find numerous examples of such references in the Court's recent jurisprudence, by both liberal and conservative justices currently on the Court. Breyer, of course, continues to cite to foreign law to argue for international agreement concerning the death penalty. Dissenting in *Glossip v. Gross* (2015), he referenced foreign law to support his objections to the Court's holding that the Eighth Amendment is not violated by officials' use of a drug protocol that does not render prisoners unable to feel all pain associated with administration of lethal injection. The Court affirmed that the death penalty is not categorically unconstitutional, and that this particular method is not cruel and unusual punishment. Breyer, joined by Ginsburg, supported the claim that the death penalty is cruel by citing foreign courts' findings that imposition of the death penalty imposes excessive delays. Further contending that the death penalty is indeed unusual, he asserted that many nations have formally abolished the death penalty, and numerous countries have abolished it in practice (*Glossip v. Gross* 2015, Breyer, J., dissenting, 2775, citing practices in Europe, Central Asia, and reports by the Amnesty International and other nonprofits). He prefaced his reference to foreign law with a long discussion of the practices of American states, and the statement, "I rely primarily upon domestic, not foreign events, in pointing to changes and circumstances to justify the claim that the death penalty, constitutionally speaking, is 'unusual'" (*Glossip v. Gross* 2015, Breyer, J., dissenting, 2775). Scalia's protests do not seem to have had much impact on Breyer's willingness to cite foreign practice to support consensus.

Kennedy has also cited global consensus when evaluating criminal penalties. Writing for the majority in *Graham v. Florida* (2010), Kennedy referenced foreign practices, reports by human rights NGOs, and an international treaty to support the Court's holding that the Eighth Amendment prohibited imposing a life-without-parole sentence on a juvenile who committed a non-homicide crime. Noting that the observation did not control the decision, he argued that this sentencing practice has been "rejected the world over," and citing *Roper, Atkins* and *Thompson,* among other cases, identified a "long-standing practice" of "noting the global consensus" (*Graham v. Florida* 2010, 80). In a statement clearly rejecting Scalia's position, Kennedy contended that international opinion is "not irrelevant" (*Graham v. Florida* 2010, 80). Kennedy listed the practices of Israel, reports by Amnesty International and Human Rights Watch, and the United Nations Convention on the Rights of the Child. Emphasizing that his argument was not based on a claim that this treaty, or any norm of international law, is binding on the Court, he argued that "the judgment of the world's nations that a particular sentencing practice is inconsistent with basic principles of decency demonstrates that the Court's rationale has respected reasoning to support it" (*Graham v. Florida* 2010, 82). Interestingly, Kennedy also referenced an Amnesty International report to support his argument that the constitutionality of certain forms of solitary confinement should be considered, an issue unrelated to the Court's holding in a death penalty case involving a challenge to the jury selection process (*Davis v. Ayala* 2015). Kennedy appears to be interested in expanding the transnational judicial dialogue, at least with regards to identifying human rights violations in criminal sentencing.

More conservative justices have also referenced foreign legal sources, but with the goal of arguing that international consensus does not exist on an issue, or at least that international opinion does not support the opposing side. Justice Alito referenced foreign practices in his dissent in *United States v. Windsor* (2013), where the majority held that a federal law refusing to recognize same-sex marriages (the Defense of Marriage Act) violated the Fifth Amendment's Due Process Clause. Arguing that substantive due process protects only "fundamental rights and liberties which are, objectively, 'deeply rooted in this Nation's history and tradition,'" Alito asserted that no state permitted such unions until 2003, and that no country allowed them until the Netherlands did so in 2000 (*United States v. Windsor* 2013, 2715). In a dissent in *Obergefell v. Hodges* (2015), Alito again referenced this evidence of foreign practice to dispute the Court's holding that states must recognize same-sex marriages. Roberts, in his dissent in *Obergefell,* cited practices on several continents (including Asia and Africa) to argue that marriage has been defined as a union of a man and a woman "across cultures and time" (*Obergefell v. Hodges* 2015, Roberts, J., dissenting, 2612). Scalia joined Roberts' and Alito's dissents in *Obergefell.* Such inconsistency certainly undermined his ability to combat the practice.

Scalia's Failure to Provide Guidelines for Learning from Foreign Nations' Practices

As noted, Scalia was inconsistent in his position concerning citation to foreign law to demonstrate the consequences of a policy choice or, in general, to learn from the approaches of foreign countries to common problems. Although justices do tend to cite countries that will likely be viewed as legitimate (i.e. the United Kingdom, Canada, Australia) (Black et al. 2014a; 2014b), they continue to make these references with few standards for when they are appropriate. For example, Breyer, a vocal advocate for learning from his fellow jurists abroad,[14] considered the jurisprudence of foreign courts when devising an appropriate level of scrutiny in free speech cases (*Ysursa v. Pocatello Education Association* 2009, Breyer, J., concurring in part, dissenting in part). Employing a rational basis standard of review, the majority held that an Idaho law prohibiting public employees from authorizing payroll deductions for union political activities did not violate the First Amendment. The Court found Idaho's justification for the policy, the interest in avoiding the reality or appearance of government favoritism with partisan politics, reasonable. Breyer argued that the Court should have applied an intermediate level of scrutiny because he viewed this prohibition as an indirect restriction on expression, reducing financing for speech. He advocated a test that examines whether the law imposes a disproportionate burden on speech, considering the government interest at stake. After citing numerous American precedents for the standard, Breyer noted that "several Constitutional courts in other nations have also used similar approaches when facing somewhat similar problems," and cited courts in Canada, South Africa, Israel, and the European Court of Human Rights. He did not attempt to explain why the approaches of these particular countries should guide the Court (*Ysursa v. Pocatello Education Association* 2009, Breyer, J., concurring in part, dissenting in part, 367).

Kennedy has not rejected the practice. For example, writing for the majority in *Brown v. Plata* (2011), he approved of the lower courts citation to foreign practices in its finding that the reduction of prison populations would not necessarily increase crime. In *Brown,* the district court had ordered California to reduce prison overcrowding because the condition led to deficiencies in medical care that violated the Eighth Amendment. The Court upheld the order, finding that the district court gave appropriate weight to the possible adverse impact on public safety, relying on statistical evidence from several states and Canada, where authorities implemented similar plans to reduce prison populations.[15] Such references to foreign law appear to be accepted by the Court.

SCALIA'S IMPACT ON THE PERCEPTION OF FOREIGN LAW REFERENCES WITHIN THE JUDICIAL HIERARCHY

Scalia's attacks on certain uses of foreign law were likely not only aimed at his colleagues on the Court. Researchers, studying his speeches and writings, have concluded that he also wanted to educate members of the legal community (Murphy 2014). He wrote dissents in the hopes that lawyers and judges would use his arguments to undermine the Court's standards with which he disagreed. These efforts could both contain the spread of such references and undermine the incentive driving his colleagues to resort to these sources. If lower courts question the legitimacy of this reasoning, Supreme Court Justices will see fewer benefits from the practice. In particular, they will not gain influence. Judges are motivated by a desire for influence, defined as "affect[ing] the thinking or work product of the judges or other actors in the legal community" (Curry and Miller 2017). In this section, I investigate the extent to which Scalia was successful in reducing influence gained by citation to foreign law. I conclude that, overall, Scalia failed in this endeavor.

Supreme Court justices understand that the impact of their opinions lies in the doctrines they produce (Clark and Lauderdale 2010), and that lower court treatments of their decisions (or lack thereof) affect the extent to which the justices' policy choices will determine outcomes in future cases (Canon and Johnson 1999). Justices want to set precedents that have their desired long-term impact, and therefore want their decisions to be cited often (Lupu and Fowler 2013; Fowler and Jeon 2008; Fowler et al. 2007). A wide array of studies have examined the impact of Supreme Court opinions.[16] The approach often depends on the specific audience of interest, which could be future high courts, the lower courts, administrative agencies, individuals and corporations who receive a benefit or suffer a disability as a result of the decision, and those indirectly affected, such as interest groups, the media, and the public at large (Canon and Johnson 1999). Judges' personal and professional acquaintances have also been considered (Baum 2006). I focus on the impact of Supreme Court references to foreign law within the federal judicial hierarchy. To my knowledge, only one study investigated the impact of citation to foreign law, and the authors looked at the effect on the Court's legitimacy with the public (Curry and Miller 2008). Employing an experimental design, Curry and Miller (2008) found that such references had a negative impact. It is not clear that members of the judiciary, as legal elites, would have the same reaction, however. I examine the impact of citation to foreign law, before and after Scalia joined the Court, on this crucial implementing audience.

To measure influence, I employ the total number of citations the precedent garners, as citation patterns are a recognized tool for this purpose (Black and Spriggs 2013; Cross 2010). Each citation communicates that a judge researched the law and made judgments about which cases to cite or not to cite, and chose to reference that case because the citation would legitimate his or her decision in some way (Fowler and Jeon 2008; Hansford and Spriggs 2006). The total number of citations conveys the extent to which the decision has influenced the outcome of later cases and played an important role in the development of the law (Cross 2010; Fowler and Jeon 2008). Even negative citations indicate that a decision presented "a powerful challenge to established positions or ways of thinking" (Curry and Miller 2017, citing Posner 2000, 387).

In developing my model, I control for factors deemed significant in prior studies of this kind. Scholars have included circuit and judge-specific characteristics, such as ideology, when studying reactions at the level of the individual lower court judge or panel (Corley and Wedeking 2014; Westerland et al. 2010; Luse et al. 2009; Benesh and Reddick 2002).[17] However, I focus on the standard set of precedent attributes included in these models because the goal of the present study is to examine the effect of a case characteristic (citation to foreign law) on the precedent's impact. The age of a precedent has been shown to affect its level of influence on future Courts and lower courts (Hitt 2016; Hansford and Spriggs 2006; Benesh and Reddick 2002). Unanimity, which expresses a clear legal answer to a question, increases the likelihood that lower courts will follow a case (Hitt 2016; Corley et al. 2013, Benesh and Reddick 2002). Similarly, ambiguous decisions are less likely to be treated positively (Hitt 2016). An ambiguous decision is one in which a majority of justices cannot agree on all of the premises for the judgment (Hitt 2016). Increases in the complexity of a case, measured by issue area or by the number of legal provisions and issues involved, are associated with a greater response (Hitt 2016; Hansford and Spriggs 2006; Benesh and Reddick 2002). Decisions addressing a circuit conflict are likely to have greater legal significance than those not resolving a controversy (Hitt 2016). Similarly, opinions that overturn a prior Supreme Court precedent or find a statute unconstitutional are likely to have a greater impact, as they alter the state of the law (Hitt 2016). Interestingly, precedent that is later overturned tends to be more authoritative, as these are cases that likely received a great deal of attention and have been influential, and are therefore more in need of revision (Fowler and Jeon 2008; Hansford and Spriggs 2006). Landmark cases—those of historical and/or social significance or salience—also tend to have a greater impact (Fowler and Jeon 2008). Such cases are generally more visible and controversial than others. Therefore, they are more likely to be treated but not necessarily followed (Corley and Wedeking 2014). This factor has been measured in a myriad of ways, including media attention to the case and whether the case has been identified as important by legal experts (Hitt 2016; Corley and Wedeking 2014; Fowler and Jeon 2008).

To this list of important precedent characteristics, I add citations to foreign law, which are justices' attempts to portray their arguments as consistent with the practices of other nations or international consensus. Such references arguably demonstrate the opinion's wide-ranging relevance, making it appear to speak to a larger issue than simply the dispute in that case, and therefore applicable to a broader set of cases. I focus on positive references to foreign law because research indicates that justices employ this tactic to support major changes to the law and ideologically motivated decisions (Black et al. 2014a; 2014b), and because Scalia specifically attacked these types of citations. As noted above, he drew attention to the reality that evidence now supports, that such references are used as thin veils to hide judges' pursuit of their policy goals. Although prior work suggests that Scalia had a significant impact on lower court citation rates (Cross 2010) and on references to legislative history (Koby 1999), with regard to foreign law, his actions were not always consistent with his words. Therefore, I contend that Scalia will not have undermined the likelihood that foreign law references will be associated with increased influence.

Hypothesis: Positive references to foreign law will be associated with an increase in the number of citations to a Supreme Court opinion before and after Scalia joined the Court.

In the next section, I present the data and methodological approach I employ to test these expectations.

Data and Analysis

The dataset for this analysis includes all Supreme Court opinions decided between 1953 and 2001. The unit of analysis is the Supreme Court precedent. I employ a variable on the use of foreign law provided by Black et al (2014a; 2014b). I obtain information on the citations to all cases by later Supreme Courts and lower federal courts from Hitt (2016), who collected original data on the treatment in the federal courts of every Supreme Court precedent promulgated from 1946 to 2010. Ending the cited cases at 2001 allows time for the precedents to move down the federal court hierarchy (Black et al. 2016). My starting point was dictated by the time frame of the Black et al. (2014a; 2014b) data. I describe the variables and methodology employed further below.

My primary dependent variables are aggregate and court-level measures taken from Hitt (2016), who obtained records of the treatment of Supreme Court decisions from *Shephard's Citations.* Hitt collected the total number of citations for each Supreme Court case at every level of the federal judicial hierarchy. The aggregate measure, *Aggregate citations*, adds the total number of citations across all three levels of the federal judicial hierarchy. Because the caseloads at each level of the hierarchy are very different, Hitt's (2016) aggregated measure equally weight a precedent's influence at every level by standardizing the counts at each level, obtaining a z-score, and then summing the z-scores. I also employ three of Hitt's (2016) court-level measures to examine whether justices find a greater benefit at one level of the judicial hierarchy than at another. *Supreme Court cites* is the total number of citations to a case, including positive, negative and neutral treatments. *Circuit court citations* provides the total for the U.S. Courts of Appeals, and *District court citations* indicates the same for this level of the courts. Hitt's (2016) findings indicate that the one can accurately measure a decision's relevance by employing any of the total count variables. Because my expectations are framed in terms of overall impact, I do not have a priori expectations as to whether or how each level may respond differently.

The central independent variable of interest is a dichotomous measure, *Positive foreign law reference,* coded 1 if the Supreme Court opinion positively cites foreign law, and 0 if otherwise (Black et al. 2014a). The authors followed the approach of *Shephard's* coding system.[18] They coded every formally decided, full opinion case, unsigned (i.e., per curium) orally argued case, and judgment of the Court handed down during their time frame. As noted above, they searched for references to all countries (using current and former names) and major international tribunals. Citations include references to: foreign court decisions; the foreign court procedures or practices; foreign law enforcement procedures; foreign constitutional provisions; foreign legislative acts; foreign informal government acts (i.e., debates); international reports or documents (i.e., a United Nations study) that mention the country searched for; or a foreign country's cultural, economic, political, or historical practices (Black et al. 2014a). The authors also generously provided data distinguishing references to solely English common law from those made to the practices of other foreign countries. This allowed me to control for any difference between the impact of generally accepted citations to English common law from that of more controversial references to foreign law. I ran tests replacing the *Positive foreign law reference* variable in my models with an indicator measuring references to positive foreign law excluding those to English common law. My overall findings were the same when using both variables. I note any differences in the results where relevant below.

I also obtained the control variables from Hitt's (2016) data set. They are measures of the precedent characteristics listed above as standard controls, and are therefore appropriate as my unit of analysis is the Supreme Court case.[19] The variable *Ambiguous decision* is included to control for the probability that courts are less likely to follow these inconsistent and complex rulings. The measure *Circuit conflict* accounts for the fact that a decision resolving such a conflict is likely to have greater significance, and therefore to be cited and followed more often. The dummy variables *Precedent altering* and *Judicial review* control for the likelihood that decisions changing the state of the law are likely to receive more citations. A dichotomous measure, *Non-unanimous case* (coded 1 if the case is not unanimous, and 0 if it is unanimous) distinguishes opinions that likely expressed a clear legal answer on an issue. The variable *Case importance,* coded 1 for cases identified as important by experts at the Legal Information Institute, controls for whether the case is considered a landmark decision. The dummy variable *Later reversed case* accounts for cases that are more authoritative. In addition, *Mandatory case,* a dummy variable, controls for precedents that probably do not deal with issues of broad national significance. An indicator, *Age of case,* is included because studies show this factor is significant. In addition, because lower courts respond to complex cases more quickly, fixed effects for Spaeth's 14 issue area categories are included.

I estimated negative binomial regression models for the court-level variables because this methodology allows for over-dispersed data (the variance exceeds the mean) (Hitt 2016; Hansford and Spriggs 2006). OLS regression models are employed for the aggregated models. I divided the dataset into cases decided before and after Scalia joined the Court, and ran the regressions on each set of data separately. In table 5.1, I compare the findings for each level of the judiciary and in the aggregate for both time periods. Due to space considerations, I do not include the fixed effects for legal issue area or the constant estimates.

Table 5.1. Impact of Foreign Law References on Citation Rates before and after Scalia Joined the Court

	Before Scalia Joined Court				After Scalia Joined Court			
	Supreme Court Citations	Circuit Court Citations	District Court Citations	Aggregate Citations	Supreme Court Citations	Circuit Court Citations	District Court Citations	Aggregate Citations
Foreign Law Reference	0.42 (0.07)***	0.40 (0.10)***	0.05 (0.16)***	0.08 (0.25)***	0.30 (0.06)***	0.04 (0.13)***	0.28 (0.14)**	0.64 (0.22)***
Ambiguous Decision	0.17 (0.09)**	-0.17 (0.09)**	-0.36 (0.16)**	-0.10 (0.16)	0.16 (0.08)**	-0.14 (0.13)	-0.42 (0.15)***	-0.14 (0.13)
Circuit Conflict	0.02 (0.05)	0.12 (0.09)	0.28 (0.16)*	0.13 (0.10)	-0.16 (0.04)	0.13 (0.07)**	0.27 (0.12)**	0.19 (0.09)**
Precedent Altering	0.87 (0.08)***	0.69 (0.14)***	0.91 (0.25)***	2.41 (0.48)***	0.79 (0.07)***	0.56 (0.12)***	0.80 (0.24)***	1.90 (0.38)***
Judicial Review	0.42 (0.05)***	0.00 (0.11)	0.03 (0.13)	0.31 (0.11)***	0.31 (0.05)***	-0.07 (0.09)	-0.15 (0.11)	0.14 (0.09)
Non-unanimous Case	0.09 (0.04)**	-0.09 (0.08)***	0.16 (0.11)	0.11 (0.08)	0.10 (0.04)***	0.11 (0.07)*	0.18 (0.10)*	0.13 (0.07)*
Mandatory Case	0.13 (0.04)**	-0.64 (0.08)***	-0.73 (0.11)***	-0.18 (0.06)***	0.21 (0.04)***	-0.60 (0.08)***	-0.70 (0.10)***	-0.12 (0.06)**
Case Importance	0.97 (0.06)***	1.08 (0.11)***	1.08 (0.14)***	2.19 (0.22)***	0.94 (0.05)***	1.02 (0.10)***	1.03 (0.12)***	1.89 (0.18)***
Later Reversed Case	0.58 (0.11)***	0.96 (0.18)***	1.09 (0.31)***	1.45 (0.49)***	0.052 (0.11)***	0.92 (0.18)***	1.07 (0.32)***	1.37 (0.48)***
Age of Case	0.01 (0.00)***	-0.04 (0.00)***	-0.06 (0.01)***	-0.01 (0.00)***	0.04 (0.00)***	-0.02 (0.00)***	-0.05 (0.00)***	0.00 (0.00)
N	4,969	4,969	4,969	4,969	6,631	6,631	6,631	6,631

Sources: Hitt (2016); Black et. al. (2014b); Spaeth (2017)

Note: Robust standard errors in parentheses. Constant and legal issue area fixed effects not reported. The court-level models are estimated via negative binomial regression. The aggregate models are estimated via OLS.

*p < 0.10, **p < 0.05, ***p < 0.01

The results for the aggregate models confirm my hypotheses. The variable *Positive foreign law reference* is significantly associated with an increase in total citations before and after Scalia joined the Court. Such references are also associated with an increase in citations by the Supreme Court and U.S. Courts of Appeals regardless of whether Scalia is on the high court's bench. The results remain the same when I control for references to English common law. Reliance upon foreign law is also associated with an increase in citations at the district level, regardless of whether Scalia is on the Court. However, the variable fails to reach significance by a small margin (0.107) when I exclude references to English common law. Therefore, I find weak evidence that Scalia's presence on the Court correlates with a decline in the significance of foreign law references at the lowest level of the federal judicial hierarchy. Overall, the relationship between references to foreign law and citations is positive and significant. I find little evidence that Scalia had any impact on the perception of the practice within the judicial hierarchy. Thus, despite Scalia's harsh criticisms, justices desiring broader influence still have an incentive to use foreign law.

DISCUSSION AND CONCLUSION

Taken together, my qualitative and quantitative findings inspire several conclusions concerning Scalia's impact on the Court's practice of citing foreign law, and on the extent to which American judges participate in the transnational judicial dialogue. First, Scalia succeeded in encouraging citations to foreign law of which he approved, those that involve deducing the intent of treaty partners and resorting to English legal history to interpret the Constitution. Second, Scalia failed to dissuade his colleagues from citing foreign law to identify consensus on an issue or to learn from the practices of other nations. Third, Scalia failed to alter the perception of the practice among members of the judiciary. Citation to foreign law is associated with increased influence, despite Scalia's attempts to breed suspicion of the practice. This incentive will continue to drive judges to reference foreign law in ways that Scalia decried.

In addition, based on my study and prior scholarly research, I argue the accusations that Scalia's extreme form of provincialism have hurt the Supreme Court's reputation abroad, place more blame on Scalia than he deserves. I accept that foreign judges believe the U.S. Supreme Court's failure to participate in the international dialogue "contribut[es] to a growing isolation and diminished influence" (L-Heureux-Dube 1998). Furthermore, researchers have found evidence consistent with the notion that the U.S. Supreme Court's hesitancy to "pay decent respect to the opinions of mankind by participating in an ongoing 'global judicial dialogue' is diminishing the appeal of American constitutional jurisprudence abroad" (Law and Versteeg 2012, 766). However, Scalia's rhetoric is not the primary cause of this phenomenon. Rather, this failure is a result of strategic calculations on the part of individual judges. If they perceive a benefit, they will cite foreign law, and if they do not, they will not participate in this global judicial dialogue. Scalia's harsh attacks did not undermine the incentive. It is unlikely that any one judge could significantly encourage or dissuade justices from employing this tactic.

Thus, although Scalia's replacement, Gorsuch, will probably continue Scalia's legacy of suspicion of foreign law, he is not likely to eliminate the practice. Like Scalia, Gorsuch is a textualist, arguing that "an assiduous focus on text, structure, and history is essential to the proper exercise of the judicial function" (Gorsuch 2016, 909). He has a fondness for quoting Blackstone, particularly when discussing the U.S. Constitution (Gorsuch 2016, 910). His opinions for the Tenth Circuit provide evidence of this propensity. For example, he cited English common law when interpreting the Fourth Amendment's protection against unreasonable searches and seizures (*United States v. Carloss* 2016, Gorsuch, J., dissenting; *United States v. Ackerman* 2016), and applying due process and equal protection principles to immigrants (*Robles v. Lynch* 2015). Therefore, he will probably continue Scalia's effort to encourage recourse to English common law for constitutional interpretation. In addition, Gorsuch has drawn on other sources of foreign law in his scholarly analyses of rights and liberties. In his book evaluating assisted suicide and euthanasia policies, he argues for retaining existing laws prohibiting these practices on the grounds that "human life is fundamentally and inherently valuable, and that the intentional taking of human life by a private person is always wrong" (Gorsuch 2006, 157). Gorsuch bases his contention on human experience, and documents it by looking not only to the Declaration of Independence and the Fourteenth Amendment of our Constitution, but by citing the principles of equality enshrined in Article 14 of the European Convention, and the "constitutions and declarations of rights in many other countries" (159). Scalia tolerated such references that built on American consensus (and to nations with a common history) in the past. He likely approved of Gorsuch's in-depth exploration of modern English cases in his book. Regardless of Gorsuch's judicial or political philosophy, however, he is likely to employ foreign law strategically to support his arguments at some point in his time on the bench when the need is great, as long as an incentive to do so remains.

Finally, I argue that Scalia succeeded in another sense. He spoke the truth, well-supported by strong scholarly evidence, that Supreme Court justices use the transnational judicial dialogue as a facade for purely ideological decision making. His ability to draw a crowd brought attention to important facts about the Supreme Court, showing the machinations of the man behind the curtain. I believe Scalia would be satisfied with this legacy.

NOTES

1. References to foreign law, for my purposes, refer to both international law and to the legal practices of other countries, including references to: the decisions of international tribunals, treaties, and the law of nations or customary international law; citations to the legal practices of other countries, such as a foreign state's court decisions, procedures or practices; law enforcement procedure; constitutions; legislative acts; informal government acts; and social, cultural, economic, or political practices (Black et al 2014a, 900). Although the normative justifications for referencing another state's laws and for citing international law differ, critics tend to lump both together when arguing against the use of foreign law in constitutional interpretation (Buys 2007) and judges arguing for their usefulness do not distinguish sharply between them (Koh 2004).

2. Scholars label the two sides of the debate as the nationalist and transnationalist positions (Farber 2007; Koh 2004). Scalia was a particularly loud voice in a line of nationalist justices condemning the practice.

3. Supreme Court justices taking this position include Jay, Marshall, Taft, Brennan, Douglas and White (Koh 2004).

4. Scholars have documented the long history of this debate. For example, in 1820, Justice Livingston disapproved of Justice Story's citation to foreign law in defining the crime of piracy, complaining that "it is not perceived why a reference to the laws of China, or to any other foreign code, would not have answered the purpose quite as well as the one which has been resorted to . . . it is the duty of Congress to incorporate into their own statutes a definition in terms, and not to refer the citizens of the United States for rules of conduct to the statute or laws of any foreign country, with which it is not to be presumed that they are acquainted." [Calabresi and Zimdahl 2005, citing *United States v. Smith*, 18 U.S. (5 Wheat.) 153, 181 (1820) (Livingston, J., dissenting)].

5. Constitution Restoration Act of 2004, S. 2323, 108th Cong. § 201 (2004) ("In interpreting and applying the Constitution . . . a court . . . may not rely upon any . . . law . . . of any foreign state or international organization or agency, other than English constitutional and common law"); H. R. Res. 568, 108th Cong. (2004) ("[J]udicial determinations regarding the meaning of the laws of the United States should not be based in whole or in part on judgments, laws, or pronouncements of foreign institutions unless such foreign judgments, laws, or pronouncements . . . inform an understanding of the original meaning of the laws of the United States." Examples of questioning of Supreme Court nominees on this subject include the Gorsuch and Roberts nomination hearings (Liptak et. al. 2017).

6. Scalia therefore joined opinions referencing foreign law to determine the meaning of the Refugee Convention's (1951) Article 33 prohibition on expelling refugees (*Sale v. Haitian Centers Council, Inc., et al.*, 1993) and the Hague Rules on the enforceability

of foreign forum selection clauses (*Vimar Seguros Y Reasurgos, S.A. v. M/V Sky Reefer* 1995).

7. Scalia joined several opinions looking to modern British practices under these circumstances (*Cooper v. Oklahoma* 1996; *Markman and Positek, Inc v. Westview Instruments Inc.* 1996).

8. The Court referenced practices in the United Kingdom, New Zealand, Australia, West Germany, France, Portugal, The Netherlands and all of the Scandinavian countries, Canada, Italy, Spain, Switzerland, and the Soviet Union.

9. The majority cited several foreign sources, including the UN Convention on the Rights of the Child and the United Kingdom's modern practice as instructive, but not controlling (*Roper v. Simmons* 2005, 575–77).

10. I calculated predicted probabilities for a dummy variable indicating whether Scalia was on the Court or not, holding the covariates at their means. The confidence intervals overlap; therefore, I report the most conservative estimates.

11. I employed Black et al.'s (2014a, 2014b) methodology, searching for the names of recognized countries around the world as listed on the State Department's list found at: http://www.state.gov/misc/list/index.htm. Because country names have changed, I also examined the previous names. In addition, I searched for international tribunals. I thank Ryan C. Black for his guidance in employing their methodology.

12. I employ a lowess smoothing line to explore the relationship between the two variables, number of citations to foreign law and the Court term. This trend was also evident, though only slightly less pronounced, when I performed a parallel analysis excluding references to English common law.

13. Predicted probabilities calculated holding covariates at their means. Because the confidence intervals overlap, I report the most conservative estimates.

14. See, for example, Stephen Breyer, Assoc. Justice, U.S. Supreme Court, The Supreme Court and the New International Law, Keynote Address at the American Society of International Law Annual Meeting (Apr. 4, 2003), available at http://www.supremecourt.gov/publicinfo/speeches/viewspeeches.aspx?Filenamesp_04-04-03.html.

15. I should note that Scalia objected to the district court's factual findings on this matter as simply policy preferences in disguise. He did not specifically object to the reference to the Canadian experience, however (*Brown v. Platt* 2011, Scalia, J., dissenting). His primary criticism was that judges are not qualified to evaluate such evidence concerning the proper functioning of the prison system.

16. For political science literature, see, for example, Luse et al. 2009; Canon and Johnson 1999; and Songer et al. 1994; for legal scholarship, one can look to any number of articles on specific doctrines, but for a wider picture see, for example, Re 2016.

17. These measures address the effects of the lower court judges' policy goals and their fear of reversal (Luse et. al. 2009; Benesh and Reddick 2002).

18. A reference that uses a foreign source of law to support a conclusion or a point is coded as positive. Conversely, a reference that criticized, questioned, limited, or distinguished a foreign source of law (or the use of such a law) is a negative reference. Language that takes neither a positive nor negative position is deemed to be neutral, and references receiving both positive and negative treatment were coded as mixed (Black et al. 2014a).

19. Although studies indicate that the ideology of the citing judges impacts citation rates, I do not employ a measure of citing court ideology because my unit of analysis is the precedent, and it would therefore have to be an aggregate measure of ideology that would not capture the variations across courts. Hansford and Spriggs (2006) found such an aggregate measure to be insignificant in their test, which employed precedent-year as their unit of analysis. They conclude that: "To more fully assess the role of ideology in this process, one would need to change the unit of analysis to include an observation for each precedent for each court for each year" (Hansford and Spriggs 2006, 121). As my interest is in examining the overall impact of positive references to foreign law, I did not take that approach.

REFERENCES

Bartl, Anthony Danilo. 2014. *The Constitutional Principles of Justice Kennedy: A Jurisprudence of Liberty and Equality.* El Paso, TX: LFB Scholarly Publishing.

Baum, Lawrence. 2006. *Judges and Their Audiences: A Perspective on Judicial Behavior.* Princeton, NJ: Princeton University Press.

Benesh, Sara C. and Malia Reddick. 2002. "Overruled: An Event History Analysis of Lower Court Reaction to Supreme Court Alteration of Precedent." *Journal of Politics* 64(2): 534–50.

Black, Ryan C. and Lee Epstein. 2007. "(Re-)Setting the Scholarly Agenda on Transjudicial Communication." *Law & Social Inquiry* 32(3): 791–807.

Black, Ryan C. and James F. Spriggs II. 2013. "The Citation and Depreciation of U.S. Supreme Court Precedent." *Journal of Empirical Legal Studies* 10(2): 325–58.

Black, Ryan C., Ryan J. Owens, and Jennifer L. Brookhart. 2014a. "We Are the World: The U.S. Supreme Court's Use of Foreign Sources of Law." *British Journal of Political Science* 46: 891–913.

Black, Ryan C., Ryan J. Owens, Daniel E. Walters, and Jennifer L. Brookhart. 2014b. "Upending a Global Debate: An Empirical Analysis of the U.S. Supreme Court's Use of Transnational Law to Interpret Domestic Doctrine." *Georgetown Law Journal* 103(1): 1–46.

Black, Ryan C., Ryan J. Owens, Justin Wedeking, and Patrick Wohlfarth. 2016. *U.S. Supreme Court Opinions and Their Audiences.* Cambridge: Cambridge University Press.

Bryant, A. Christopher. 2011. "Foreign Law as Legislative Fact in Constitutional Cases." *Brigham Young University Law Review* 4: 1005–40.

Buys, Cindy G. 2007. "Burying Our Constitution in the Sand? Evaluating the Ostrich Response to the Use of International and Foreign Law in U.S. Constitutional Interpretation." *Brigham Young University Journal of Public Law* 21(1): 1–55.

Calabresi, Steven G. and Stephanie Dotson Zimdahl. 2005. "The Supreme Court and Foreign Sources of Law: Two Hundred Years of Practice and the Juvenile Death Penalty Decision." *William and Mary Law Review* 47(3): 743–909.

Canon, Bradley C. and Charles A. Johnson. 1999. *Judicial Policies: Implementation and Impact.* 2nd ed. Washington, DC: CQ Press.

Clark, Tom S. and Benjamin Lauderdale. 2010. "Locating Supreme Court Opinions in Doctrine Space." *American Journal of Political Science* 54(4): 871–90.

Corley, Pamela C., Robert M. Howard, and David C. Nixon. 2005. "The Supreme Court and Opinion Content: The Use of the Federalist Papers." *Political Research Quarterly* 58(2): 329–40.

Corley, Pamela C. Amy Steigerwalt, and Artemus Ward. 2013. *The Puzzle of Unanimity: Consensus on the United States Supreme Court.* Stanford: Stanford University Press.

Corley, Pamela C. and Justin Wedeking. 2014. "The (Dis)Advantage of Certainty: The Importance of Certainty in Language." *Law and Society Review* 48(1): 35–62.

Cross, Frank B. 2010. "Determinants of Citations to Supreme Court Opinions (and the Remarkable Influence of Justice Scalia)." *Supreme Court Economic Review* 18(1): 177–202.

Curry, Brett and Banks Miller. 2008. "Looking for Law in All the Wrong Places? Foreign Law and Support for the U.S. Supreme Court." *Politics and Policy* 36(6): 1094–124.

———. 2017. "Case Citation Patterns in the U.S. Courts of Appeals and the Legal Academy." *Justice Systems Journal* 38(2): 164–82.

Dorsen, Norman. 2005. "The Relevance of Foreign Legal Materials in U.S. Constitutional Cases: A Conversation between Justice Antonin Scalia and Justice Stephen Breyer." *International Journal of Constitutional Law* 3(4): 519–41.

Epstein, Lee and Jack Knight. 1998. *The Choices Justices Make.* Washington, DC: CQ Press.

Farber, Daniel A. 2007. "The Supreme Court, the Law of Nations, and Citations of Foreign Law: The Lessons of History." *California Law Review* 95: 1335–65.

Fowler, James H. Timothy R. Johnson, James F. Spriggs II, Sangick Jeon, and Paul J. Wahlbeck. 2007. "Network Analysis and the Law: Measuring the Legal Importance of Supreme Court Precedents." *Political Analysis* 15: 324–46.

Fowler, James H., and Sangick Jeon. 2008. "The Authority of Supreme Court Precedent." *Social Networks* 30: 16–30.

Gorsuch, Neil M. 2006. *The Future of Assisted Suicide and Euthanasia.* Princeton, NJ: Princeton University Press.

Gorsuch, Judge Neil M. 2016. "Of Lions and Bears, Judges and Legislators, and the Legacy of Justice Scalia: Sumner Canary Lecture at Case Western Reserve University School of Law." *Case Western Reserve Law Review* 66(4): 905–20.

Gray, David C. 2007. "Why Justice Scalia Should Be a Constitutional Comparativist . . . Sometimes." *Stanford Law Review* 59(5): 1249–80.

Hansford, Thomas G. and James F. Spriggs. 2006. *The Politics of Precedent on the U.S. Supreme Court.* Princeton, NJ: Princeton University Press.

Hume, Robert J. 2006. "The Use of Rhetorical Sources by the U.S. Supreme Court." *Law and Society Review* 40(4): 817–43.

Hitt, Mathew P. 2016. "Measuring Precedent in the Judicial Hierarchy." *Law and Society Review* 50(1): 57–81.

Koby, Michael H. 1999. "The Supreme Court's Declining Reliance on Legislative History: The Impact of Justice Scalia's Critique." *Harvard Journal on Legislation* 36: 369–95.

Koh, Harold Hongju. 2004. "International Law as Part of Our Law." *The American Journal of International Law* 98(1): 43–57.

Law, David S. and Mila Versteeg. 2012. "The Declining Influence of the United States Constitution." *New York University Law Review* 87: 762–858.

L'Heureux-Dube, Claire. 1998. "The Importance of Dialogue: Globalization and the International Impact of the Rehnquist Court." *Tulsa Law Review* 34(1): 15–40.

Liptak, Adam, Charlie Savage, Matt Flegenheimer, and Carl Hulse. 2017. "Highlights from Judge Gorsuch's Confirmation Hearing." *New York Times.* March 22, 2017. https://www.nytimes.com/2017/03/22/us/politics/what-to-watch-will -democrats-be-more-aggressive-with-neil-gorsuch.html?_r=0. Last visited September 7, 2017.

Lupu, Yonatan and James H. Fowler. 2013. "Strategic Citations to Precedent on the U.S. Supreme Court." *The Journal of Legal Studies* 42(1): 151–86.

Luse, Jennifer K., Geoffrey McGovern, Wendy L. Martinek, Sarah C. Benesh. 2009. "Such Inferior Courts: Compliance by Circuits with Jurisprudential Regimes." *American Politics Research* 37(1): 75–106.

Murphy, Bruce Allen. 2014. *Scalia: A Court of One.* New York: Simon and Shuster.

O'Brien, David M. 2006. "More Smoke Than Fire: The Rehnquist Court's Use of Comparative Judicial Opinions and Law in the Construction of Constitutional Rights." *Journal of Law and Politics* 22: 83–112.

Parrish, Austen L. 2007. "Storm in a Teacup: The U.S. Supreme Court's Use of Foreign Law." *University of Illinois Law Review* 2: 637–80.

Posner, Richard A. 2000. "An Economic Analysis of the Use of Citations in the Law." *American Law and Economics Review* 2: 381–406.

Re, Richard M. 2016. "Narrowing Supreme Court Precedent from Below." *The Georgetown Law Journal* 104: 921–71.

Scalia, Antonin. 1997. *A Matter of Interpretation: Federal Courts and the Law.* Princeton, NJ: Princeton University Press.

Scalia, Antonin, and Bryan A. Garner. 2012. *Reading the Law: Interpretation of Legal Texts.* Saint Paul, MN: Thomson/West.

Simon, Stephen A. 2013. "The Supreme Courts Use of Foreign Law in Constitutional Rights Cases: An Empirical Study." *The Journal of Law and Courts* 1(2): 279–301.

Slaughter, Anne-Marie. 1994. "A Typology of Transjudicial Communication." *University of Richmond Law Review* 29: 99–137.

Songer, Donald R., Jeffrey A. Segal, and Charles M. Cameron. 1994. "The Hierarchy of Justice: Testing a Principal-Agent Model of Supreme Court-Circuit Court Interactions." *American Journal of Political Science* 38(3): 673–96.

Spaeth, Harold J. Lee Epstein, et al. 2017. Supreme Court Database, Version 2017 Release 1. URL: http://Supremecourtdatabase.org. Last visited September 6, 2017.

Tribe, Lawrence H. 2016. "The Legacy of Antonin Scalia—the Unrelenting Provoker." *Boston Globe*, February 17, 2016. https://www.bostonglobe.com/opinion /2016/02/17/the-legacy-antonin-scalia-unrelenting-provoker/mH40dhHDvEPXCz yXCLfxqI/story.html. Last visited September 6, 2017.

Waters, Melissa A. 2005. "Justice Scalia on the Use of Foreign Law in Constitutional Interpretation: Unidirectional Monologue or Co-Constitutive Dialogue." *Tulsa Journal of Comparative and International Law* 12(1): 149–61.

Westerland, Chad, Lee Epstein, Jeffrey A. Segal, Charles Cameron, and Scott Comparato. 2010. "Strategic Defiance and Compliance in the U.S. Courts of Appeals." *American Journal of Political Science* 54: 891–905.

Wilkinson, Hon. J. Harvie III. 2004. "The Use of International Law in Judicial Decisions." *Harvard Journal of Law and Public Policy* 27: 423–29.

Young, Ernest A. 2005. "Foreign Law and the Denominator Problem." *Harvard Law Review* 119: 148–67.

Zaring, David. 2006. "The Use of Foreign Decisions by Federal Courts: An Empirical Analysis." *Journal of Empirical Legal Studies* 3(2): 297–331.

TABLE OF CASES

Abbott v. Abbott, 560 U.S. 1 (2010).

Air France v. Saks, 470 U.S. 392 (1985).

Almendarez-Torres v. United States, 523 U.S. 224 (1998).

Atkins v. Virginia, 536 U.S. 304 (2002).

Betterman v. Montana, 136 S.Ct. 1609 (2016).

Boggs v. Boggs, 520 U.S. 833 (1997).

Boumediene v. Bush, 553 U.S. 723 (2008).

Browning Ferris v. Kelco, 492 U.S. 257 (1989).

Brown v. Plata, 563 U.S. 493 (2011).

Burson v. Attorney General, 504 U.S. 191 (1992).

Chauffeurs, Teamsters and Helpers, Local No. 391 v. Terry et al., 494 U.S. 558 (1990).

Citizens United v. Federal Elections Commission, 558 U.S. 310 (2010).

Cooper v. Oklahoma, 517 U.S. 348 (1996).

Coy v. Iowa, 487 U.S. 1012 (1988).

Davis v. Ayala, 135 S.Ct. 2187 (2015).

Dean v. United States, 556 U.S. 568 (2009).

Eastern Airlines, Inc. v. Floyd, 499 U.S. 530 (1991).

Eastern Enterprise v. Apfel, 524 U.S. 498 (1998).

Gasperini v. Center for Humanities, 518 U.S. 415 (1996).

Glossip v. Gross, 135 S.Ct. 2726 (2015).

Graham v. Florida, 560 U.S. 48 (2010).

Gustafson v. Alloyd Company, Inc., 513 U.S. 561 (1995).

Hosanna-Tabor Evangelical Lutheran Church and School v. Equal Employment Opportunity Commission, 132 S.Ct. 694 (2012).

Immigration and Naturalization Service v. St. Cyr, 533 U.S. 289 (2001).

Kiobel v. Royal Dutch Petroleum Co., 133 S.Ct. 1659 (2013).

Lawrence v. Texas, 539 U.S. 558 (2003).

Lozano v. Alvarez, 134 S.Ct. 1224 (2014).

Markman and Positek, Inc. v. Westview Instruments, Inc., 517 U.S. 370 (1996).

Match-E-Be-Nash-She-Wish Band of Pottawatomi Indians v. Patchak, 132 S.Ct. 2199 (2012).

McDonald v. Chicago, 561 U.S. 742 (2010).

McIntyre v. Ohio Elections Commission, 514 U.S. 334 (1995).

Negusie v. Holder, 555 U.S. 511 (2009).

New York Times Co. v. Tasini, 533 U.S. 483 (2001).

Obergefell v. Hodges, 135 S.Ct. 2584 (2015).

Olympic Airways v. Husain, 540 U.S. 644 (2004).

Oregon v. Ice, 555 U.S. 160 (2009).

Pepper v. United States, 562 U.S. 476 (2011).

Planned Parenthood v. Casey, 505 U.S. 833 (1992).

Printz v. United States, 521 U.S. 898 (1997).

Rasul v. Bush, 542 U.S. 466 (2004).

Robles v. Lynch, 803 F.3d 1165 (10th Cir. 2015).

Roe v. Wade, 410 U.S. 113 (1973).

Roper v. Simmons, 543 U.S. 551 (2005).

Safford Unified School District v. Redding, 557 U.S. 364 (2009).

Sale v. Haitian Centers Council, Inc., et al., 509 U.S. 155 (1993).

Sosa v. Alvarez-Machain, 542 U.S. 692 (2004).

Stop the Beach Renourishment, Inc. v. Florida Department of Environmental Protection, 560 U.S. 702 (2010).

Thompson v. Oklahoma, 487 U.S. 815 (1988).

Tull v. *United States*, 481 U.S. 412 (1987).

United States v. Ackerman, 831 F.3d 1292 (10th Cir. 2016).

United States v. Carloss, 818 F.3d 988 (10th Cir. 2016).

United States v. Gaudlin, 515 U.S. 506 (1995).

United States v. Windsor, 133 S.Ct. 2675 (2013).

Vimar Seguros Y Reasurgos, S.A. v. M/V Sky Reefer, 515 U.S. 528 (1995).

Washington v. Glucksberg, 521 U.S. 702 (1997).

Williams v. Illinois, 132 S.Ct. 2221 (2012).

Ysursa v. Pocatello Education Association, 555 U.S. 353 (2009).

STATUTES CITED

Alien Tort Statute, 28 U.S.C. § 1350 (1789).

Securities Act, 15 U.S.C. § 77 (1933).

Chapter 6

The Anti-Madison

Antonin Scalia's Theory of Politics

Howard Schweber

This chapter examines the late Justice Scalia's thinking about politics. More specifically, I will consider Scalia's understanding of constitutional norms of political practice. A particular constitutional design for political institutions depends on a concomitant idea of what political processes should look like. Conceptions of federalism, separation of powers, and equal protection imply norms of representation, discourse, and the political process, what I will refer to in this chapter as "constitutionalist politics." The term is chosen to avoid confusion with the phrase "constitutional politics." "Constitutional politics" refers to the political debates surrounding the role of the Constitution and its interpretations. "Constitutionalist politics" as used here refers to the norms that the Constitution prescribes for the practice of politics. One very obvious example is the Fourteenth Amendment's declaration that participation in the process of voting may not be restricted on the basis of race. What other norms of political practice does the Constitution contain? What was Scalia's response to that question, how was his response different from those offered by others, and what is his legacy in this particular area of constitutional jurisprudence?

The idea of constitutionalist politics may be expressed in terms of necessary conditions, as "what characteristics are political processes required to have in order for this constitutional system to work as envisioned?" This was the form in which Federalist writers most often addressed the question. Madison's description in *Federalist* 62 of the need for a bicameral national legislature to prevent Congress from overwhelming the other branches is an example. (Madison 1787a). In Madison's conception, an effective system of separation of powers and checks and balances among the branches of the national government was a necessary condition for constitutionalist politics.

Alternatively, the argument can be interpretive: "what characteristics of political processes does this constitutional text implicitly assume, and how does the answer to this question guide us in the tasks of textual interpretation?" This is a common approach to problems such as reasoning from silence in the constitutional text or determining implications from constitutional structure, as in *Printz v. United States* (1997) when Scalia indicated that the absence of a textual proscription on "commandeering" provided a mandate for the justices to look elsewhere for unstated but enforceable principles of federalism, specifically in historical practices, the implications of constitutional structure, and past precedents.

Yet a third iteration of the argument is both normative and legalistic: "What characteristics of a political process does this constitution require and make enforceable by proper authorities?" For a good example of the last version, consider what would happen if the Republican Guaranty Clause were treated as both substantive and judicially enforceable, as in Chief Justice Taney's comment in *Luther v. Borden* that "Unquestionably a military government, established as the permanent government of the State, would not be a republican government, and it would be the duty of Congress to overthrow it" (*Luther v. Borden* 1849, 45). Left unaddressed is whether there might be a judicial remedy to Congress' failure to perform its constitutional "duty," but the main point is that whether the proper authority in such a case is Congress or the courts or both, the requirement of republican government at some point becomes enforceable, making an understanding of the meaning of "republican" necessary. Another example was the justification for the announcement of the constitutional principle of "one man, one vote" in *Wesberry v. Sanders* (1964). The Court in that case looked to the requirement in Article I, section 12, of the Constitution that the members of Congress be elected by "the People of the United States." Translating this democratic principle into a norm of constitutionalist politics led to the conclusion that all votes should count equally and that unnecessary infringements on the right to vote would violate the Constitution. None of those conclusions is necessarily required by the appearance of the terms "the People" and "elected," it is only as a matter of the expression of constitutionalist norms that enforceable requirements are found to inhere in the constitutional text. Yet a third example appeared in Justice Ginsburg's majority opinion upholding Arizona's use of a referendum to create a nonpartisan districting commission. Confronted by an argument that this practice violated the constitutional requirement that the State's "legislature" control the electoral process, Ginsburg appealed to republican principles (*Arizona State Legislature v. Arizona Independent Redistricting Commission* 2015, 35). "[T]he core principle of republican government," namely, "that the voters should choose their representatives, not the other way around." Here,

Justice Ginsburg was using constitutionalist political theory used as a guide to interpretation (reading the word "legislature"). Her discussion included originalist review of historical texts, but those texts were used as sources of constitutionalist principles, not doctrine. Noteworthy is that there was no historical practice of referenda.

In very sharp contrast to these examples, I will argue that the best understanding of Scalia's answer to this question is as a fundamental rejection of Madison's normative conception of representative democracy. Scalia's anti-Madisonian theory of constitutionalist politics inheres in his rejection of two key political propositions. First, I will focus on Madison's famous discussion of "factions," meaning the constitutionally appropriate forms of political interest expression and more generally the idea of structural constraints on the political process. Madison held above all that the Constitution's success depended on the promise of preventing political factions from becoming fixed lines of enmity and instruments of majoritarian domination. By contrast, Scalia's conception of democratic decision making involved competition across precisely those sorts of permanent and tribalistic lines of division, and a strong preference that the majority will determine the scope of minority rights without interference. Second, I will consider Madison's concern with the need for virtue in political representatives. Where Madison saw the essential purpose of elections as the selection of virtuous individuals, with a particular understanding of "virtuous" as commitment to the public good over private interest, Scalia concluded that the Constitution actively precludes any attempts to preserve virtue in the electoral process and by extension in political processes generally. The need for structures to prevent factional domination and the need for virtue in leaders were the two central elements to Madison's idea of constitutionalist politics. In both these respects Scalia's view was fundamentally anti-Madisonian.

It may seem that there is some irony in describing Scalia as an anti-Madisonian theorist. In fact the irony is more apparent than real. In the first place, Scalia identified himself primarily as a textualist. "What I look for in the Constitution", he wrote, "is precisely what I look for in a statute: the original meaning of the text, not what the original draftsmen intended" (Scalia 1997, 38). Originalism was Scalia's preferred method for addressing questions the text left unresolved. Madison's ideas of constitutionalist politics were central to his arguments in favor of the Constitution, but they do not appear explicitly in the text (although to be sure Scalia could have invoked the same reasoning from silence approach that he relied upon for his *Printz* opinion).

Separately and independently, to the extent that Scalia's constitutionalist politics are drawn from originalist sources they are as often anti-federalist than Federalist. For example, in 2004 Scalia employed a description of

Anti-Federalist fears of a standing army to establish the idea of an individual right to bear arms. "The fear that the federal government would disarm the people in order to impose rule through a standing army or select militia was pervasive in Anti-Federalist rhetoric" (*Dist. Of Columbia v. Heller* 2004). In Scalia's reasoning, the Antifederalists would likely not have accepted the Constitution if they had not conceived of the Second Amendment as guaranteeing an individual right, and therefore modern courts are obliged to follow that original Anti-Federalist understanding in order to enforce the constitutional bargain.

Regardless of the merits of one or another particular originalist argument, it is certainly the case that among the writers (and lawyers, voters, merchants, farmers, mechanics, and slaves) of the founding generation there were deep disagreements, and a commitment to "originalism" by no means necessarily equates to a commitment to Madison's theory of constitutionalist politics.

CONSTITUTIONALIST POLITICS IN THE U.S. SUPREME COURT

There is nothing original in the suggestion that constitutional visions contain prescriptions for politics, nor that these prescriptions imply a role for courts. In *Federalist* 78 Hamilton commented extensively on the connection. "It is not otherwise to be supposed that the Constitution could intend to enable the representatives of the people to substitute their WILL to that of their constituents. It is far more rational to supposed that the courts were designed to be an intermediate body between the people and the legislature, in order, among other things, to keep the latter within the limits of their assigned authority" (Hamilton 1787). Other Federalist writers like James Wilson and Samuel Chase similarly viewed the constitutional order as expressions of political norms, as in Wilson's criticism of the compact theory of federalism as "not politically correct" in *Chisholm v. Georgia* (1793), or Chase's appeal to the social contract in *Calder v. Bull* (1798): "An act of the legislature (for I cannot call it a law) contrary to the great first principles of the social compact cannot be considered a rightful exercise of legislative authority." In this view, legislation that was not "republican" was outside the scope of legitimate public authority altogether.

At times these political conceptions lead to specific doctrinal conclusions about what the Constitution permits or requires. That was true of Chief Justice Warren's discussion of representation in *Reynolds v. Sims* (1964) and Justice Clark's invocation of the same concept in *Baker v. Carr* (1962). "[The majority's] decision today supports the proposition for which our forebears fought and many died, namely that, to be fully conformable to the principle of right, the form of government must be representative. That is the keystone upon which our government was founded and lacking which no republic can survive" (*Baker v. Carr* 1962, 261–62). In the same case, Justice Brennan's limitation of the political question doctrine to cases involving separation of powers concerns (as opposed to federalism concerns) likewise involved the application of a principle of constitutional governance to the determination of an uncertain doctrinal question. Representation, accountability, and separation of powers are classic examples of political norms found by these justices to inhere in the provisions of the Constitution.

In one of the less-noted passages in Rufus Peckham's *Lochner* majority, he spoke of the political context of the case as he saw it. "It is impossible for us to shut our eyes to the fact that many of the laws of this character, while passed under what is claimed to be the police power for the purpose of protecting the public health or welfare, are, in reality, passed from other motives." (*Lochner v. New York* 1905, 64). In *Lochner* and numerous other cases the justices portrayed the Constitution as a bar to "unreasonable" or "arbitrary" legislation. Ideas of strict scrutiny announced in *Skinner v. Oklahoma* (1942) and *Korematsu v. United States* (1944) further refined the idea that the Constitution defines the outer bounds of legitimate politics in terms of motivations as well as means. That is, the Constitution was understood not only to set limits on government actions but equally as setting limits on what counts as a proper motivation for government action, what kinds of justifications are acceptable in defense of a particular choice of means. Early equal protection cases likewise explored the idea of an improper democratic motive, as in Justice Henry Billings Brown's dictum in *Plessy v. Ferguson*. "[E]very exercise of the police power must be reasonable, and extend only to such laws as are enacted in good faith for the promotion for the public good, and not for the annoyance or oppression of a particular class" (*Plessy v. Ferguson* 1896, 550). Brown's conclusion that the segregation law he was reviewing did not violate this principle was wildly dishonest, but the principle itself stands as a declaration of constitutionally required limitations on the democratic process. One may debate the question of whether the Constitution prohibits political appeals based on a desire to harm a racial minority, but the principle is established and accepted that legislation cannot be based on that motivation.[1]

Equally explicit invocations of constitutionalist political norms appear in discussions of the First Amendment. To explain the reach of the Establishment Clause, Chief Justice Burger appealed to a key element in Madison's theory of destructive factions. "Ordinarily, political debate and division, however vigorous or even partisan, are normal and healthy manifestations of our democratic system of government, but political division along religious lines was one of the principal evils against which the First Amendment was intended to protect" (*Lemon v. Kurtzman* 1971, 622). Discussing his idea of free speech, Justice Kennedy invoked the idea of democracy as "the duty to engage in a rational civic discourse" (*Schuette v. Coalition to Defend Affirmative Action, Integration and Immigration Rights* 2014). Conversely, fighting words are deemed unworthy of protection because they are "no essential part of any exposition of ideas" (*Chaplinsky v. New Hampshire* 1942, 572). These comments all invoke constitutionalist norms of democratic discourse.

The very operations of political systems themselves are frequently the subject of constitutional adjudication. The model of politics as interest group pluralism is characterized by a neutral with respect to political or policy outcomes. In Oliver Wendell Holmes Jr.'s expression of this view, "the Constitution was "made for people of fundamentally differing views" (*Lochner* 1905, Holmes dissenting), an idea also exemplified in his metaphor of a competitive "market" in ideas for First Amendment freedoms. (*Abrams v. United States* 1919, 630). The market metaphor suggests interest group pluralism as a model of democratic competition. But even this pluralist or market model conceives of the Constitution as establishing procedural limitations. The analogy to the marketplace is instructive. Just as markets are regulated to ensure fair competition, competitive democratic politics is subject to restrictions to ensure the integrity of that competition (*United States v. Carolene Products* 1938).[2] And just as an individual's view of antitrust principles may be both driven by and reflective of her understanding of properly functioning capitalist markets, so too an individual's ideas about what is and is not properly a matter for constitutional argument reveals and is driven by an underlying notion of what that politics ought to look like (Posner 1992).

Recognizing this relationship between constitutional doctrine and constitutionalist politics can help explain apparent inconsistencies. To take one example that will be explored later, Justice Scalia's relatively restrictive attitude toward police may be explained by his relatively libertarian notions of individual liberty while his acceptance of authoritarian exercises of state authority in other areas are reflective of his acceptance of the legitimacy of inter-group domination as the outcome of democratic politics. In the First Amendment context, in fact, these two elements come together, as Scalia's near-absolutist protection of free expression in a political context serves both to enable individuals to exercise their freedoms and to ensure that legitimate (in his view) political contestation is not limited or distorted. Rights claims by their nature involve consideration of the limits of proper democratic politics: "The very purpose of a Bill of Rights was to withdraw certain subjects from the vicissitudes of political controversy, to place them beyond the reach of majorities and officials, and to establish them as legal principles to be applied by the courts" (*West Virginia Bd. of Educ. v. Barnette* 1943, 639). This singularly unoriginal observation has consequences when one realizes that while sometimes justices proceed from an understanding of rights to determine the limits of politics, in Scalia's case it is equally accurate to say that he proceeded from a view of politics to determine the scope of rights.

Scalia's Anti-Madisonian Theory of Constitutionalist Politics

In the American constitutional tradition, we make frequent reference to the ideas of James Madison and with good reason. No one among the framers thought more deeply about the connection between the Constitution as a blueprint for governance and the Constitution as a limitation on the concentration of power in government. Most famously, Madison made two separate and potentially inconsistent arguments relevant to this discussion: that the Constitution depends on structural systems to decrease the effects of ambition, and that the Constitution depends on the selection of virtuous individuals who will set the public good above their own interests. Both elements are expressed in *Federalist* 10, where Madison identified a theory of factions as a central element of his idea of constitutional practice. "Among the numerous advantages promised by a well-constructed Union, none deserves to be more accurately developed than its tendency to break and control the violence of faction." Specifically, Madison was concerned with the danger that a majoritarian faction would capture the system of government and use their power to deprive minorities of their liberties. Madison's solution was a large republic, a novel approach that in his view combined the themes of structural design and virtuous leadership.

> Does the advantage consist in the substitution of representatives whose enlightened views and virtuous sentiments render them superior to local prejudices and schemes of injustice? It will not be denied that the representation of the Union will be most likely to possess these requisite endowments. Does it consist in the greater security afforded by a greater variety of parties, against the event of any one party being able to outnumber and oppress the rest? In an equal degree does the increased variety of parties comprised within the Union, increase this security. Does it, in fine, consist in the greater obstacles opposed to the concert and accomplishment of the secret wishes of an unjust and interested majority? Here, again, the extent of the Union gives it the most palpable advantage. (Madison 1787b)

Thus Madison worked from two distinct theories: a theory of institutional design to prevent majority capture, and a theory of virtue. Both of these concerns led Madison to normative commitments that he believed to be essential to the Constitution—such as his call for a national veto on all state legislation—and both applied to politics at all levels. That is, the design of the government and the design of the political system that would select it were both grounded in normative commitments to rule by virtuous elite representatives and constraining structures designed to enforce norms of political competition.

In a letter to the Marquis de Lafayette in 1792, Madison expanded on the implications of his theory for the relationship between government and political parties, and by extension the role of government in preserving constitutionalist politics.

> In every political society, parties are unavoidable. A difference of interests, real or supposed, is the most natural and fruitful source of them. The great object should be to combat the evil: 1. By establishing a political equality among all. 2. By withholding unnecessary opportunities from a few, to increase the inequality of property, by an immoderate, and especially an unmerited, accumulation of riches. 3. By the silent operation of laws, which, without violating the rights of property, reduce extreme wealth towards a state of mediocrity, and raise extreme indigence towards a state of comfort. 4. By abstaining from measures which operate differently on different interests, and particularly such as favor one interest at the expense of another. 5. By making one party a check on the other, so far as the existence of parties cannot be prevented, nor their views accommodated. If this is not the language of reason, it is that of republicanism. (Madison 1792)

These political prescriptions are readily recognizable as the equivalents of Madison's principles of checks and balances and his insistence on the importance of virtue among representatives.

By very sharp contrast, Scalia's constitutionalism was grounded in a set of assumptions about constitutional practice that rejected both of the elements of the Madisonian conception. The Constitution, in Scalia's view, not only permitted but required that wealth be allowed to dominate political discussions, that factions be allowed to form on the basis of mutually inimical tribal identities, that majorities be permitted to dominate minorities, and that parties be permitted to game the system without interference from courts or voters.

Turning to the other core Madisonian principle of constitutionalist politics, Scalia was overtly hostile to the idea of government by virtuous elites, and found efforts to ensure that outcome constitutionally suspect. In particular, Scalia rejected the proposition that there is a constitutionally legitimate public interest in preventing domination of the system by powerful interests, precisely the phenomenon of "capture" that Madison feared.

Scalia's Theory of Factions: Democracy as Domination

"The majority has mistaken a *Kulturkampf* for a fit of spite" (*Romer v. Evans* 1996, 620). Even among the frequently provocative and gnomic pronunciations of the late Justice Scalia, this one stands out. In the specific context of the case the meaning is plain enough; Scalia was accusing the majority of mistaking a legitimate political conflict for an illegitimate act of discrimination. In terms of the outcome of the case, then, the sentence simply stated Scalia's disagreement with the majority's ruling. But in fact this sentence illustrates something much deeper about Scalia's jurisprudence that reaches far beyond the particular case. Across a range of areas Scalia was motivated by a particular conception of democratic politics, and that recognizing this conception provides considerable interpretive purchase on his arguments. Furthermore, I will argue that one of Scalia's most powerful legacies may be the adoption of that conception of politics—often unarticulated, at times likely without examination—by self-styled judicial conservatives.

In *Romer*, the Supreme Court reviewed an amendment to the Colorado constitution, adopted by referendum, that prohibited state or local authorities from adopting any measure that would have the purpose or effect of prohibiting discrimination on the basis of sexual orientation. Uninitiated readers who encounter that description tend to suffer vertigo: this was not an amendment prohibiting discrimination, nor an amendment requiring discrimination, nor an amendment necessarily allowing discrimination, it was an amendment that directly regulated the politics *around* issues of discrimination by restricting the available avenues for seeking protection through constitutional entrenchment. As the majority noted, the effect of the amendment was that individuals seeking protection from discrimination based on sexual orientation would have to succeed in re-amending the state constitution rather than simply securing the enactment of ordinary legislation. To the majority, this was a sleight of hand designed to obscure the fact that the true purpose of the amendment was to ensure that discrimination would go unchecked. According to Justice Kennedy's evaluation, "the amendment seems inexplicable by anything but animus toward the class that it affects; it lacks a rational relationship to legitimate state interests" (*Romer* 1996, 632).

It was that characterization of the provision as "bare animus" that Justice Scalia described as "spite." There is an important point, here. At least for purposes of this discussion, Justice Scalia appeared to agree that if "bare animus" had been an accurate description of the motivation behind the amendment it might have been constitutionally invalid, but in his mind the amendment served other, entirely legitimate interests that are properly matters for contestation in democratic politics. It is that implicit vision of legitimate democratic politics that is so interesting. Scalia was famous for insisting that he rejected his colleagues "judicial activism" and would leave many issues to the resolution of the democratic process, but he rarely directly addressed what he thought that process should consist of and what limits, if any, the Constitution might impose on political practices.

As a descriptor for democratic politics, the choice of *Kulturkampf* is mystifyingly obscure. The term *Kulturkampf* was coined to describe efforts to rid German politics of the influence of the Catholic Church. Between 1871 and 1887, secular liberal politicians in the Prussian state parliament and the Reichstag adopted a series of laws aimed at asserting state control over religious institutions and curtailing the activities of clergy. These laws went far beyond anything that would be considered tolerable in the American constitutional tradition, including the direct assertion of state control over religious education and practices: clergy could be imprisoned for discussing state affairs from the pulpit; clergy were excluded from participating in education (the primary school system had previously been largely run by the Catholic Church); half a dozen specific orders beginning with the Jesuits were banned outright and their members expelled from the country; the government took control over the qualifications of clergy, their appointment and dismissal, and ecclesiastical discipline; Prussia established a new Royal Court for Ecclesiastical Affairs; German Catholic clergy were made legally answerable only to political authorities; and in numerous other ways state authorities attempted to exert direct control over religious affairs. By the end of the period all of the bishops in Prussia had been imprisoned or exiled, a quarter of parishes had no priests, more than 1,800 priests had been imprisoned or exiled along with thousands of parishioners convicted of aiding clergymen, and half of all the monks and nuns had fled Prussia. One of the results of the *Kulturkampf* was a wave of German Catholic immigration to the United States (Blackbourn 2002).

Justice Scalia could not have been unaware of this history, nor could he have approved of the antireligious *Kulturkampf*. So what did he mean by choosing that term to describe the kind of politics to which the members of the Court owe nearly absolute deference? Even if Scalia's point was that this kind of religious repression was a regrettable but unavoidable "constitutional evil" (Graber 2006), the specific choice of terminology remains obscure.

The explanation appears in a passage in which Scalia laid out the core of his anti-Madisonian theory of faction.

> Because those who engage in homosexual conduct tend to reside in disproportionate numbers in certain communities, and, of course, care about homosexual-rights issues much more ardently than the public at large, they possess political power much greater than their numbers, both locally and statewide. Quite understandably, they devote this political power to achieving not merely a grudging social toleration, but full social acceptance, of homosexuality . . . homosexuals are as entitled to use the legal system for reinforcement of their moral senti-

ments as is the rest of society. But they are subject to being countered by lawful, democratic countermeasures as well. . . . That is where Amendment 2 came in. It sought to counter both the geographic concentration and the disproportionate political power of homosexuals by (1) resolving the controversy at the statewide level, and (2) making the election a single-issue contest for both sides. It put directly, to all the citizens of the State, the question: Should homosexuality be given special protection? They answered no. The Court today asserts that this most democratic of procedures is unconstitutional. (*Romer* 1996, 645–56, 647)

There is an extraordinary amount of unarticulated political prescription packed into those passages, captured in Scalia's use of the encomium "most democratic of procedures." First, consider the proposition that "those who wish to engage in homosexual conduct . . . possess political power much greater than their numbers." The description of a minority group as concentrated in certain cities and politically engaged is familiar (one may be mildly surprised that he did not add "cosmopolitan" to his list of descriptors). But what is much more revealing is Scalia's articulation of the idea that democratic politics is a conflict for supremacy among identity-based groups seeking advantage, in this instance "homosexuals" and "the rest of society." Note that Scalia did not describe the competition as one between "those who favor protections for homosexuals" and "those who opposed protections for homosexuals," which would have been the more accurate and precise description of the competing interests at stake in the conflict. Instead, Scalia referred to the competing positions in terms of a binary opposition between two tribalistic, identity-based factions. Scalia did not consider the existence of heterosexual supporters of protections for homosexuals, nor of homosexuals who opposed such protections, because here, as elsewhere, Scalia assumes that democratic politics is *and ought to be* a conflict among identity-based factions. Scalia positively embraces the idea of democratic politics as a conflict for supremacy between essentially tribal groups. In this case the political struggle was between homosexuals trying to force acceptance on an unwilling heterosexual majority and the heterosexual majority trying to stop them. As an account of American politics this description is reductionist to the point of absurdity; as a theory of constitutionalist politics it is the antithesis of Madison's prescription.

This observation finally makes sense of Scalia's choice of the term *Kulturkampf* at the outset of his discussion. Political competition is competition for control of the sovereign power, conducted between fixed and permanently opposing factions. For Scalia, in other words, the "legitimate democratic politics" that is shielded from constitutional intervention is exemplified by the very kinds of conflicts that Madison decried as the illness of democracy that the Constitution was designed to ameliorate. At the same time, another element of Scalia's anti-Madisonian conception concerned the limits of majority rule. As was noted earlier, a key element in Madison's discussions of structural checks in a republican system was his fear of majoritarian tyranny resulting from "capture" of government. Scalia, by contrast, viewed majoritarian capture as not only legitimate but as the most desirable end of constitutionalist politics. Consequently, far from viewing majority capture as a constitutional problem to be prevented, Scalia considered it his role to ensure that the channels for majoritarian capture remained open.

But Scalia went even further. He insisted that one of the legitimate functions of politics is to determine when and how to express a community's moral disapproval.

> Of course it is our moral heritage that one should not hate any human being or class of human beings. But I had thought that one could consider certain conduct reprehensible—murder, for example, or polygamy, or cruelty to animals—and could exhibit even "animus" toward such conduct. Surely that is the only sort of "animus" at issue here: moral disapproval of homosexual conduct. . . . The Colorado amendment does not, to speak entirely precisely, prohibit giving favored status to people who are *homosexuals;* they can be favored for many reasons-for example, because they are senior citizens or members of racial minorities. But it prohibits giving them favored status *because of their homosexual conduct—that* is, it prohibits favored status *for homosexuality.* (*Romer* 1996, 644, emphasis in original)

In fact, the provision at issue had nothing to do with conduct; its effect, for example, was not triggered by a judicial ruling to the effect that an individual had or had not engaged in homosexual conduct. The statement that the amendment "prohibits giving them favored status *because of their homosexual conduct*" was simply false. Nonetheless, as a starting point for the analysis of constitutionally acceptable politics Scalia laid down a clear position: expression of disapproval for conduct *or the persons who are presumed to want to engage in such conduct* is a legitimate state purpose, and securing such expression of disapproval is a legitimate political goal. Accepting morals legislation as a legitimate exercise of States' police powers is not, itself, an expression of an anti-Madisonian conception of politics. Indeed, it is an element of the traditional understanding of police powers as the power to legislation for "health, welfare, safety, and morals." The extent to which the adoption of the Fourteenth Amendment alters this understanding is a doctrinal issue that does not turn on a particular conception of majoritarian politics. But the position that Scalia asserted went far beyond a minimalist conception of rights or equal protection by virtue of his description of constitutionalist politics. Scalia rejected outright the idea that "bare animus"—disapproval of a category of persons—was an improper democratic motive, a principle that even Justice Brown acknowledged in *Plessy*. Again, the choice of the term *Kulturkampf* is remarkable; one may presume that in the absence of specific constitutional rules to the contrary, expressions of majoritarian disapproval for Catholics because such persons are presumed to want to engage in Catholic behavior would be equally exemplary of democracy in action.

Scalia's analysis of race-based affirmative action displayed a similar understanding of constitutionalist politics. The *Carolene Products* Footnote 4 principle that vulnerable minorities might require protection was articulated in the idea of a "suspect" or "protected" class. In Scalia's analysis, "suspect class" became "suspect classification," a rule prohibiting differential treatment by race regardless of whether the intent was to harm or benefit a vulnerable group (*Adarand Constructors, Inc. v. Pena* 1995). Scalia's explanation for his position varied. Confronted by a city-level program of preferential contracting, he invoked the Madisonian fear of majoritarian capture in the States.

A sound distinction between federal and state (or local) action based on race rests not only upon the substance of the Civil War Amendments, but upon social reality and governmental theory. It is a simple fact that what Justice Stewart described in *Fullilove* as "the dispassionate objectivity [and] the flexibility that are needed to mold a race-conscious remedy around the single objective of eliminating the effects of past or present discrimination"—political qualities already to be doubted in a national legislature, are substantially less likely to exist at the state or local level. The struggle for racial justice has historically been a struggle by the national society against oppression in the individual States. (*Richmond v. J. A. Croson Co.* 1989, 520)

But in his *Adarand* opinion and consistently thereafter when reviewing affirmative action programs, Scalia abandoned that reasoning, insisting that the same standards must apply to state and federal government and entirely rejecting the distinction between efforts by a majority to harm or to benefit a vulnerably minority. And the suggestion that the federal government can be relied upon to avoid the dangers of political capture in the states was wildly inconsistent with his positions in cases involving questions of federalism.

Regardless of one's evaluation of Scalia's jurisprudence in cases involving racial classifications, in other contexts Scalia made it clear that his guiding norm was not merely to permit majoritarian moral preference as a basis for legislation but actually to maximize the possibility of majoritarian capture. In *Employment Division v. Smith*, Scalia authored the notoriously controversial majority opinion that said that there is no obligation on states' to provide religious exemptions to the operation of generally applicable law. While that holding aroused considerable controversy, it is the comments that Scalia included in his discussion that are most interesting from the perspective of constitutionalist politics.

> [T]o say that a nondiscriminatory religious practice exemption is permitted, or even that it is desirable, is not to say that it is constitutionally required, and that the appropriate occasions for its creation can be discerned by the courts. It may fairly be said that leaving accommodation to the political process will place at a relative disadvantage those religious practices that are not widely engaged in; but that unavoidable consequence of democratic government must be preferred to a system in which each conscience is a law unto itself or in which judges weigh the social importance of all laws against the centrality of all religious beliefs. (*Employment Division v. Smith* 1990, 890)

This is an inversion of the reasoning that Jackson depended on in *Barnette* when he concluded that the identification of constitutional "rights" is precisely intended to "withdraw certain subjects from the vicissitudes of political controversy, to place them beyond the reach of majorities and officials." In *Smith*, Scalia did not first establish an argument for the proposition that there was no constitutional right at issue and then explained that the issue was therefore left to the democratic process. Instead he started with the desire to ensure the majority's ability to control the democratic process as the reason for finding there was no constitutionally protected right.

By contrast, consider Scalia's signature contribution to current thinking about protected and unprotected speech, his majority opinion in *R.A.V. v. St. Paul* (1992). Once again, a model of politics as unfettered conflict between fixed groups vying for control emerges as the key to his reasoning. *R.A.V.* involved a St. Paul ordinance that made it a misdemeanor to place "on public or private property a symbol, object, appellation, characterization or graffiti, including, but not limited to, a burning cross or Nazi swastika, which one knows or has reasonable grounds to know arouses anger, alarm or resentment in others on the basis of race, color, creed, religion or gender." Scalia concluded that the ordinance was overbroad, a position shared by a clear majority of the justice. Separately, Scalia used the opportunity to develop a new theory about the nature of "unprotected" speech, ruling that where the regulation of otherwise unprotected speech is directed at suppressing a particular viewpoint is unconstitutional.

> [T]o validate such selectivity (where totally proscribable speech is at issue) it may not even be necessary to identify any particular "neutral" basis, so long as the nature of the content discrimination is such that there is no realistic possibility that official suppression of ideas is afoot. (We cannot think of any First Amendment interest that would stand in the way of a State's prohibiting only

those obscene motion pictures with blue-eyed actresses.) Save for that limitation, the regulation of "fighting words," like the regulation of noisy speech, may address some offensive instances and leave other, equally offensive, instances alone. (*R.A.V.* 1992, 390)

Scalia's conclusion that viewpoint discrimination is constitutionally problematic even in the context of unprotected speech was controversial in itself. But the more problematic element of Scalia's analysis arose from his application of his test to the case before him, and the implications of that exercise for his understanding of constitutionalist political norms. First, Scalia addressed the question of content discrimination.

Displays containing abusive invective, no matter how vicious or severe, are permissible unless they are addressed to one of the specified disfavored topics. Those who wish to use "fighting words" in connection with other ideas—to express hostility, for example, on the basis of political affiliation, union membership, or homosexuality—are not covered. The First Amendment does not permit St. Paul to impose special prohibitions on those speakers who express views on disfavored subjects. (*R.A.V.* 1992, 391)

Moving on from there, Scalia argued that the case at hand involved viewpoint discrimination, a conclusion that is essentially always fatal in free speech analysis.

In its practical operation, moreover, the ordinance goes even beyond mere content discrimination, to actual viewpoint discrimination. Displays containing some words—odious racial epithets, for example—would be prohibited to proponents of all views. But "fighting words" that do not themselves invoke race, color, creed, religion, or gender-aspersions upon a person's mother, for example—would seemingly be usable *ad libitum* in the placards of those arguing *in favor* of racial, color, etc., tolerance and equality, but could not be used by those speakers' opponents. One could hold up a sign saying, for example, that all "anti-Catholic bigots" are misbegotten; but not that all "papists" are, for that would insult and provoke violence "on the basis of religion." St. Paul has no such authority to license one side of a debate to fight freestyle, while requiring the other to follow Marquis of Queensberry rules. (*R.A.V.* 1992, 391–92)

The legal vocabulary becomes extremely slippery here. "Viewpoint" has become "disfavored topics," blurring the traditional distinction between viewpoint and content. More important, the logic of the analogy that Scalia presents as the entirety of his analysis of the case is revealingly flawed. If the issue is a comparison of viewpoints, then the opposite of "anti-Catholic bigots" would be "people who reject anti-Catholic bigotry," not "Catholics." By the same token, if the concern is with viewpoints then the opposite of "proponents of racial segregation" is "opponents of racial segregation," not "African-Americans," and the opposite of "opponents of equal rights for homosexuals" is "supporters of equal rights for homosexuals," not "homosexuals." It is as though Scalia was unable to conceive of a non-Catholic opponent of religious bigotry, a non-African-American opponent of racism, or a heterosexual who rejects homophobia. Just as in *Romer*, in Scalia's description of the sides in a political debate are reduced to a binary opposition between two tribal groups competing for supremacy. The kinds of fixed and inimical factions that Madison feared were, for Scalia, the ideal expression of proper democratic politics. The limits of the Free Speech Clause, in turn, had to be understood to protect those politics from Madisonian efforts to limit their influence in democratic politics.

It is interesting to note that comparing Scalia's opinions in *R.A.V.* and *Smith* in terms of a simple test of more or less government power yields a contradiction. In one case Scalia argued in favor of the exercise of government power, in the other he rejected such an exercise. That contradiction evaporates, however, when we step back from focusing on the outcome of democratic politics to the process, that is, to the politics themselves. Seen this way the two opinions are perfectly consistent, as each maximizes the anything goes libertarianism of political competition in response to efforts to find contraints grounded in a normative conception of what constitutionalist politics should look and sound like.

Yet another illustration of Scalia's anti-Madisonian conception appeared in his dissenting opinion in the same-sex marriage case, *Obergefell v. Hodges* (2015). Scalia's most famous comment in that opinion had to do with the role of courts in a democracy. "This practice of constitutional revision by an unelected committee of nine, always accompanied (as it is today) by extravagant praise of liberty, robs the People of the most important liberty they asserted in the Declaration of Independence and won in the Revolution of 1776: the freedom to govern themselves." There is a great deal that can be said about this statement, but one interesting aspect is Scalia's description of "the most important liberty . . . the freedom to govern themselves." This is a classic expression of what Benjamin Constant called "the liberty of the ancients" (Constant 1819), the idea that what matters is who rules us rather than how they rule. To ascribe this view to the generation of the Constitution's adoption is extremely questionable. Historians and political scientists have demonstrated many times over that the vocabulary of the constitutional debates combined elements of traditional republicanism, liberalism, British legalism, and many other ways of conceiving of republican liberty (Kramnick 1988). The primary author of the Declaration of Independence was adamant that protection of individual rights against the will of a self-governing people was his most central concern, as the phrase "endowed by their Creator with certain inalienable rights" manifestly and eloquently declares.

So there is something disturbingly thin and unexamined about Scalia's description of "the freedom to govern themselves" in this passage. Certainly it was Scalia's view (as it was not Madison's) that restrictions on democracy should be kept to a minimum. That much is not contentious as a reading of Scalia's thoughts. But in a later passage Scalia affirmatively described the form and character of the democratic politics that he valorized.

> Until the courts put a stop to it, public debate over same-sex marriage displayed American democracy at its best. Individuals on both sides of the issue passionately, but respectfully, attempted to persuade their fellow citizens to accept their views. . . . Win or lose, advocates for both sides continued pressing their cases, secure in the knowledge that an electoral loss can be negated by a later electoral win. That is exactly how our system of government is supposed to work.
> (*Obergefell* 2015, Scalia dissenting, op. 2)

No political scientist will fail to recognize the reference to Dahl's "democratic bargain" (Dahl 1970), the argument that participants in a democratic system accept the legitimacy of unwelcome outcomes based on the premise that at some future date their preferences may be reflected in public policy. And on questions of policy making there is a widely shared consensus that this is, indeed, how our system "is supposed to work." But from a Madisonian perspective that is not the end of the question. *How* the politics of decision making occurs, *on what basis* a decision is reached, and *whether* the question is one properly left to majority determination are the critical questions. Dahl, for example, proposed that individuals who feel most strongly about an issue should have the most say in its resolution (2006). Political scientists might argue that the reliance on referenda produces precisely that outcome. From a constitutional perspective, is that an appropriate way to determine a question of legal rights?

The Madisonian tradition emphasizes the idea that where the process of decision making is called into question we have the most reason to fear majoritarian factions precisely because the channels of political decision making are at issue. In the most famous footnote in American legal history (or possibly any history), Justice Harlan Fiske Stone identified one of the situations in which courts may be called to scrutinize government actions. "It is unnecessary to consider now whether legislation which restricts those political processes which can ordinarily be expected to bring about repeal of undesirable legislation is to be subjected to more exacting judicial scrutiny under the general prohibitions of the Fourteenth Amendment than are most other types of legislation." Stone followed this tentative identification of an area of special concern with citations to earlier cases involving voting rights, speech rights, rights to political organization, and rights to peaceable assembly (*United States v. Carolene Products* 1938, 152n).

It is not only judges who have considered the question of what the Constitution demands in terms of democratic practices and what the role of courts might be in response to those demands. Among other famous treatments of the question, John Hart Ely, in *Democracy and Distrust*, emphasized the idea that courts have a special role to play in the American constitutional system in this regard (Ely 1980). In the political science literature, theorists of interest group pluralism—the form of political competition Scalia seemed to accept—consistently found it necessary to ground the system of competition in Madisonian limiting principles. The late Theodore Lowi concluded his magisterial study of interest group politics with the conclusion that the preservation of constitutional norms required a turn to juridical politics. Lowi was expressing a very Madisonian concern with the danger of capture, identifying the locus of that capture in agencies and bureaucracies and the agents of capture in the form of interest groups (Lowi 2009). David Truman's description of American government as competition among interest groups depended on the assumption that the government would establish conditions for competition, conditions that reflect constitutionalist norms of politics (Truman 1951). By contrast, Scalia's model of politics was pure interest group competition without any of the ameliorating constitutionalist norms that democratic theorists like Dahl, Lowi and Truman assumed. Instead, in his descriptions of constitutionalist politics, Scalia not only accepted but actively valorized a model of tribalistic competition for majoritarian supremacy that was the opposite of Madison's conception of constitutionalist politics, a kind of identity group-based political equivalent to *laissez-faire* theories of market economics.

The anti-Madisonian dimensions of Scalia's thinking become even more clear when we consider Scalia's response to the second of Madison's most important concerns, the need for virtue in representation. In Scalia's view, the Constitution not only did not depend on such virtue, it did not permit efforts by courts or by legislatures to limit corruption.

Scalia's Anti-Madisonian Theory of Virtue, Corruption, and the Democratic Process

If one of Madison's fears was majoritarian capture, the other was corruption. In the language of republicanism the opposite of "virtue" is "corruption," exemplified in the pursuit of self-interest at the expense of the public good.

"The aim of every political Constitution, is or ought to be first to obtain for rulers men who possess most wisdom to discern, and most virtue to pursue, the common good of society; and in the next place, to take the most effectual precautions for keeping them virtuous whilst they continue to hold their public trust" (Madison 1787c). Applied to the key American innovations of representative republican government, this meant that the primary function of elections was for the mass of the people to choose the most virtuous and public-spirited among them to serve as their representatives. As was noted at the outset, Madison's fellow Federalist author, Hamilton, explicitly conceived of federal courts as regulating the relationship between electors and representatives. More generally, however, it was critical to Madison's conception of constitutionalist politics that the processes of selection and accountability operate to ensure virtue in leaders separate from the need for structural systems to channel ambition or avarice.

For Scalia the implications of the Constitution were quite nearly the opposite: any attempt to prevent corruption in representatives was to be viewed with the greatest suspicion, and only the most narrowly defined, legalistic definition of "corruption" as the *quid pro quo* exchange of money for a specific action could even be recognized as a legitimate concern. The role of the courts, for Scalia, was to *prevent* any attempt to promote the selection of virtuous leaders, however that term might be defined.

The most emphatic discussion of Scalia's anti-Madisonian conception of the role of virtue in politics appeared in cases involving attempts to regulate campaign finance. In 1990, Justice Marshall delivered a majority opinion that explained why the State of Michigan was justified in limiting campaign contributions by corporations. Marshall began by identifying the relevant state interests, "preventing corruption or the appearance of corruption are the only legitimate and compelling government interests thus far identified for restricting campaign finances." Reviewing the various special legal prerogatives that attach to the corporate form, Marshall concluded that Michigan could reasonably have concluded that corporations would exert an "unfair" degree of influence on elections. "[T]he political advantage of corporations is unfair because [t]he resources in the treasury of a business corporation are not an indication of popular support for the corporation's political ideas. They reject instead the economically motivated decisions of investors and customers. The availability of these resources may make a corporation a formidable political presence, even though the power of the corporation may be no reflection of the power of its ideas." As a result, said Marshall, courts had previously recognized that "the compelling governmental interest in preventing corruption" justified restrictions on corporate political expenditures separate and apart from limits on campaign contributions (*Austin* 1990, 659).

Scalia wrote one of his famously biting dissents. He acknowledged that a fear of corruption might justify limits on campaign contributions. "Certain uses of "massive wealth" in the electoral process—whether or not the wealth is the result of "special advantages" conferred by the State—pose a substantial risk of corruption which constitutes a compelling need for the regulation of speech. Such a risk plainly exists when the wealth is given directly to the political candidate, to be used under his direction and control" (*Austin* 1990, 682). But Scalia denied outright the proposition that similar dangers might arise from independent expenditures, on the grounds that only a direct contribution to a campaign posed the danger of *quid pro quo* corruption. That last observation identified the core of Scalia's position: his denial that any form of corruption other than the exchange of payment for specific services could be legitimately recognized as a threat to the democratic process.

> The Court does not try to defend the proposition that independent advocacy poses a substantial risk of political "corruption," as English-speakers understand that term. Rather, it asserts that that concept (which it defines as "financial quid pro quo' corruption") is really just a narrow subspecies of a hitherto unrecognized genus of political corruption. "Michigan's regulation," we are told, "aims at a different type of corruption in the political arena: the corrosive and distorting effects of immense aggregations of wealth that are accumulated with the help of the corporate form and that have little or no correlation to the public's support for the corporation's political ideas" . . . the concept that government may restrict the speech of some elements of our society in order to enhance the relative voice of others is wholly foreign to the First Amendment, which was designed to secure the widest possible dissemination of information from diverse and antagonistic sources, and to assure unfettered interchange of ideas for the bringing about of political and social changes desired by the people. (*Austin* 1990, 684)

As was often the case, the exuberance of Scalia's prose ran ahead of its analytical rigor. Any number of "English speakers" past and present have had a much broader understanding of "corruption" than financial *quid pro quo* transactions (Teachout, 2016). Similarly, one does not need to be a specialist in political communication to recognize that the amplification of some views by purchasing advertising can have the effect of shutting out other, alternative views rather than ensuring "the widest possible dissemination of information". It is difficult to avoid being impressed at the careless ease with which Scalia first raises and then dismisses empirical claims about what practices will or will not maximize a normatively desirable outcome.

In fact, the important thing to recognize about the passage quoted above is not that it is self-contradictory, but rather that it is merely irrelevant to the real work of the argument. Scalia's appeal to free speech principles was not driven by a calculation of what would maximize the range of ideas or voices to which the public was exposed. Instead, Scalia was specifically motivated to ensure that certain views would carry extra weight *precisely by virtue of the fact* that they were held by powerful business corporations.

> Why should Michigan voters in the 93d House District be deprived of the information that private associations owning and operating a vast percentage of the industry of the State, and employing a large number of its citizens, believe that the election of a particular candidate is important to their prosperity? . . . It is important to the message that it represents the views of Michigan's leading corporations *as corporations,* occupying the "lofty platform" that they do within the economic life of the State—not just the views of some *other* voluntary associations to which some of the corporations' shareholders belong. (*Austin* 1990, 694)

This is literally an argument in favor of domination by wealthy elites as a characterizing aspect of ideal democratic politics. The reference to corporations as employers of "large numbers of its citizens" being heard expressing their views "as corporations occupying the lofty platform that they do within the economic life of the State" comes within a hair of endorsing the idea that employers should be able to threaten the economic futures of their employees in order to coerce their political support, a tactic often associated with the nineteenth-century political machinations. It is important to recognize that Scalia is not merely saying that corporate employers cannot be prevented from using their positions to "influence" their employees, he is positively endorsing the idea as an exemplar of democratic politics. It is not enough that voters hear the voices of corporate shareholders; they must know the preferences of their corporate employers as a condition of constitutionalist democratic politics.

Campaign contributions and free speech issues were not the only contexts in which Scalia laid out his anti-Madisonian conception of corruption. Gerrymandering—the practice of designing voting districts in ways that favor a party—has also been an occasional subject of consideration by the Supreme Court during Justice Scalia's tenure. In this context, interestingly, Scalia retreated from his absolutist position of rejecting any constitutional limit on political practices other than those specified in the Fifteenth Amendment. Instead he relied on a separation of powers argument. In 2004 Scalia suggested that a Madisonian concern with antidemocratic practices required a congressional response. Article I, section 4, gives Congress the authority to overrule State regulations of elections. Scalia pointed out that federal legislation had been enacted repeatedly, including the Apportionment Act of 1842 establishing the system of single-member, winner-take-all districts, and subsequent federal laws enacted in 1872, 1901, and 1911. Most importantly, Scalia insisted that he was entirely sympathetic to constitutional concerns about gerrymandering even though he did not regard courts as the proper authority to resolve such problems. Responding to Justice Stevens' dissenting opinion Scalia wrote, "Much of his dissent is addressed to the incompatibility of severe partisan gerrymanders with democratic principles. We do not disagree with that judgment. . . . The issue we have discussed is not whether severe partisan gerrymanders violate the Constitution, but whether it is for the courts to say when a violation has occurred, and to design a remedy" (*Vieth v. Jubelirer* 2004, 292).

To that point, Scalia's argument appeared to be focused on judicial restraint and the difficulty of creating judicial standards for certain categories of political controversy. But another, very different dimension of the argument appeared in Salia's response to Justice Breyer. Justice Breyer proposed a judicially enforceable standard of "unjustified" district-drawing. Scalia argued that Breyer's standard could not be specified because Breyer ultimately depended on the idea that there would be no "neutral" explanation for a districting decision. "But of course there *always is* a neutral explanation—if only the time-honored criterion of incumbent protection." To the extent that he acknowledges the theoretical possibility that gerrymandering might pose a problem, that recognition is undercut by his description of the process as "an excess of an ordinary and lawful motive" (*Vieth* 2004, 286). The idea that "incumbent protection" constitutes a legitimate criterion for drawing legislative districts makes a mockery of the idea that "severe partisan gerrymanders" might be incompatible with "democratic principles." In Madison's view, structural designs of democratic systems should serve to safeguard against the dangers of ambition, partisanship, and self-interest. In Scalia's view, the idea that structural elements of our democratic system serve constitutionalist ends was entirely absent.

In *Vieth* Scalia presented his argument as one about the absence of judicially manageable standards. All of which raises a question: What, if anything, would Scalia accept as evidence of a "deviation from democratic principles" so severe as to justify judicial intervention? In fact, however, even that question turns out to be overstated. As it turns out, in Scalia's view, the relevant question is: What deviations from democratic principles are sufficiently extreme that the Constitution *permits* efforts to counter their effects by legislatures?

In *Citizens' United v. FEC* (2010), Justice Kennedy wrote the majority opinion that established the right of business corporations to make unlimited expenditures for the purpose of influencing electoral outcomes. Perhaps because Kennedy had already covered many of the issues, Scalia's concurring opinion did not feature a wide-ranging discussion of constitutional history and doctrine. He did, however, take the opportunity to reassert his commitment to the idea that "corruption," like its opposite, "virtue," is essentially irrelevant concepts in constitutional evaluation of political practices.

> The dissent also claims that the Court's conception of corruption is unhistorical. The Framers "would have been appalled," it says, by the evidence of corruption in the congressional findings supporting the Bipartisan Campaign Reform Act of 2002. For this proposition, the dissent cites a law review article arguing that "corruption" was originally understood to include "moral decay" and even actions taken by citizens in pursuit of private rather than public ends. It is hard to see how this has anything to do with what sort of corruption can be combated by restrictions on political speech. Moreover, if speech can be prohibited because, in the view of the Government, it leads to "moral decay" or does not serve "public ends," then there is no limit to the Government's censorship power. (*Citizens United* 2010, 391)

The dissenting opinion of Justice Stevens was the primary focus of Scalia's disagreement, but Scalia's description of Stevens' argument as depending solely on a single law review article's reference to moral decay was misleading. "Congress," wrote Stevens, "crafted BCRA in response to a virtual mountain of research on the corruption that previous legislation had failed to avert." The terms "corrupt" or "corruption" appear eighty times in Stevens' opinion. In explaining his position Stevens appealed to a historical understanding of political "corruption."

> On numerous occasions we have recognized Congress' legitimate interest in preventing the money that is spent on elections from exerting an "undue influence on an officeholder's judgment" and from creating "the appearance of such influence," beyond the sphere of *quid pro quo* relationships. Corruption can take many forms. Bribery may be the paradigm case. But the difference between selling a vote and selling access is a matter of degree, not kind. . . . Corruption operates along a spectrum, and the majority's apparent belief that *quid pro quo* arrangements can be neatly demarcated from other improper influences does not accord with the theory or reality of politics. (*Citizens United* 2010, 447–48)

By contrast, Scalia's rejection of any legitimate interest in ensuring the integrity of elections or public trust in their outcomes is a statement that political dominance is a sign of properly functioning constitutionalist politics.

Scalia's Anti-Madisonian Legacy

I have described Scalia's view of constitutionalist politics as fundamentally anti-Madisonian based on his rejection of Madison's two core tenets:

that there is a need to control the processes of politics to avoid the danger of majoritarian tyranny, and that there is a need to promote virtue and avoid corruption in the selection of elected representatives. Concerning the idea of factions, where Madison feared the creation of fixed and inimical factions engages in competition for supremacy Scalia embraced precisely that model as the epitome of constituitionalist politics. Scalia's view on these question appears across multiple areas: in his valorization of majoritarian politics in *Romer v Evans*; in his repeated descriptions of democracy as an unbridled competition among groups; in his insistence that religious minorities had no right to be free from unequal treatment by the majority, and by his general abandonment of Madison's concern—expressed in footnote 4 of *Carolene Products*—that the democratic process is most in need of constitutional check when a majority seeks to impose its will to the detriment of a vulnerable minority.

On the question of whether pursuing virtue and concomitantly avoiding "corruption" was an element of constitutionalist politics, Scalia was vehement and scathing in his insistence that there could be no legitimate interest in pursuing either of those goals except in the narrowest imaginable circumstances of a direct exchange of money for a specific legislative vote. Anything else was not merely not contrary to the mandate of the Constitution, in Scalia's view the Constitution affirmatively required courts to protect a model of democratic politics as a bare-knuckled brawl for supremacy among unequally empowered groups. In Scalia's view, this system of political norms was the only one consistent with the constitutional mandate for democratic self-rule. The predictable outcome of domination by those groups more powerful than others by virtue of numbers or wealth or local concentration was an inevitable and welcome outcome of the system. In other words, Justice Scalia did not merely take the position that it would be wrong to read the Constitution to imply a Madisonian vision of constitutionalist politics, he explicitly and repeatedly declared his belief that the Constitution requires an extremely anti-Madisonian version of politics as a foundational element of American constitutionalism.

What is the legacy of Scalia's anti-Madisonian notion of constitutionalist politics? The question is difficult to answer. While one may easily find examples of other justices or judges adopting positions consistent with Scalia's or citing his opinions, that fact by itself does not demonstrate influence rather than coincidence of views, nor does it necessarily address the question of how long Scalia's influence may last. There are suggestive indications, however, that Scalia's views are likely to have a significant impact among the self-described "conservative" judges and justices.

One place to look is a debate that is very much an element of both judicial and public attention, the debate over whether the Constitution imposes limits on political gerrymandering. A brief filed in a Virginia gerrymandering case gives a glimpse of what happens when Scalia's view of constitutionalist politics is given weight. In response to a determination that Virginia's legislative districts had been drawn with impermissible racially discriminatory intent, the Virginia Republican Party submitted an alternative plan. Here is an excerpt from the brief in favor of the proposed plan.

> When "faced with the necessity of drawing district lines by judicial order, a court, as a general rule, should be guided by the legislative policies underlying" a state plan—even one that was itself unenforceable—"to the extent those policies do not lead to violations of the Constitution or the Voting Rights Act . . . both of Intervenor-Defendants' proposed remedial plans dramatically outperform Plaintiffs' Alternative Plan on the Legislature's principles" that "inarguably . . . played a role in drawing" Enacted District 3; namely, "protect[ing] incumbents" and preserving cores to maintain the 8 Republican to 3 Democrat ratio established in 2010. Indeed, there is no dispute that maintaining the 8–3 partisan division, by protecting all incumbents of both parties and preserving all district cores, was the Legislature's top discretionary priority. (*Personhuballah v. Alcorn* 2015)

It is difficult to imagine any lawyer being willing to attach his or her name to such an argument without the shelter of Scalia's *Vieth* opinion. More generally, Scalia's strident rejection of any Madisonian concerns about the political process as an element of constitutional reasoning is an essential precursor to this extraordinary but legally likely correct argument.

On the Supreme Court itself, one clear indication of Scalia's influence in this particular context may be found in the arguments of Chief Justice Roberts. During oral arguments in the most recent gerrymandering case the Court was presented with an enormous amount of data compiled by political scientists in an attempt to satisfy Scalia's (and others') concern for a judicially cognizable standard for finding an "excess of an ordinary and lawful motive." Roberts' comment in response to the data presented would have been appropriate to a vintage Scalia opinion: "The whole point is you're taking these issues away from democracy and you're throwing them into the courts pursuant to—and it may be simply my educational background, but I can only describe as—sociological gobbledygook" (*Gill v. Whitford* 2017).

Earlier, in 2014, Roberts penned a majority opinion in which Scalia joined that adopted the same narrow view of what constitutes a constitutionally legitimate public interest in combatting political corruption. "Ingratiation and

access . . . are not corruption. They embody a central feature of democracy.
. . . Any regulation must instead target what we have called quid pro quo"
corruption or its appearance" (*McCutcheon v. FEC* 2014, 1441). Madisonian
concerns with a politics driven by self-interest or domination are not only
judicially incomprehensible, they are constitutionally impermissible. Roberts
was partially quoting his own earlier opinion in *Citizens United.* In that same
case—again in an opinion joined by Scalia—Roberts asserted the remarkable
proposition that "corporate democracy" can be relied upon to ensure accurate
representation of shareholders' views, quoting an earlier opinion by Justice
Powell. The fact that the words are originally Powell's points to the issue
of whether one can assign a specific influence to Scalia on this issue, but it
is noteworthy that the invocation of corporate democracy applies the same
black box deliberate ignorance of processes to corporate governance that
Scalia had earlier applied to democratic politics.

The current justice who has most vocally identified himself as a devotee of
Scalia's constitutional reasoning is Neal Gorsuch. In a 2016 essay Gorsuch
presented a classic straw man argument: either a judge must follow Scalia's
version of originalism or else embrace a role as "pragmatic social-welfare
maximizer." According to Gorsuch, if the view of a judge as a social-welfare
maximizer is rejected then the only alternative is to follow Scalia's lead
(Gorsuch 2016, 918). It is easy to see echoes of Scalia's arguments from
legerdemain in *R.A.V.* and *Romer* in this style of analysis.

There are signs that on the specific question of gerrymandering the Court,
including Roberts, may be ready to accept Scalia's *Vieth* position at his word
and therefore establish judicial remedies in response to the discovery of a
workable standard for "excess." In December 2017 the Court accepted a
second gerrymandering case to go with *Gill v. Whitford*, which has caused
observers to speculate that the Court is moving toward reopening the issue
(Barnes 2017). But there is no indication that Scalia's basic notion that political manipulation of districts as a constitutionally protected practice will be
called into question. And while the outcomes of recent cases involving equal
protection and free speech have been varied, there is no indication that any
of the conservative justices of the Court are interested in departing from the
path that Scalia blazed.

In other areas, too, Scalia's legacy is likely to be keenly felt. In 2018, the
Supreme Court is expected to rule on one or more cases involving claims that
religious objections to providing services to homosexuals should trump state
anti-discrimination laws. Legal doctrines aside, as a matter of constitutionalist politics Scalia's influence can be seen strongly in support of the States: in
his position that majority preferences trump minority religious practices and
that conflicts of issues of this kind are best understood as tribalistic competi-

tions between groups defined by sexual orientation seeking political dominance. Conversely, arguments supporting the constitutionality of state laws *permitting* business owners to discriminate against homosexuals where their actions are motivated by religious beliefs is both an articulation of the other side of the *Smith* coin (Scalia's acknowledgment that majoritarian religious practices are the ones most likely to be protected) and an expression of his view of democratic politics. More narrowly, in the earlier discussion the one situation in which Scalia appeared to invoke Madisonian principles was in his rejection of racial affirmative action. One possible interpretation of that departure from the norm might be that in Scalia's view race was a unique category, not because of a peculiar vulnerability of a discrete and insular minority but because of the specific historical context and textual treatment of racial discrimination in the Reconstruction Amendment. Echoes of that understanding appeared during oral arguments in *Masterpiece Cakeshop v. Colorado Civil Rights Commission*, 16–111. U.S. Solicitor General Noel Francisco, asked whether his position would protect religiously-inspired discrimination on the bases of race, gender, or national origin, described that racial case as unique. "I think pretty much everything but race would fall in the same category" (*Masterpiece Cakeshop,* oral argument 2018, 32). This proposed unique treatment of race as a category of classification is not based on a Madisonian fear of majoritarian tyranny, it is a formal and unique case. For "pretty much everything" else the Scalian conception of constitutionalist politics holds sway in the view of the current Department of Justice.

The mention of the Department of Justice points to what is likely the most lasting, most important, and least quantifiable element of Scalia's legacy in this area. The idea that American constitutionalist politics is exemplified by bare-knuckled conflicts for supremacy among fixed factions is entirely characteristic of the politics of the Trump administration and state administrations and campaigns who share a similar ideology. This is not merely a matter of partisanship in the traditional sense of the word, it is a matter of deliberated tearing away long-accepted norms that reflected Madisonian concerns. In the modern era no member of the Court has done as much to encourage and legitimate that project than Antonin Scalia.

NOTES

1. For a discussion of the proposition that the US Constitution implies constraints on legitimate political discourse, see Schweber 2011.

2. For an extended discussion of the idea that the scope of judicial review should be considered in light of the integrity of political processes see Ely, 1980.

REFERENCES

Barnes, Robert. 2017. "Supreme Court Will Take Up a Second Gerrymandering Case This Term." *Washington Post*. Dec. 8, 2017. https://www.washingtonpost.com/. politics/courts_law/2017/12/08/4fde65f4-dc66-11e7-b1a8-62589434a581_story .html?utm_term=.f42cc8c86832.

Blackbourn, David. 2002. *History of Germany, 1780–1918: The Long Nineteenth Century*, 2nd ed. Hoboken, NJ: Blackwell Press.

Bellamy, Richard. 2007. *Political Constitutionalism: A Republican Defense of the Constitutionality of Democracy*. Cambridge: Cambridge University Press.

Constant, Benjamin. 1819. "The Liberty of the Ancients Compared with That of the Moderns." http://oll.libertyfund.org/titles/constant-the-liberty-of-ancients-com pared-with-that-of-moderns-1819.

Dahl, Robert. 1970. *After the Revolution: Authority in a Good Society*. New Haven, CT: Yale University Press.

———. 2006. *A Preface to Democratic Theory, Expanded Edition*. Chicago: University of Chicago Press.

Ely, John Hart. 1980. *Democracy and Distrust*. Cambridge, MA: Harvard University Press.

Gorsuch, Hon. Neil M. 2016. "Of Lions and Bears, Judges and Legislators, and the Legacy of Justice Scalia." *Case Western Reserve Law Review* 66: 905–20.

Graber, Mark. 2006. *Dred Scott and the Problem of Constitutional Evil*. Cambridge: Cambridge University Press.

Hamilton, Alexander. 1787. *Federalist* 78. http://avalon.law.yale.edu/18th_century/ fed78.asp. Last accessed December 20, 2017.

Kramnick, Isaac. 1988. "The Great National Discussion, the Discourse of Politics in 1787." *The William and Mary Quarterly* 45: 3–32.

Lowi, Theodore J. 2009. *The End of Liberalism: The Second Republic of the United States*, 40th Anniversary Edition. New York: Norton.

Madison, James. 1787a. *Federalist* 62. http://avalon.law.yale.edu/18th_century/fed10 .asp.

———. 1787b. *Federalist* 10. http://avalon.law.yale.edu/18th_century/fed10.asp

———. 1787b. *Federalist* 57. http://avalon.law.yale.edu/18th_century/fed57

———. Letter to Marquis de Lafayette January 23, 1792. http://press-pubs .uchicago.edu/founders/documents/v1ch15s50.html

Posner, Richard A. 1992. "Legal Reasoning from the Top Down and from the Bottom Up: The Question of Unenumerated Constitutional Rights," *University of Chicago Law Review* 59: 433–50.

Putnam, Robert D., Robert Leonardi, Raffaella Y. Nanetti. 1994. *Making Democracy Work: Civic Traditions in Modern Italy*. Princeton, NJ: Princeton University Press.

Scalia, Antonin. 1997. *A Matter of Interpretation*. Princeton, NJ: Princeton University Press.

Schweber, Howard. 2011. *The Language of Liberal Constitutionalism*. Cambridge, MA: Cambridge University Press.
Teachout, Zephyr. 2016. *Corruption in America: From Benjamin Franklin's Snuff Box to Citizens United*. Cambridge, MA: Harvard University Press.
Truman, David. 1951. *The Governmental Process*. Oxford: Oxford University Press.

TABLE OF CASES

Abrams v. United States, 250 U.S. 616 (1919).
Adarand Constructors, Inc. v. Pena, 515 U.S. 200 (1995).
Arizona State Legislature v. Arizona Independent Redistricting Commission, No. 13–1314 (2015), slip op.
Austin v. Michigan Chamber of Commerce, 494 U.S. 652 (1990).
Baker v. Carr, 369 U.S. 186 (1962).
Calder v. Bull, 3 U.S. 386, 388 (1798).
Chaplinsky v. New Hampshire, 315 U.S. 568, 572 (1942).
Chisholm v. Georgia, 2 U.S. 419, 462 (1793).
Citizens' United v. FEC, 558 U.S. 310 (2010).
Dist. Of Columbia v. Heller, 554 U.S. 570 (2004).
Employment Division v. Smith, 494 U.S. 872 (1990).
Gill v. Whitford, transcript of oral argument available at https://www.oyez .org/cases/2017/16-1161, last viewed March 5, 2018.
Korematsu v. United States, 323 U.S. 214 (1944).
Lemon v. Kurtzman, 403 U.S. 602, 622 (1971).
Lochner v. New York, 198 U.S. 45, 64 (1905).
Luther v. Borden, 48 U.S. 1, 45 (1849).
Masterpiece Cakeshop v. Colorado Civil Rights Commission, transcript of oral argument. https://www.supremecourt.gov/oral_arguments/argument_transcripts/2017/16-111_f314.pdf, last viewed Jan. 9, 2018.
McCutcheon v. FEC, 134 S.Ct. 1434, 1441 (2014).
Obergefell v. Hodges, 576 U.S. ___ , slip op. No. 14–556. (2015).
Personhuballah v. Alcorn, Civil Action No.: 3:13-cv-678, "Intervenor-Defendants' Brief in Support of Their Proposed Remedial Plans" (E.D. Vir. 2015).
Plessy v Ferguson, 163 U.S. 537, 550 (1896).
Printz v. United States, 521 U.S. 898, 904–05 (1997).
R.A.V. v. St. Paul, 503 U.S. 377 (1992).
Reynolds v. Simms, 377 U.S. 533 (1964).
Richmond v. J.A. Croson Co., 488 U.S. 469, 520 (1989).
Romer v. Evans, 517 U.S. 620, 636 (1996).

Schuette v. Coal. to Defend Affirmative Action, Integration & Immigration Rights, 572 U.S. ___ (2014).

Skinner v. Oklahoma, 316 U.S. 535 (1942).

United States v. Carolene Products, 304 U.S. 144 (1938).

Vieth v. Jubilerer, 541 U.S. 267 (2004).

Wesberry v. Sanders, 376 U.S. 1 (1964).

West Virginia Bd. Of Educ. v. Barnette, 319 U.S. 624, 639 (1943).

Chapter 7

Justice Scalia and the Legal Conservative Movement

An Exploration of Nino's Neoconservatism

Jesse Merriam

Over the past ten years, there have been several books on the legal conservative movement ("LCM")—the social movement by which conservative and libertarian lawyers have sought to push the judiciary, legal academy, and bar toward the right. In Steven Teles's (2008) groundbreaking book on the LCM, Teles focused on the importance of conservative and libertarian "intellectual entrepreneurs" and "network entrepreneurs" in structuring the movement's coalitions and advancing the movement's agenda (18). Teles identified Scalia as one of the most significant LCM figures, largely due to his involvement in promoting originalism (one of the most important LCM ideas) and creating the Federalist Society (indisputably the most important LCM network).

In her recent book on the LCM, Amanda Hollis-Brusky similarly described the Federalist Society as a "political epistemic network" that has enabled conservative and libertarian lawyers to bind themselves together around a particular set of beliefs on the separation of powers, federalism, and originalism (Hollis-Brusky 2016, 13). Like Teles, Hollis-Brusky points to Scalia as a critical figure in creating and expanding this political epistemic network.

Scalia has thus become known as "[t]he *dean of the modern conservative legal movement*" (O'Donnell 2010). Some scholars and pundits have even extended this beyond law to apply to the conservative movement as a whole. For example, after Justice Scalia's untimely death in February 2016, Maggie Gallagher at *National Review* proclaimed that Scalia was "one of the four greats of the conservative movement," with Barry Goldwater, Ronald Reagan, and William F. Buckley being the other three (Gallagher 2016). Adam Liptak similarly described Scalia as "a leader of a conservative intellectual renaissance" (Liptak 2016).

There has, however, been little exploration of Scalia's particular *type* of conservatism. While there have been many studies exploring where various

Supreme Court justices are located on the ideological spectrum, and these studies have generally placed Scalia as the second most conservative justice on the Rehnquist and Roberts Courts, behind only Justice Thomas (Epstein et al. 2016.), it is still unclear what type of conservative he was. The few scholars who have sought to characterize Scalia's conservatism have assigned radically different designations, such as "very conservative" (Witt 1986, 149), a "traditionalist" (Presser 2016, 403), a "neoconservative" (Feldman 2012), a "Hamiltonian" (Staab 2006), and a "right-wing reactionary" (Brisbin 1998, 6). Some scholars have even found in Scalia significant strains of liberalism, which some have attributed to Scalia's consistent originalism (Dorsen 2017; Schultz and Smith 1996, 80), and others to his inconsistent originalism (Barnett 2006).

This chapter will draw from these works on the LCM and Scalia's legacy to provide a more thorough exploration of Scalia's legal and political ideology, as well as his contributions to the LCM. The first part of the chapter will explore the antecedent intellectual and political trends within the conservative movement that led to Scalia's rise in the political and legal world, ultimately leading to his appointment to the Supreme Court in 1986. This part will focus on: (a) the young Scalia's support of Barry Goldwater, who represented the early *National Review* model of conservatism, marked in the domestic sphere by a radical suspicion of federal authority and a traditionalist view of interpersonal relations, and (b) Scalia's affiliation with neoconservatism in the late 1970s, a new approach to conservatism that represented a substantial departure from the Goldwater conservatism that had initially drawn Scalia right-ward in the 1960s.

The second part of the chapter will examine how neoconservative values and strategies overlapped with Scalia's thinking about the law. Here, the chapter will consider his thirty-year career as a Supreme Court justice, in addition to his extrajudicial writing, in exploring Scalia's views on five topics at the core of his conservatism—originalism, federalism, executive power, affirmative action, and church-state relations.

The picture of the LCM that will emerge from this chapter is of a movement that is much more dynamic than is typically assumed, having undergone substantial changes, in both its strategy and agenda, over the last fifty years. Scalia was at the heart of this dynamism, a neglected point in much of the scholarship exploring Scalia's role in the movement. Indeed, Teles overlooks Scalia's role as an "intellectual entrepreneur" in *transforming* the conservative movement, and especially its legal subsidiary, into a *neo*conservative movement. Likewise, Hollis-Brusky neglects the extent to which Scalia's contributions to the Federalist Society *defined* a new conservative agenda and identity, and how this "political epistemic network" served to construct and police the boundaries of conservatism. The chapter will conclude with a brief discussion of what Scalia's political and legal trajectory reveals about the future of conservatism and the LCM, particularly in light of the 2016 populist revolt against the neoconservative establishment to which Scalia was so closely linked.

ANTONIN SCALIA AND THE
EARLY CONSERVATIVE MOVEMENT

The "conservative movement" generally refers to the post-war coalition that emerged among three types of political thinkers and activists: (1) cultural traditionalists such as Russell Kirk and Richard Weaver, (2) libertarians such as Frank Meyer and F. A. Hayek, and (3) anti-communist "cold warriors" such as Whittaker Chambers and James Burnham (Nash 1976). This coalition was solidified through William F. Buckley's creation of *National Review*, leading one Buckley biographer to proclaim that "[t]he conservative movement was born on November 19, 1955, the publication date of the first issue of the *National Review*" (Bogus 2011, 141). Antonin Scalia was nineteen years old at the time and there were few signs that this Georgetown University undergraduate would end up being a conservative, let alone one of the movement's leaders.

Scalia was born in 1936 and was raised in an Italian-American household in Elmhurst, Queens, an ethnically diverse, working- and middle-class neighborhood. Scalia's father, a Sicilian immigrant and lover of literature, was a professor of Romance languages at Brooklyn College. His parents, like most Italian-Americans in New York City at the time, were "staunch Democrats" (Murphy 2014/2015). In fact, Scalia would later recount that he showed serious support for a political candidate only once in his life and that was when "he went door-to-door for his uncle Vince Panaro, a Democrat, in local campaigns in the 1950s" (Biskupic 2009/2010, 71).

Nevertheless, there were some signs that the young Scalia would eventually migrate toward the right, at least on religious issues. A fellow student from his Jesuit high school remembered Scalia as being "[a]n archconservative Catholic" (Molotsky 1986). His Catholic conservatism soon came into conflict with the liberalization of the Catholic Church under the Second Vatican Council in the early 1960s.

Some scholars have sought to link Scalia's emerging conservatism to his possible attendance of Herbert Wechsler's controversial 1958 "neutral principles" lecture at Harvard Law School, a lecture in which Wechsler provocatively criticized the recent *Brown v. Board of Education* (1954) decision. Even though Scalia was a Harvard Law student at the time, he later insisted that he did not attend the lecture, "a claim that many [have] questioned" (Murphy 2014/2015, 38).

In any event, whether or not the young Scalia attended Wechsler' lecture, the link between Scalia's emerging conservatism and the Wechsler' *Brown* critique seems too attenuated to draw such a strong causal inference. The more plausible explanation is that Scalia migrated toward the right after his graduation from law school in 1960 as a result of the coinciding of the liberalization of the Catholic Church, and the rise of a new form of conservatism through *National Review* and Barry Goldwater's 1964 presidential run.

A *NATIONAL REVIEW* CONSERVATIVE
AND BARRY GOLDWATER SUPPORTER

In 1961, Scalia began his legal career at the Cleveland, Ohio, office of the elite law firm—Jones, Day, Cockley and Reavis—where he quickly became known as the most conservative lawyer in the office. According to one partner, the young Scalia was a "hard-core Goldwater person," even in 1963, before the Goldwater movement had developed significant momentum. Another partner at the firm described Scalia as "one of the first Bill Buckley-type conservatives" and a "big *National Review* fan" (Murphy 2014/2015, 46). Although one should not read too much into Scalia's support of Goldwater or *National Review* in his late twenties, it is nevertheless worth considering what type of conservatism Goldwater and *National Review* represented at this time, given that Scalia was known at his law firm as a particularly forceful advocate for this radical brand of conservatism, which in the early 1960s was certainly not the norm for a young elite lawyer from New York City (Murphy 2014/2015).

One relevant point is that while *National Review* was overwhelmingly Catholic in the 1950s and 1960s, and featured many articles on how Christianity was central to American conservatism, other cultural factors besides Scalia's faith may have played a role in his emerging identification as a political conservative. During this period, much of the legal writing at *National Review* focused on how the civil rights movement, including *Brown v. Board of Education* (1954), threatened the American constitutional order (Kersch 2011b). The *National Review* criticisms of *Brown* and the civil rights movement ranged the conservative gambit, including arguments based on federalism (Meyer 1956), originalism (Kilpatrick 1963), freedom of association (Weaver 1957), and even racial superiority (*National Review Editorial* 1957).

That is not to imply, of course, that Scalia supported *National Review* specifically *because* of its opposition to the civil rights movement. But it is equally difficult to draw the inference that a young lawyer in the 1960s could be a "big *National Review* fan" without at least having some sympathy for the magazine's most salient and provocative legal position at the time. In this sense, it may be helpful to understand Scalia's right-ward drift in his twenties as part of a larger national trend among white Catholics away from the more socially progressive dimensions of the Democratic Party. That is, Scalia migrated toward the right at precisely the period in which "Catholic ethnic neighborhoods" followed Southern whites in "the backlash against liberal social policies" (Gottfried 2012, 35).

It is especially telling that Scalia was a "hard-core Goldwater person," instead of a supporter of Nelson Rockefeller, the moderate New York governor and namesake for the so-called "Rockefeller Republicans" (i.e., the liberal Northeastern contingent of the Republican party in the 1960s). On this issue, Scalia squarely fell in line with *National Review*, which had long supported Goldwater and had helped propel the Arizona Senator to the national stage through his hugely successful 1960 book, *The Conscience of a Conservative*, ghostwritten by L. Brent Bozell, a *National Review* contributor and Buckley's brother-in-law. As many scholars of the conservative movement have noted, the acrimonious and contentious nomination of Goldwater over Rockefeller represented the beginning of the ideological link between the Republican Party and *National Review*-style conservatism (Nash 1976).

Scalia's support of Goldwater was remarkable for a native New Yorker. In the presidential election, Goldwater suffered an enormous defeat, losing to Lyndon B. Johnson by a staggering 486–52 margin in the electoral college, a loss that was especially pronounced in the Empire State: Goldwater garnered only 31 percent of the New York vote, as opposed to Johnson's 69 percent. Even more strikingly, the 1964 election was the only presidential election in American history in which a Democratic presidential candidate carried every single New York State county. To put that in perspective, in the shocking 2016 presidential election, Hillary Clinton garnered 59 percent of the votes in New York State, against Donald Trump's 37 percent, and Trump won the vast majority of the counties. So a New Yorker supporting Goldwater in 1964 was taking a much more radical position than one supporting Trump in 2016.

In considering Scalia's political beliefs as a young lawyer, it is also worth noting that Goldwater was so controversial among moderate Republicans partly because of his opposition to the Civil Rights Act of 1964, which contributed significantly to the rise of the Republican Party in the South. Indeed, Goldwater's only victories, besides in his home state of Arizona, were in the Deep South, thus becoming the first post-Reconstruction Republican presidential candidate to win Alabama, Georgia, Louisiana, Mississippi, and South Carolina. According to the conventional account of mid-century electoral politics, many white Southerners switched to the Republican Party because they were disenchanted with the Democratic Party platform, principally due to its expansion of federal programs in reaching out to African American voters. While some conservatives have recently challenged this account and claimed it was actually conservative economic policies, rather than racial resentment, that led many white Southerners to make this switch (Williamson 2012), civil rights and race relations were undeniably significant forces in making the South more Republican.

Again, one should not infer too much about the young Scalia's views on these subjects from his support of Goldwater, but in conjunction with his being drawn to the *National Review* conservatism at this time, in concert with many other white Catholics, it strongly indicates that, if he was not hostile toward the civil rights movement, he was at the very least not sympathetic.

Scalia's appointment to the Supreme Court many years later was indirectly part of this racialization of American conservatism. In 1968, under the advice of Pat Buchanan, President Richard Nixon broadened the so-called "Southern Strategy" to become a "Silent Majority Strategy," which would also include Northern "white ethnics"—namely, "Irish, Italians, Poles" (Klein 2017). Buchanan's Silent Majority Strategy led not only to a complete electoral transformation of the South (Texas was the only state south of the Mason-Dixon to vote in 1968 for the Democratic candidate, Hubert Humphrey) but also to significant advances for the Republican Party in the Northeast. Almost twenty years later, in 1985, Buchanan wrote a White House memorandum advising President Reagan to nominate Scalia over Robert Bork specifically because of the role that working-class, Italian-Americans had come to play in the new "white ethnic" Republican Party coalition—specifically how Italian-Americans could "provide[] the GOP its crucial margins of victory in New Jersey, Connecticut, and New York" (Buchanan memo). Scalia's Italian ancestry was reportedly the deciding factor in Reagan's decision to choose Scalia over Bork (Murphy 2014/2015, 124).

In Scalia's appointment, the traditionalist Buchanan did, to some extent, get the combative and confrontational populist he wanted, but as we will discuss in the second half of this chapter, Scalia's populism would end up being much more neoconservative than traditionalist. Before we explore Scalia's jurisprudence, however, it will be helpful to examine what neoconservatism—a controversial and often misunderstood area of conservative thought—represents in the conservative movement and its legal applications.

THE AMERICAN ENTERPRISE INSTITUTE
AND THE RISE OF NEOCONSERVATISM

Scalia's first political appointment arose in 1971, when at the age of 35 and only four years after joining the UVA Law faculty, Scalia was appointed by

President Nixon to be general counsel for the Office of Telecommunications Policy. Three years later, Nixon nominated Scalia to be assistant attorney general for the office of legal counsel, a nomination that President Gerald Ford sustained after Nixon resigned from office. Scalia served in this position for two years, taking on several important executive-power issues. After Ford's loss to Jimmy Carter in 1976, Ford joined the right-leaning American Enterprise Institute ("AEI"), bringing with him several officials from the Ford administration, including Scalia. Scalia joined AEI at a critical period, when the think tank was at the core of the neoconservative ascendancy within the conservative movement, a topic of significant relevance to understanding Scalia's eventual role as an intellectual entrepreneur in shaping the LCM.

Neoconservatism is an intellectual and political movement that emerged in the late 1960s and early 1970s, largely as a response to the rise of the New Left (Ehrman 2006, 610). The early neoconservatives were predominately (though not exclusively) Jewish New Yorkers who, up until the 1960s, had been Trotskyites and committed members of the Democratic Party (ibid.). Over the 1970s, many of these thinkers became disenchanted with the New Left and began identifying with "vital center" liberalism, often times referring to themselves as "right-wing liberals." Irving Kristol, known as the "godfather" of neoconservatism, famously defined a neoconservative as "a *liberal who has been mugged by reality*" (Kristol 1983). The term "neoconservative" is often traced to 1973, when the left-wing political theorist Michael Harrington coined the term in describing the political orientation of Kristol's quarterly journal, *The Public Interest* (Bronitsky 2014).

The first generation of neoconservatives departed from the New Left most fundamentally on two issues: urban policy (generally relating to affirmative action) and foreign affairs (generally relating to Israel). These issues became of particular concern to neoconservatives after "the 1967 Six-Day War in the Middle East and the eruption of anti-Semitism among black and Hispanic 'community activists' during New York City's 1968 teacher's strike" (Shapiro 2006, 171).

Many of the early neoconservatives were social scientists and their writing was often quite technical in nature, focusing on how various Great Society programs had bad consequences for their intended beneficiaries (Friedman 2007, 120). Over the course of the 1970s, however, neoconservatives became more critical of the entirety of these programs, not just bits and pieces of technical details. As this group of social scientists moved right-ward, many conservative organizations moved left-ward to appeal to this influential group of thinkers.

AEI was one of those right-leaning organizations that moved in the neoconservative direction in the early 1970s, a transition that began when the AEI president, William Baroody Sr., took an interest in some of the policy ideas coming out of Kristol's *The Public Interest* (Friedman 2007, 131). In 1972, Kristol came "out of the conservative closet" (Goodman 1981) by becoming the first of the neoconservatives to announce a switch to the Republican Party. That year, Baroody recruited Kristol to become one of the first AEI research fellows (Stahl 2016, 83).

The other leading neoconservatives at the time still identified as Democrats, and many had been highly involved in the LBJ administration as well as the Hubert Humphrey and Scoop Jackson campaigns. Kristol was at the center of recruiting leading neoconservatives to join AEI so that they could get to "know and understand conservative Republicans" (Vaïsse 2011, 206). For Kristol, this exchange between neoconservative Democrats and conservative Republicans was critical to transforming American conservatism to become more electorally appealing and intellectually sophisticated. As Kristol bluntly put it, "Jews can offer political conservatism . . . *an intellectual vigor and cultural buoyancy it has so sadly lacked until now.*" According to Ben Wattenberg, one of the early recruits Kristol brought to AEI, Kristol was "at the center where the neoboys' network interconnects" (Goodman 1981). Through his connections, Kristol "helped transform [AEI] into a neoconservative hotbed" (Feldman 2012, 53), eventually making AEI "one of the largest neocon foundations" (Gottfried 2007).

This AEI "takeover" marked the beginning of a major rift between traditional conservatives and neoconservatives (Vaïsse 2011, 206). AEI's hiring of Kristol "enraged Goldwater conservatives" (Friedman 2012, 131), because the Goldwater conservatives had been the traditional backers of AEI, and many Goldwater conservatives suspected that "questions of affirmative action and meritocracy apart, almost all of the neoconservatives remained liberals on most domestic policy issues" (Vaïsse 2011, 207).

In locating Scalia's jurisprudence on the conservative spectrum, which we will do in the second part of this chapter, it is important to have a clear understanding of what exactly divided traditional conservatism from neoconservatism, a divide that is too often ignored in commentary on American conservatism and the LCM. Here, it is important to note that I will be using "traditional conservatives" as a broad category, including the various elements of the *National Review* conservative movement that predated the emergence of neoconservatism. This most prominently includes the two pillars of 1950s and 1960s *National Review*-style conservatism—cultural traditionalists (e.g., Kirk) and libertarians (e.g., Meyer). The division between this older conservatism and neoconservatism can best be placed in three categories.

First, on issues relating to ethnicity, religion, and immigration, neoconservatives took a much more egalitarian and inclusive position than traditional conservatives. Whereas traditional conservatives generally opposed mass immigration in favor of highly homogeneous and small communities rooted in organic bonds and attachments, neoconservatives overwhelmingly favored the fluidity, diversity, and mobility that increasingly characterized post-war America. At the same time, however, neoconservatives disagreed with the New Left in that neoconservatives rejected the relativization of culture and values that had come to accompany this diversity. Neoconservatives generally urged for diverse populations to be unified by a strong non-racial (and even anti-racial) *American* identity, to fulfill America's exceptional nature as "the first universal nation"—*i.e.*, a nation built not by and for a certain group of people but on a set of abstract ideas or propositions (Wattenberg 1991).

Second, whereas traditional conservatives were highly suspicious of federal authority, and therefore favored dismantling much of the administrative state, neoconservatives were largely accepting of the federal welfare state. But the neoconservatives emphasized, much more than liberals, the need for the government to partner with the private sector in distributing goods and benefits so as to achieve the "good intentions" of these programs (Kristol 2003).

Finally, whereas many traditional conservatives had been isolationists opposing the use of American military force except for when necessary for the direct advancement of American interests, neoconservatives believed that "American exceptionalism" meant that the United States had not only the authority but also the moral duty to promote democracy and American culture across the globe. Neoconservatives therefore favored a "muscular, assertive liberalism" that would be "internationalist [and] assertive around the world" (Wattenberg 1991), so that the United States, and its version of liberal democracy, would represent the "end of history" (Fukuyama 1992).

Three critical events arose in the 1980s and early 1990s to facilitate the neoconservative triumph over the identity, views, and agenda of the conservative movement. The first major conflict between traditional conservatives and neoconservatives arose in 1981, when President Reagan nominated Mel Bradford to be chairman of the National Endowment for the Humanities. Neoconservatives such as Irving Kristol and Norman Podhoretz vehemently opposed Bradford (who was an accomplished Southern academic known for his scholarship favoring local government and regional identities) for being too conservative, particularly on civil rights issues (Gordon 2010, 34). As the *New York Times* reported at the time, "Kristol picked up the phone . . . to talk to some acquaintances in Washington about the [Bradford] appointment," and as a result, "[t]he job went instead to Kristol's choice, William Bennett, of the neoconservative National Humanities Center" (Goodman 1981).

Five years later, at a 1986 Philadelphia Society conference designed to bring traditionalists and neoconservatives together, Stephen Tonsor, a traditionalist and historian at the University of Michigan, lambasted neoconservatives for exercising so much influence over the conservative movement within just a few years of their conversion to conservatism. In particularly striking and evocative language, Tonsor compared the neoconservatives to a "town whore [who] gets religion" and then "begins to tell the minister what he ought to say in his Sunday sermons." This language led many attendees to charge Tonsor with anti-Semitism, a charge that only intensified after Tonsor turned his speech into a *National Review* article, *Why I Am Not a Neoconservative* (Klingenstein 2003).

Finally, as acrimony between traditionalists and neoconservatives escalated with the first Iraq War, Buckley decided in 1991 to dedicate an entire issue of the *National Review* (turned into a book in 1993) to the task of rooting out suspected anti-Semites from the conservative movement, which had the effect of banishing many traditionalists from *National Review* (Buckley 1993). Over the twenty-five years since the Buckley cleansing, neoconservative views have generally (though not entirely) controlled the *National Review*—a turnaround that enabled, for example, neoconservatives to make the striking claim that traditionalists were "unpatriotic" and not true conservatives for following their anti-interventionist views in opposing the second invasion of Iraq (Frum 2003).

As neoconservatives prevailed in each of these conflicts, Goldwater conservatives generally adapted to and assimilated to the transition, leading many over time to adopt neoconservative views on pluralism, federal authority, and foreign affairs. In turn, many neoconservatives did the same with regard to some conservative views, such as on abortion and gun rights. Due to this cross-pollination, neoconservatism has become a largely anachronistic term, having become generally synonymous with the conservative movement itself.

Scalia, as we will soon discuss, may be best understood as one of those Goldwater/early *National Review* conservatives who ended up adopting neoconservative positions on many important issues. While it is unclear to what extent his ultimate neoconservative views represented a departure from his earlier Goldwater/*National Review* conservatism, and it is similarly unclear whether Scalia made this transition unwittingly in tracking the overall current of American conservatism, or for more politically opportunistic reasons, it is nevertheless clear that Scalia ended up assimilating decidedly neoconservative views on issues like federal power, civil rights, and church-state relations. And Scalia did not just assimilate these views; he played an early and important role as the leading LCM intellectual entrepreneur in *framing neoconservatism in legal terms*.

An important step in this path was Scalia's affiliation with AEI at a time when the think tank was actively rebranding itself in the neoconservative mold and recruiting leading neoconservative thinkers. While at AEI, Scalia was personally and highly involved in the intellectual cross-pollination between conservative Republicans and neoconservative Democrats that Kristol had set out to create (Staab 2006, 13; Brisbin 1998, 23). And although Scalia worked out of the AEI office with Kristol only for several months, before taking a faculty position in 1977 at the University of Chicago Law School, his relationship with AEI and Kristol continued well beyond that, principally through Scalia's role as editor of AEI's bimonthly magazine, *Regulation* (now run by the libertarian think tank Cato). The *Regulation* editorial board included several leading neoconservative thinkers, such as Kristol and Jeane Kirkpatrick (who became Reagan's ambassador to the United Nations). For a period, Scalia served as coeditor of *Regulation*, along with the economist Murray Weidenbaum (who became Reagan's chairman of the Council of Economic Advisors). Scalia eventually became sole editor of the journal, a position he maintained in his five years as a law professor at the University of Chicago.

At the time, the University of Chicago was known as a "bastion of conservatism," due its affiliation with the law and economics movement in the law school and Straussianism in its political science department (Staab 2006, 14)—making it quite fitting that this is where Scalia would take his most significant steps in furthering and shaping the LCM.

THE HOROWITZ REPORT,
THE FEDERALIST SOCIETY,
AND THE RISE OF THE LCM

As conservatives came into power with the election of Ronald Reagan, elite lawyers and think tanks began strategizing how they could use this opportunity to push back against the Warren Court Revolution. A particularly significant event in this movement arose in 1980 when the Scaife Foundation funded Michael Horowitz, a well-connected and elite conservative lawyer, to develop a strategy as to how legal conservatives could mobilize a counterliberal movement. Horowitz (who ended up becoming Reagan's chief counsel of the Office of Management and Budget and is currently a senior advisor at the Religion Action Center of Reform Judaism) wrote a lengthy report that was widely "distributed to conservative donors and activists," eventually becoming the LCM blueprint (Teles 2008, 67).

Horowitz prescribed legal conservatives to follow five basic tenets, which essentially boiled down to one overriding principle: in order to recruit idealistic young elite lawyers into the movement, legal conservatives had to represent themselves as the "good guys," and to do this, legal conservatives had to take on progressively oriented causes that targeted sympathetic populations, such as "ghetto school children" and "ghetto public housing residents" (Teles 2008, 72).

Scholars of the LCM have noted Horowitz's influence on the movement (Teles 2008; Decker 2016), but these scholars have neglected the relationship between the Horowitz report and the neoconservative trajectory within the conservative movement. In particular, it is important to understand the Horowitz report in light of contemporaneous efforts by neoconservatives like Jack Kemp to diversify the Republican Party regionally and ethnically by branding it the "party of civil rights," largely through policies like free-enterprise zones and school vouchers (Tanenhaus 2014).

Scholars of the LCM can best understand the Horowitz report in light of this current running through neoconservatism and the larger conservative movement in the 1980s. It is only by understanding this larger trajectory that LCM scholars can understand, for example, what inspired one of the LCM's most important intellectual entrepreneurs, Clint Bolick, to structure legal conservatism as a resuscitation of the civil rights movement (Bolick 1988). In a panel before Kristol's Institute for Educational Affairs, which was created "to funnel corporate money into conservative organizations" (Teles 2008, 314n14), Horowitz urged big business to invest in creating conservative litigation firms that will protect "the interest of America's poor, vulnerable, and minority population" (Horowitz 1981). This became the model for Bolick's Institute for Justice, one of the LCM's most important networks.

Horowitz was also largely responsible for creating what is indisputably the LCM's most important network: the Federalist Society. The same year that Horowitz's Scaife report was published, three law students (two at Chicago and one at Yale) began discussing the possibility of creating the first conservative legal organization. These formerly liberal students were discouraged to find that, despite the Reagan Revolution sweeping the nation, they had no faculty, student, or professional groups through which to explore their increasingly conservative political beliefs. Two years later, in 1982, these students formally created the Federalist Society, with ideological guidance and financial support from both Horowitz and Kristol (Teles 2008, 141).

The only figure more important than Kristol and Horowitz in getting the Federalist Society off the ground was Antonin Scalia. In 1982, Scalia became the Society's first faculty advisor, after two of his students (David McIntosh and Lee Liberman Otis) approached him about leading the Chicago chapter. Scalia helped these students get their first Federalist Society office (in the AEI building, in 1983). Even more importantly, Scalia used his relationship with Kristol to help the Federalist Society obtain from Kristol's Institute an initial $20,000 grant (Biskupic 2009/2010, 78), and a subsequent $50,000 grant (Friedman 2007, 132), which was the institute's most important achievement before it became defunct (Teles 2008, 314n14).

The Federalist Society was also Scalia's most significant achievement during his five years at Chicago Law. The Federalist Society put Scalia at the center of the relationship between the growing neoconservative network and the Reagan administration. Scalia had made clear to his D.C. connections that he wanted a position in the Reagan administration. After he interviewed for, but was not offered, the position of solicitor general, Scalia was "bitterly disappointed" (Biskupic 2009/2010, 74). But as a result of the rejection he became even more determined to end up on the D.C. Circuit, which would provide the most likely path to the U.S. Supreme Court. In 1982, he made the remarkable decision to turn down an offer to serve on the Seventh Circuit, because he was waiting for a D.C. Circuit appointment. This audacious move ultimately worked in his favor. Later that year, Scalia was offered a coveted D.C. Circuit judgeship, and four years later—based partly on an important White House memo by Federalist Society founder and former Scalia student, Lee Liberman Otis—President Reagan nominated Scalia to serve on the U.S. Supreme Court.

JUSTICE SCALIA'S CONSERVATIVE JURISPRUDENCE

Although providing a detailed account of Scalia's thirty-year career on the Supreme Court is well outside the scope of this chapter, the remaining pages will take a brief and general look at how Scalia addressed five topics at the center of his conservative legacy: originalism, federalism, executive power, affirmative action, and church-state relations. We will see in this part of the chapter that Scalia's legal ideology certainly had a traditionalist (specifically Catholic) strain, but scholars who treat Scalia simply as a traditionalist are overlooking a major part of his political development and jurisprudence. Drawing from his Supreme Court opinions, in conjunction with his extrajudicial writings when applicable, this chapter will show how Scalia was a critical agent in developing a neoconservative legal agenda.

ORIGINALISM

Paul Brest, a liberal constitutional scholar, first coined the term "originalism" in 1980 to describe the "familiar approach to constitutional adjudication that accords binding authority to the text of the Constitution or the intentions of its adopters" (Brest 1980). Brest considered this "familiar approach" to be "misguided" but he nevertheless conceded that it had long been a part of American constitutional jurisprudence. As Jonathan O'Neill has ably demonstrated, originalism, as a distinct form of constitutional interpretation, is traceable all the way back to the founding (O'Neill 2005/2007, 5). Although this familiar approach was temporarily overshadowed by legal realism and its assault on legal formalism in the first half of the twentieth century, interest in a history-based constitutionalism surged back in the 1960s, largely as a response to the Warren Court's progressive activism.

At first the resurgence appeared in nonacademic venues, such as the writing of *National Review*'s James Kilpatrick and L. Brent Bozell, and the statements of politicians like Senator Sam Ervin (D-NC). But in the 1970s, this interest migrated from the political sphere into the legal academy, most significantly with Robert Bork's groundbreaking article, "Neutral Principles and Some First Amendment Problems" (1971), and then Raoul Berger's equally important book, *Government by Judiciary: The Transformation of the Fourteenth Amendment* (1977). These academic explorations of originalism focused on the "intent" of the framers and unapologetically defended originalism as central to the conservative effort to "forestall[] legal liberalism" (O'Neill 2005/2007, 168).

Over the nearly twenty years between Scalia's first academic job at UVA Law in 1967 and his appointment to the U.S. Supreme Court in 1986, a time in which originalism experienced rapid growth as a distinct interpretive methodology in the scholarship of Bork and Berger and public statements by Attorney General Ed Meese, Scalia's academic and professional work was conspicuously devoid of historical analysis. Indeed, as we will discuss below, Scalia wrote three articles as a Chicago Law professor on controversial constitutional law topics (federalism, affirmative action, and church-state relations) and none of these articles even bothered to consider the original meaning of the Constitution as it relates to these hot-button topics. Likewise, in his four years on the D.C. Circuit, "his work . . . evidenced no single jurisprudential principle or philosophy" (Murphy 2014/2015, 116).

Scalia's first explicit foray into originalism did not arise until June 14, 1986, when, at the age of fifty, Scalia gave a speech on the subject to the Attorney General's Conference on Economic Liberties. When Scalia gave that now-famous 1986 speech, Scalia knew that he and Bork were both being considered for the Supreme Court vacancy left by Chief Justice Burger's retirement, and the speech was unmistakably designed to persuade the Reagan administration that Scalia's "public meaning" approach, which focused on the meaning available to the public at the time of a constitutional provision's ratification, "was different, and even better, than Bork's 'original intent' theory" (Murphy 2014/2015, 125). Two days after giving the speech, Scalia was nominated to the Supreme Court (125).

Scalia may not have foreseen the implications of his "public meaning" approach, but he is now considered the critical figure in moving away from Borkian "original intent" originalism and toward what is often referred to as "new originalism"—which seeks to extract an objective meaning from the constitutional language itself, as opposed to Bork's approach of focusing on the framers' intent as the source of constitutional meaning. There has been abundant literature on new originalism, and there has been some scholarship on the role of originalism in the development of American conservatism (Kersch 2011; Post and Siegel 2006). But overlooked in all of this scholarship is how Scalia's "public meaning" originalism, and its eventual role in birthing new originalism, can be understood in the context of broader shifts within the conservative movement.

Scalia's creation of "public meaning" originalism fits with the rise of neo-conservatism in two important and related ways. One, Scalia's "public meaning" originalism and neoconservatism are compatible with progressive values in a way that the more rigid "original intent" originalism and traditionalist conservatism are not. Two, Scalia's "public meaning" originalism facilitated the redemptive and mythic project at the core of the neoconservative movement and its notion of American exceptionalism. Below, we will explore each of these points in turn.

As for the first similarity between Scalia's originalism and neoconservatism, it is important to recall that neoconservatives generally accepted the egalitarian premises of Great Society programs but criticized these programs on technical grounds for having "unintended bad consequences"—neoconservatives therefore sought to make these programs operate more efficiently through government partnerships with the private market. Likewise, in the realm of law, neoconservatives, unlike traditionalist conservatives, criticized the Warren Court not because of its substantive outcomes (which neoconservatives generally favored) but because of the allegedly poor legal reasoning the Warren Court used to justify those outcomes (Kersch 2009).

Scalia's creation of "public meaning" originalism facilitated a similar shift within legal conservatism. Because "public meaning" is a more capacious concept than "original intent," Scalia's originalism, and the new originalism movement that it eventually created, functioned just like neoconservatism in permitting the use of formally conservative means (i.e., the language of originalism) to justify substantively liberal ends. For example, employing Scalia's "public meaning" originalism, legal conservatives have argued that originalism requires such progressive policies as open borders (Somin 2013), desegregation (McConnell 1995), same-sex marriage (Calabresi and Begley 2016), and bodily autonomy (Barnett 2003).

As a result of the adaptability of "public meaning" originalism to progressive causes, the left-right divide in law has become largely about form and not substance. This is illustrated in how the leading LCM organization, the Federalist Society, refuses to take any policy stances, and originalism has become the LCM's unifying principle (Hollis-Brusky 2016, 20). This in sharp contrast with how countervailing liberal organizations, such as the ACLU or ACS, operate in pursuit of explicitly liberal goals.

The second important way in which Scalia's "public meaning" originalism fits with the rise of neoconservatism within the broader conservative move-ment has to do with the redemptive promise of "public meaning" originalism and its power in facilitating the "American exceptionalism" agenda at the core of neoconservatism. As discussed above, a significant feature of the neoconservative movement was the effort to create a unifying American religion cleansed of social hierarchy, ethnic identity, and atavistic faith—and refurbished with an unflinchingly optimistic, patriotic, and egalitarian spirit.

Before the rise of originalism, Abraham Lincoln, the great unifier, had played this role for many neoconservative thinkers, with the leading example being Harry Jaffa (Jaffa 2004). But after Scalia's "public meaning" original-ism eliminated the theory's anchor to the concrete and granular intentions of particular historical figures, originalism itself could become the unifying force behind the American identity and mythic narrative. The breadth of Sca-lia's "public meaning" originalism held the promise of creating an American creed sufficiently general and ethereal that it was untethered to a particular ethos, region, or epoch.

Freed from this anchor to the particularity of the past, Scalia's "public mean-ing" originalism paved the way for the Constitution to be worshipped as a uni-fying and egalitarian document. Indeed, employing Scalia's "public meaning" originalism, legal conservatives have developed the Janus-like flexibility of defending the Constitution as fundamental to the American tradition and charg-ing liberals with being unconstrained activists, while at the same time adapting to each new liberal change that transforms that tradition (Merriam 2018).

Understanding "public meaning" originalism in this way reveals a profound lesson about both originalism and Scalia's legacy. Although some scholars have observed how originalism has serviced the conservative agenda, (Post and Siegel 2006), and some have noted Scalia's role in this process (Teles 2008), scholars have neglected how the shift in originalism theory initiated by Scalia operated, in accord with the rise of neoconservatism, to make legal conserva-tism less concrete and tradition-oriented, and more abstract and adaptable.

In the remaining pages, we will explore how Scalia used the flexibility in his "public meaning" originalism to justify distinctly neoconservative positions on federalism, executive power, affirmative action, and church-state relations.

FEDERALISM

Some Scalia critics, on both the left and right, have charged Scalia with be-ing inconsistent in his federalism jurisprudence, largely due to his decision in *Gonzales v. Raich* (2005), where he concurred with the liberal justices in upholding the federal government's authority to apply federal drug laws to the intra-state use and manufacture of medical marijuana. Some critics have likewise charged Scalia with being inconsistent in his commitment to federalism due to his expansive interpretations of the Dormant Commerce Clause, Taxing and Spending Clause, and Supremacy Clause.

These portrayals of Scalia's federalism jurisprudence are not entirely accurate. When Scalia's extra-judicial writings on federalism are analyzed against his thirty-year career on the Supreme Court, it becomes evident that Scalia was both consistent *and* non-originalist in this important area of law. Indeed, Scalia consistently took the view that federal power is not to be opposed but rather should be marshalled for good (which for Scalia means conservative) purposes. For example, unlike Justice Thomas, who has suggested that the "substantial effects" prong of the Court's Commerce Clause analysis is illegitimate, thereby drawing into question such important civil rights victories as *Heart of Atlanta Motel Inc. v. United States* (1964) and *Katzenbach v. McClung* (1964), Justice Scalia never went this far in challenging the Court's Commerce Clause jurisprudence. To the contrary, although Justice Scalia at times questioned the wisdom of *Wickard v. Filburn* (1942), Scalia (unlike Thomas) never provided a serious attack against the thrust of the Supreme Court's expansion of federal authority during the New Deal and civil rights movement.

Justice Scalia's position on federalism was perhaps most evident in his pre-judicial writing. Consider, for example, how Scalia argued repeatedly in his articles for the neoconservative AEI publication, *Regulation*, that big business should favor rather than oppose an expansive federal power because such a power could subsume discordant state regulation and thereby reduce transaction costs (Staab 2006, 15). Scalia's most significant pre-judicial writing on federalism arose in the first Federalist Society conference, in 1982, when he presented *The Two Faces of Federalism*, which chastised traditional conservatives for thinking of federalism as a timeless legal philosophy, rather than as a time-bound legal *strategy*. Pointing to Hamilton's nationalist view of federal power, but without even mentioning Jefferson's or Madison's important writings on the subject, Scalia accepted in that article the neoconservative principles supporting the expansion of federal authority during the New Deal and civil rights movement. Based on these principles, Scalia concluded that the "anti-federalist philosophy on the part of conservatives seems simply wrong" and Scalia urged conservatives "as Hamilton would have urged [them]—to keep in mind that the federal government is not bad but good" (Scalia 1982).

Scalia therefore prescribed conservative lawyers to think about federalism strategically by seeking federalism limitations when liberals were in power, but then embracing a Hamiltonian view of federal authority when conservatives were in power. During the conference, Scalia even suggested that the Reagan administration should consider such intrusive federal intervention as a regulation of intra-state abortion services, a ban on state economic regulation, and a restriction prohibiting state courts from developing new tort theories (Staab 2006, 240).

Understood against the background of his pre-judicial scholarship, Scalia's federalism jurisprudence on the Supreme Court is quite coherent. Indeed, given the views expressed in his 1982 article, Scalia's departure from the conservative position in *Gonzales v. Raich* (2005) should not come as a surprise. Nor should it come as a surprise that Scalia voted for preemption at a significantly higher rate (63 percent) than any other justice on the Rehnquist Court (Staab 2006, 243). Although Scalia's 67 percent pro-preemption rate was only fourth on the Roberts Court (Merriam 2017, 1007), Scalia was tied for first, with a pro-preemption rate of 89 percent, in cases involving tort reform on that business-friendly Court (1009).

It is also worth mentioning that even when Scalia did consider historical materials in his federalism jurisprudence, it was almost always a "tilted" originalism, based principally on constitutional nationalists like Alexander Hamilton, Chief Justice John Marshall, and Justice Joseph Story, as well as the more nationalist elements of Madison's mixed federalism legacy. Scalia consistently dismissed, often times without even as much as a reference, constitutional localists like Thomas Jefferson, John Randolph, John Taylor, St. George Tucker, and Abel Upshur.

Importantly, this represented a reversal of the early *National Review* conservative movement, which, particularly in the writings of traditionalists like Russell Kirk and Richard Weaver, had looked to these latter thinkers as true conservatives and had condemned nationalists like Hamilton and Marshall as centralizing liberals (Nash 1976, 303). As discussed above in categorizing the three differences between traditional conservatism and neoconservatism, neoconservatives held a radically more expansive view of federal power, and therefore favored the more mercantile, consolidationist, Northern legacy of Hamilton and Lincoln, over the more agrarian, disaggregated, Southern legacy of Jefferson and Randolph. The conservative movement did not embrace this Hamiltonian approach to federalism until the 1980s, when neoconservative views on federal authority became the dominant view within American conservatism. Scalia was thus marching perfectly in line with the neoconservatives in advocating a broader view of federal power in the late 1970s and early 1980s.

In sum, while scholars may be right as applied to some areas of law like criminal procedure in portraying Scalia's deviations from the Court's conservative justices as illustrations of his rule-of-law commitment to originalism

(Dorsen 2017), this is certainly not right as applied to his federalism jurisprudence. Indeed, there is nothing in originalist theory or practice that warrants Scalia's favoring, for example, Hamilton's and Story's over Tucker's and Upshur's radically different understandings of federal power. This strongly suggests that it was not Scalia's originalism, but his neoconservative and decidedly anti-traditionalist view of federal power, that led him to reach his centralist understandings of the Commerce Clause, Taxing and Spending Clause, and Supremacy Clause.

EXECUTIVE POWER

A similar pattern of following neoconservatism over originalism is evident in Scalia's executive-power jurisprudence, as well as in his pre-judicial writings on administrative law, which defended a broad view of executive power as applied to varied regulatory contexts. I will not delve into this area of law as much as I do in the other sections in this part of the chapter, because Scalia's executive-power views have already been ably explored in James Staab's excellent profile of Justice Scalia as a Hamiltonian. In that book, Staab argues that "in the post-New [D]eal era (and arguably in the history of the Supreme Court), no one on the nation's highest court has surpassed Scalia as a consistent defender of a Hamiltonian conception of the presidency" (Staab 2006, 91). The only justices whom Staab considers to be close in espousing such a muscular view of the presidency are Chief Justices John Marshall, William Howard Taft, and Warren Burger (129n13).

In Staab's view, Scalia's Hamiltonian vision of the presidency is apparent in Scalia's decisions holding that the president has the unchecked authority: (1) to act as the "sole organ" in foreign affairs, (2) to make treaties and executive agreements, (3) to make military decisions as "commander in chief," (4) to withhold national-security information from the public, and (5) to be immune from liability (95). Scalia's aggressive view of executive power was most prominently on display in the Guantanamo Bay decisions, such as *Hamdan v. Rumsfeld* (2006) and *Boumediene v. Bush* (2008), where Scalia provocatively claimed that judicial limitations on executive discretion "*will almost certainly cause more Americans to be killed.*" To this list, Staab also could have included Scalia's contribution to, and consistent defense of, the *Chevron* doctrine, which requires courts to defer to an administrative agency's reasonable interpretations of its administrative power, a doctrine that has vastly expanded the administrative state (Scalia 1989).

Staab's analysis overlooks, however, that traditional conservatives have long condemned such aggressive exertions of executive power, out of a concern that it would lead to an expansive and unconstrained use of federal authority, particularly in leading to a loss of national sovereignty to foreign entanglements (Nash 1976/1996/2006). Whereas in the domestic sphere one of the sharpest conflicts between neoconservatives and traditional conservatives has been over the scope of federal power in local affairs, in foreign relations the sharpest conflict has in local affairs been over executive power and interventionism. As mentioned above, neoconservatives have departed sharply from the traditional conservative suspicion of foreign adventurism. And as neoconservatives have gained more power within the conservative movement, the Cold War exception to conservative isolationism has become the rule, transforming the GOP into a more interventionist and globally oriented party.

Although this robust view of executive power may be defensible on policy or even legal grounds, it certainly is not necessitated by originalism, given the divergent views of executive authority articulated during the Philadelphia Convention, ratification debates, and first few presidential administrations (Staab 2006, xxx). Scalia's decision to adopt the Hamiltonian position on executive power was a *choice*, and it was a choice, moreover, that marked a substantial transition within the conservative movement—highlighting the critical role Scalia played as an LCM intellectual entrepreneur in articulating and transforming the agenda and identity of legal conservatism.

AFFIRMATIVE ACTION

The one domestic policy issue most responsible for pushing neoconservatives to the right was the emergence of identity politics within the New Left, particularly in the form of affirmative action. Although neoconservatives and traditional conservatives both opposed affirmative action, they did so for radically different reasons. Traditionalists opposed affirmative action as part of their general objection to federal intervention in local and private social relations. Because traditionalists favored the organic communal bonds that they believed to be essential to social cohesion and moral virtue, they opposed all federal legislation that interfered with the freedom of association, including such landmark civil rights achievements as the Civil Rights Act of 1964 and the Fair Housing Act of 1968.

Neoconservatives, by contrast, did not object to, but rather praised, these legislative achievements. They nevertheless opposed affirmative action as a betrayal of the civil rights movement's promise of color-blind justice. This line of argumentation appeared most prominently in *Commentary* (the leading neoconservative publication of the 1970s), where writers like Norman Podheretz argued persistently and consistently that affirmative action would result in the same quota system that gentiles had used to deprive so many Jews of elite positions in the first half of the twentieth century.

Scalia adopted a similar argument against affirmative action in his 1979 law review article, *Disease as a Cure*, published just a year after the Court's first major decision on the subject, in *Regents of University of California v. Bakke* (1978). In highly sardonic and acerbic language, Scalia unapologetically attacked Justice Powell's controlling concurrence in *Bakke*, which had invalidated the UC-Davis affirmative action program as an impermissible quota but also pronounced in *dictum* that more individualized and holistic preferences should be upheld as constitutional. Scalia's blunt hostility toward identity politics would later become a central part of his Supreme Court jurisprudence, but what distinguished this article from how Justice Scalia would later attack affirmative action is that the article did not even so much as mention the applicable Fourteenth Amendment text, history, and precedent.

Instead of consulting conventional legal sources, then-Professor Scalia based his argument against affirmative action almost entirely on policy reasoning. Indeed, Scalia concluded that he was "opposed to racial affirmative action for reasons of both principle and practicality." And his primary reason of principle was *not* that color-blindness is a constitutional or even a moral virtue, but rather that affirmative action punishes the *wrong* whites. That is, Scalia objected to affirmative action, because instead of restoring justice to African Americans by penalizing "the Powells, the Whites, the Stewarts, the Burgers" (i.e., the WASPs who have profited from African American subjugation), affirmative action had the deleterious effect of punishing *all* whites. Most problematically for Scalia, affirmative action penalized the "many white ethnic groups that came to this country in great numbers relatively late in its history—Italians, Jews, Irish, Poles—who not only took no part in, and derived no profit from, the major historic suppression of the currently acknowledged minority groups, but were, in fact, themselves the object of discrimination by the dominant Anglo Saxon majority" (Scalia 1979, 152).

Just as Podhortez did in the pages of *Commentary*, Scalia explicitly framed his argument against affirmative action in terms of his own ethnic background—particularly how, as an Italian-American, Scalia was entirely innocent of any wrongdoing in causing America's racial inequalities. Echoing the neoconservative civil rights position, Scalia proclaimed that in such matters he was more on the side of African Americans than on the side of the WASPs, "because [African Americans] have (many of them) special needs, and they are (all of them) my countrymen and (as I believe) my brothers." Scalia simply objected to "ethnic whites" bearing the burden of redressing these "special needs," a burden that he argued should fall squarely on "the Wisdoms and the Powells and the Whites" (Scalia 1979, 152).

In highly evocative language, Scalia compared this division between "ethnic whites" and WASPs to a scene from the *Lone Ranger* in which the white Texan encounters danger with a group of bellicose Native Americans. Scalia explained how the Lone Ranger (the white Texan) looked to Tonto (his "faithful Indian companion") and asked "what should we do?" As Scalia recounted, Tonto's response was, "[W]hat [sic] you mean, 'we,' white man?" (Scalia 1979, 151). Scalia's point, of course, was that "ethnic whites" were in the position of Tonto and African Americans were wrongly grouping these innocent ethnic whites in with the actual WASP wrongdoers. This support for affirmative action, but only as applied to the responsible WASPs, was a prominent theme in neoconservative arguments at the time.

After Scalia's conversion to originalism in 1986, his arguments against affirmative action morphed into the claim that the practice is categorically barred by the original meaning of the Fourteenth Amendment, which Scalia claimed required absolute color-blindness, a guarantee that he grounded in Justice Harlan's famous *Plessy* dissent and in the Declaration of Independence. As he wrote in *City of Richmond v. J.A. Croson Co.* (1989), "[t]he relevant proposition is not that it was blacks, or Jews, or Irish who were discriminated against, but that it was individual men and women, 'created equal,' who were discriminated against." This use of the Declaration as a source of Fourteenth Amendment meaning is quite curious, especially because Scalia often argued, *contra* political theorists like Harry Jaffa, that the Declaration lacks enforceable legal meaning (Shain 2007).

But an even more bewildering component of Scalia's race jurisprudence is that he embraced decisions like *Brown v. Board of Education* (1954) and *Loving v. Virginia* (1967) and yet was staunchly against affirmative action. This is puzzling as an originalist matter because the historical evidence strongley suggests that the Fourteenth Amendment ratifiers supported benefits programs designed exclusively for African Americans, such as The Freedmen's Bureau (1865) but they were vociferously and explicitly against integration and interracial marriage (Balkin 2005). In other words, originalism would seem to require exactly the opposite of Scalia's positions on these matters.

Just as in the federalism and executive-power contexts, we see in Justice Scalia's race jurisprudence that his views did not fit the commands of originalism as much as the neoconservative agenda on civil rights and affirmative action. Moreover, just as in the federalism and executive-power contexts, his legal views on affirmative action had been formed well before he was on the bench and well before he had developed any originalist commitments. Once on the Supreme Court, he used the flexibility of his "public meaning" originalism to express those very same policy views in more historically grounded terms.

Our last topic of discussion, church-state law, will reveal the same relationship in Justice Scalia's First Amendment jurisprudence.

CHURCH-STATE LAW

One of Justice Scalia's most persistent criticisms of legal liberalism was its insistence on a wall of separation between church and state. Many scholars have pointed to Scalia's vituperative writing on church-state law as evidence that Scalia's originalism, or perhaps his Catholic traditionalism, animated his jurisprudence. While a strong case could be made for either claim, a close examination of his church-state jurisprudence reveals that a more compelling account is the one developed in this chapter—that Scalia was an LCM intellectual entrepreneur who used his capacious "public meaning" originalism to redefine conservatism and advance a distinctly neoconservative agenda.

Just as in the subjects discussed above, Scalia had expressed his views on church-state law well before he was appointed to the federal bench. In 1978, when Scalia was at AEI, he provided congressional testimony supporting the constitutionality of a proposed federal college tuition tax credit. Scalia testified that, under governing Supreme Court precedent, the credit could include religious colleges as a part of a generally available tax benefit. And even though it was not necessary to his testimony, Scalia took the opportunity to complain about "the utter confusion of Supreme Court pronouncements in the church-state area" (Scalia 1978). A few years later, when Scalia was a law professor at Chicago, he turned his testimony into an article on church-state law, which appeared as a chapter in a book on private education (Gaffney 1981).

Once on the Court, Scalia made church-state doctrine a central part of his assault on legal liberalism, with his favorite target being the tripartite Establishment Clause test established in *Lemon v. Kurtzman* (1971). Scalia complained about the *Lemon* test principally for two reasons. One, the three prongs were highly manipulable, leading to inconsistent adjudication, which was anathema to Scalia's commitment to consistency as forming the cornerstone of the rule of law. Two, the *Lemon* test was based on the notion that there is a wall of separation between church and state, a concept that is often traced to Thomas Jefferson's views on church-state relations, which were highly unrepresentative of how many of the framers viewed the First Amendment. Indeed, Justice Scalia was quick to note that many of the founding-era leaders, such as Presidents Washington and Adams, believed that religion plays a vital and salutary role in the public sphere.

These are certainly valid criticisms, but Scalia's own church-state jurisprudence, on both the Establishment Clause and Free Exercise Clause, was arguably just as inconsistent with regard to the original meaning of those provisions. Consider, for example, how many historians have found that the Establishment Clause was originally understood as a federalism directive, barring the federal government from interfering with state positions on church-state relations, which varied at the founding from Massachusetts's relatively strong establishment regime to Rhode Island's disestablishment regime (a point explicitly observed in the First Amendment drafting). For this reason, many scholars have claimed that, as an originalist matter, it does not make sense to incorporate the Establishment Clause through the Fourteenth Amendment to apply to the states, a position that Justice Thomas has adopted in several opinions. Justice Scalia, by contrast, has thought of the Establishment Clause as creating a limited individual right to be free from denominational discrimination when the government funds religion, and to be free from sectarian government endorsements of religion outside of the broad monotheistic parameters of the Abrahamic faiths when the government communicates religious messages.

Just as in the subjects discussed above, we can see in Justice Scalia's Establishment Clause jurisprudence more neoconservatism than originalism. A good illustration of this arose in *Lee v. Weisman* (1992), in which the Court held, 5–4, that a public school violated the Establishment Clause by having a Rabbi solemnize a graduation ceremony with a short "prayer within the embrace of what is known as the Judeo-Christian tradition." In dissent, Justice Scalia argued that this short Judeo-Christian prayer was permissible because it was non-denominational and the attendees were not forced to participate in the benediction.

Scholars have analyzed this doctrinal part of Scalia's opinion at length, but in his concluding paragraph, Scalia made a policy argument that scholars have largely ignored. Here, Scalia argued that, in a religiously and ethnically diverse nation such as ours, prayer is useful to creating "an affection[] for one another." For example, Scalia noted, "[t]he Baptist or Catholic who heard and joined in the simple and inspiring prayers of Rabbi Gutterman on this official and patriotic occasion was inoculated from religious bigotry and prejudice in a manner that cannot be replicated." Therefore, Scalia concluded, it is "as senseless in policy as it is unsupported in law . . . [t]o deprive our society of that important unifying mechanism."

In considering Scalia's policy reasoning in *Lee* about how Judeo-Christian public displays should be permissible because they serve an "important unifying mechanism" and reduce "bigotry and prejudice," it is worth remembering that the very notion of a "Judeo-Christian" tradition was alien to the Founders. In fact, the term was not used in this sense until the 1940s, as part of American war propaganda to distinguish the United States from the ethnocentric fascism of Germany and the atheistic communism of the Soviet Union. The term was not popularized until 1952, when a month before his inauguration President Eisenhower identified America as being unified by "the Judeo-Christian" religion whose central precept is the Declaration's proposition that "all men [are] created equal." And the term did not appear in a U.S. Supreme Court opinion until *U.S. v. Seeger* (1965).

Scalia's policy reasoning in *Lee* does not fit comfortably with founding-era views on church-state relations but it does fit with the neoconservative agenda with regards to America's "exceptionalism" as the "first universal nation."

Consider one more example of Justice Scalia's neoconservative use of the Establishment Clause, how almost twenty-five years after the *Lee* decision, Justice Scalia expanded his view of the "Judeo-Christian tradition" to include Islam in two Ten Commandments cases decided the same day—*Van Orden v. Perry* (2005) (upholding a Ten Commandments monument displayed on the Texas State Capitol grounds) and *McCreary County v. ACLU of Kentucky* (2005) (invalidating framed copies of the Ten Commandments displayed in a Kentucky courthouse).

Dissenting in the *McCreary* case, Justice Scalia argued that the Kentucky display should be permissible, just like the monument in *Van Orden*, because both displays were consistent with the nation's tradition of endorsing monotheistic messages that are "scrupulously nondenominational." Moreover, Scalia wrote, the Ten Commandments are consistent with "[t]he three most popular religions in the United States, Christianity, Judaism, and Islam—which combined account for 97.7 percent of all believers." As scholars have noted, that Scalia's revision of the American tradition to include Islam complimented President Bush's was particularly striking because it coincided with the Bush II Administration's War on Terror effort to depict Islam as part and parcel to the American "Judeo-Christian" heritage—as one of the three religions "that traces its origins back to God's call on Abraham" (Bush 2002, 2052).

In Justice Stevens's *Van Orden* dissenting opinion, Justice Stevens turned Scalia's own originalism into a weapon, marshalling it against Scalia's reasoning in *McCreary*. Pointing to two of Scalia's heroes—John Marshall and Joseph Story—Justice Stevens noted the irony of Scalia's sudden disinterest in their constitutional understandings. As Stevens wrote, the "inclusion of Jews and Muslims inside the category of constitutionally favored religions surely would have shocked Chief Justice Marshall and Justice Story."

Stevens emphasized how Justice Story had written at length in his *Commentaries* (a work that, as alluded to above, greatly influenced Scalia's federalism jurisprudence) about the importance of Christianity to the American heritage. Moreover, Stevens explained, Story wrote in the *Commentaries* that the entire purpose of the Establishment Clause was "to exclude all rivalry among Christian sects, and to prevent any national ecclesiastical establishment," so as to protect America's Christian identity. For this reason, Stevens noted, "for nearly a century after the Founding, many accepted the idea that America was not just a *religious* nation, but 'a Christian nation,'" as the Supreme Court explicitly asserted in *Church of Holy Trinity* v. *United States* (1892). Put simply, Stevens concluded, "[t]he original understanding of the type of 'religion' that qualified for constitutional protection under the Establishment Clause likely did not include those followers of Judaism and Islam."

Stevens also could have noted the poor sociology underlying Scalia's argument. Scalia's claim that there is a Christian-Jewish-Islamic monotheistic tradition in the United States, on the ground that these religions currently combine for "97.7 percent of all believers," is certainly a strange basis for a long-held tradition, given that Muslims and Jews had a marginal presence in the United States until well into the twentieth century. And even if current demographic percentages mattered in identifying a constitutional tradition (which is itself a highly dubious claim), it surely would have been more compelling for Scalia to say there is *only* a Christian tradition in the United States, given that, even today, almost all of that 97.7 percent are Christian, with Jews and Muslims currently combining for less than 3 percent of the overall population (Pew Research Center 2014).

As Stevens powerfully argued, Scalia's originalism was simply twenty-first-century political conservatism projected back on to the Establishment Clause. Indeed, just as the term "Judeo-Christian" initially served as an American war measure in the 1940s, and Justice Scalia likewise invoked this tradition in *Lee* as a unifying device during the culture wars of the 1990s, Scalia's expansion of this heritage to include Islam in his 2005 *McCreary* dissent can be understood as working in concert with the Bush II democratization efforts in the Middle East. In other words, Scalia's *McCreary* construction of the American Christian-Jewish-Islamic monotheistic tradition makes most sense, not by looking to the founding era, but by following the Bush II foreign policy agenda.

None of this is to say that Scalia was necessarily wrong that a nation needs to be unified by a religion. And perhaps Scalia and the neoconservatives were right that a broad and patriotic monotheism can provide this function. But just as is the case with his federalism, executive power, and race-relations jurisprudence, Scalia's position on church-state law seems to have little to do with the original meaning of the Constitution, and much more to do with the current meaning of conservatism.

CONCLUSION

In 1986, when news of Scalia's nomination first circulated among the White House staff, Pat Buchanan reportedly had the most enthusiastic reaction, screaming "Yes!" and "pump[ing] his fists in the air" (Biskupic 2009/2010, 109). This may have been because Buchanan was one of Scalia's most ardent advocates within the Reagan White House, as part of Buchanan's hope to build a more populist, hard-nosed, and combative right wing on the Court (107).

There were certainly ways in which Buchanan got the populist pugilist he wanted. Scalia's dissenting opinions were unlike anything the Court had ever seen, completely unmatched in their vituperative and incisive wit. And at times Scalia took on a populist tone in attacking the liberal elite establishment, just as Buchanan had hoped, most passionately in abortion and gay-rights cases. But while Scalia astutely observed the cultural clash emerging between liberal elites and religious conservatives, he did not foresee the extent to which this might soon transmogrify into a class, regional, and even ethnic conflict. Ironically, the Republican Party that emerged *after* Scalia's death on February 13, 2016, looks much more like the movement that Buchanan sought to create through the Scalia appointment thirty years earlier.

In *Obergefell v. Hodges* (2015), one of Scalia's last (and most bitter) opinions, Scalia noted the Court's regional, class, and religious disproportionality. "Four of the nine are natives of New York City," he charged. But Scalia was one of those four, and his brand of conservatism reflected his New York identity. To be sure, Scalia's affirmative action opinions may not always have celebrated diversity, and it may be that at one point the young Scalia was more of a traditionalist who was hostile toward the civil rights movement and its transformation of American life. But in many ways Scalia was a true believer in the American experiment to make one out of many, a particularly important part of his legacy as many, on both the left and right alike, seem to be losing their faith in this uniquely American experiment. This diversity, Scalia said in a 1987 speech to B'Nai B'Rith, is what makes America "a symbol of light and of hope for the world," and it is what made his New York experience of growing up in "a melting pot" so "wonderful" (Scalia 2017, 25). New York was in Scalia's core, and when conservatism ramified along regional and cultural lines, Scalia's conservatism turned out to be more Hamiltonian than

Jeffersonian, more living constitutionalist than originalist, more Acela Express than Middle America.

This chapter thereby affirms to some extent Stephen Feldman's treatment of Scalia as a neoconservative (Feldman 2012), an account that certainly provides a fuller and more accurate picture of Scalia than the conventional account of Scalia as a traditionalist. But because Feldman treats neoconservatism as an unqualifiedly right-wing movement, and overlooks the extent to which neoconservatism made American conservatism more liberal on social and cultural issues, Feldman's work misses a large part of Scalia's legacy. Just as this should complicate how we think about Justice Scalia as "[t] he *dean of the modern conservative legal movement*" (O'Donnell 2010), it should also complicate how we think about legal conservatism and the conservative movement in general.

Three areas for further study, in particular, follow from this chapter. One, the analysis in this chapter provides the basis for further exploration of the relationship between conservatism and originalism. Liberal scholars have mounted powerful arguments against originalism on the ground that it is not only conceptually flawed, but also inconsistently practiced, by both scholars and judges alike (Segall 2015). Scholars of the LCM have similarly noted the "redemptive" rather than "restorative" ways in which conservatives have sought to use the Declaration of Independence as a promissory note on the shortcomings of prior generations (Kersch 2011a, 272). The analysis in this chapter suggests a related but heretofore unexplored feature of originalism—that it has been used as a tool not only for creating the LCM "political epistemic network" but also for purging elements from that network that no longer have a desirable place in light of coalitional and ideological shifts within the larger conservative movement. The flexibility inhering in Scalia's "public meaning" originalism can be understood as more "redemptive" than "restorative," functioning to construct, tailor, and police the changing boundaries of conservatism.

Two, this chapter helps us understand the LCM as a highly dynamic and temporally contingent movement, a phenomenon that should be explored in future LCM studies. By tracing the genealogy of some of the LCM's leading intellectual and network entrepreneurs, this chapter has highlighted how much change within the LCM arose from the contingencies of 1970s and 1980s electoral politics, conservative movement coalitional realignments, and individual career ambitions and opportunities. Future work on Scalia and the LCM would benefit from being more attentive to how LCM intellectual and network entrepreneurs have operated in accord with changing currents in the conservative movement and Republican Party.

Three, the dynamism revealed in this chapter has profound implications for scholarship depicting the LCM as a right-wing counterrevolution that has taken the law back from the left (Hollis-Brusky 2016; Chemerinsky 2010). A closer examination of Scalia's neoconservative contributions to the LCM, and his neoconservative jurisprudence on the Court, suggests that the conservative counterrevolution supposedly mounted under the LCM was not much of a revolution after all—at least not one against the liberal legal establishment.

REFERENCES

Balkin, Jack. 2005. "Bad Originalism." *Balkinization*. https://balkin.blogspot.com/2005/05/bad-originalism.html

Barnett, Randy E. 2006. "Scalia's Infidelity: A Critique of Faint-Hearted Originalism." *University of Cincinnati Law Review* 75(7): 7–24.

———. 2002–2003. "Justice Kennedy's Libertarian Revolution: *Lawrence v. Texas.*" *Cato Supreme Court Review*: 21–41. https://scholarship.law.georgetown.edu/facpub/838.

Biskupic, Joan. 2009/2010. *American Original: The Life and Constitution of Supreme Court Justice Antonin Scalia.* Repr. New York: Sarah Crichton Books.

Bogus, Carl T. 2011. *Buckley: William F. Buckley Jr. and the Rise of American Conservatism*. New York: Bloomsbury Press.

Bolick, Clint. 1988. *Changing Course: Civil Rights at the Crossroads.* Piscataway, NJ: Transaction Publishers.

Bonitsky, Jonathan. 2014. "The Brooklyn Burkeans." *National Affairs*. https://www.nationalaffairs.com/publications/detail/the-brooklyn-burkeans. Last visited: Feb. 25, 2018.

Brest, Paul. 1980. "The Misconceived Quest for the Original Understanding." *Boston University Law Review* 60: 204–38.

Brisbin Jr., Richard A. 1998. *Justice Antonin Scalia and the Conservative Revival.* Baltimore: The Johns Hopkins University Press.

Buchanan, Patrick J. 2017. *Nixon's White House Wars: The Battles That Made and Broke a President and Divided America Forever.* New York: Crown Publishing Group.

———. 2004/2005. *Where the Right Went Wrong.* Repr. New York: St. Martin's Griffin.

Buckley, William F. 1992/1993. *In Search of Anti-Semitism.* Repr. New York: Continuum International Publishing Group.

Bush, George W. 2002. Public Papers of the Presidents of the United States, George W. Bush, 2002, Bk. 1, January 1 to June 30, 2002. Washington, DC: U.S. Government Printing Office.

Bush, George W. 2002. Remarks at an Iftaar Dinner, November 7, 2002. In Public Papers of the Presidents of the United States, George W. Bush, 2002, Bk. 1, January 1 to June 30, 2002. Washington, DC: US Government Printing Office.

Calabresi, Steven G. and Hannah M. Begley. 2016. "Originalism and Same-Sex Marriage." *University of Miami Law Review* 70: 648–707.

Chemerinsky, Erwin. 2010. *The Conservative Assault on the Constitution*. New York: Simon & Schuster.

Cohen, Arthur A. 1969. "The Myth of the Judeo-Christian Tradition." *Commentary*, https://www.commentarymagazine.com/articles/the-myth-of-the-judeo-christian-tradition/.

Decker, Jefferson. 2016. The Other Rights Revolution: Conservative Lawyers and the Remaking of American Government. New York: Oxford University Press.

Dorsen, David M. 2017. *The Unexpected Scalia: A Conservative Justice's Liberal Opinions*. New York: Cambridge University Press.

Ehrman, John. 2006. "Neoconservatism." In *American Conservatism: An Encyclopedia*, ed. Bruce Frohnen, Jeremy Beer, and Jeffery O. Nelson, 610–14. Wilmington, DE: Intercollegiate Studies Institute.

Feldman, Stephen M. 2012. *Neoconservative Politics and the Supreme Court: Law, Power, and Democracy*. New York: New York University Press.

Friedman, Murray. 2007. *The Neoconservative Revolution: Jewish Intellectuals and the Shaping of Public Policy*. New York: Cambridge University Press.

Frum, David. 2003. "Unpatriotic Conservatives." *National Review*. https://www.nationalreview.com/2003/03/unpatriotic-conservatives-david-frum/.

Fukuyama, Francis. 1992/2006. *The End of History and the Last Man*. Repr. New York: Free Press.

Gallagher, Maggie. 2016. "Why I Wept for Justice Scalia." *National Review*. https://www.nationalreview.com/2016/02/antonin-scalia-funeral-ceremony/.

Goodman, Walter. 1981. "Irving Kristol: Patron Saint of the New Right." *New York Times*. http://www.nytimes.com/1981/12/06/magazine/irving-kristol-patron-saint-of-the-new-right.html?pagewanted=all.

Gordon, David. 2010. "Southern Cross." *The American Conservative*. https://www.theamericanconservative.com/articles/southern-cross/.

Gottfried, Paul E. 2012. *Leo Strauss and the Conservative Movement in America*. New York: Cambridge University Press.

———. 2007/2007. *Conservatism in America: Making Sense of the American Right*. Repr. New York: Palgrave Macmillan.

———. 1988/1993. *The Conservative Movement: Social Movements Past and Present*. Revised ed. Repr. New York: Twayne Publishers.

Hollis-Brusky, Amanda. 2016. *Ideas with Consequences: The Federalist Society and the Conservative Counterrevolution*. New York: Oxford University Press.

Horowitz, Michael. 1981. "In Defense of Public Interest Law." In *Institute for Education Affairs, Perspectives on Public Interest Law*. Foundation Officers Forum Occasional Papers 2: 7–8.

Jaffa, Harry V. 2004. *A New Birth of Freedom: Abraham Lincoln and the Coming of the Civil War*. Lanham, MD: Rowman & Littlefield.

Kersch, Ken I. 2011a. "Beyond Originalism: Conservative Declarationism and Constitutional Redemption." *Maryland Law Review* 71: 229–82.

———. 2011b. "Ecumenicalism through Constitutionalism: The Discursive Development of Constitutional Conservatism in National Review, 1955–1980." *Studies in American Political Development* 25(1): 86–116.

——. 2009. "Neoconservatism and the Courts: The Public Interest, 1965–1980." In *Ourselves and Our Posterity: Essays in Constitutional Originalism.* ed. Bradley C. S. Watson, 247–96. Lanham, MD: Rowman & Littlefield.

Kilpatrick, James J. 1963. "Civil Rights and Legal Wrongs," *National Review.* 24 September.

Kilpatrick, James J. Aug. 12, 1969. "A Very Different Constitution." *National Review.*

Klein, Joe. 2017. "Patrick Buchanan Reveals Himself to Be the First Trumpist." *New York Times.* https://www.nytimes.com/2017/05/08/books/review/nixons-white-house-wars-patrick-j-buchanan.html?mtrref=www.google.com&mtrref=www.nytimes.com. Last visited: Feb. 25, 2018.

Klingenstein, Susanne. 2003. "'It's Splendid When the Town Whore Gets Religion and Joins the Church': The Rise of the Jewish Neoconservatives as Observed by the Paleoconservatives in the 1980s." *Shofar* 21(3): 83–89.

Kristol, Irving. 2003. "The Neoconservative Persuasion." *The Weekly Standard.* http://www.weeklystandard.com/the-neoconservative-persuasion/article/4246.

——. 1983. *Reflections of a Neoconservative: Looking Back, Looking Ahead.* New York: Basic Books.

——. Sept. 14, 1972. "Why Jews Turn Conservative." *Wall Street Journal.*

Liptak, Adam. 2016. "Antonin Scalia, Justice on the Supreme Court, Dies at 79." *New York Times.* https://www.nytimes.com/2016/02/14/us/antonin-scalia-death.html?mtrref=www.google.com.

Liptak, Adam and Alicia Parlapiano. 2016. "How Clinton's or Trump's Nominees Could Affect the Balance of the Supreme Court." https://www.nytimes.com/interactive/2016/09/25/us/politics/how-clintons-or-trumps-nominees-could-affect-the-balance-of-the-supreme-court.html?mtrref=undefined. *New York Times.*

McConnell, Michael W. 1995. "Originalism and the Desegregation Decisions." *Virginia Law Review* 81: 947–1140.

Merriam, Jesse. 2018. "Countering the Counterrevolution Narrative." *Modern Age* 60(1): https://home.isi.org/countering-counterrevolution-narrative.

——. 2017. "Preemption as a Consistency Doctrine." *William & Mary Bill of Rights Journal* 25(3): 981–1045.

Meyer, Frank S. May 30, 1956. "The Revolt against Congress." *National Review.*

Molotsky, Irvin. 1986. "The Supreme Court: Man in the News: Judge with Tenacity and Charm: Antonin Scalia." *New York Times.* http://www.nytimes.com/1986/06/18/us/the-supreme-court-man-in-the-news-judge-with-tenacity-and-charm-antonin-scalia.html.

Murphy, Bruce Allen. 2014/2015. *Scalia: A Court of One.* Repr. New York: Simon & Schuster.

Nash, George H. 1976/1996/2006. T*he Conservative Intellectual Movement in America Since 1945.* Wilmington, DE: Intercollegiate Studies Institute.

National Review Editorial. Aug. 24, 1957. "Why the South Must Prevail." *National Review.*

O'Donnell, Michael. 2010. "Scalia v. The World: On Antonin Scalia." https://www.thenation.com/article/scalia-v-world-antonin-scalia/. *The Nation.* Last visited: Feb. 25, 2018.

O'Neill, Johnathan. 2005/2007. *Originalism in American Law and Politics: A Constitutional History* (The Johns Hopkins Series in Constitutional Thought). Repr. Baltimore: The Johns Hopkins University Press.

Pew Research Center. 2014. "U.S. Religious Landscape Study." http://www.pew forumorg/religious-landscape-study/. Last visited: Feb. 25, 2018.

Posner, Richard A. and Eric J. Segall. 2016. "Faux Originalism." *Green Bag* 200(2): 109–13.

Post, Robert and Reva Siegel. 2006. "Originalism as a Political Practice: The Right's Living Constitution." *Fordham Law Review* 75(2): 545–74.

Preston, Andrew. 2012. "A very young Judeo-Christian tradition." *Boston Globe*. https://www.bostonglobe.com/ideas/2012/06/30/very-young-judeo-christian-tradi tion/smZoWrkrSLeMZpLou1ZGNL/story.html.

Scalia, Antonin. 2017. *Scalia Speaks: Reflections on Law, Faith, and Life Well Lived*. Ed. Christopher J. Scalia, and Edward Whelan. New York: Crown Forum.

———. 1982. "The Two Faces of Federalism." *Harvard Journal of Law and Public Policy* 6: 19–22.

———. 1981. "On Making It Look Easy by Doing It Wrong: A Critical View of the Justice Department, in Private Schools and the Public Good: Policy Alternatives for the Eighties." Ed. Edward McGlynn Gaffney Jr. Notre Dame, TN: University of Notre Dame Press.

———. 1979. "The Disease as Cure: 'In Order to Get beyond Racism, We Must First Take Account of Race.'" *Washington University Law Quarterly* 1979(1): 147–57.

———. 1978. *Testimony on the Constitutionality of Tuition Tax Credits*. Washington, DC: American Enterprise Institute, Reprint Number 84, March 1978.

———. 1989. "Judicial Deference to Administrative Interpretations of Law." *Duke Law Journal* (3): 511–21.

Schultz, David A. and Christopher E. Smith. 1996. *The Jurisprudential Vision of Justice Antonin Scalia* (Studies in American Constitutionalism). Lanham, MD: Rowman & Littlefield.

Segall, Eric J. 2015. "Will the Real Justice Scalia Please Stand Up?" *Wake Forest Law Review* (5): 101–8. Shain, Barry. 2007. "Harry Jaffa and the Demise of the Old Republic." *Modern Age* 49(4): 476–89.

Shapiro, Edward S. 2006. "Commentary." In *American Conservatism: An Encyclopedia*, ed. Bruce Frohnen, Jeremy Beer, and Jeffery O. Nelson, 171–2. Wilmington, DE: Intercollegiate Studies Institute.

Somin, Ilya. 2013. "Immigration and the US Constitution." *Open Borders*. https://openborders.info/blog/immigration-and-the-us-constitution/.

Staab, James B. 2006. *The Political Thought of Justice Antonin Scalia: A Hamiltonian on the Supreme Court*. Lanham, MD: Rowman & Littlefield.

Stahl, Jason. 2016. *Right Moves: The Conservative Think Tank in American Political Culture since 1945*. Chapel Hill: The University of North Carolina Press.

Tanenhaus, Sam. 2014. "Can the G.O.P. Be a Party of Ideas?" *New York Times*. https://www.nytimes.com/2014/07/06/magazine/can-the-gop-be-a-party-of-ideas .html?mtrref=www.google.com&mtrref=www.nytimes.com&gwh=63A2BB4BD3 274CBD5817641B401518E4&gwt=pay.

Teles, Steven. 2008. *The Rise of the Conservative Legal Movement*. Princeton, NJ: Princeton University Press.

Vaïsse, Justin. 2011. *Neoconservatism: The Biography of a Movement*. Cambridge: Harvard University Press.

Wattenberg, Ben J. 1990. *The First Universal Nation*. New York: Free Press.

———. Dec. 13, 1990. C-SPAN interview. https://www.c-span.org/video/?15600-1/the-universal-nation.

Weaver, Richard. July 13, 1957. "Books in Review: Integration Is Communization." *National Review*.

West, Thomas G. 2017. *The Political Theory of the American Founding: Natural Rights, Public Policy, and the Moral Conditions of Freedom*. New York: Cambridge University Press.

Wiliamson, Kevin D. 2012. "The Party of Civil Rights." *National Review*. https://www.nationalreview.com/2012/05/party-civil-rights-kevin-d-williamson/.

Witt, Elder. 1986. *Different Justice: Reagan and the Supreme Court*. Washington, DC: Congressional Quarterly, Incorporated.

TABLE OF CASES

Boumediene v. Bush, 553 U.S. 723 (2008).

Brown v. Board of Education of Topeka, 347 U.S. 483 (1954).

Church of Holy Trinity v. United States, 143 U.S. 457 (1892).

City of Richmond v. J.A. Croson Co., 488 U.S. 469 (1989).

Gonzales v. Raich, 545 U.S. 1 (2005).

Hamdan v. RumsfeldI, 548 U.S. 557 (2006).

Heart of Atlanta Motel, Inc. v. United States, I 379 U.S. 241 (1964).

Katzenbach v. McClung, 379 U.S. 294 (1964).

Lee v. Weisman, 505 U.S. 577 (1992).

Lemon v. Kurtzman, 403 U.S 602, 622 (1971).

Loving v. Virginia, 388 U.S. 1 (1967).

McCreary County v. ACLU of Kentucky, 545 U.S. 844 (2005).

Obergefell v. Hodges, 576 U.S. ___ (2015).

Regents of University of California v. Bakke, 438 U.S. 265 (1978).

United States v. Seeger, 380 U.S. 163 (1965).

Van Orden v. Perry, 545 U.S. 677 (2005).

Wickard v. Filburn, 317 U.S. 111 (1942).

Chapter 8

Justice Scalia and the Originalist Fallacy

Stephen M. Feldman

The late Justice Antonin Scalia famously advocated for originalism as the only legitimate and apolitical method of constitutional interpretation. He failed to advance his cause, however, in multiple ways. He neither adequately explained nor justified originalism. He did not apply originalism consistently in Supreme Court cases. And he often failed to persuade his colleagues to follow his originalist reasoning. Ironically, Scalia's greatest success was political: He might be our most Machiavellian Supreme Court justice. Although he was extremely conservative and persistently decided cases in accord with his political views, he persuaded numerous scholars, judges, and much of the general public to believe that originalism was a legitimate and politically neutral interpretive methodology (Greene 2016, 155–57, 183–84; Morris 2016).

THE EVOLUTION OF ORIGINALISM

In reaction to the ostensible liberal activism of the Warren and early-Burger Courts, conservatives such as Raoul Berger, Robert Bork, and Attorney General Edwin Meese began to argue that constitutional interpretation should be grounded on the framers' intentions (Levy 1988, xii–xiii). For instance, Bork asserted in 1971 that the Court, for the most part, should enforce only those rights that "text or history show the framers actually to have intended [to protect] and which are capable of being translated into principled rules" (Bork 1971, 17). These early originalists sought to secure the political high ground by maintaining that their methodology was objective and politically neutral while liberal justices corrupted the judicial process by deciding in accord with their personal values or political preferences (Department of Justice Office of Legal Policy 1988, 1).

This original-intent approach—now sometimes referred to as old originalism—provoked powerful criticisms. A multimember group such as the framers, critics pointed out, does not have a stable and determinate intention. An individual might have a single discernible intent, but a group does not; group members are likely to entertain varied intentions (Brest 1980). While such criticisms mounted, Antonin Scalia articulated a conservative approach to *statutory* interpretation: textualism. Scalia explained that "[s]tatutes should be interpreted . . . not on the basis of the unpromulgated intentions of those who enacted them . . . but rather on the basis of what is the most probable meaning of the words of the enactment, in the context of the whole body of public law with which they must be reconciled" (Scalia 1986, 103). Thus, just as originalists were struggling to defend their reliance on the framers' intentions in constitutional interpretation, Scalia was repudiating a similar reliance on legislators' intentions in statutory interpretation. Perhaps seeing a way to separate himself from Bork, Scalia's conservative colleague on the District of Columbia Court of Appeals, Scalia in 1986 began to advocate for a modification of originalist methodology (Murphy 2014, 101–7). Instead of seeking the original intent of the framers, Scalia sought the original meaning of the constitutional text. In other words, he brought his form of textualism to constitutional interpretation. The framers' statements were not "irrelevant," he added; they could be "strong indications of what the most knowledgeable people of the time understood the words to mean" (Scalia 1986, 103). Nevertheless, Scalia would subsequently emphasize that "[w]hat I look for in the Constitution is precisely what I look for in a statute: the original meaning of the text, not what the original draftsmen intended" (Scalia 1997, 38). Scalia's original-meaning approach—now referred to as new originalism—quickly overtook the original-intent approach as the predominant originalist methodology. In fact, Bork himself soon was advocating for the new originalism (Bork 1990, 6, 144).

Just over three months after Scalia introduced his form of originalism, he was sitting on the Supreme Court. In his new role as a justice, he continued to elaborate and advocate for originalism. As he explained in a concurring opinion: "I take it to be a fundamental principle of constitutional adjudication that the terms in the Constitution must be given the meaning ascribed to them at the time of their ratification" (*Minnesota v. Dickerson* 1993, at 379–80). Over time, Scalia would flesh out his method. The discovery of the original meaning of the constitutional text, for instance, often would require extensive historical research. Scalia admitted that this research task could be difficult and sometimes might be "better suited to the historian than the lawyer" (1989a, 857). He explained:

[I]t is often exceedingly difficult to plumb the original understanding of an ancient text. Properly done, the task requires the consideration of an enormous mass of material—in the case of the Constitution and its Amendments, for example, to mention only one element, the records of the ratifying debates in all the states. Even beyond that, it requires an evaluation of the reliability of that material—many of the reports of the ratifying debates, for example, are thought to be quite unreliable. And further still, it requires immersing oneself in the political and intellectual atmosphere of the time—somehow placing out of mind knowledge that we have which an earlier age did not, and putting on beliefs, attitudes, philosophies, prejudices and loyalties that are not those of our day. (1989a, 856–57)

Despite the apparent impediments to discerning original meaning, Scalia insisted that "for the vast majority of [constitutional] questions the answer is clear" (Scalia 1989a, 863). How could Scalia so confidently assert his ability to discover the original meaning? Often, he simply bypassed the complicated and obscure sources of original meaning and relied on dictionary definitions, citing and quoting dictionaries from around the time of the framing (Garner and Scalia 2012, 72). For example, in his "judicial magnum opus" (Murphy 2014, 385), the Second Amendment decision, *District of Columbia v. Heller* (2008), Scalia repeatedly invoked founding-era dictionaries (at 581–84, 587–88). In a typical passage parsing the Second Amendment text—"the right of the people to keep and bear Arms, shall not be infringed"—Scalia wrote: "Before addressing the verbs 'keep' and 'bear,' we interpret their object: 'Arms.' The 18th-century meaning is no different from the meaning today. The 1773 edition of Samuel Johnson's dictionary defined 'arms' as '[w]eapons of offence, or armour of defence'" (at 581).

Besides the difficulties with historical research, new originalists encountered additional methodological obstacles in their quest for constitutional meaning. Some new originalists argued that judges and other constitutional interpreters should seek to discern how the ratifiers or the wider public understood the constitutional text (at the time of ratification) (Bork 1990, 6, 143–44; Kay 1988, 246–47). For example, in a subsequent Second Amendment decision, *McDonald v. City of Chicago* (2010), Justice Clarence Thomas (concurring in part and concurring in the judgment) discussed the original meaning of the Privileges or Immunities Clause in the Fourteenth Amendment. From his perspective, "what the *public* most likely thought the Privileges or Immunities Clause to mean" at the time of ratification was determinative (at 835). Yet, critics pointed out that an emphasis on the ratifiers or the general public raised numerous problems, many of which echoed the problems of old originalism (focusing on the framers' intentions) (Bennett and Solum 2011, 104–5). There were more than 1,000 delegates to the various state ratifying conventions. How could one possibly discern a single coherent meaning for any constitutional provision from such a large mass of diverse individuals (Lawson and Seidman 2006, 61–67)? If an interpreter focused on the general public, how did he or she account for the fact that much of the founding-era public was either ignorant of or apathetic about the Constitution and its meaning (Somin 2012)?

Such difficulties led to a further refinement of originalism. The problem for new originalists was to develop a method that would ostensibly cleanse interpretation of historical ambiguities and other impurities. Originalists sought the unadulterated meaning of the constitutional text. Scalia, along with many other new originalists, settled on a reasonable-person methodology. They began to ask the following question: How would a hypothetical reasonable person, when the Constitution was adopted, have understood the text (Barnett 1999, 620–21; Lawson and Seidman 2006, 48)? A veritable "all-star roster of originalist scholars" have "endorsed reliance upon the reasonable person in constitutional interpretation" (Lawson and Seidman 2006, 48n11). In a book published in 2012, Scalia (along with coauthor, Bryan A. Garner) defined original meaning accordingly: "The understanding of [the constitutional text] reflecting what an informed, reasonable member of the community would have understood at the time of adoption according to then-prevailing linguistic meanings and interpretive principles" (Garner and Scalia 2012, 435).

Even if new originalists were able to discern a purified constitutional meaning—for example, through a reasonable-person method—they still needed to confront a separate obstacle, which Scalia fully acknowledged. Namely, originalism might lead to constitutional results inconsistent with Supreme Court precedents. In such cases, should the judge follow originalism or *stare decisis*? For example, if originalism could not justify an iconic decision such as *Brown v. Board of Education* (1954), should the Court repudiate *Brown*? Scalia, referring to himself as a "faint-hearted originalist," admitted that he would sometimes depart from originalist meaning to remain consistent with key precedents (Scalia 1989a, 862–64). As he explained, "*stare decisis* is not *part* of my originalist philosophy; it is a pragmatic *exception* to it" (Scalia 1997, 140). Yet, in the 1988 lecture where Scalia coined the phrase, faint-hearted originalist, he explained that cases pitting originalism against precedent were unlikely to arise (Scalia 1989a, 864). Subsequently, in 2008, he would dismiss the problem as an "academic question" (Murphy 2014, 169). And in a 2011 interview, he recanted his self-categorization as faint-hearted; he said he would follow originalism regardless of *stare decisis* (Coyle 2013, 165).

SCALIA'S JUSTIFICATIONS FOR ORIGINALISM

According to Scalia, why did he advocate for an originalist approach to constitutional interpretation? He repeatedly emphasized that the law, including constitutional law, should be predictable and consistent (Scalia 1989b, 1178–79; 1989a, 855). To attain predictability and consistency, judges need to respect and uphold legal rules, which was why Scalia argued that the rule of law must be "the law of rules" (Scalia 1989b, 1187). Judges should not exercise personal or political discretion when deciding cases. Of course, Scalia and the originalists were not the first judges or scholars to insist that judicial decision making must be apolitical. From the late-nineteenth century Langdellian legal scientists, who argued that judges should mechanically apply legal rules without regard for justice, to the post-World-War-II legal process scholars, who argued that judges should decide constitutional cases pursuant to neutral principles, legal scholars have maintained that politics corrupt adjudication (Langdell 1879, viii–ix; Wechsler 1959; Bickel 1986, 25–26, 49–59).

Following in those anti-politics footsteps, Scalia and other originalists declared that originalism is the only interpretive method that constrains judges within the rule of law. Scalia wrote: "You can't beat somebody with nobody" (Scalia 1989a, 855). The renowned originalist scholar, Randy Barnett, elaborated: "It takes a theory to beat a theory and, after a decade of trying, the opponents of originalism have never congealed around an appealing and practical alternative" (Barnett 1999, 617). Originalism was the default winner in the interpretive race because it was, in the end, the only theory in the competition—at least according to Scalia and other originalists.

The degree to which Scalia and other originalists denigrated their critics—often pejoratively denounced as non-originalists—was extraordinary. For Scalia, the failure of so-called non-originalists to agree on a single interpretive method that supposedly led to predictable and consistent judicial results was fatal. He sarcastically asked: "Are the 'fundamental values' that replace original meaning to be derived from the philosophy of Plato, or of Locke, or Mills [*sic*], or Rawls, or perhaps from the latest Gallup poll" (Scalia 1989a, 855)? He asserted that non-originalists argued "to the effect that (believe it or not) words have no meaning" (856). Scalia categorized some non-originalists as Living Constitutionalists. To counter their views, Scalia liked to proclaim that the Constitution is "dead, dead, dead" (Gentilviso 2013). One should not believe "that the proponents of the Living Constitution follow the desires of the American people in determining how the Constitution should evolve," Scalia sneered, as was his wont. "They follow nothing so precise; indeed, as a group they follow nothing at all" (Scalia 1997, 44).

Why, from Scalia's perspective, must we categorize the Constitution as dead rather than alive? The dead Constitution is Scalia's metaphorical description of a crucial originalist point, "the fixation thesis," as Lawrence Solum more precisely referred to it (Bennett and Solum 2011, 4; Barnett 2009, 660). Constitutional "meaning remains fixed," Scalia explained; "words must be given the meaning they had when the text was adopted" (Garner and Scalia 2012, 78, 428). Thus, the dead Constitution, with its fixed meanings, contrasts sharply with the so-called "Living Constitution, a body of law that (unlike normal statutes) grows and changes from age to age, in order to meet the needs of a changing society" (Scalia 1997, 38). The insurmountable problem, then, with the Living Constitution, according to Scalia, is that it invests judges with unbounded discretion: "[I]t is the judges who determine those [societal] needs and 'find' that changing law" (38).

Such personal discretion in constitutional interpretation was unacceptable to Scalia. He demanded objectivity, and his new originalism, focused on a reasonable person's outlook at the time of ratification, ostensibly uncovered objective constitutional meaning (17, 29). Scalia committed so strongly to the supposed existence of an objective and fixed meaning for the constitutional text that he claimed to develop "the science of construing legal texts" (3). In his *Heller* opinion, he wrote: "Constitutional rights are enshrined with the scope they were understood to have when the people adopted them, whether or not future legislatures or (yes) even future judges think that scope too broad [or, for that matter, too narrow]" (554 U.S. at 634–35). Constitutional change can occur only through formal constitutional amendments. A more flexible approach to constitutional interpretation, according to Scalia, would contravene democracy. Originalism is the only interpretive method, Scalia wrote, "compatible with the nature and purpose of a Constitution in a democratic system" (Scalia 1989a, 862; 1997, 40). Because the Constitution was democratically ratified and is the supreme law of the land, it must take priority over inconsistent legislative and executive actions. Hence, in *Heller*, Scalia insisted that the ostensibly objective and fixed meaning of the Second Amendment took certain legislative or "policy choices off the table," including the District of Columbia's "absolute prohibition of handguns held and used for self-defense in the home" (554 U.S. at 636). If one believes Scalia, the Court could have reached no other legitimate decision.

Finally, Scalia and numerous other originalists invoke history itself as justifying their interpretive approach (Garner and Scalia 2012, 78–82). The legal historian, Johnathan O'Neill, stated that "[t]he originalist approach was present in American constitutional law and thought since the country's founding" (O'Neill 2005, 5). This invocation of history makes sense given that originalists advocate for relying on history—namely the original meaning—when interpreting the Constitution. Should not a history-based interpretive method be grounded in history, particularly in the history of the framing era (McGinnis and Rappaport 2009, 787)? Scalia and other originalists have maintained that James Madison, perhaps the most important framer, used originalist methods (Garner and Scalia 2012, 80–81; McDowell 2010, 250–51, 261–62; Barnett 1999, 625–26). Moreover, as with other originalists, Scalia insisted that original-meaning originalism remained the predominant method of constitutional interpretation from the framing until sometime in the mid-twentieth century (Garner and Scalia 2012, 81–82). From Scalia's perspective, then, his reasonable-person originalism would return us to the nation's original method of constitutional interpretation.

CRITICISMS OF SCALIA'S ORIGINALISM

Scalia's implementation of originalism failed on multiple grounds. It did not lead to predictable and consistent case results; it contravened history; and it did not identify fixed objective constitutional meanings and thus did not produce apolitical judicial decisions.

Predictability and Consistency: The Cases

Scalia applied originalist methodology sporadically and reached decisions that were inconsistent with or unpredictable from an originalist perspective.

Tenth Amendment and Congressional Power Cases

In congressional power and Tenth Amendment cases, Scalia often departed from the most reasonable readings of text and history to reach politically conservative decisions limiting Congress's power. The Court relied on the Tenth Amendment in two anti-commandeering decisions: *New York v. United States* (1992), and *Printz v. United States* (1997). In *New York*, the Court invalidated a federal statute that mandated state governments either to regulate the disposal of low-level radioactive waste pursuant to congressional directives or to take title to the waste and then pay for any subsequent damages. Scalia joined Justice Sandra Day O'Connor's majority opinion, which began by suggesting that the Court would follow an originalist approach, bereft of political concerns. "Our task," O'Connor wrote, "consists not of devising our preferred system of government, but of understanding and applying the framework set forth in the Constitution. 'The question is not what power the Federal Government ought to have but what powers in fact have been given by the people'" (at 157). Unsurprisingly, then, O'Connor discussed the constitutional framing. Specifically, she emphasized that, early in the constitutional convention, the framers needed to choose between two overarching frameworks that would structure further discussions at the convention: the Virginia Plan, and the New Jersey Plan. The Virginia Plan would invest the national government with the power to regulate and tax the people directly without state governments acting as intermediaries—a power denied the national government under the Articles of Confederation. Under the Articles, the national government had been able to regulate and tax the people only indirectly, if state governments cooperated by imposing the desired national regulations. The New Jersey Plan would echo the Articles, allowing the national government to regulate and tax the people indirectly, with the state governments acting as intermediaries (at 163–66). The framers chose the Virginia Plan. Based partly on this history, the Court concluded that the Constitution empowered Congress to regulate the people but *not* the states. The disputed regulation of low-level radioactive waste was, from this perspective, an impermissible congressional attempt to regulate or commandeer state legislatures, echoing the defeated New Jersey Plan (at 166).

The Court's reasoning turned history on its head, as Justice John Paul Stevens observed, concurring in part and dissenting in part. The framers chose the Virginia Plan and rejected the New Jersey Plan precisely because they wanted to *expand* national powers beyond those granted under the Articles. The New Jersey Plan would have left the national government with powers inadequate to govern, as had been true under the Articles. "Nothing in that history suggests that the Federal Government may not also impose its will upon the several States," Stevens explained. "The Constitution enhanced, rather than diminished, the power of the Federal Government" (at 210). The majority opinion misconstrued the history by concluding that the choice of the Virginia Plan limited rather than expanded congressional power.

Scalia wrote the majority opinion in *Printz*, invalidating a federal statute that required state and local executive officers (police) to perform background checks on prospective buyers of handguns. He began with a strange statement coming from an originalist: "Because there is no constitutional text speaking to this precise question, the answer . . . must be sought in historical understanding and practice, in the structure of the Constitution, and in the jurisprudence of this Court" (at 905). If Scalia had followed his originalist methodology, then presumably he should have deferred to the legislature. "The principle that a matter not covered is not covered is so obvious that it seems absurd to recite it" (Garner and Scalia 2012, 93). When the constitutional text is silent, the legislature should be free to decide policy. Of course, deference to the legislature in this case would have led the Court to uphold the disputed (liberal) gun-control statute. Thus, despite the silent text, Scalia inquired into historical understandings and practices, as if there were relevant constitutional text to be interpreted. He ostensibly uncovered "the original understanding of the Constitution" by examining the actions of the first Congresses and statements of the framers (at 910, 905–11). Plus, he explicitly invoked *New York v. United States* and its erroneous historical argument concluding that the national government can directly regulate the people but not the states (at 919–21). In short, the anti-commandeering rule of the Tenth Amendment, articulated in *New York* and *Printz*, might be good policy (though I would argue against it), "but the rule is not based on the text or history of our Constitution" (Segall 2015, 102).

In related Supreme Court decisions limiting the scope of congressional power under the Commerce Clause, Scalia again wavered when confronted with ostensible originalist conclusions that he found distasteful (Greene 2016, 162). In the landmark 1995 decision, *United States v. Lopez* (1995), which imposed formalist limits on Congress's commerce power, Scalia joined the majority opinion but refused to join Thomas's concurrence, which followed originalist methodology to conclude that Congress should have even less power than the majority allowed (at 584). In the subsequent *Gonzales v. Raich* (2005), Scalia joined the progressive justices in upholding a congressional statute proscribing the possession of marijuana. Scalia concurred in the judgment and did not join the majority opinion, but he refused to join Thomas's originalist dissent concluding that Congress lacked the power to enact this statute under the Commerce Clause and the Necessary and Proper Clauses (at 57–59).

Equal Protection Cases

In equal protection cases, Scalia failed to inquire into the original understanding of the Fourteenth Amendment. A prominent example is *Bush v. Gore* (2000), which resolved the 2000 presidential election. Scalia purportedly was determined to install George W. Bush rather than Al Gore as the next president regardless of the legal arguments (Murphy 2014, 265–80). The Florida Supreme Court had ordered manual recounts of the votes cast for president in several different counties. The U.S. Supreme Court reversed with a 5-to-4 decision and ordered the termination of the recounts (at 532–33). A conservative bloc of five justices, the Court majority, held that the state of Florida had violated equal protection because different counties and different recount teams had used divergent standards to determine voter intent, which state law established as the criterion for determining votes (at 530–31). This equal protection reasoning was not only strikingly novel but also disregarded substantial discrepancies in the original counting of votes—discrepancies that arose because of the diverse and unequally effective procedures used in different counties. For instance, some counties used punch-card ballots while other counties used more modern optical-scan systems, even though punch-cards produced a far higher percentage of nonvotes (ballots that did not register votes in the machines) (at 541n4, Stevens, J., dissenting). If anything, the recount procedure would have produced a more equal and fair tallying of the votes. When subsequently pressed to explain this decision, Scalia had a stock answer: "Get over it" (Murphy 2014, 277–78). He accused the Florida Supreme Court of being politically motivated while claiming the mantle of political neutrality for the U.S. Supreme Court (278).

In equal protection cases challenging affirmative action programs, Scalia voted consistently for conservative outcomes, invalidating affirmative action, while disregarding originalism. In *City of Richmond v. J.A. Croson Company* (1989), Richmond instituted a plan mandating that contractors with the city subcontract at least 30 percent of the dollar amount of any prime contract to minority business enterprises. The Court invalidated this program, with a majority of justices (Scalia, O'Connor, Rehnquist, White, and Kennedy) agreeing for the first time on a single standard of judicial review for affirmative action. Under this rigorous judicial standard, strict scrutiny, the Court will uphold an affirmative action program only if the government proves that the program is narrowly tailored to achieve a compelling government purpose. Even so, O'Connor's plurality opinion left wiggle room. She suggested that strict scrutiny might not be appropriate for *all* affirmative action programs and that, even if strict scrutiny was applied, governments might sometimes be able to satisfy it (488 U.S. at 495–96, 504, 509–11). Scalia concurred in the judgment and refused to join O'Connor's opinion because, from his perspective, state and local governments could never constitutionally use race-conscious affirmative action programs. From his perspective, strict scrutiny should be fatal for all affirmative action programs (at 520–28).

The Court narrowed the wiggle room in *Adarand Constructors, Inc. v. Pena* (1995), which involved a federal affirmative action program resembling the municipal plan invalidated in *Croson*. Clarence Thomas had replaced Thurgood Marshall in 1991 and created a solid bloc of conservative justices on the Court. In *Adarand*, the conservative bloc held that strict scrutiny must be applied in all cases of affirmative action (at 227). Pursuant to the facts, O'Connor's majority opinion concluded that the federal government could not satisfy strict scrutiny, but that, in the right circumstances, the government might be able to adopt an affirmative action program passing constitutional muster. Specifically, the redress of past invidious discrimination could amount to a purpose compelling enough to satisfy strict scrutiny (at 237–38).

Scalia, concurring in part and concurring in the judgment, again disagreed with O'Connor's qualification of strict scrutiny. "In my view, government can never have a 'compelling interest' in discriminating on the basis of race in order to 'make up' for past racial discrimination in the opposite direction," Scalia explained. "Individuals who have been wronged by unlawful racial discrimination should be made whole; but under our Constitution there can be no such thing as either a creditor or a debtor race" (at 239).

In other words, Scalia insisted that the Equal Protection Clause mandates that all levels of government be color-blind. From Scalia's perspective, equality is purely formal, prohibiting racial classifications, but numerous commentators have argued that the Fourteenth Amendment instead mandates an anti-caste or anti-subordination principle that would harmonize with affirmative action (Siegel, R. B. 2004; Segall 2015, 104–5). During Reconstruction, Congress enacted multiple statutes that solely benefitted African Americans (Siegel, S. A. 1998, 558–62; Schnapper 1985, 754). These congressional actions suggest that the original meaning of the Equal Protection Clause allows race-conscious affirmative action programs, at least if created and implemented by the federal government. Whether this reasoning would extend to state and local affirmative action is unclear, but the crucial point is that Scalia never confronted this history. In affirmative action cases, he completely ignored his ostensible commitment to originalist methodology (Greene 2016, 163; Segall 2015, 104–5).

Free-Expression Cases

Likewise, in First Amendment free-expression cases, Scalia consistently disregarded history and originalism. To take one example, Scalia wrote the majority opinion in *Brown v. Entertainment Merchants Association* (2011), which invalidated a state law prohibiting "the sale or rental of 'violent video games' to minors" (at 789). Scalia largely followed a standard doctrinal analysis for a free speech issue. He invoked the self-governance rationale, a traditional philosophical justification for protecting expression, to suggest that the Court should presume that video games are constitutionally protected expression (at 790). He marched through the traditional low-value categories, such as fighting words and obscenity, which specify types of speech beyond First Amendment protections (or with limited protections), and concluded that violent video games do not fit into any of the pre-existing low-value categories (at 791–93). Finally, he considered whether the government could satisfy strict scrutiny. Scalia admitted that protecting children from portrayals of violence might be a compelling state interest, but he nonetheless concluded that the regulation in this case was not narrowly tailored to achieve that end.

The regulation of video games was, for instance, under-inclusive because it still allowed children to be exposed to depictions of violence in sources other than video games (at 799–804).

Interestingly, Justice Thomas dissented and argued that an originalist approach to the First Amendment revealed that the disputed expression was constitutionally unprotected (at 821). In this instance, Thomas correctly analyzed the history, even if his originalist analysis could not reveal a definitive meaning for the First Amendment. Thomas reasoned that the founding generation would have understood that speech to minors was filtered through the parents; children did not have unrestricted First Amendment rights to receive information (at 822–24). More broadly, from the framing era through the early twentieth century, free expression was widely understood to allow government restrictions in pursuit of the common good or general welfare. Hence, throughout this time period lasting more than a century, courts allowed governments to punish speech or writing that was likely to produce bad tendencies or harmful consequences because such expression undermined virtue and contravened the common good (Feldman 2008, 46–290). Courts during that time would have concluded that the government could prevent children from being exposed to violent forms of entertainment, including video games if they had existed.

Over the past thirty years, some of the most important free-expression cases have involved campaign finance restrictions, including limits on corporate political spending. Scalia repeatedly maintained that corporations have expansive First Amendment rights to spend on political campaigns—rights equivalent to those enjoyed by individual citizens (*McConnell v. Federal Election Commission* 2003, at 256–62, Scalia, J., concurring in part, concurring in the judgment in part, and dissenting in part). *Citizens United v. Federal Election Commission* (2010) was the most prominent of these campaign finance decisions. In a 5-to-4 decision, the conservative bloc invalidated statutory limits on corporate spending for political campaign advertisements. Justice Anthony Kennedy's majority opinion did not rely extensively on historical sources, though he concluded with an originalist flourish: "There is simply no support for the view that the First Amendment, as originally understood, would permit the suppression of political speech by media corporations" (at 353). Justice Stevens's dissent criticized the majority on originalist grounds (at 425–32), so Scalia wrote a concurrence largely responding to Stevens's dissent. The crux of Scalia's argument was that the original meaning of the First Amendment could not be construed to deny corporations full constitutional rights to express political viewpoints (at 385–93).

Scalia's history was startling wrong in two ways. First, he incorrectly equated conceptions of free expression from the framing era with conceptions from the mid- to late twentieth century. Consequently, he wrote in his concurrence: "[I]f speech can be prohibited because, in the view of the Government, it leads to 'moral decay' or does not serve 'public ends,' then there is no limit to the Government's censorship power" (at 391). But as mentioned above, the framers' generation recognized that governments could punish expression that was likely to produce bad tendencies or harmful consequences. That is, the government could limit expression exactly because it might undermine morals or, more broadly, because it contravened public ends or the common good. This narrow interpretation of free expression continued until the 1930s, when significant shifts in American views of democracy led the Court to transform free expression into a constitutional lodestar (Feldman 2008, 395–401; White 1996, 300–301).

Second, Scalia incorrectly asserted that the framers' generation would not have differentiated corporations from individual citizens for purposes of free expression (at 391–93). Scalia seemingly read the history through the lens of twenty-first-century neoliberal market fundamentalism, but the framers were not even full-fledged capitalists, much less laissez-faire ideologues. The constitutional protection of slavery as a legal institution underscores that the framing generation was not committed to a capitalist free-market economy. Capitalism is based on the drive for profit in a competitive free market. Slavery is the antithesis of a free market; it is coerced labor (Heilbroner and Singer 1984, 9–12, 132). Without doubt, slavery enabled slave owners to accumulate capital in a commercial market economy and thus facilitated the eventual emergence of capitalism. Regardless, throughout the pre-Civil War decades, slavery skewed the natural movement of capital among various productive and profitable market activities. Slavery constrained the marketplace as well as constraining human freedom (Beckert 2014, 98–135; Davis 1975, 346–54). Slavery, in fact, was consistent with a premodern economy. At the time of the American founding, England was developing a theory of contract based on marketplace values, but this innovation would not be adopted in any American states until the early nineteenth-century, well after the ratification of the Constitution. In late eighteenth-century America, notions of fairness and equity limited the assignability and enforcement of contracts. Contract law, in fact, emerged as a separate common-law realm in the United States only after the turn into the nineteenth century (Hall 1989, 119–23; Horwitz 1977, 180–81; McDonald 1985, 113–14).

Unsurprisingly, the framers' generation did not conceptualize corporations in a way that would even resemble the profit-driven multinational behemoths that dominate the twenty-first-century marketplace. During the early decades of nationhood, corporations could be formed only when legislatures specially chartered them—general incorporation laws did not exist—and legislatures rarely granted such special state charters. Legislatures almost never granted corporate charters to businesses that focused solely on profit-making. Instead, in a manifestation of the lingering premodern mercantilist outlook, states would charter corporations that promoted the common good by performing a function useful to the public. For example, corporate charters were typically granted for the building of infrastructure, including roads, bridges, and canals, as well as for the operation of ferries, banks, and insurance companies (Friedman 1985, 179–81; Hurst 1970, 14–17; Maier 1993, 51–55, 84). In the end, Scalia's suggestion in *Citizens United* that the framing generation would have viewed corporations as indistinguishable from individual citizens for purposes of free expression is so ahistorical as to be nonsensical (Feldman 2015b).

The three realms of constitutional cases discussed in this section—the Tenth Amendment and congressional power; equal protection; and free expression—all illustrate that Scalia applied originalist methodology sporadically and reached decisions that were apparently inconsistent with, or unpredictable from, an originalist perspective. The same is true in other constitutional realms. For example, Scalia's expansive interpretation of the Eleventh Amendment and its grant of state sovereign immunity is "famously anti-textual" (Segall 2015, 103). In the Establishment Clause realm, Scalia never subscribed to Thomas's originalist analysis, which concluded that state and local governments, unlike the federal government, can establish religions overtly and explicitly without violating the First Amendment (*Elk Grove Unified School District v. Newdow* (2004), at 49–51 (Thomas, J., concurring in the judgment)). Unpredictability and inconsistency, though, were not the only problems with Scalia's originalism.

History and Originalism

The historical difficulties encountered by originalism are insurmountable (Cross 2013, 107–18; Wood 1988). All forms of originalism, including Scalia's, appeal to history to resolve constitutional ambiguities. Instead of more present-minded and apparently open-ended interpretive approaches, originalists claim that history, in some shape or form, can reveal a fixed and objective constitutional meaning. Constitutional interpretation, as such, is ostensibly purified.

If one listens to professional historians, however, historical research leads to complexity rather than to univocal and determinate factual nuggets. When a historian confronts a textual document, he or she does not seek to understand its surface meaning because, from the historian's standpoint, any such surface meaning is either insignificant or nonexistent. Texts, to historians, "are slippery, cagey, and protean, reflecting the uncertainty and disingenuity of the real world" (Wineburg 2001, 66). A text is never *merely* or *simply* what is "set down on paper" (66–67). A historian wants to appreciate and reconstruct the social context surrounding a text. If successful, the historian can begin to glimpse the subtexts, the meanings hidden below the surface of the document—meanings that often are far more important than any superficial ones floating on the surface. A historian who ignores subtext is likely to skew or warp the significance of a document.

Originalists attempt to use "history without the historicism" (Griffin 2008, 1888). Historicism stresses that all human actions, thoughts, and events occur in a context of contingent and changing social, cultural, and political arrangements (White 2002, 506). The contexts and the contingencies engender, for a historian, the subtexts, the layers of underlying meaning. But originalists disregard context, contingency, and subtext. They want to find a fixed objective meaning, when a historical text, such as the Constitution—especially, the Constitution, which forged a nation in a political crucible—is roiling with subtexts. The framing era was especially dynamic, as individuals contested shifting practices in and ideas about government and the economic marketplace (Rakove 1996; Wood 1969; Griffin 2016, 60). But originalists resemble naive students rather than historians. While historians seek "to engage" with a text, situating it "in a social world" and digging for subtexts, students instead view texts more simply, as "serving as bearers of information" (Wineburg 2001, 76). Thus, unsurprisingly, the originalist Randy Barnett tellingly declared: "[O]riginal public meaning is an objective fact that can be established by reference to historical materials" (Barnett 2009, 660).

Scalia and other originalists have persistently oversimplified historical research into the Constitution. Scalia invoked dictionary definitions from the framing period as if those definitions resolved constitutional disputes. But in an originalist's hands, the dictionary becomes a tool for ignoring complexity and other historical sources (Cornell 2011, 334–37). "Dictionaries are mazes in which judges are soon lost," Richard Posner wrote. "A dictionary-centered textualism is hopeless" (Posner 2012, 20). Even when originalists do not fall back on dictionaries, they cherry-pick their sources and blatantly omit contrary evidence that would complicate their conclusions (Cornell 2011, 301; Posner 2012, 20). Scalia's concurring opinion in *Citizens United*, discussed above, typified his truncated inquiry into history. He concluded that the original meaning of the First Amendment fixed expansive free-speech rights for corporations. In reaching that conclusion, however, he ignored the history of free expression suggesting that courts interpreted free speech and a free press far more narrowly in the late eighteenth and early nineteenth than in the late twentieth and early twenty-first centuries. He also ignored economic history and, in particular, the role of corporations in the marketplace during the early years of nationhood. Ignore all those complexities, and anyone might readily reach a simple but wrongheaded conclusion.

Originalists' overarching problems with historical research might help explain a more specific historical difficulty encountered by Scalia and many other originalists. Recall, numerous originalists have refined the historical inquiry by asking the following question: How would a hypothetical reasonable person, when the Constitution was adopted, have understood the text? Moreover, many of these reasonable-person originalists, including Scalia, have claimed that their method is grounded in the history of the framing period. According to Scalia, his reasonable-person originalism would return us to the nation's original method of constitutional interpretation. This crucial historical assertion is wrong in two ways. First, as a general matter, the framing generation did not endorse any single univocal approach to constitutional interpretation (Cornell 2009, 1101; Treanor 2009, 985–86). Any statements about the Constitution and its interpretation from that era, whether by key framers such as Madison or by lesser known delegates to state ratifying conventions, must be understood within the political context of the time—from the closely contested state battles over ratification to the controversial decisions implementing the Constitution in the 1790s (Maier 2010; Elkins and McKitrick 1993).

Second, while the reasonable-person construct is a widely accepted legal standard today, it was not at the time of the founding or for many years afterward. Jurists and scholars in the latter decades of the eighteenth century and the early years of the nineteenth century viewed "reason" as a principle internal to the law, including natural law. Judges would invoke the faculty of reason to discern the law and guide decision making. Consequently, judges would sometimes ask whether the law was reasonable. Occasionally, though infrequently, a judge would invoke a "reasonable man" (or "prudent man"), but judges did not generally conceive of these terms as manifesting a legal standard of judgment, liability, or otherwise (Calnan 2005, 157, 213–18, 275).

Lawyers and judges nowadays often invoke the reasonable person as a generalized legal standard establishing an individual's duty of care in a wide variety of circumstances, but jurists during the early decades of nationhood discerned duties of care as established in the status-relationships of the disputants. The common law attached a specific duty of care to many occupations. For example, innkeepers owed a particular duty of care to protect lodgers, while ferrymen owed a duty of safe transportation to travelers. In civil liability (tort) cases, structured around common-law writs or forms of action such as trespass or trespass on the case, judges (or juries) would be unlikely to conclude that a defendant was negligent (pursuant to a reasonable-person standard), but might conclude that the defendant neglected to fulfill a duty in accordance with his distinct status (Calnan 2005, 235, 279; White 1977, 685). In early constitutional cases, jurists might invoke reason as a guide to interpretation, but they would not have asked how a reasonable man would have understood the constitutional text. In fact, one can search in vain through framing-era newspapers, dictionaries, the statements of framers and ratifiers, congressional declarations, and legal treatises for some invocation of the reasonable man as a generalized legal standard of duty or interpretation (Feldman 2014, 304–49). The reasonable man emerged as a generalized legal standard of care or liability, governing interactions among strangers, only in the early to mid-eighteenth century (and the "reasonable *person*" replaced the "reasonable *man*" as a predominant legal standard only in the late twentieth century [Bernstein 1997, 465–67]).

The Politics of Originalism

Scalia's implementation of originalism was unpredictable and inconsistent as well as contrary to history. Why, then, did he so strongly advocate for and claim to apply originalism? The short answer: politics.

Some commentators attribute Scalia's unpredictability and inconsistency to his being a self-proclaimed faint-hearted originalist (Scalia 1989a, 862–64). But from Scalia's perspective, his occasional acquiescence to precedent did not diminish the importance of, or his commitment to, originalism. He was merely recognizing that, as a practical matter, some precedents were so deeply entrenched or widely relied upon that they should not be over-ruled (Scalia 1997, 140). There are two drawbacks to this defense of faint-heartedness. First, as mentioned above, Scalia himself dismissed the potential conflict between stare decisis and originalism as academic, and subsequently, he recanted his faint-heartedness altogether (Murphy 2014, 169; Coyle 2013, 165). But if the potential conflict was only academic, then it follows that Scalia never decided a case where he confronted an actual tension between precedent and original meaning. In reality, at least according to Scalia, he never had to choose between *stare decisis* and originalism. His faint-heartedness, therefore, could not explain his unpredictability and inconsistency because it (faint-heartedness) was merely an abstract or hypothetical problem.

Second, Scalia's qualification of originalism with faint-heartedness—even if it was only academic—undermines many of his justifications for being an originalist in the first place. Scalia insisted that originalism uncovers the objective meaning of the Constitution. Therefore, originalism constrains judges and prevents them from imposing their own values or political preferences. Originalism supposedly produces predictability and consistency because originalist judges follow the rule of law. But as even Randy Barnett admits, a faint-hearted originalism is no originalism at all (Barnett 2006). Originalism has no bite if a judge can choose to ignore it when it contravenes practical considerations such as *stare decisis* (Greene 2016, 151). The rule of law is defeated, at least from an originalist perspective.

In fact, as discussed above, historical research into the framing period cannot uncover fixed and determinate constitutional meanings. Historical research reveals subtexts, subtleties, and complexities. Numerous Supreme Court decisions illustrate that different justices in a single case can claim to follow originalist sources but arrive at different conclusions. In the *Heller* decision, Scalia supposedly used an originalist analysis and held that the Second Amendment protected an individual right to own and possess firearms. Yet, Stevens' *Heller* dissent relied extensively on historical sources and concluded that Scalia's originalist conclusion was incorrect (554 U.S. at 641–62). Likewise, in *Citizens United*, Scalia's originalist concurrence diverged from Stevens' originalist dissent. Scalia also frequently refused to join Thomas's originalist opinions (Coyle 2013, 165–66), such as when Thomas argued that the Establishment Clause did not apply to state and local governments (*Elk Grove Unified School District v. Newdow* 2004, at 49–51, Thomas, J., concurring in the judgment).

The key point is that the indeterminacy of historical analysis facilitated Scalia's voting to decide cases in accord with his political preferences (Posner 2012, 19; Segall 2015, 101). As Stevens wrote in his dissent in *McDonald v. City of Chicago* (2010), "It is hardly a novel insight that history is not an objective science, and that its use can therefore 'point in any direction the judges favor'" (at 907). Of course, Scalia did not hesitate to declare that his originalist methodology produced politically neutral decisions: He was above politics. But all Supreme Court decision making—in fact, all constitutional interpretation—is partly political. The fixation thesis of originalism is invalid. No theory or method can reduce constitutional interpretation to an apolitical and objective exercise, like an arithmetic problem, concluding with a fixed and determinate result (Feldman 2005; 2015a; Berger 2013; Tribe 1997). Hence, Scalia correctly observed that no other theory could eliminate politics from Supreme Court adjudication, but he incorrectly asserted that originalism could do so.

Scalia repeatedly claimed that he sometimes voted to reach a liberal decision, thus proving that his decision-making process was, in fact, apolitical. Two flag desecration cases were among his favorite examples (Garner and Scalia 2012, 17). *Texas v. Johnson* (1989) invalidated a conviction under a state flag desecration statute; Scalia joined the majority opinion written by the liberal Justice William Brennan. Congress responded by enacting a federal statute prohibiting flag destruction, and again, in *United States v. Eichman* (1990), Scalia joined a majority opinion holding the statute unconstitutional. Afterward, Scalia frequently insisted that his votes in those cases contravened his personal preferences. "If it were up to me, I would put in jail every sandal-wearing, scruffy-bearded weirdo who burns the American flag," Scalia proclaimed. "But I am not king" (Bomboy 2015).

Unfortunately for Scalia, the flag desecration cases put the lie to his supposed commitment to originalism, his apolitical bona fides, and his belief in constitutional objectivity. *Johnson* and *Eichman* were not the first flag desecration cases to reach the Court. In *Halter v. Nebraska*, decided in 1907, the Court upheld the conviction under a state flag desecration statute of defendants who sold bottled beer affixed with labels bearing the flag. The majority opinion discussed free expression at length as an aspect of due process liberty rather than as a First Amendment right per se. "[A] state possesses all legislative power consistent with a republican form of government," the Court wrote, "therefore each state . . . may, by legislation, provide not only for the health, morals, and safety of its people, but for the common good, as involved in the well-being, peace, happiness, and prosperity of the people" (at 40–41). Thus, "[i]t is familiar law that even the privileges of citizenship and the rights inhering in personal liberty are subject, in their enjoyment, to such reasonable restraints as may be required for the general good" (at 42). In other words, the Court followed the standard narrow interpretation of free expression that courts had been articulating throughout the nineteenth century. Governments could punish speech or writing that was likely to produce bad tendencies or harmful consequences because such expression undermined virtue and contravened the common good. In fact, the Nebraska flag desecration law resembled those in two-thirds of the then forty-five states. "[A] duty rests upon each state," the *Halter* Court reasoned, "to encourage its people to love the Union with which the state is indissolubly connected" (at 43). To the extent that original meaning should matter, *Halter* resonated with the understanding of free expression from the framing era, while Scalia's conception of the First Amendment vis-à-vis flag desecration fit the post-1930s enshrinement of free expression as a constitutional lodestar (Feldman 2008, 46–290, 395–401).

Scalia claimed that originalism is the only method of constitutional interpretation consistent with democracy because only originalism is politically neutral (Scalia 1989a, 862; Scalia 1997, 40). All other methods of interpretation, according to Scalia, allow the justices to substitute their own personal or political preferences for the judgments of the elected representatives of the people. Ironically, though, it was Scalia who invoked originalism to ostensibly justify Court decisions invalidating legislative enactments. Stevens described *Heller* as a "law-changing decision" (at 679, Stevens, J., dissenting). "Until today, it has been understood that legislatures may regulate the civilian use and misuse of firearms so long as they do not interfere with the preservation of a well-regulated militia," Stevens explained. "The Court's announcement of a new constitutional right to own and use firearms for private purposes upsets that settled understanding" (at 679). Perhaps, no case has intruded more directly into the democratic process than *Bush v. Gore*. By preventing a manual recount of the votes cast for president in several Florida counties, Scalia and the other conservative justices placed George W. Bush into the presidency. Numerous scholars, even those who believe that the Court ordinarily follows the rule of law, argued that this case could not be explained in any way other than as a raw power grab (Gillman 2001, 2–5, 185–89; Sunstein 2001, 759).

In short, if one searches for consistency in Scalia's Supreme Court votes and opinions, one will not find it in an unwavering commitment to originalist methods and the history of the original understanding. Instead, consistency lies in Scalia's conclusions: He could be reliably counted on to reach the conservative outcome in almost every case. Scalia invoked originalism to accomplish precisely what he claimed originalism banished: He allowed his (conservative) politics to shape his votes and opinions (Posner 2012, 18; Greene 2016, 152).

CONCLUSION:
AN ALTERNATIVE TO ORIGINALISM

Scalia and other originalists have persistently claimed that originalism is the only possible approach to constitutional interpretation. This claim is patently untrue. Many constitutional scholars have adopted a pluralist or eclectic approach to constitutional interpretation (Feldman 2014; Bobbitt 1991). Other scholars refer to common-law constitutionalism, living constitutionalism, and a flexible pragmatism—all of which resonate with a pluralist or eclectic approach (Farber and Sherry 2002; Strauss 2010; 1996; Fallon 1987). In fact, historical evidence shows that a pluralist approach to constitutional interpretation predominated during the early decades of nationhood. Judges, scholars, and even the framers drew upon a shifting variety of factors, including original meaning, framers' intentions, practical consequences, judicial precedents, and so forth, when interpreting the Constitution (Feldman 2014, 317–49).

In the 1793 *Chisholm v. Georgia* decision, the issue was whether Article III allowed a citizen of one state to sue another state in federal court. The case might be viewed not only as the Court's first constitutional decision but also as the Court's first foray into a volatile political controversy. The underlying political issues were twofold: first, the case rekindled Anti-Federalist fears that the new centralized government would overwhelm state sovereignty, and second, the case, if decided against Georgia, might cause creditors to stampede into federal court suing state governments for large sums of money (McCloskey 1960, 34–35). The Court, with opinions delivered seriatim, held that the state was unprotected by sovereign immunity and, therefore, subject to suit. In so deciding, the Court buttressed national power at the expense of state sovereignty. The ensuing political uproar was so deafening that the Eleventh Amendment, prohibiting similar suits, was proposed almost immediately and ratified within two years (Schwartz 1993, 20–22).

The multiple opinions in *Chisholm* show numerous interpretive approaches. Several justices appear to refer to the public meaning of the text, as discerned in various ways. For instance, the lone dissenter, Iredell, stated that the Constitution should have a "fair construction," such that "every word in the Constitution may have its full effect" (at 449–50). All of the justices in the majority appear to suggest that the text has a plain (public) meaning. Justice William Cushing, for instance, reasoned that the case "seems clearly to fall within the letter of the Constitution" (at 467). Justice James Wilson, the most sophisticated legal scholar on the Court, inquired into the public meaning based on the people's intentions, while also suggesting the text had a plain meaning (at 464–66). Chief Justice John Jay, after declaring that he would look to the Constitution's "letter and express declaration," explained that the text's meaning is based on "ordinary and common" usage, though he then suggested that congressional understanding and action manifested such usage (at 474, 477).

If one were to focus solely on these multiple emphases on the Constitution's public and plain meaning, one could readily conclude that the justices followed an original-meaning approach to interpretation. Such a conclusion, however, would be mistaken. At least two justices, and maybe a third, looked elsewhere in their efforts to ascertain constitutional meaning. Both Wilson and Jay stressed that the Constitution's underlying purposes should inform its interpretation. Both justices drew, in particular, on the preamble's "declared objects" or purposes (at 465, 474–75). Wilson reasoned that the Court should interpret the Constitution to further such purposes: "to form an union more perfect . . . 'to establish justice' . . . 'to ensure domestic tranquility'" (at 465). Likewise, Jay explained that because he was obliged to attend to "the design of the Constitution," he must therefore construe Article III in light of the injunction "to establish justice" (at 474–76).

Wilson also mentioned "the general texture of the Constitution," suggesting an attention to the fabric of the whole—the location of a particular provision relative to other provisions (at 465). Jay, interestingly, emphasized the advantageous practical consequences of allowing states to be sued. The extension of the federal judicial power "to such controversies, appears to me to be wise, because it is honest, and because it is useful. . . . It is useful . . . because it leaves not even the most obscure and friendless citizen without means of obtaining justice from a neighbouring State" (at 479). Jay continued by listing four more favorable consequences (at 479). Meanwhile, Iredell suggested, albeit ambiguously, that the framers' intentions might be relevant (at 432).

One remarkable case, *Ogden v. Saunders*, decided in 1827, nicely illustrates not only that the justices, as a group, used a wide variety of interpretive approaches, but also that individual justices applied multiple interpretive strategies. The majority held that the congressional bankruptcy power, under Article I, section 8, clause 4, was not exclusive, and that a state bankruptcy statute did not violate the Contract Clause so long as it applied to contracts entered subsequently to the legislative enactment. What rendered the case extraordinary was that the justices issued five opinions—one each by the four majority justices, William Johnson, Robert Trimble, Smith Thompson, and Bushrod Washington, and one by the dissenting Chief Justice John Marshall, joined by Gabriel Duvall and Joseph Story—even though the Court long ago had abandoned the practice of issuing seriatim opinions. Partly because they were so closely divided, the justices momentarily returned to the seriatim approach. Given that the Marshall Court decided most significant cases unanimously, with Marshall writing the Court's opinion, this case provides a rare view into the interpretive approaches of the respective justices.

Johnson and Trimble invoked public meaning, based on how the people actually understood the Constitution (at 278–79, 290, 329). Johnson, for instance, emphasized "the sense put upon [the Constitution] by the people when it was adopted by them" (at 290). Both justices believed that contemporary constructions of the document provided the best evidence of public meaning. Johnson gleaned such evidence from legislative actions taken after ratification, while Trimble quoted from the *Federalist Papers* to illustrate "the contemporary construction" given during the ratification process (at 290, 329). Johnson explained that "the contemporaries of the constitution have claims to our deference on the question of right, because they had the best opportunities of informing themselves of the understanding of the framers of the constitution, and of the sense put upon it by the people when it was adopted by them" (at 290).

Apparently consistent with a public meaning approach, two justices, Johnson as well as Thompson, suggested that some constitutional provisions had a plain meaning (at 274–75, 302–3). Thompson, for example, wrote: "If this provision in the constitution was unambiguous, and its meaning entirely free from doubt, there would be no door left open for construction" (at 302). He then referred to "the plain and natural interpretation" of the Contract Clause (at 303). Reasoning inversely, so to speak, Johnson found it significant that "nothing . . . on the face of the Constitution" directly prohibited states from enacting bankruptcy laws (at 274). Washington emphasized the textual arrangement of the words within particular provisions (at 267–68). Johnson and Trimble also thought that the fabric of the whole Constitution was relevant to interpretation (at 275, 288–89, 329–31). "The principle," Trimble wrote, "that the association of one clause with another of like kind, may aid in its construction, is deemed sound" (at 329).

Four justices, Washington, Johnson, Thompson, and Trimble, relied on the framers' intentions (at 256, 258, 274–75, 280, 302–5, 329, 331). Trimble referred to the framers as "sages," while Washington wrote: "I have examined both sides of this great question with the most sedulous care, and the most anxious desire to discover which of them, when adopted, would be most likely to fulfil the intentions of those who framed the constitution of the United States" (at 256, 331). Related to framers' intentions, Washington and Johnson believed that the Constitution's overall purposes should inform its interpretation, while Thompson considered "the reason and policy" of particular provisions to be relevant (at 265, 274, 303).

Three justices, Washington, Johnson, and Thompson, suggested that natural law principles should inform constitutional interpretation (at 258, 266, 282, 303–4). Two justices, Johnson and Marshall (dissenting), reasoned that the history of the political problems that provoked the Philadelphia convention was germane to constitutional interpretation (at 274, 276–77, 339, 354–55). Marshall, for instance, emphasized that state government corruption in the 1780s produced unjust debtor relief laws, which engendered the inclusion of the Contract Clause in the Constitution (at 354–55). Two justices, Johnson and Thompson, believed that the justices could legitimately consider practical consequences when interpreting the Constitution (at 276, 300, 313). At one point, when considering what constituted an "obligation" under the Contract Clause, Thompson contemplated whether a particular interpretation would "facilitate commercial intercourse" (at 300). Finally, two justices, Johnson and Thompson, examined judicial precedents concerning disputed constitutional meanings (at 272, 296). Thompson, for instance, considered prior state court interpretations of the Contract Clause to be relevant (at 296).

In sum, the five justices writing opinions in *Ogden* employed a dizzying array of interpretive strategies. No justice relied on only one exclusive interpretive approach, whether public meaning or otherwise. Every justice used multiple approaches. Justice Washington explicitly admitted that, in his view, constitutional interpretation was not mechanical, and constitutional meaning was not objective and determinate. He explained his interpretive judgment: "I should be disingenuous were I to declare, from this place, that I embrace [a particular interpretation of the Contract Clause] without hesitation, and without a doubt of its correctness. The most that candour will permit me to say upon the subject is, that I see, or think I see, my way more clear on the side which my judgment leads me to adopt, than on the other, and it must remain for others to decide whether the guide I have chosen has been a safe one or not" (at 256).

Despite the assertions of Scalia and other originalists, a coherent pluralist practice of constitutional interpretation is widely followed today and deeply rooted in American history. To be sure, pluralists (or eclectics) generally do not claim that their approach is apolitical or objective or reveals a fixed and determinate constitutional meaning. Such claims are impossible to fulfill. In fact, originalist claims to accomplish these goals turn out, upon examination, to be rhetorical strategies oriented to gaining political advantage, usually an attempt to legitimate a conservative legal or judicial conclusion. Ironically, nobody demonstrates the fallacy of originalism more so than Scalia himself. If an avowed originalist such as Scalia could not implement originalist methods and reach originalist conclusions—he failed to deliver, after all, in case after case after case—then we can reasonably conclude that originalism is not a feasible approach to constitutional decision making.

Of course, despite the problems inherent in originalism, Supreme Court justices, lower court judges, and constitutional scholars can continue to claim the originalist mantle of neutral and apolitical decision making. On the current Court, Justices Thomas and Neil Gorsuch openly claim to be originalists (and other conservative justices sometimes invoke originalism). In fact, Gorsuch sees Scalia as a model justice, a "lion of the law" (Gorsuch 2016, 905–6, 920; Savage 2017). Gorsuch, then, claims to decide cases in accord with "cold neutrality," which in application translates into cold conservatism (Gorsuch 2016, 920; Epstein et al. 2016).

Even so, because originalism does not lead to fixed and determinate constitutional meanings, it can, in theory, be invoked to support progressive outcomes. Indeed, a small number of progressive scholars have argued for a modified form of originalism (Balkin 2011). Nevertheless, any ostensible constitutional method that emphasizes political intentions and meanings from the framing period will tilt in a conservative direction. During the framing and ratification and for decades afterward, women, racial minorities, and many religious minorities were precluded from participation in the polity. Their respective interests, values, and perspectives will therefore be ignored or downplayed under most originalist analyses. Finally, even if originalism can, in theory, be turned toward progressive goals, it is most often applied in practice as a subterfuge for conservative conclusions. That political insight is ultimately Scalia's true legacy.

REFERENCES

Balkin, Jack M. 2011. *Living Originalism*. Cambridge, MA: Belknap Press of Harvard University Press.

Barnett, Randy E. 1999. "An Originalism for Nonoriginalists." *Loyola Law Review* 45: 611.

———. 2006. "Scalia's Infidelity: A Critique of 'Faint-Hearted' Originalism." *University of Cincinnati Law Review* 75: 7.

———. 2009. "The Misconceived Assumption about Constitutional Assumptions." *Northwestern University Law Review* 103: 615.

Beckert, Sven. 2014. *Empire of Cotton: A Global History*. New York: Vintage Books.

Bennett, Robert W., and Lawrence B. Solum. 2011. *Constitutional Originalism: A Debate*. Ithaca, NY: Cornell University Press.

Berger, Eric. 2013. "Originalism's Pretenses." *University of Pennsylvania Journal of Constitutional Law* 16: 329.

Bernstein, Anita. 1997. "Treating Sexual Harassment with Respect." *Harvard Law Review* 111: 445.

Bickel, Alexander M. 1986. *The Least Dangerous Branch*. New Haven: Yale University Press.

Bobbitt, Philip. 1991. *Constitutional Interpretation*. Cambridge, MA: B. Blackwell.

Bomboy, Scott. 2015. "Justice Antonin Scalia Rails Again about Flag-Burning 'Weirdoes.'" *Constitution Daily*, 12 November.

Bork, Robert H. 1971. "Neutral Principles and Some First Amendment Problems." *Indiana Law Journal* 47: 1.

———. 1990. *The Tempting of America*. New York London: Free Press Collier Macmillan.

Brest, Paul. 1980. "The Misconceived Quest for the Original Understanding." *Boston University Law Review* 60: 204.

Calnan, Alan. 2005. *A Revisionist History of Tort Law: From Holmesian Realism to Neoclassical Rationalism*. Durham, NC: Carolina Academic Press.

Cornell, Saul. 2009. "*Heller*, New Originalism, and Law Office History: 'Meet the New Boss, Same as the Old Boss'." *U.C.L.A. Law Review* 56: 1095.

———. 2011. "The People's Constitution vs. The Lawyer's Constitution: Popular Constitutionalism and the Original Debate Over Originalism." *Yale Journal of Law and the Humanities* 23: 295.

Coyle, Marcia. 2013. *The Roberts Court: The Struggle for the Constitution*. New York: Simon & Schuster.

Cross, Frank B. 2013. *The Failed Promise of Originalism*. Stanford, CA: Stanford Law Books.

Davis, David Brion. 1975. *The Problem of Slavery in the Age of Revolution, 1770–1823*. Ithaca, NY: Cornell University Press.

Department of Justice Office of Legal Policy. 1988. *Guidelines on Constitutional Litigation*.

Elkins, Stanley and Eric McKitrick. 1993. *The Age of Federalism*. New York: Oxford University Press.

Epstein, Lee, et al. 2016. "President-Elect Trump and His Possible Justices." *New York Times*, 15 December.

Fallon, Richard H. 1987. "A Constructivist Coherence Theory of Constitutional Interpretation." *Harvard Law Review* 100: 1189.

Farber, Daniel A., and Suzanna Sherry. 2002. *Desperately Seeking Certainty: The Misguided Quest for Constitutional Foundations.* Chicago: University of Chicago Press.

Feldman, Stephen M. 2005. "The Rule of Law or the Rule of Politics? Harmonizing the Internal and External Views of Supreme Court Decision Making." *Law and Social Inquiry* 30: 89.

———. 2008. *Free Expression and Democracy in America: A History.* Chicago: University of Chicago Press.

———. 2014. "Constitutional Interpretation and History: New Originalism or Eclecticism?" *B.Y.U. Journal of Public Law* 28: 283.

———. 2015a. "Fighting the Tofu: Law and Politics in Scholarship and Adjudication." *Cardozo Public Law, Policy & Ethics Journal* 14: 91.

———. 2015b. "Is the Constitution Laissez Faire? The Framers, Original Meaning, and the Market." *Brooklyn Law Review* 81: 1.

Friedman, Lawrence M. 1985. *A History of American Law.* New York: Simon & Schuster.

Garner, Bryan A. and Antonin Scalia. 2012. *Reading Law: The Interpretation of Legal Texts.* St. Paul, MN: Thomson/West.

Gentilviso, Chris. 2013. "Scalia: Constitution Is 'Dead, Dead, Dead.'" *Huffington Post*, 29 January.

Gillman, Howard. 2001. *The Votes That Counted: How the Court Decided the 2000 Presidential Election.* Chicago: University of Chicago Press.

Gorsuch, Neil. 2016. "Of Lions and Bears, Judges and Legislators, and the Legacy of Justice Scalia." *Case Western Reserve Law Review* 66: 905.

Greene, Jamal. 2016. "The Age of Scalia." *Harvard Law Review* 130: 144.

Griffin, Stephen M. 2008. "Rebooting Originalism." *University of Illinois Law Review* 2008: 1185.

———. 2016. "Justice Scalia: Affirmative or Negative?" *Minnesota Law Review Headnotes* 101: 52.

Hall, Kermit L. 1989. *The Magic Mirror: Law in American History.* New York: Oxford University Press.

Heilbroner, Robert L. and Aaron Singer. 1984. *The Economic Transformation of America: 1600 to the Present.* San Diego: Harcourt Brace Jovanovich.

Horwitz, Morton. 1977. *The Transformation of American Law, 1780–1860.* Cambridge, MA: Harvard University Press.

Hurst, James Willard. 1970. *The Legitimacy of the Business Corporation in the Law of the United States, 1780–1970.* Charlottesville: University Press of Virginia.

Kay, Richard S. 1988. "Adherence to the Original Intentions in Constitutional Adjudication: Three Objections and Responses." *Northwestern University Law Review* 82: 226.

Langdell, Christopher C. 1879. *A Selection of Cases on the Law of Contracts*. Boston: Little Brown, and Company.

Lawson, Gary, and Guy Seidman. 2006. "Originalism as a Legal Enterprise." *Constitutional Commentary* 23: 47.

Levy, Leonard W. 1988. *Original Intent and the Framers' Constitution*. New York: Macmillan.

Maier, Pauline. 1993. "The Revolutionary Origins of the American Corporation." *William & Mary Quarterly* 50: 51.

———. 2010. *Ratification: The People Debate the Constitution, 1787–1788*. New York: Simon & Schuster.

McCloskey, Robert G. 1960. *The American Supreme Court*. Chicago: University of Chicago Press.

McDonald, Forrest. 1985. *Novus Ordo Seclorum: The Intellectual Origins of the Constitution*. Lawrence: University Press of Kansas.

McDowell, Gary L. 2010. *The Language of Law and the Foundations of American Constitutionalism*. New York: Cambridge University Press.

McGinnis, John O. and Michael B. Rappaport. 2009. "Original Methods Originalism: A New Theory of Interpretation and the Case against Construction." *Northwestern University Law Review* 103: 751.

Morris, Benjamin. 2016. "How Scalia Became the Most Influential Conservative Justice Since the New Deal." *FiveThirtyEight*, 14 February.

Murphy, Bruce Allen. 2014. *Scalia: A Court of One*. New York, NY: Simon & Schuster.

O'Neill, Johnathan. 2005. *Originalism in American Law and Politics: A Constitutional History*. Baltimore: Johns Hopkins University Press.

Posner, Richard A. 2012. "The Spirit Killeth, but the Letter Giveth Life." *New Republic*, 13 September, 18.

Rakove, Jack N. 1996. *Original Meanings: Politics and Ideas in the Making of the Constitution*. New York: A.A. Knopf.

Savage, David G. 2017. "Scalia's Views Mixed with Kennedy's Style: Meet Neil Gorsuch, Trump's Pick for the Supreme Court." *L.A. Times*, 31 January.

Scalia, Antonin. 1986. "Address before the Attorney General's Conference on Economic Liberties." In *Original Meaning Jurisprudence: A Sourcebook*, Office of Legal Policy, appendix C. Washington, DC: U.S. Department of Justice.

———. 1989a. "Originalism: The Lesser Evil." *University of Cincinnatti Law Review* 57: 849.

———. 1989b. "The Rule of Law as a Law of Rules." *University of Chicago Law Review* 56: 1175.

———. 1997. *A Matter of Interpretation: Federal Courts and the Law*. Edited with commentary by Amy Gutmann et al. Princeton, NJ: Princeton University Press.

Schnapper, Eric. 1985. "Affirmative Action and the Legislative History of the Fourteenth Amendment." *Virginia Law Review* 71: 753.

Schwartz, Bernard. 1993. *A History of the Supreme Court*. New York: Oxford University Press.

Segall, Eric J. 2015. "Will the Real Justice Scalia Please Stand Up?" *Wake Forest Law Review Online* 50: 101.

Siegel, Reva B. 2004. "Equality Talk: Antisubordination and Anticlassification Values in Constitutional Struggles Over *Brown*." *Harvard Law Review* 117: 1470.

Siegel, Stephen A. 1998. "The Federal Government's Power to Enact Color-Conscious Laws: An Originalist Inquiry." *Northwestern University Law Review* 92: 477.

Somin, Ilya. 2012. "Originalism and Political Ignorance." *Minnesota Law Review* 97: 625.

Strauss, David A. 1996. "Common Law Constitutional Interpretation." *University of Chicago Law Review* 63: 877.

———. 2010. *The Living Constitution*. Oxford ; New York: Oxford University Press.

Sunstein, Cass. 2001. "Order Without Law." *University of Chicago Law Review* 68: 757.

Treanor, William Michael. 2009. "Against Textualism." *Northwestern University Law Review* 103: 983.

Tribe, Laurence H. 1997. "Comment." In *A Matter of Interpretation: Federal Courts and the Law*. Edited with commentary by Amy Gutmann et al., 65–94. Princeton, NJ: Princeton University Press.

Wechsler, Herbert. 1959. "Toward Neutral Principles of Constitutional Law." *Harvard Law Review* 73: 1.

White, G. Edward. 1977. "The Intellectual Origins of Torts in America." *Yale Law Journal* 86: 671.

———. 1996. "The First Amendment Comes of Age: The Emergence of Free Speech in Twentieth-Century America." *Michigan Law Review* 95: 299.

———. 2002. "The Arrival of History in Constitutional Scholarship." *Virginia Law Review* 88: 2002.

Wineburg, Sam. 2001. *Historical Thinking and Other Unnatural Acts: Charting the Future of Teaching the Past*. Philadelphia: Temple University Press.

Wood, Gordon S. 1969. *The Creation of the American Republic, 1776–1787*. Chapel Hill: University of North Carolina Press.

———. 1988. "The Fundamentalists and the Constitution." *N.Y. Review of Books*, 18 February, 33.

TABLE OF CASES

Adarand Constructors, Inc. v. Pena, 515 U.S. 200 (1995).

Brown v. Board of Education, 347 U.S. 483 (1954).

Brown v. Entertainment Merchants Association, 564 U.S. 786 (2011).

Bush v. Gore, 531 U.S. 98 (2000).

Chisholm v. Georgia, 2 U.S. (Dall.) 419 (1793).

Citizens United v. Federal Election Commission, 558 U.S. 310 (2010).

City of Richmond v. J.A. Croson Company, 488 U.S. 469 (1989).

District of Columbia v. Heller, 554 U.S. 570 (2008).

Elk Grove Unified School District v. Newdow, 542 U.S. 1 (2004).
Gonzales v. Raich, 545 U.S. 1 (2005).
Halter v. Nebraska, 205 U.S. 34 (1907).
McConnell v. Federal Election Commission, 540 U.S. 93 (2003).
McDonald v. City of Chicago, 561 U.S. 742 (2010).
Minnesota v. Dickerson, 508 U.S. 366 (1993).
New York v. United States, 505 U.S. 144 (1992).
Ogden v. Saunders, 25 U.S. (12 Wheat.) 213 (1827).
Printz v. United States, 521 U.S. 898 (1997).
Texas v. Johnson, 491 U.S. 397 (1989).
United States v. Eichman, 496 U.S. 310 (1990).
United States v. Lopez, 514 U.S. 549 (1995).

Chapter 9

The Jurisprudence of Justice Scalia

Common-Law Judging Behind an Originalist Façade

Ronald Kahn and Gerard Michael D'Emilio

Undoubtedly the late Justice Antonin Scalia was a larger-than-life figure in American jurisprudence. Viewed as the intellectual anchor of the Supreme Court's so-called "conservative wing," Justice Scalia leaves a monumental legacy, revolutionizing all facets of legal studies and judicial commentary. But whether Scalia *as a justice* was an exemplar of the originalist jurisprudence for which he advocated is a question that deserves vigorous consideration in light of his recent death. This chapter will argue that, while Scalia's opinions embody aspects of the judicial philosophy he delineated in scholarly publications, they often fail to reflect ideal originalism—a pragmatic reality that Scalia himself readily acknowledged, and happily so. Moreover, Scalia, though a uniquely dynamic member of the Court, was *not* unique as a Supreme Court justice. That is, Court decision making is more intrinsic to the institution than specific to each justice, and Scalia's opinions are no exception. Rather, the late justice by and large deploys a variant of what we refer to as "Model 2" decision making, the bidirectional, mutual construction process that both characterizes non-originalist jurisprudence and is a facet of the Supreme Court itself as an institution. That Scalia did not escape this offers useful data about his tenure of the Court.

The chapter proceeds in three parts. Part I explores Scalia's judicial philosophy as laid out in his own words and writings. Part II explores Scalia in majority and dissent, striving to find patterns and ultimately to assessing whether his jurisprudence is fairly (and best) described as "originalist"—and, more broadly, whether his jurisprudence "in action" aligns with the judicial philosophy he writes about. Part III offers a reconceptualization, viewing Scalia through a different decision-making theory in an attempt to make more cohesive and meaningful analysis. Upon doing this, Scalia looks far more like his colleagues than an outlier or defender of a particular constitutional theory.

PART I: JUSTICE SCALIA—IN HIS OWN WORDS

Perhaps most synonymous with Scalia's name is "originalism," the interpretive methodology of which the late justice was arguably the vanguard. But whereas his avowed commitment to originalism was at times aggressive in his judicial opinions—more on this later—Scalia was far more equivocal when the robes came off.

For Scalia, judicial opinions vary in greatness by their degree of historicity—that is, whether original understandings are central to the underlying logic (Scalia 1989b, 849–52). Scalia's preferred approach to judicial decision making involves a years-long historical investigation—indeed, Scalia admits that it may be "a task sometimes better suited to the historian than the lawyer"—aimed at gleaning the right answer from as much source material as can be examined (851–52, 856–57). Ignoring any troubling implications from this admission, Scalia sets out to justify originalism's worth by attacking the deficiencies of *non*-originalism, hoping to leave originalism as the only game in town.

Non-originalism produces judicial opinions "rendered not on the basis of what the Constitution originally meant, but on the basis of what . . . judges currently th[ink] it desirable for it to mean" (Scalia 1989b, 852). And for justification these non-originalists turn to Marshall's statement in *McCulloch v. Maryland*—"we must never forget that it is a constitution we are expounding"—which, to Scalia, reveals non-originalism's central deficiency:

> The principal theoretical defect of nonoriginalism . . . is its incompatibility with the very principle that legitimizes judicial review. . . . Nothing in the text of the Constitution confers upon the courts the power to inquire into, rather than passively assume, the constitutionality of federal statutes. . . . Central to [judicial review's legitimacy] . . . is the perception that the Constitution, though it has an effect superior to other laws, is in its nature the sort of "law" that is the business of the courts—an enactment that has a fixed meaning ascertainable through the usual devices familiar to those learned in the law. If the Constitution were not that sort of a "law," but a novel invitation to apply current societal values, what reason would there be to believe that the invitation was addressed to the courts rather than to the legislature? (Scalia 1989b, 854)

Justifying judicial review requires conceptualizing the Constitution as fixed in meaning, such that constitutional interpretation is really more investigation than interpretation. To this non-originalism's open-endedness is anathema. Moreover, non-originalism sets out to further restrict democratic government, rather than unleash it (Scalia 1997, 41). In Scalia's eyes, "devotees of The Living Constitution do not seek to facilitate social change but to prevent it" (40–42).

Beyond non-originalism's theoretical frailty is also the "practical difficulty" of its big-tent heterogeneity (Scalia 1989b, 855). If law is to maintain "consistency and predictability," says Scalia, "there must be general agreement not only that judges reject one exegetical approach (originalism), but that they adopt another" (855). Yet non-originalists lack a consensus as to this alternative approach, which follows from the fact that they define themselves as *against*, rather than *for*, something (855). While acknowledging that originalism is not monolithic, Scalia nevertheless points out that, unlike non-originalism, originalism "by and large represents a coherent approach, or at least an agreed-upon point of departure" (855).

But while Scalia slices through non-originalism, he offers a notably tepid defense of originalism's virtues. First are the practical problems of applying originalism, compounded by Scalia's frank admission that the ideal originalist opinion might require years—and different personnel than justices unschooled in history—to complete (860–61).[1] As well, Scalia recognizes that pure originalism is "medicine that seems too strong to swallow" and, consequently, is often diluted through such tools as *stare decisis* (861).

Moreover, Scalia's advocacy for originalism is in tension with his broader comments on the "textualism" anchoring his statutory interpretation. On statutes, Scalia takes aim at those who insist that "the judge's object . . . is to give effect to 'the intent of the legislature'":

The evidence suggests that . . . we do not really look for subjective legislative intent. We look for a sort of "objectified" intent—the intent that a reasonable person would gather from the text of the law, placed alongside the remainder of the *corpus juris*. . . . And the reason we adopt this objectified version is, I think, that it is simply incompatible with democratic government, or indeed, even with fair government, to have the meaning of a law determined by what the lawgiver meant, rather than by what the lawgiver promulgated. . . . Government by unexpressed intent is simply tyrannical. (Scalia 1997, 16–17)

The "practical threat" of this search for legislative intent "is that, under the guise or even the self-delusion of pursuing unexpressed legislative intents, common-law judges will in fact pursue their own objectives and desires, extending their lawmaking proclivities from the common-law to the statutory field" (Scalia 1997, 17–18). This principle—"that laws mean whatever they ought to mean, and that unelected judges decide what that is"—is "incompatible with democratic theory" (22).

Looming over this discussion, however, is a key question: given that originalism—Scalia's method of constitutional interpretation—turns so much on the thoughts of the founding generation, how can Scalia square it with the plain-language textualism he subscribes to in statutory interpretation? The late justice offers an answer (and perhaps not a satisfactory one):

> I will consult the writings of some men who happened to be delegates to the Constitutional Convention—Hamilton's and Madison's writings in *The Federalist*, for example. I do so, however, not because they were Framers and therefore their intent is authoritative and must be the law; but rather because their writings, like those of other intelligent and informed people of the time, display how the text of the Constitution was originally understood. . . . What I look for in the Constitution is precisely what I look for in a statute: the original meaning of the text, not what the original draftsmen intended. (Scalia, 1997, 38)

In other words, originalism is merely a species of textualism. "[T]he Great Divide with regard to constitutional interpretation," says Scalia, "is not that between Framers' intent and objective meaning, but rather between *original meaning* (whether derived from Framers' intent or not) and *current* meaning" (38). Yet this is a surprisingly feeble response—even if we assume original meaning is what originalism is after, how is one to discover this meaning without resorting to subjective interpretations and understandings?[2]

Enter Scalia's "faint-hearted originalism." Scalia asserts that most originalists are faint-hearted, accounting for the fact that "the sharp divergence" between originalism and non-originalism in their theoretically pure forms "does not produce an equivalently sharp divergence in judicial opinions" (Scalia 1989b, 862). Indeed, Scalia jettisons much of the theoretical rigor in a moment of candor:

> The inevitable tendency of judges to think that the law is what they would like it to be will . . . cause most errors in judicial historiography to be made in the direction of projecting upon the age of 1789 current, modern values—so that as applied, even as applied in the best of faith, originalism will (as the historical record shows) end up as something of a compromise. Perhaps not a bad characteristic for a constitutional theory. (864)

This defense of originalism is quite pragmatic, and strikingly so coming from the often-strident Scalia. Scalia admits both that "it may indeed be unrealistic to have substantial confidence that judges and lawyers will find the correct historical answer to . . . refined questions of original intent" *and* that "one cannot realistically expect judges . . . to apply [originalism] without a trace of constitutional perfectionism" (Scalia 1989b, 863). That is, not only are judges unlikely to adequately perform the historical exegesis originalism demands, but they are also likely to decide cases based on modern, subjective viewpoints, projecting contemporary mores onto "the past." To this tepid endpoint Scalia offers a shrug, muttering that originalism is intrinsically worth deploying—even if poorly (864).

Ultimately, Scalia falls back on an institutional-policy rationale for originalism:

> [E]ven if one assumes . . . that the Constitution was originally meant to expound evolving rather than permanent values, . . . I see no basis for believing that supervision of the evolution would have been committed to the courts. . . . [O]riginalism seems to me more compatible with the nature and purpose of a Constitution in a democratic system. A democratic society does not, by and large, need constitutional guarantees to insure that its laws will reflect "current values." Elections take care of that quite well. The purpose of constitutional guarantees . . . is precisely to prevent the law from reflecting certain changes in original values that the society adopting the Constitution thinks fundamentally undesirable. (862)

As non-originalists appeal to America's "fundamental values," they exacerbate the greatest "danger in judicial interpretation of the Constitution"—"that the judges will mistake their own predilections for the law" (Scalia 1989b, 863). At the core of Scalia's originalism, then, is his deep-seated discomfort with judicial review in a democratic system. "Originalism," he argues, "does not aggravate the principal weakness of the system [of judicial review], for it establishes a historical criterion that is conceptually quite separate from the preferences of the judge himself" (864).

Scalia's reservations about judicial review spill over into his general methodology of jurisprudential analysis. Scalia eschews an incremental, "one case at a time" approach to judicial decision making in favor of establishing bright-line rules that, even if awkward at the margins, clearly organize and regulate actions (Scalia 1989a, 1175–78). Turning from Thomas Paine to Aristotle, Scalia links the "general rule of law" central to a democratic system of government to a jurisprudence guided not by fact-bound, case-by-case adjudication, but rather by broader principles of decision that corral wide swathes of future cases (1176–77).

While Scalia accepts that the quest for the "perfect" judicial decision for the facts at hand has some utility, he offers a series of countervailing values that justify a more "formalist" or bright-line jurisprudence. The first might be classed as "legitimacy":

> When a case is accorded a different disposition from an earlier one, it is important, if the system of justice is to be respected, not only that the later case *be* different, but that it *be seen to be so*. When one is dealing . . . with issues so heartfelt that they are believed by one side or the other to be resolved by the Constitution itself,

it does not greatly appeal to one's sense of justice to say: "Well, that earlier case had nine factors, this one has nine plus one." Much better, even at the expense of the mild substantive distortion that any generalization introduces, to have a clear, previously enunciated rule that one can point to in explanation of the decision. (Scalia 1989a, 1178)

Moreover, Scalia points to institutional restraints as supporting a bright-line approach to decision making: because the Supreme Court can and will hear only a relatively miniscule slice of cases, the need for systemic uniformity counsels against a minimalist jurisprudence (1178–79). Finally, Scalia cites predictability, an essential component in the rule of law, as needing "clear, general principle[s] of decision" established as early as possible, rather than opaque, multi-factor tests (1179).

Scalia also attacks the premise that incremental jurisprudence is somehow more restrained than its bright-line counterpart:

[W]hen, in writing for the majority of the Court, I adopt a general rule, and say, "This is the basis of our decision," I not only constrain lower courts, I constrain myself as well. If the next case should have such different facts that my political or policy preferences regarding the outcome are quite the opposite, I will be unable to indulge those preferences; I have committed myself to the governing principle. . . . Only by announcing rules do we hedge ourselves in. (1179–80)

Thus, much like with his arguments for originalism, Scalia justifies his bright-line jurisprudence by waiving about his activist judge, unconstrained by the law and giving in to his or her personal proclivities and political preferences. What's more, this bright-line jurisprudence, in constraining judges, also *emboldens them* when they are called upon (by the constitutionally-ordered democratic system) to "stand up to what is generally supreme in a democracy: the popular will" (Scalia 1989a, 1180).

Scalia's jurisprudential thinking, then, might be boiled down into a few, broad observations:

1. Justice Scalia is deeply concerned with judicial encroachment on a robust, majoritarian democracy he believes to be the core of the American republic. Much of his constitutional theory springs from a belief in the illegitimacy of judicial review—and of the common-law system as a whole. Judge-made law cannot coexist with democracy, in Scalia's eyes, absent strong textual and institutional checks that assure that the Court remains the least dangerous branch.
2. Scalia is a textualist, and he likely would say that his originalism is a species of this broader theory. In the constitutional space, this textualism is synonymous with original meaning, which is some amalgam of public

understanding of constitutional provisions at the time they were drafted and ratified. This theory is necessary to make judicial action legitimate.

3. Scalia's arguments are primarily offered from a negative posture: that is, they are justified by what they are *not*—they are *not* non-originalism. He spills much of his ink in attacking non-originalism rather than building out the details of an originalist jurisprudence.

4. Scalia, while being somewhat doctrinally rigid, is realistic and pragmatic. He admits, quite jarringly, that originalism in practice is likely to exhibit a hearty dose of personal viewpoint—and this is simply the inescapable human condition. As well, he expresses doubt that originalism can really be practiced given the time constraints of modern decision making, not to mention the fact that judges are not necessarily equipped to engage in rigorous historical analysis.

5. Scalia loves bright lines—perhaps the standout feature of his writings. Harshness at the margins is the price of the predictability, reliability, and legitimacy that come with such bright lines. Formalism for Scalia is a positive—a sign of a strong democracy—rather than a drawback. And, no surprise, bright lines hedge in judges (where they should be restricted) and empowers them (where the Constitution gives them power).

These principles are important, but only when examined against Scalia's actual judicial opinions. The central question, then, is to what extent does Scalia follow some or all of these principles in his decision making, and does his adherence change in any way depending on the substantive area in which he is operating? It is to these considerations that we turn.

PART II: JUSTICE SCALIA—IN HIS OPINIONS

This analysis of Scalia's opinions is admittedly cursory, a fuller examination requiring far more paper. However, some significant, if general, observations may be had by looking at some of the late justice's "greatest hits," be they majority, concurring, or dissenting opinions. We begin with Scalia's majority opinion in *District of Columbia v. Heller*, dealing with whether the Second Amendment protects an individual right to bear arms for non-militia purposes. Next, we examine Scalia's dissents in *Casey, Lawrence, Windsor,* and *Obergefell*—what are his gay and reproductive rights dissents. Finally, we turn to one of the late justice's more recent First Amendment cases: his majority opinion in *Brown v. Entertainment Merchants Association.* By conducting this brief survey, one can see that Scalia no doubt adheres to his jurisprudential principles—but not always comprehensively or consistently.

The Second Amendment: *District of Columbia v. Heller*

One would expect Scalia's majority opinion in *Heller* to be an exemplar of originalist jurisprudence, giving trenchant empirical evidence of Scalia's originalism "on the ground." However, *Heller* lacks the fire and fierce logic that are often hallmarks of Scalia's well-known dissents. Overall, his opinion more resembles typical common-law decision making rather than the originalism outlined in Scalia's theoretical work.

In *Heller*, Scalia begins with textualism: the starting point is the Second Amendment's natural division between "its prefatory clause" ("A well-regulated Militia, being necessary to the security of a free state") and its "operative clause" ("the right of the people to keep and bear Arms, shall not be infringed") (*District of Columbia v. Heller* 2008, 577). But in starting with the operative clause, returning to the prefatory clause only to "ensure that [his] reading of the operative clause is consistent with the [Amendment's] announced purpose," Scalia arguably loads the dice (*Heller* 2008, 557–78). Framing this are Scalia's guiding principles of constitutional interpretation: the Constitution's "words and phrases were used in their normal or ordinary . . . meaning" and "[n]ormal meaning . . . excludes secret or technical meanings *that would not have been known to ordinary citizens of the founding generation*" (576–77). Thus, the text of the Second Amendment controls—but the text as understood by "the founding generation."

Because the operative clause speaks of a "right of the people," Scalia commences "with a strong presumption that the . . . right is exercised individually" (579–81). Scalia moves on to "keep and bear arms," surveying a smattering of founding-era documents—and more modern case law—to conclude that the phrase refers to a general right to possess firearms not limited to military-style weaponry or militia-related use (581–92). Scalia asserts that the Amendment's historical background confirms this meaning and is salient "because it has always been widely understood that the Second Amendment . . . codified a *pre-existing* right" (592).[3] Having cemented the operative clause's meaning, Scalia allows the prefatory clause an (ultimately fruitless) opportunity to rebut. But perhaps what stands out most is that Scalia's citations are not exclusively from the founding era, turning to modern-day law review articles, twentieth-century Supreme Court precedent, and Joseph Story (the closest to the founding) as authorities for his reading (595–98).

All this throat-clearing drives toward the key denouement: Scalia's reading of the prefatory and operative clauses *together*. Scalia's reading is grounded in backdoor intentionalism, the two clauses fitting together "once one knows the history that the founding generation knew" (598). His holistic reading focuses primarily on English tactics for eliminating militias, which relied on disarming citizens; consequently, the right to bear arms was codified in the English Bill of Rights (*Heller* 2008, 598). So too in America, where the founding generation "understood . . . that the right helped to secure the ideal of a citizen militia, which might be necessary to oppose an oppressive military force if the constitutional order broke down" (598–99).

So, power to the prefatory clause? Not quite. With his indelible confidence—and no citation—Scalia muses that "most [founding-era citizens] undoubtedly thought [the right to bear arms] even more important for self-defense and hunting" (599). Thus, Scalia's textualist interpretation of the Second Amendment ends up relying on a background principle that is extratextual, operating "behind the curtain" of the constitutional text.

This extratextual justification continues in Scalia's explication of "how the Second Amendment was interpreted from immediately after its ratification through the end of the 19th century" (605–19).[4] But this section suffers from two fundamental defects. First, it seems to contravene textualism, as it relies on a plethora of secondary sources that state subjective interpretations, rather than a widely-shared, objective understanding. Second, Scalia surveys *centuries* of commentary, rather than confining his study to founding-era documents recounting the drafters' viewpoints.

The problems emerge immediately. In his discussion of "Postratification Commentary," Scalia relies on "[t]hree important founding-era legal scholars" for the proposition that the Second Amendment "protect[s] an individual right unconnected with militia service." But Scalia's direct evidence is ambiguous at best—and oftentimes barely from the "founding period" to boot—and where he attempts to augment the persuasive value of these scholars, he cites interpretive sources from decades *after* the founding (*Heller* 2008, 605–10). The remainder of Scalia's historical survey is dedicated to pre- and post-Civil War sources, along with Supreme Court precedent (610–26). The persuasive value of these sources is irrelevant, though—at least from the standpoint of Scalia's originalism. Indeed, such historical sources are salient only if one allows that jurists engage in common-law decision making—from which Scalia sets himself apart. Thus, Scalia's lengthy historical analyses read as undisciplined and cursory, not so much distillations of original understandings as advocacy drawing on vague traditionalism and a selectively-edited historical record.

Justice Stevens's pointed dissent brings these problems into sharp relief. Key to Stevens's dissent is its deployment of the analytical devices used by Scalia. Stevens's thorough and disciplined historical argument at the very least offers a substantial counterpoint to Scalia's—and, more likely, reveals both the deficiencies of Scalia's opinion and the shortcomings of his broader jurisprudential theory. For Stevens, the prefatory clause "identifies the preservation of the militia as the Amendment's purpose; it explains that the militia is necessary to the security of a free State; and it recognizes that the militia must be 'well regulated'" (*Heller* 2008, 640).[5] Stevens contrasts this phrasing with state constitutions, which often explicitly included references to self-defense and hunting (642). Thus, "[t]he contrast . . . confirms that the Framers' single-minded focus in crafting the constitutional guarantee 'to keep and bear Arms' was on military uses of firearms . . . viewed in the context of service in state militias" (643).

Stevens's analysis of the operative clause is similarly incisive. In "to keep and bear arms," Stevens sees "a unitary right: to possess arms if needed for military purposes and to use them in conjunction with military activities" (646). Stevens cites a myriad of founding-era sources to bolster this reading, along with general linguistic authorities (646–51). Thus, "[w]hen each word in the text is given full effect, the Amendment is most naturally read to secure to the people a right to use and possess arms in conjunction with service in a well-regulated militia" (651). As Stevens trenchantly notes, "not a word in the constitutional text even arguably supports the Court's overwrought and novel description of the Second Amendment as 'elevat[ing] above all other interests the right of law-abiding, responsible citizens to use arms in defense of hearth and home'" (*Heller* 2008, 652).

Stevens additionally takes issue with Scalia's generic historical survey (662). On Scalia's reliance on the English Bill of Rights, Stevens—rightly— observes that the English right "tells us little about the meaning of the Second Amendment" because it was "adopted in a different historical and political context and framed in markedly differently language" (664–65). And as to Scalia's use of post-ratification commentary, Stevens deploys a healthy skepticism, dismissing these sources as offering little insight into the founding-era meaning of the Amendment (666–71).

In closing, Stevens notes the irony behind Scalia's purportedly originalist opinion:

> The Court . . . declar[es] that it is not the proper role of this Court to change the meaning of rights "enshrine[d]" in the Constitution. But the right the Court announces was not "enshrined" in the Second Amendment by the Framers; it is the product of today's law-changing decision. The majority's exegesis has utterly failed to establish that as a matter of text or history, "the right of law-abiding, responsible citizens to use arms in defense of hearth and home" is "elevate[d] above all other interests" by the Second Amendment. (679)

In other words, it is Scalia, rather than the four dissenting justices, that reinterpret the Second Amendment to give it modern-day salience.

Scalia's Dissents: *Casey, Lawrence, Windsor,* and *Obergefell*

From *Planned Parenthood v. Casey* through *Obergefell v. Hodges,* Justice Scalia consistently lambasts what he views as the illegitimacy of the majority (or, for *Casey*, plurality) opinions. Always in dissent, Scalia's opinions in this area lack the lengthy historical and textual analyses in his plurality opinions, such as *Heller*, and instead lean heavily on institutionalist arguments, emphasizing themes of tradition, legitimacy, majoritarian democracy, and self-governance.

Take Scalia's dissent in *Planned Parenthood v. Casey*. Scalia's gripe with the majority opinion—and with its predecessor, *Roe v. Wade*—can be summed up in one word: democracy (*Casey* 1992, 979). This abortion right—which Scalia acknowledges is a liberty interest, broadly speaking—falls under majoritarian governance because "(1) the Constitution says absolutely nothing about it, and (2) the longstanding traditions of American society have permitted it to be legally proscribed" (980).

The balance of Scalia's dissent draws on the dominant themes of his theoretical writings, attacking *Casey*'s plurality with his criticisms of non-originalist jurisprudence. First up in Scalia's crosshairs: the plurality's "reasoned judgment" used to interpret the Constitution (981–84). Scalia makes great hay out of the plurality's somewhat florid language in an effort to discredit the plurality's persuasive power and expose that "only personal predilection," rather than "reasoned judgment . . . supports the Court's decision" (983–84). Second, Scalia attacks the "standardless nature" of the plurality's "undue burden" threshold, arguing that such a threshold merely invites judges to engage in preferentially-weighted fact finding geared toward reaching their desired outcomes (991–93).

But Scalia saves his most pointed criticism for last, castigating the plurality's argument that the American polity, to ensure a government of laws, has found in the Court a vanguard of constitutional values:

> The Imperial Judiciary lives. It is instructive to compare this Nietzschean vision of us unelected, life-tenures judges—leading a Volk who will be "tested by following," and whose very "belief in themselves" is mystically bound up in their "understanding" of a Court that "speak[s] before all others for their constitutional ideals"—with the somewhat more modest role envisioned for these lawyers by the Founders. (*Casey* 1992, 996)

The Court, in Scalia's eyes, remains legitimate only while it reads text and renders decisions based on "society's traditional understanding of that text" (1000). When the Court instead makes value judgments (and Scalia would class *Roe* and *Casey* as value judgments), "then a free and intelligent people's attitude toward us can be expected to be (*ought* to be) quite different" (1000–1).

In some ways Scalia's dissent in *Lawrence v. Texas* is merely an extension of his *Casey* dissent, as he clearly sees both cases as fruit of the same poisonous tree. And Scalia goes for the low-hanging fruit of the majority opinion's expansive language at the outset:

> The Court's claim that *Planned Parenthood v. Casey* "casts some doubt" upon the holding in *Bowers* [*v. Hardwick*] . . . does not withstand analysis. . . . And if the Court is referring not to the holding of *Casey*, but to the dictum of its famed sweet-mystery-of-life passage ("At the heart of liberty is the right to define one's own concept of existence, of meaning, of the universe, and of the mystery of human life"): That "casts some doubt" upon either the totality of our jurisprudence or else . . . nothing at all. I have never heard of a law that attempted to restrict one's "right to define" certain concepts; and if the passage calls into question the government's power to regulate *actions based on* one's self-defined "concept of existence, etc.," it is the passage that ate the rule of law. (*Lawrence* 2003, 588)

Such a broad conceptualization of constitutional liberties is "easy pickings" for Scalia, who admits to no such facility in constitutional analysis. For substantive due process, Scalia subscribes to the holding of *Washington v. Glucksberg*: "that *only* fundamental rights which are 'deeply rooted in this Nation's history and tradition' qualify for anything other than rational-basis scrutiny," absent explicit inclusion in the constitutional text (588). Thus, in *Lawrence's* majority Scalia sees only results-oriented decision making— anathema to his skepticism of judicial review and preference for majoritarian democracy (591).

Similarly, Scalia's institutional philosophy is on full display in the opening words of his *United States v. Windsor* dissent, echoing his preference for majoritarian processes and a narrow reading of due process liberty rights:

> This case is about power in several respects. It is about the power of our people to govern themselves, and the power of this Court to pronounce the law. Today's opinion aggrandizes the latter, with the predictable consequence of diminishing the former. . . . The Court's errors . . . spring forth from the same diseased root: an exalted conception of the role of this institution in America. (*Windsor* 2013, 2697–98)

In the majority opinion, Scalia sees a "black-robed supremacy" wholly foreign to the founding-era fixation on self-rule (*Windsor* 2013, 2698).

Beyond bemoaning the majority's "nonspecific hand-waving . . . that th[e] law is invalid (maybe on equal-protection grounds, maybe on substantive-due-process grounds, and perhaps with some amorphous federal component playing a role)," Scalia trains particular ire toward the majority's assertion that a bare desire to harm cannot be a predicate for legislative action (2698).

For Scalia, "the majority has declared open season on any law that (in the opinion of the law's opponents and any panel of like-minded federal judges) can be characterized as mean-spirited" (2698). Here the late justice returns to majoritarian democracy, accusing the majority of "impos[ing] change by adjudging those who oppose it . . . enemies of the human race" (2709). Scalia's brewing frustration boils over in a rather remarkable rewriting of passages from the majority opinion to make them applicable to state marriage laws limited to opposite-sex couples (2709–11).

Scalia's *Obergefell v. Hodges* dissent acts as an epilogue to his *Windsor* opinion. He admits that the decision in the case—that marriage includes same-sex couples—is "not of immense personal importance" to him (*Obergefell* 2015, 2626). Instead, Scalia's target is the "Court's threat to American democracy":

> Today's decree says that my Ruler, and the Ruler of 320 million Americans coast-to-coast, is a majority of the nine lawyers on the Supreme Court. The opinion in these cases is the furthest extension in fact—and the furthest extension one can even imagine—of the Court's claimed power to create "liberties" that the Constitution and its Amendments neglect to mention. This practice of constitutional revision by an unelected committee of nine, always accompanied . . . by extravagant praise of liberty, robs the People of the most important liberty they asserted in the Declaration of Independence and won in the Revolution of 1776: the freedom to govern themselves. (*Obergefell* 2015, 2626–27)

For Scalia, the answer is simple: "[w]hen the Fourteenth Amendment was ratified in 1868, every State limited marriage to one man and one woman, and no one doubted the constitutionality of doing so" (2628). As same-sex marriage "is not expressly prohibited by the Fourteenth Amendment's text, and . . . bears the endorsement of a long tradition of open, widespread, and unchallenged use dating back to the Amendment's ratification," states can allow or disallow such a classification as they see fit (2629).

Of course Scalia does not end there, as he spends several more pages discussing the "hubris reflected in [the majority's] judicial Putsch" (2629). Scalia attacks the majority's "pretentious" and "egotistic" tenor and content, picking apart individual sentences in an attempt to demonstrate their absurdity (2630). But Scalia's real gripe is more straightforward: the majority opinion lacks the formalistic line-drawing—what he would call "logic and precision"—that he sees as a necessary component of good jurisprudence (2630).

Thus, these dissents focus on one thing: majoritarian democracy. While Scalia may be remembered for the salty counterarguments he laces through these dissents, the key point he makes throughout is that the liberty interests at issue in these cases are subject to the whims of the people, as their textual foundation requires more than a historical exegesis for justification. In other words, Scalia's originalism makes an appearance in his narrow reading of Due Process and Equal Protection principles, but it is his conceptualization of the Court's institutional role in American political development that drives his arguments.

Scalia and Free Speech: *Brown v. Entertainment Merchants Association*

Scalia's free speech opinions (at least when he writes for the majority) are arguably the *least* explicitly originalist. Indeed, one might say that Scalia seems most like a conventional exponent of the common law when dealing with the First Amendment, concerning himself more with the Court's precedents than on the original understanding of the Amendment and how that understanding might apply to the facts at hand.

In *Brown*, Scalia and the Court considered whether California's prohibition on the sale of "violent video games" to minors was constitutional under the First Amendment (*Brown* 2011, 788–89). Beginning from the uncontroverted premise that video games qualify as speech, Scalia engages in a fairly pedestrian, "by-the-numbers" analysis that turns on longstanding Court precedent, rather than any intimate look at text or original understandings (790). Scalia gives the Amendment's general principle: that "government has no power to restrict expression because of its message, its ideas, its subject matter, or its content" (790–91). Only for a few narrow categories of speech that have been traditionally recognized does this principle not apply (790–91). And the Court does not have the power to create additional categorical exemptions; evading the First Amendment requires a "long . . . tradition of proscription," and while some traditions may yet be unrecognized by the Court, speech restrictions must nevertheless be rationalized upon such a traditional basis, rather than a free-standing balancing of social values and costs (791–92). Unlike with other rights recognized by the Court, Scalia holds that "esthetic and moral judgments about art and literature . . . are for the individual to make, not for the Government to decree, *even with a mandate or approval of a majority*" (*Brown* 2011, 791–92).

Scalia cites to a year-old Court case as controlling, holding that no such tradition of proscription protects California's video games restrictions (791–92). As well, in rejecting California's argument that the state may create "a wholly new category of content-based regulation that is permissible only for speech directed at children," Scalia quotes Court precedent for the proposition that "minors are entitled to a significant measure of First Amendment protection, and only in relatively narrow and well-defined circumstances may government bar public dissemination of protected materials to them" (794). For additional authority, Scalia turns to the nation's history of allowing children to engage with violent *books*, noting that school reading lists include literature rife with gore, brutality, and general suffering (794–96).

Having found numerous examples in culture and precedent to support his conclusion, Scalia turns to the applicable legal test: where a law "imposes a restriction on the content of protected speech, it is invalid unless . . . it passes strict scrutiny—that is, unless it is justified by a compelling government interest and is narrowly drawn to serve that interest" (*Brown* 2011, 799). Scalia focuses on the tailoring portion of the analysis, looking for the level of fit between the state's avowed interests—preventing harm to minors and aiding parents in protecting their children—and the legal restriction on the sale of violent video games to minors (799–805). Immediately skeptical, Scalia proceeds by pointing out the ways in which the law is "wildly underinclusive" and "vastly overinclusive" (801–5). "Legislation such as this, which is neither fish nor fowl," says Scalia, "cannot survive strict scrutiny" (805).

Perhaps what makes his opinion notable, though, is that Justice Thomas—Scalia's purported fellow traveler in originalism—*dissents* from the Court's conclusion, doing so on expressly originalist grounds. This is clear from the opening line of Thomas's dissent: "The Court's decision today does not comport with the original public understanding of the First Amendment" (*Brown* 2011, 821). In his mind, the answer could not be clearer. Given that "[t]he practices and beliefs of the founding generation establish that 'the freedom of speech,' as originally understood, does not include a right to speak to minors (or a right of minors to access speech) without [parental consent]," Thomas argues that California's statute comports with the First Amendment (821).

Thomas's dissent is remarkable in several respects, not least of which is the fact that he begins with the same interpretive principle that Scalia follows in *Heller*: "When interpreting a constitution provision, 'the goal is to discern the most likely public understanding of [that] provision at the time it was adopted'" (822). Thomas shares Scalia's observation that the First Amendment, from its inception, exempted particular narrow classes of speech from its protections, but for Thomas, these classes *include* "speech to minor children bypassing their parents" (822). Thomas reaches this conclusion because of "historical evidences show[ing] that the founding generation believed parents had absolute authority over their minor children and expected parents to use that authority to direct the proper development of their children" (822).

What follows is a lengthy historical exegesis (indeed, Scalia should have been thrilled given the rigor and thoroughness of Thomas's historical narrative). Thomas offers an overview of the founding generation's attitudes toward children—both before and after the Revolutionary War (823–25). Thomas also examines Locke and Rousseau, prominent founding-era political thinkers, who "were a driving force behind the changed understanding of children and childhood" (824–26). In light of "great concern about influences on children," "the founding generation understood parents to have a right and duty to govern their children's growth" (*Brown* 2011, 827–34). "In light of this history, the Framers could not possibly have understood 'the freedom of speech' to include an unqualified right to speak to minors" (835). Consequently, for Thomas, California's statute comports with the First Amendment (839).[6]

Summary

This brief survey offers some broad takeaways on Scalia's as-applied jurisprudence. First, in cases like *Heller*, where Scalia is the most overtly "originalist," the late justice shares more with his non-originalist counterparts than one might expect. That is, bearing the moniker of "originalist" does not necessarily imply a wholly unique legal methodology in practice—far from it. While Scalia turns to founding-era sources in his textual arguments, the balance of his opinion is dedicated to post-ratification commentary and past precedents, standard devices of non-originalist or more "common-law" jurisprudence. As well, critical turning points in the argument often hang on the fewest citations, suggesting that Scalia is simply making arguments whose weight depends on their persuasiveness. Not a bad thing—and, really, what Stevens is arguing *all* justices do—but different than the exegesis-type decision making Scalia lays out in his theoretical writings.

In his gay and reproductive rights dissents, Scalia is laser-focused on judicial overreach and majoritarian democracy. As well, Scalia deploys a narrower textualism in crafting counterexamples to undercut the logic of the Court's majorities. But taking "potshots" at the language and arguments in these cases is less than convincing, and Scalia throughout tends to lose persuasive value by resorting to overwrought or overly emotional diatribes. While the late justice will be remembered for his dissent zingers, the critical take home from these dissents is the principle of judicial restraint flowing from narrowly-construed (yet broadly-worded) constitutional provisions, like equal protection and due process.

In *Brown*, as an example of Scalia's First Amendment jurisprudence, Scalia is at his most formalist, drawing bright lines and offering clear rules of decision. Yet Scalia is also at his least originalist, instead arguing more from a common-law, or even non-originalist, posture. Thomas's dissent in *Brown* clarifies this, as it offers an originalist counterpoint that could have easily been written by Scalia, particularly after reading *Heller*. Instead, Scalia writes for the majority in *Brown*, deciding the case based on recent Court precedent and clear tests that, if effectuating the Amendment's purpose, do not enjoy any explicit license from the Amendment's text.

Thus, Scalia's opinions suggest that, while the late justice certainly draws on aspects of his theoretical writings in his decision making, Scalia was neither consistent nor comprehensive in how he decided cases and moved through doctrinal areas. Whereas one doctrinal area evinces emphasis on judicial minimalism and legislative primacy, another reverses this paradigm based on traditionalist arguments wrapped in a plausible reading of constitutional text. Scalia's writings, then, are of limited value in classifying and analyzing his actual jurisprudence, as the late justice was not rigidly originalist in his decision making—a fact he seemed to acknowledge in admitting the inherent pragmatism of being a judge (and a human being). We turn now to an alternative framework for analyzing Scalia's opinions.

PART III: JUSTICE SCALIA—IN REALITY?

The past work of one of these authors[7] has argued that the Supreme Court engages in a dynamic, mutual construction process in which the world outside the Court—the social, political, and economic realities of the lived lives of persons—is brought into the Court and engaged alongside the Court's internal legal rules and precedents (Kahn 2006). This contrasts with unidirectional models of Court action, which posit either that the Court makes decisions based on internal, legalist rationales—with "originalism" being a textbook example—or external factors such as political parties, coalitions, electoral pressures, or the ideological predispositions of the justices—with attitudinalist, strategic, and critical legal theories exemplifying this thinking. These models fall short, however, because they fail to embrace the reality of the Court's decision-making process. We refer to these unidirectional arguments as "Model 1" and the bidirectional model that we advocate for—objectively and normatively—as "Model 2."

The hallmark of Model 2 bidirectional decision making is the social construction process (SCP), the continuous and mutually constitutive dynamic relationship between internal/legalistic and external factors. Engaging in the SCP blends normative and empirical elements and, therefore, is simultaneously inward- (legal) and outward- (society) looking. Because the SCP is bidirectional, legal principles and the world outside the Court become symbiotic and mutually construct each other. Through this lens, one recognizes that internal polity and rights principles—that is, Court concepts of liberty interests and democratic self-rule—gain meaning through their application to the social, political, and economic world outside the Court. Through a process of analogy, the Court considers whether a legal concept, such as liberty, should be extended to a group that heretofore has been denied specific rights.

Moreover, this process results in a legal objectivity that, along with other factors, provides a relative autonomy for the Supreme Court from political pressures and institutions. The legal objectivity of the SCP and the attendant Court autonomy are politically significant. For non-originalists, the SCP is the basis for claims of Court legitimacy and uniqueness among governmental institutions; for originalists, like Scalia, it is the basis for undercutting the Court's legitimacy. The SCP also helps explain why a moderate-conservative Court in a conservative political era expanded the jurisprudential basis for the right of abortion—moving from a concept of privacy (in *Roe v. Wade*) to one of personhood (in *Planned Parenthood v. Casey*)—and extended autonomy and marriage rights to gay Americans in cases like *Lawrence*, *Windsor*, and *Obergefell*. Because Supreme Court decision making cannot be segmented into internal or external elements, Model 1 approaches to studying the Supreme Court resting on such segmentation—that is, on a vision of "law" versus "politics"—are wanting. Thus, Model 2 thinking has major implications for the role of the Supreme Court in American society and American political development.

The SCP has several core elements: (1) it is simultaneously empirical and normative, or inward- and outward-looking; (2) the "interpretive turn" is the process through which the mutual construction process occurs; (3) a special kind of legal objectivity is inherent in the process; (4) the process is cumulative; and (5) the components of this process, including its objectivity, lead to the relative autonomy of the Supreme Court from political institutions.

The SCP is empirical because justices engage in the application of legal concepts to the lived lives of citizens. The process is also normative: the empirical only gains meaning through application of core evaluative standards derived from what justice, liberty, and equality have meant in the past and present, with a concern for what rights and justice might mean in the future. In other words, Supreme Court decision making is simultaneously internal ("inward looking") and external ("outward looking"). Internal influences include the law itself (be it the Constitution, statutes, or settled common law) and judicial norms and procedures. The process is also external or outward looking to social, political, institutional, cultural, historical, and intellectual forces.

At the core of Supreme Court decision making is an "interpretive turn" in which the normative and empirical are mutually constructed through a consideration of "internal" legal principles and the "external" lived lives of citizens. Resulting from this interpretive turn are social constructions resting on precedential social facts—the facts of a case at hand now suffused with the legal principles at issue. These social constructions become "pictures in precedents" of rights principles, growing and changing as the Court grapples with new facts and the changing social, political, and economic realities outside its walls.

This process also produces objectivity to Court decisions, such that they cannot be explained simply on the basis of internal or external factors. Supreme Court decision making is objective because the Court engages in an analogical process of deciding whether a right defined in prior cases should apply in the case before the Court. This process is a defining characteristic of the Supreme Court and of the rule of law itself. Moreover, engaging in a disciplined and robust SCP adds to the legitimacy of the Court and the rule of law because it allows the Court to place its decision making among competing claims within the nation's political culture. Moreover, the role of the SCP in Court decision-making is closely linked to the place of the Supreme Court in American political development. This suggests that the bidirectionality inherent to the Court occurs at several levels: (1) internally, as the Court considers polity and rights principles in past precedents; (2) in cases, as the court mutually constructs the internal legal doctrine and the lived lives of citizens outside the Court; and (3) institutionally or systemically, as the Court engages as a unique American institution with other electorally-accountable political institutions.

Critically, all justices, originalists and non-originalists alike, agree to follow precedent, consider polity and rights principles in making constitutional choices, and engage in analogical reasoning. All see themselves as dealing with the normative and empirical in ways that are special to courts. All see themselves as engaging in a process of interpretation. Both originalists and non-originalists acknowledge that Supreme Court decision making has normative and empirical elements, and that it is both inward- and outward-looking. Where they differ primarily pertains to what should be included in the SCP. The conflict between the originalists and non-originalists is over the relationship between the internal and external (and the normative and empirical). The outward-looking "empirical" of originalist justices may vary among them, but, for most, it is far more limited than for non-originalists. The "external" reference point for most originalists is the narrow time frame of the founding era. Originalists reject that outward-looking components of Court decision making moving beyond founding periods of the Constitution and its amendments. But an implication is that, apart from these specific differences, originalists accept many of the qualities of non-originalist decision making.

Implications

So—what does this all have to do with Justice Scalia? Re-conceptualizing Scalia through the lens of Model 2, bidirectional decision making offers a more fruitful and accurate analytical lens for his jurisprudence than does originalism. Moreover, Model 2 decision making has implications for *originalism* itself.

To summarize, Model 2 envisions a bidirectional, mutual construction process between internal Court precedent and legal rules *and* the social, economic, and political realities outside the Court. As well, mutual construction occurs at the internal Court level, as justices grapple with polity and rights principles inherent in different substantive areas of the law. Through this social construction process the law is applied to the facts of the case at hand, with an eye toward past applications in lines of cases that have preceded the Court's current consideration. Emerging from this process are precedential social facts, which are carried on through substantive legal areas as legally-suffused factual archetypes. The Court, in subsequent cases, reflect back on these precedential facts when dealing with the specific details of a controversy, employing the analogic framework that typifies common-law jurisprudence to determine whether the controversy of the day comports or deviates from critical precedential findings. Put simply, there is dialecticism to Court decision making, where the Court is cognizant of the changing social, political, and economic landscape while bound and informed by the decisions and determinations of past precedents.

When positioned within this idiom, Scalia's jurisprudence remains unique, but it also cannot be described as *contra* the common law. Scalia no doubt puts faith first and foremost in the legalistic traditions of the forum he dominated for three decades. His vocal advocacy for text-centered decision making and historical constitutionalism might be classed as narrowly formalistic or inward-looking (that is, unidirectional in focus). But this does a disservice to Scalia's jurisprudence, for he also took cognizance of the facts at hand in a case, along with the reality of the world outside the Court. His First Amendment decisions display this, particularly *Brown*. There Scalia analogized to past precedents in grappling with video games' interaction with the First Amendment. Indeed, in all of Scalia's opinions there is a keen awareness—for better or worse—of the world outside the Court's walls.

From a decisional standpoint, however, the "originalist" factor takes hold at this "outside-in" point in the late justice's decision making. What separates Scalia from, say, Justices Kennedy or Ginsburg or Kagan (to name a few) is that his bidirectionality is frozen at particular historical moments. Scalia brings the outside world into the Court, but it is the outside world of 1791 or 1868, not today's outside world. This is a byproduct of his reified notion of textual meaning: the constitutional text is a placeholder for chronologically-fixed subjective understandings, such that mutual construction occurs on one temporal plane (a sort-of two-dimensional, rather than three-dimensional, bidirectionality).[8]

However, it is important to note that even Scalia admits that modern viewpoints inevitably find their way into avowedly originalist readings of text, suggesting that the bidirectionality inherent to the Court is inescapable, even if it primarily occupies the internal/legal side of the dichotomy. But more accurately, Scalia accepts the social construction process more fully than he may admit, as the interaction of internal and external factors naturally flows from such guiding principles as limiting due process rights to those deeply rooted in American history and tradition. In order to realize such a principle, one must make value judgments about what traditions count, what constitutes being deeply rooted, and whether the rights being sought in the case at hand comport with the traditions selected. Even if Scalia limits his data set to the founding era, it is fair to say that he remains constrained by the Model 2, bidirectional decision-making characteristic of the Court as an institution.

Notably, though, such reality calls into question unidirectional criticisms of Scalia as purely ideological, masking a conservative policy agenda with faux impartiality in decision making. Scalia himself argues against this characterization: in his eyes, he was just calling "balls and strikes," as it were, and his fixation on bright lines and formalistic jurisprudence was an outgrowth of this belief that his mission was ostensibly nonpartisan. Moreover, Scalia questioned the typical association between non-originalism and progressive policy wants, arguing in part that such "living constitutionalism" did not always result in expansion of individual liberties or some generic "freedom" (Scalia 1989b, 862; 1997, 40–43). First, classifying any justice as driven solely or predominantly by policy preferences is difficult—not to mention of limited empirical value—in light of the Court's inherent bidirectionality, which acts as an institutional context influencing judicial decision making. As well, Scalia's vast output as a justice is hardly homogenous: unidirectional critics might strain to reconcile their characterization of Scalia as nakedly partisan with his majority-supporting vote in a case like *Texas v. Johnson*, which extended First Amendment protection to flag burning, a "liberal" policy position. Finally, unidirectional criticisms of Scalia—and in general—are overly simplistic, too quickly conflating the late justice's formalism or originalism with a partisan conservatism, when these concepts rather should be disaggregated and examined case-by-case. If anything, that Scalia's opinions are uneven when examined against idealized originalism or formalism speaks to the overarching influence of Model 2, as well as the fruitlessness of explaining justices' opinions by this or that factor external to the Court.

More broadly, the foregoing observations about Scalia certainly have implications for how useful originalism itself is as a constitutional theory. Scalia renders decisions as a common-law judge, plain and simple. Yes, he may disagree with Justice Stevens, but such is the nature of judging—indeed, Justice Stevens might argue that such disagreements prove his point about the impossibility of unemotional, purely objective decision making. Ironically, Scalia's *Heller* opinion is a case in point of this common-law adjudication: for all of Scalia's historical fixation, his "originalist" justifications are decidedly more "traditional" (read: general) than "framers' intent" (read: specific). That is, Scalia examines a broad swatch of historical sources in order to discern the nation's "majority view" on the Second Amendment, rather than looking to specific writings of the men who authored and discoursed on the Second Amendment at the time it was ratified. This is not originalist in the pure sense, though it does show that Scalia's adjudicatory admixture is more heavily populated with tradition-based arguments. And where Scalia *does* attempt to be narrowly originalist, the opinion is at its least convincing. The textual analysis seems strained in parts, the citations are uneven, and the argument on the whole reads as more results-oriented than process-focused and diligent.

Where Scalia may be best remembered—in his vibrant and feisty dissents—one might argue his purest originalism is on display. But these dissents are difficult to analyze fully, given that they focus on picking apart sections of majority opinions, rather than offering fully-realized counterarguments. And on the whole these dissents revolve around one theme: majoritarian democracy and the illegitimacy of judicial review (maybe, in Scalia's terms, judicial activism or supremacy). But this is not "originalist"—rather, Scalia organizes his thoughts in these dissents around an overweening polity principle of deference to majorities in the Due Process and Equal Protection space. Compare this with the Second Amendment, where the *rights* principle trumps the polity principle of deference, with the corresponding result being a more active Court.

Finally, Scalia does not shirk precedent—which his colleague, Justice Thomas, is more willing to do. In his First Amendment decisions, Scalia is content to draw lines left and right—but he fundamentally operates within an analytical framework that really emerged only in the last sixty years. That is, Scalia fits firmly in the common-law tradition when examining First Amendment issues, even if he is more overtly reactionary when it comes to such things as gay rights or reproductive freedom.

Moreover, his disagreement with other justices arguing from "originalist" grounds demonstrates that one of originalism's claims to superiority—predictability and objective legitimacy—is not as strong as Scalia asserts. When originalism loses the aegis of truth which its adherents ascribe to it, then, it appears as one of many normative, unidirectional theories of constitutional decision making, a creature of the legal academy rather than a framework for judging. And though Scalia values tradition and history in particular substantive fields, he nevertheless follows the basic judging playbook: apply legal principles to the facts at hand, analogize and distinguish particular cases and ideas, and reaching a decision based on a mix of legal principles, tradition, policy, and pragmatic considerations. That Scalia prefers bright-line rules over incremental decision making is merely a difference in degree rather than type.[9]

And this, of course, merely relates to the judge being human, to the judge failing to escape his or her own subjective bents, viewpoints, and life experiences. To this reality, Scalia was no exception.

CONCLUSION

Nothing here should diminish the impact Justice Scalia has had on the practice and theory of law. His tenure on the Court was of immense consequence, synonymous with a conservative revolution in politics and American culture at the time of his confirmation. But in his efforts to set himself apart from his colleagues, to justify the jurisprudential philosophy to which he held fast, the late justice reveals a great deal about the Supreme Court as an institution, as well as the decision-making process inherent to it. While Scalia's contributions to legal academia have had immense influence in spurring a renaissance of originalist theorizing, his decisions not only cut back against the practicability of such theories, but also call into question the efficacy of such legal theory in explaining what the Court does as an institution. But whether originalism remains an accurate descriptor of Scalia's jurisprudence—or whether originalism offers much to jurisprudence in general—Scalia, regardless of what "wing" of the Court he occupied, made meaningful and dialogue-spurring contributions. If he was a man truly dedicated to democracy and self-rule, then surely this decades-long discussion must make him smile.

NOTES

1. Scalia notes that the perfect originalist opinion "might well take thirty years and 7,000 pages." That the modern Supreme Court dedicates even *less* time to deciding cases than it did in past decades only exacerbates this difficulty.

2. *See* Dennis Goldford, *The American Constitution and the Debate over Originalism* (New York: Cambridge University Press), 2005, (employing hermeneutics and linguistic theory in criticizing originalism's claim to textual authority and interpretive legitimacy).

3. This conceptualization of the Amendments has ramifications for constitutional textualism—that is, if the Amendments are merely stand-ins for "natural rights" predating the Amendments, to what source do we truly look for authoritative guidance on American liberties? Is the Constitution merely a placeholder for some celestial body of freedoms and obligations, or does this almost passing comment reveal a more fundamental tension between Scalia's textualism and his broader constitutional jurisprudence?

4. "[E]xamination of a variety of legal and other sources to determine *the public understanding* of a legal text in the period after its enactment or ratification," says Scalia, "is a critical tool of constitutional interpretation" (*Heller* 2008, 605).

5. Stevens argues that the Amendment's preamble "both sets forth the object of the Amendment and informs the meaning of the remainder of its text" (*Heller* 2008, 643).

6. Scalia points out that Thomas ignores Supreme Court precedent—twentieth-century precedent—in denying minors First Amendment liberties (*Brown* 2011, 795). But Thomas retorts, framing the case's central question as "not whether certain laws might make sense to judges or legislators today, but rather what the public likely understood 'the freedom of speech' to mean when the First Amendment was adopted" (835). Thomas "believe[s] it is clear that the founding public would not have understood the freedom of speech' to include speech to minor children bypassing their parents" (835). Citing nothing less than a Scalia dissent, Thomas asserts that the absence of precedent for a particular state control does *not* establish a constitutional right (835).

7. Ably assisted by his research assistant-*cum*-co-author and collaborator!

8. In addition to *Heller*, one sees originalism's "atextuality" in Scalia's concurrence in *Citizens United v. Federal Election Commission*, an interesting data point given the non-originalist tones of Scalia's Brown opinion. Concurring primarily to criticize Justice Stevens's dissent, Scalia in *Citizens United* makes broad assumptions about the First Amendment's meaning from hazy historical evidence. Stevens rightly pushes back on two fronts. First, he calls into question Scalia's evidence, offering counterexamples showing the founding generation's discomfort with corporations. This evidence is salient to the founding-era meaning of the First Amendment—that is, the Amendment, as the founding generation understood it, did not contemplate corporations as protected speakers. Second, Stevens attacks the originalist mission overall as nothing but cover for subjective judgments. In other words, Scalia's non-specific historical exegesis allows him to construct the First Amendment as he likes. For Stevens, this is not a problem in particular; rather, the issue is that originalism claims an objective rightness that simply is not there, and Scalia, like his colleagues, must rest on persuasiveness as the critical criterion of his opinions.

9. Worth noting here is Judge Posner's central criticism of Scalia: that the late justice was inherently pragmatic, inconsistent in deploying formalism, and ultimately driven by ideology (Posner 2008; Posner 2003). Posner's critique certainly has merit, but it only takes the discussion so far. That is, one can criticize Scalia's formalism and consistency without reaching the conclusion that he is inherently driven by policy preferences. Moreover, it is important to separate the consistency of Scalia's jurisprudence from his use of formalism overall. Certainly cases like *R.A.V. v. St. Paul* and *Employment Division v. Smith* are good examples of Scalia drawing bright lines, even when those lines appear needlessly overwrought or produce opaque internal logic. Posner might fairly call out Scalia's inconsistent *use* of formalism across decades of cases, and Scalia himself seems more amendable to a broader pragmatism in his academic writing. But there is more to the story than an overweening background principle of political ideology. Even if Scalia's judicial philosophy is less monolithic than he presents it to be—and less important in light of Model 2—it nevertheless is still significant in explaining his decisions, at least as one factor among others.

REFERENCES

Kahn, Ronald. 2006. "Social Constructions, Supreme Court Reversals, and American Political Development: *Lochner*, *Plessy*, *Bowers*, but Not *Roe*. In *The Supreme Court and American Political Development*, edited by Ronald Kahn and Ken I. Kersch. 67–113. Lawrence, KS: University Press of Kansas.

Posner, Richard (2003). *Law, Pragmatism, and Democracy*. Cambridge, MA: Harvard University Press.

Posner, Richard (2008). *How Judges Think*. Cambridge, MA: Harvard University Press.

Scalia, Antonin. 1997. "Common-Law Courts in a Civil-Law System: The Role of United States Federal Courts in Interpreting the Constitution and Laws." In *A Matter of Interpretation*. Princeton, NJ: Princeton University Press.

———. 1989. "The Rule of Law as a Law of Rules." *University of Chicago Law Review* 56.

———. 1989b. "Originalism: The Lesser Evil: *University of Cincinnati Law Review* 57.

TABLE OF CASES

Brown v. Entertainment Merchants Association, 564 U.S. 786 (2011).

District of Columbia v. Heller, 554 U.S. 570 (2008).

Lawrence v. Texas, 539 U.S. 558 (2003).

McCulloch v. Maryland, 17 U.S. 316 (1819).

Obergefell v. Hodges, 135 S.Ct. 2584 (2015).

Planned Parenthood of Southeastern Pennsylvania v. Casey, 505 U.S. 833 (1992).

United States v. Windsor, 133 S.Ct. 2675 (2013).

Washington v. Glucksberg, 521 U.S. 702 (1997).

Chapter 10

Justice Scalia and Oral Arguments at the Supreme Court

Timothy R. Johnson, Ryan C. Black,
and Ryan J. Owens

Supreme Court oral arguments feel lonelier these days without Justice Scalia's booming baritone voice. The conservative wing's interruptions seem less common and, certainly, less piercing. The gallery's laughs seem quieter and less frequent even when humor graces the Court's otherwise dry legal discussions. Justice Scalia cast a long shadow over the law. And for some, a Court without Scalia feels like a once majestic tree shorn of its leaves.

While Scalia's judicial legacy is sure to be discussed by many scholars, across many dimensions, for many decades, we focus on Scalia's influence over the only public part of the Court's decision-making process: oral argument.[1] Scalia's behavior (both good and bad) during oral argument has taken on nearly mythical status. Immediately after his death, Court watchers rushed to describe Scalia's influence on oral argument. For example, former solicitor general (and former Scalia clerk) Paul Clement remarked: "Justice Scalia fundamentally changed oral argument before the Supreme Court" (Clement 2016). Similarly, Harvard Law professor Richard Lazarus suggested: "When you prepared for oral argument, you tended to focus tremendously on him because he could transform an argument" (cited in Kendall and Bravin 2016, n.p.). Carter Phillips, an attorney who argued regularly before the Court, declared: "oral argument . . . changed completely after [Scalia] went on the bench" (Fuchs 2016). Perhaps unsurprisingly, Scalia's colleagues agreed. Justice Alito, no wilting flower himself, asserted that Scalia turned oral argument into "a contact sport" (Alito 2017, 1605).

Is this conventional wisdom correct? Did Scalia really reverse the axis upon which oral argument spun? Did he really have the outsized effects attributed to him? The goal of this chapter is to answer these questions empirically. To do so we examine more than 2,800 oral argument transcripts from cases before, during, and after Scalia's tenure on the bench. These data yield more than 316,000 justice-speaking "turns" during which a total of 8.7 million words were spoken. Using these data, we seek to document the extent of Scalia's impact on this most public aspect of the Court's work. More specifically, we ask:

- How often did Scalia speak compared to his colleagues, how verbose was he?
- How often did Scalia interrupt his colleagues and the attorneys as compared to his colleagues?
- How humorous and harsh was Scalia during oral argument as compared to his colleagues?
- Did Scalia's behavior have an effect on his colleagues and, if so, how?

Answering these questions adds a key layer to scholarly accounts of how and why oral arguments play an important role in the decisions Supreme Court justices make. Indeed, research demonstrates that information gathered from these proceedings affects the policy justices set in their opinions (Johnson 2004), that justices may signal how they will decide based on the number of questions they ask (Johnson et al. 2009) and by the tone of those questions (Black et al. 2011), and that justices can and do strategically interrupt their colleagues when asking questions or making comments (Black et al. 2012). If the dynamic changed when Scalia joined the bench in 1986 than his presence certainly had an effect on each of these phenomena. In turn, when he died midway through the 2015 term, the dynamics then changed again—in terms of who dominates the proceedings and who interrupts whom. Thus, understanding perhaps the most loquacious justice to ever sit on the bench provides insight into how oral arguments ultimately affect case outcomes.

This chapter unfolds as follows. First, in an effort to provide readers a sense of the role Scalia might have played at oral arguments, we begin by describing how these proceedings generally operate. We then delineate the reasons justices ask questions and make comments during these public hearings. Next, we transition to our empirical examination of Scalia's behavior and whether his 1986 appointment altered how the justices behaved during oral arguments. To do so, we address the four bullet points displayed above. So that there is no confusion about our results, we state up front that the data show Scalia played a significant role in oral arguments and had an effect on his colleagues in several areas. He asked more questions, displayed more humor, interrupted more often, and used more unpleasant words than his colleagues. And, an initial assessment of the justices' behavior in his absence suggests that his remaining colleagues are seeking to fill the void left when Scalia departed.

ORAL ARGUMENT AT THE U.S. SUPREME COURT

The U.S. Supreme Court normally sits for oral arguments between the first Monday in October and the last week in April. It schedules cases for oral argument in two-week sittings. During each sitting, the Court hears two (although sometimes one or three) arguments per day on Mondays, Tuesdays, and Wednesdays. It hears the first case of the day at 10:00 a.m. and the second at 1:00 p.m. Generally, the Court allots one hour of argument time for a case, with the petitioner and respondent attorneys each speaking for thirty minutes. In highly salient cases, the Court sometimes sets a case for more than an hour (e.g., oral argument in *Bush v. Gore* [2000] lasted an hour and a half, while oral argument in *National Federation of Independent Business v. Sebelius* [2012] lasted six and one-half hours). In addition to the attorneys who argue for each litigant, the Court occasionally allows an interested non-party (*amicus curiae*, or "friend of the Court") to share oral argument time.

At precisely 10:00 a.m. on argument days, the justices enter the Courtroom through the red velvet curtains behind the bench. The Court Marshal then rises to proclaim:

> The Honorable, the Chief Justice and Associate Justices of the Supreme Court of the United States. Oyez! Oyez! Oyez! All persons having business before the Honorable, the Supreme Court of the United States, are admonished to draw near and give their attention, for the Court is now sitting. God save the United States and this Honorable Court![2]

After the Court announces any opinions and concludes motions for admissions to the bar, the chief justice bangs his gavel, calls the first case to order, and invites the petitioner's attorney to begin his or her argument. This attorney does so by declaring: "Mr. Chief Justice, and may it please the Court." To prevent attorneys from exceeding their allotted time, the lectern shows two lights: a white light and a red light. The white light illuminates when the attorney has five minutes left to argue. When the red light illuminates, it signals the attorney's argument time is finished. At that point, the attorney must quickly complete his or her thought and stop. Occasionally, such as when the justices have been particularly loquacious in their questioning, the Chief may extend counsel's time by a few minutes.

Once the attorney begins an argument, justices can interrupt to ask questions as often as they want. In fact, sometimes they interrupt immediately. Consider *City and County of San Francisco v. Sheehan* (2015). Counsel said one word before Justice Scalia interrupted:

> *Christine Van Aken*: Thank you, Mr. Chief Justice, and may it please the Court. This—

> *Antonin Scalia*: Ms. Van Aken, before you go any further.

In most cases, justices interrupt counsel with near impunity. For example, in *Elonis v. U.S.* (2015), Justice Breyer interrupted attorney John Elwood six times in a row. However, after Breyer's sixth interruption, Elwood had enough:

> *John Elwood*: Well, the thing is, though—

> *Stephen Breyer*: I wouldn't have asked it if I didn't want your view, so what is your view?

> *John Elwood*: I'm trying hard to give it to you.

So curious are the justices that the Supreme Court's own guide for counsel advises:

> It has been said that preparing for oral argument at the Supreme Court is like packing your clothes for an ocean cruise. You should lay out all the clothes you think you will need, and then return half of them to the closet. When preparing for oral argument, eliminate half of what you initially planned to cover. Your allotted time passes quickly, especially when numerous questions come from the Court. (Clerk of the Court 2015, 5)

Firsthand accounts from attorneys arguing before the Court suggest that even the "take half" advice is overly optimistic. One first-time attorney was advised to have prepared only a five-minute presentation for his case (i.e., the equivalent of packing only one-sixth of his suitcase). As for how his ocean voyage went, "about fifty seconds into my presentation I was interrupted by a question, and after that the questions continued to come, one after another, for the next twenty-eight minutes. I never did get to say what I wanted to say. The five-minute presentation went unused" (Riback 2003, 148).

The modern bench is quite different from the Court's early days when great lawyers such as Daniel Webster, John Calhoun, William Pinkney, Francis Scott Key (the same man who wrote the Star Spangled Banner), and Henry Clay often appeared before the justices. Then, oral arguments were elaborate oratories. More importantly, they provided the justices with their only source of information about a case because attorneys rarely, if ever, submitted written briefs (Black and Owens 2012; Johnson 2004). Consequently, following English practices, the justices placed no time limitation on the argument sessions. The result of this norm was that advocates sometimes spoke for many hours over multiple days.[3] In *McCulloch v. Maryland* (1819) for instance, Daniel Webster and five other attorneys argued for a full nine days. The justices rarely interrupted the advocates with questions or comments (Johnson et al. 2009, but see Warren 1922). They learned primarily from the information given to them by the attorneys at oral argument.

Today's justices, on the other hand, have little patience for rhetorical flashes and extended discussion. They want attorneys to get to the nub of the problem quickly. Justices ask many questions for a variety of reasons. What are some of these reasons? Surely they ask questions to learn about the facts and relevant precedents pertaining to a case but are there other motivations for questions? It is to this topic that we now turn.

The Purpose and Strategy of Oral Argument

Justices can ask any question, or make any comment they would like, at any time during oral argument.[4] Despite the attorneys' best efforts at making a coherent and persuasive argument, the justices often interrupt them with questions, comments, and hypothetical scenarios related to the case. Across the more than 2,800 cases in our thirty-five years of data (1982–2017), justices averaged about 112 speaking turns per argument (this comports with previous findings including Black, Johnson, and Wedeking 2012; Johnson 2004). Given that the vast majority of arguments are sixty minutes long, this means a justice is speaking roughly once every thirty seconds for the entire hour. Put plainly, today's Court is a hot bench.

Why justices on today's Court speak so often is no great mystery. We posit four common sense reasons for such behavior. First, justices want information about the facts and law involved in cases (Johnson 2004). They decide cases of national importance but often have limited information relevant to such cases. In many cases the facts are unclear and need explication. Other times a precedent is not clear and needs further discussion. During oral argument, the justices have time to ask attorneys questions about such issues and demand answers on the spot. Consider Justice Kennedy's comments in *McDonnell v. U.S.* (2016):

Anthony Kennedy: Can you tell me the posture of the case with reference to under Virginia law, the government the Governor's authority or lack of authority to tell the university, you will engage in this research or you will not engage?

Noel Francisco: Sure, Your Honor. He—

Anthony Kennedy: What is the state of the law, and do—do the parties agree on this point?

Oral arguments offer justices a useful tool to examine the facts of cases and the relevant legal doctrine closely during a time when attorneys can provide answers to their questions.

Second, justices ask questions to learn about the policy implications of a decision (Johnson 2004). The policy ramifications of cases are often unclear, as are the unintended consequences of a ruling. By following up with attorneys about the logical implications (and limiting principles) of their arguments, justices can better determine the consequences of their votes. Consider the following exchange between an exasperated Justice Breyer and petitioner's counsel in *Hernandez v. Mesa* (2017):

Stephen Breyer: . . . you have a very sympathetic case. We write some words. And those words you're delighted with because you win. That isn't the problem. The problem is other people will read those words, and there are all kinds of things that happen . . . what are the words that we write that enable you to win, which is what you want, and that avoid confusion, uncertainty, or decide these other cases the proper way? That's the question you've been given three times, and—and I certainly [would] like to know your answer.

Breyer wanted to know what would happen in numerous cases down the road if the Court ruled in favor of Hernandez. In essence, what would the policy implications and unintended consequences be? Like asking facts about the case, justices will try to extract such information from the attorneys.

Third, oral arguments allow justices to ask questions about the preferences of the executive and legislative branch officials (Ringsmuth and Johnson 2013). The solicitor general often participates in these proceedings—even when the United States is not a party to the case. In this capacity, justices can ask questions to learn what the executive branch thinks of a case. Such information is important to the justices because it is often the federal executive branch that is charged with implementing the Court's decisions. Justices can likewise ask attorneys questions about Congress and public opinion. For example, in *INS v. Chadha* (1983), Justice O'Connor asked Eugene Gressman, counsel for the House of Representatives, a question about how Congress used its powers over aliens; another justice asked about the executive's involvement in the process (Johnson 2004). Even when government lawyers do not argue the case, justices can ask private counsel questions about Congress, the president, and other political actors. Such information better allows justices to place themselves within broader policy and legal debates, and understand how key political actors will respond to their decisions. And for a branch of government that relies so heavily on the others, that information can be useful.

Finally, justices use oral arguments to learn what their colleagues think about a case. It is no secret that justices begin thinking about how they will vote on a case early—usually well before oral argument (Black et al. 2012; Ringsmuth and Johnson 2013). By asking questions during oral argument, justices can test drive arguments to see how they work with their colleagues. They can play devil's advocate to observe their colleagues' responses. In addition, they can directly rebut a colleague's point by answering for the attorney. Justices use oral argument like low orbit military satellites, collecting information about others in preparation for a future event.

Perhaps it is no surprise, then, that most contemporary justices find it useful to participate regularly at oral argument. And no one seemed to relish this part of the Court's decision-making process more than Justice Scalia. He once quipped that "things can be put in perspective during oral argument in a way that they can't in a written brief" (O'Brien 2000, 260). Elsewhere he suggested that, "[oral argument] provides information and perspective that the briefs don't and can't contain" (Scalia and Garner 2008, 139). So let us now move to Justice Scalia's behavior at oral argument. How did it compare to his colleagues? Did Scalia have the effects commonly believed? We describe the data we utilize to answer these questions.

Studying Oral Argument

To gain empirical leverage on oral argument, Justice Scalia's behavior during it, and his possible influence on it, we downloaded the voice-identified oral argument transcripts from the Oyez Project (www.oyez.org) from the 1982 term to the 2016 term. We began in 1982 because it provides us with four terms worth of data prior to Scalia's ascension to the bench. This process generated a total of just over 316,000 justice turns across around 2,800 cases. In total, we examine all orally argued cases for the four terms before Scalia joined the bench, the thirty terms in which Scalia sat on the bench, and the term and a half of cases since his death.

Beyond our counts of the utterances and words used by the justices, we returned to the transcripts and used two dictionary-based approaches to determine the number of words and the emotional nature of those words.[5] First, we employed the *Dictionary of Affect in Language* (hereafter DAL) (Whissell et al. 1986; Whissell 1989) to gauge the emotional content of the justices' words. Whissell (1989) argues that emotion in language can be described adequately and efficiently in terms of a two-dimensional space defined by the pleasantness and activation of words (see also Plutchik 1994; Russell 1978). This continuum allows scholars to determine the overall emotive nature of words.[6] Very unpleasant words are defined as those words in the tenth percentile (or lower) of pleasantness. Some representative examples include chaos, failed, hostile, nightmare, and phony. By contrast, very pleasant words are defined as those words in the ninetieth percentile (or higher) of pleasantness. Examples include confidence, favorable, quality, and respect. (Whissell et al. 1986). The DAL includes a total list of 8,743 words, of which 11 percent are coded as very unpleasant and 10 percent are coded as very pleasant. It is "an accurate description of English word-usage patterns" (Whissell 1999) and has proven a highly reliable and valid way to capture affect in language (Sigelman and Whissell 2002a; Dubois 1997). Contemporary research has also applied to show that the use of emotional language during oral argument by the justices helps forecast their eventual votes (Black et al. 2011). Finally, it provides an objective and replicable measure of the emotional content of language.[7]

Second, we utilize a similar list of words that comes from the Linguistic Inquiry and Word Count (LIWC) program (Pennebaker and King 1999; Tausczik and Pennebaker 2009). LIWC analyzes "attentional focus, emotionality, social relationships, thinking styles," and other features of language (Tausczik and Pennebaker 2009, 24). LIWC is also a dictionary-based approach, which is to say it counts the number of words in a document that fall into one of a number of categories. The internal and external validity of LIWC has been established in a series of publications (see, e.g., Pennebaker and King 1999; Tausczik and Pennebaker 2010; Frimer et al. 2015), and it has also been used in judicial politics scholarship (Owens and Wedeking 2011). Our analysis focuses on LIWC's affective language category, which includes a total of 919 words or word stems. Specifically, we examine the amount of positive emotion and negative emotion words Scalia and his colleagues used at oral argument. We examine two indicators from LIWC: the percent of positive and negative words used at oral argument.

An Empirical Analysis of Questions and Verbosity

According to many Court watchers, oral argument changed on the first Monday of October 1986. When Antonin Scalia joined the high court it was immediately clear he would be no wallflower during oral arguments. In his first session on October 6, 1986, Scalia waited just fifteen minutes to ask a question. And, as was often the case during his time on the Court, his question focused on something that had escaped his colleagues' attention. He wondered aloud about standing—and whether one of the parties enjoyed it.[8] In his line of questioning, Scalia repeatedly forced the attorney in *Hodel v. Irving* (1987) to respond to the standing question, so much so that Justice Blackmun noted Scalia was "hung up" on it (Johnson 2009).

This anecdote demonstrates how, even early on, Scalia played the role of the indefatigable hound dog during oral arguments. In his first term he asked more questions than any of his colleagues. One study counted the number of questions each of the justices asked in a two-week session during the 1986 term (Adler 1987; Alito 2017). Even though Scalia was the junior justice, he asked 30 percent (126 total) of *all* the questions. In comparison, Justice Powell, who had been on the Court nearly fourteen years, asked only one question in these cases (Adler 1987, 18).[9] Our data affirm these earlier findings in a broader context.

Consider figure 10.1, which depicts the distribution of speaking turns of each justice in our sample of cases. The horizontal lines identify the average for a justice. For the most part, the number of times each of the justices in our sample spoke comports with conventional wisdom about their oral argument behavior. Scalia spoke significantly more often than each of his colleagues but, while he was the most active questioner during oral argument, he also had the most variation in terms of his *expected* level of activity. For instance, in *FEC v. Wisconsin Right to Life* (2006), he asked 119 questions; in *BP America v. Burton* (2006) he asked 102 questions. Despite this variation, even a "slow" day for Justice Scalia eclipsed many of his colleagues. Scalia's twenty-fifth percentile value—roughly eighteen questions—is approximately equal to former Chief Justice Rehnquist's median level of questioning and is equivalent to the seventy-fifth percentile value for Justice O'Connor. What is more, we note that a session of eighteen questions asked by Justice Alito would be deemed a low outlier for Scalia. The point is that Scalia was quite prolific.

Figure 10.1 places Scalia in perspective and demonstrates that justices from various parts of the Court's ideological spectrum have spoken quite often in the past quarter century. Indeed, Chief Justice John Roberts is a close second to Scalia while Justices Byron White, Stephen Breyer, and Sonia Sotomayor round out the top five speakers by turn. These four represent, respectively, members of the conservative wing (Roberts), the moderate wing (White), and the liberal wing (Breyer and Sotomayor). Being voluble does not correlate with justices' ideological leanings.

Bear in mind that the *number of turns* is not a mirror image of the *number of words spoken*, though there is a correlation. That is, turns and words are not the same. Figure 10.2 shows that, while Scalia spoke the most often (i.e., had the most turns), Justice Breyer was slightly more garrulous, using the most

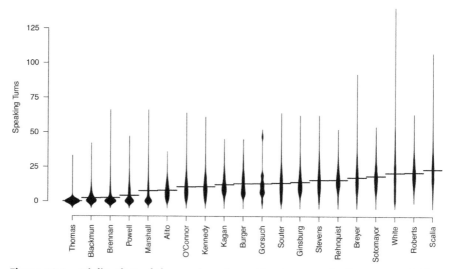

Figure 10.1. Violin plots of the number of speaking turns per justic per case (1982–2017). The solid horizontal bars within a specific density estimate provide the means for a specific justice.

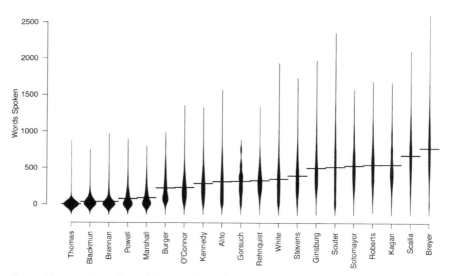

Figure 10.2. Violin plots of the number of words spoken per justice per case (1982–2017). The solid horizontal bars within a specific density estimate provide the mean for a specific justice.

words per oral argument. Not surprisingly, Justice Scalia was a close second to Breyer. Chief Justice Roberts and Justice Sotomayor again come in the top five. Justice Elena Kagan, however, supplants Justice White.

Understanding how his colleagues' speaking patterns compare to Scalia is important, but we are even more interested in whether Scalia's oral argument behavior affected his colleagues' behavior. In other words, did his penchant for questioning rub off on his colleagues? Did Scalia push so hard that his colleagues responded in kind? Kendall and Bravin (2016) suggest "Justice Scalia's active questions from the conservative side have been balanced out in recent years by the court's liberal members, including Sotomayor and Kagan." More generally, Lazarus (cited in Kendall and Bravin 2016) is certain that: "Spurred on by Scalia, the number of questions asked by the justices has steadily increased during oral argument." Totenberg (2016) agrees and suggests that, because of Scalia, his colleagues "took a more active approach to questioning."

Figure 10.3 allows us to answer this question. During the Roberts Court era, Alito spoke more often in Scalia's absence, as did Kagan, Breyer, and Sotomayor. Other justices spoke less. Roberts and Kennedy spoke somewhat less than they had prior to Scalia leaving and, surprisingly, Ginsburg spoke significantly less after Scalia's departure. Perhaps this is an indication of her strong friendship with Scalia, or perhaps it is a function of her age. Whatever the reason, she was much less active after Scalia left the Court.

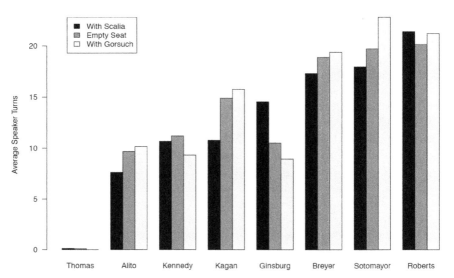

Figure 10.3. **Bar graph of the average number of utterances per justice per case with Scalia on the bench (1986–2016), after he left the bench (February 2016–April 2017), and with the addition of Justice Neil Gorsuch (April–June 2017).**

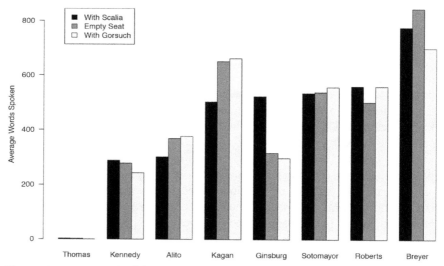

Figure 10.4. Bar graph of the average words spoken per justice per case with Scalia on the bench (1986–2016), after he left the bench (February 2016–April 2017), and with the addition of Justice Neil Gorsuch (April 2017–June 2017).

What is more, figure 10.4 shows a similar dynamic in terms of the number of words each justice used during oral argument. Indeed, this figure shows the emerging dominance of Kagan at oral argument. Not only did she speak more often after Scalia's death, she also used more words. The same could be said about Alito, who may have believed he should lend assistance to the suddenly quieter conservative bloc on the Court.

To understand Scalia's effect more generally, figure 10.5 depicts the interaction of turns and words and highlights three "states of the world" for each justice: (a) the justice's behavior prior to Scalia's departure; (b) the justice's behavior after Scalia's death but before Justice Gorsuch joined the Court; and (c) the justice's behavior after Gorsuch joined the Court. The arrows show the progression through those three states. For example, Justice Breyer's activity went up after Scalia died but then dropped back down to a bit below his "with Scalia" levels after Gorsuch joined.

Strikingly, figure 10.5 highlights just how significant the Scalia departure was for Kagan and Ginsburg. Kagan seemed to take off after Scalia's passing. It is becoming clear that she has taken on a considerably more important role in oral argument than before Scalia's death. Indeed, her number of turns increased as did her number of words used. Conversely, Ginsburg seems still to be in mourning. She asks fewer questions and employs fewer words since her good friend left the bench. Interestingly, while Breyer has not backed down in terms of the number of speaking turns (in fact, he's actually increased), he

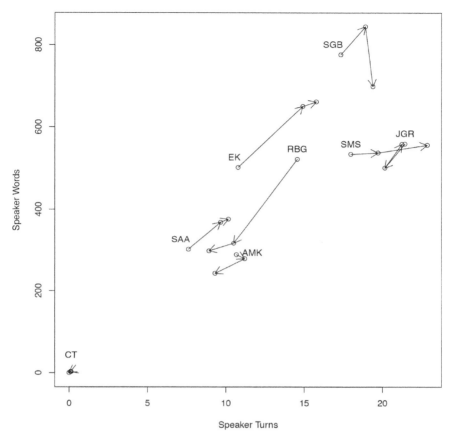

Figure 10.5. The interaction of the average number of turns per justice per case with the average number of words spoken while Scalia was on the Court, after his death, and after Gorsuch replaced him.

seems to have become less wordy in his questions. Time will tell whether or not he continues this trend.

Taken together, these findings demonstrate that Scalia had a significant impact by how he behaved during oral arguments and in terms of his colleagues' speaking turns and words spoken. For some, he had the effect of making them speak more while for others he seemed to quiet them with his willingness to speak so often. In the aggregate, this section makes clear Scalia's presence went a long way toward making the U.S. Supreme Court a hot bench.

Interruptions from the Bench

Scalia also was considered to be a "serial interrupter" of his fellow justices (Black et al. 2012) and was known to even speak over his colleagues who were in mid-sentence of their own questions. One study indicates more than 7 percent of Scalia's utterances interrupted another colleague who was trying to ask a question or make a point to counsel (Black et al. 2012). This penchant for interruptions did not go unnoticed by his colleagues, as a number of anecdotes demonstrate suggest. Consider *Tulsa Professional Collection Services, Inc. v. Pope* (1988). Roughly one-third of all Scalia's comments during these oral arguments interrupted counsel. Perhaps not surprisingly, Blackmun recorded the following in his notes: "Scalia is interrupting intolerably again!" In *Stansbury v. California* (1994) Chief Justice Rehnquist had to play traffic cop to deal with Scalia's interruption:

> *Anthony Kennedy*: The problem I have is that at eleven different points it engages in a discussion of matters that are quite irrelevant to that standard, and I'm not quite—
>
> *Antonin Scalia*: —Well, I hope you don't concede it's irrelevant. Do you concede it's irrelevant? It can't be conveyed if it doesn't exist, can it? How can you convey that he is the focus of the investigation, if in fact he is not the focus of the investigation? It is not a sufficient condition, but it is a necessary condition, isn't it, and that makes it relevant, it seems to me.
>
> *William H. Rehnquist*: Why don't you first answer Justice Kennedy's question, and then Justice Scalia?

Sometimes, Rehnquist was more aggressive and actually rebuked Scalia for his behavior. In one case, Rosen (2007) suggests Rehnquist shook his finger at Scalia for interrupting Kennedy. In another case—*U.S. v. R.L.C.* (1992)—Rehnquist was, himself, Scalia's victim. When Rehnquist began to ask counsel a question, Scalia blurted over the top of him. Chief Justice Rehnquist admonished him: "Just a minute, Justice Scalia, I think I started before you did." In his oral argument observations of the case, Blackmun noted the Chief's irritation, writing: "CJ tells AS t[o] shut up while he is asking a q[uestion]."[10] While the Chief actually used tamer language, the same point obtains: Scalia sometimes annoyed his colleagues with his penchant to speak over them.

The question is, though, were these cases outliers, or did Scalia regularly interrupt his colleagues and the lawyers? The data, which we present in figure 10.6, may be surprising. To generate these data we again mined the argument transcripts for the presence of an interruption. We follow Black, Johnson, and Wedeking (2012) and Johnson, Black, and Wedeking (2009) to define an interruption as when two (or more) consecutive turns are from a justice, with no intervening participation by an attorney.

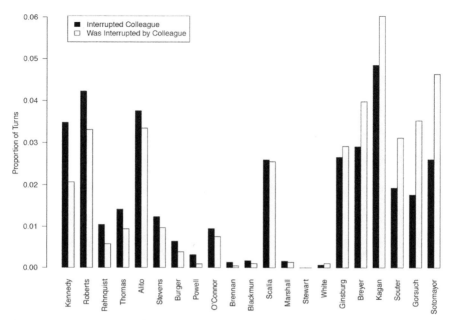

Figure 10.6. Bar graph of the proportion of utterances where a justice either interrupted (black bars) a colleague or was interrupted (white bars) by another colleague.

To be sure, Scalia interrupted his colleagues a fair amount of time. Roughly 3 percent of his speaking turns interrupted one of his colleagues. How to interpret this, of course, lies in the eye of the beholder. On the one hand, *when he spoke*, Scalia did not interrupt his colleagues as much as some other justices, including Roberts, Kennedy, Alito, Breyer, and Kagan. On the other hand, figure 10.6 reflects the *proportion* of turns in which the justice interrupted a colleague. For someone like Scalia, who spoke frequently, 3 percent reflects a large raw number of interruptions.

More generally, our data also allow us to examine whether Scalia's presence changed the culture on the bench with regards to interrupting behavior. That is, once the genie was out of the bottle, did Scalia's colleagues follow suit and start interrupting at a higher rate than before he was on the Court. The data, which we show in the two panels of figure 10.7, say no. The horizontal axis in both figures shows the Court term. The vertical axis in the top panel portrays the proportion of cases where at least one interruption took place. In the bottom panel we show the relative frequency of interruptions, as a proportion of the total number of speaking turns across an entire term. In other words, the top panel shows the basic prevalence of

At Least One Interruption Takes Place

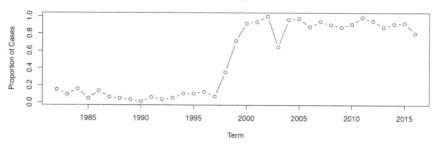

Overall Frequency of Interruptions

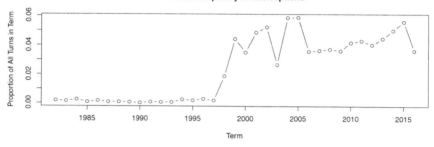

Figure 10.7.   Proportion of cases with at least one interruption between the justices (top panel) and proportion of all turns in a term that were interruptions (bottom panel) from (1982–2017).

any interruptions whereas the bottom panel provides additional data on the magnitude of interruptions.

Quite interestingly, prior to the late 1990s, interruptions were not common on the Court. To wit, before the Court's 1998 term, they never occurred in more than 20 percent of the orally-argued cases. Starting in 1998, however, both their prevalence and magnitude increased dramatically. In the span of just three terms, at least one interruption was occurring in the vast majority of cases. Lest the reader think the Court had devolved into chaos and knife fights, however, it is important to bear in mind, per the bottom panel, that the overall proportion of justice speaking turns that constituted interruptions is still low—at most only 6 percent. We are, so far as we know, the first to identify this dramatic change in the Court's behavior. Although a full accounting of the causes of this change are beyond the scope of this chapter, we suspect it might have something to do with the increased ideological polarization on the Court taking place in the late 1990s. This mirrors, of course, what was happening with the elected branches of government with the impeachment of President Clinton in December 1998.

Returning to the role of Scalia, although we only have a small sample of cases since Scalia's death, it seems his departure has led to fewer interruptions on the Court in the aggregate. Figure 10.7 shows a modest dip in the number of cases with at least one interruption after Scalia's death and a much bigger drop in the number of all justice utterances defined as an interruption of a colleague. In other words, these two most recent dips coincide with Scalia's death. We caution the reader to not insinuate too much from this finding, because we have little data since his death, but it is suggestive and worthy of future study.

Combined, figures 10.6 and 10.7 suggest that Scalia was among the most ardent interrupters during his time on the bench. This is no surprise given the anecdotes we cite prior to the data. That said, what we take away from the data is that while Scalia might have been the serial interrupter of the 1990s and 2000s, our data show the torch has been passed to Kagan. Regular interruptions now come from justices on the right *and* the left.

Scalia and the Tone of Oral Argument: The Sweet (Humor) and the Sour (Negative Tone)

Because he was known for his dry wit, we examine the emotional tone of Scalia's questions from the bench. He has, after all, been labeled as the wittiest of his colleagues (Wexler 2005) and also as the most sarcastic and biting (Hasen 2015). We first examine his use of humor during oral arguments and then turn to the tone of his utterances.

Scalia and Humor

When it comes to attorneys using humor in the Court, the expression "Do as I say, not as I do" seems appropriate. Most Court experts recommend attorneys do not attempt humor at the austere Court. The justices agree. The Court itself, speaking through the clerk of the court, indicates to attorneys that, "Attempts at humor usually fall flat" (Clerk of the Court 2015, 10). In other words, attorneys are warned to not make jokes before the bench. This does not mean humor is not a part of oral arguments, however. In fact, justices often draw laughter when they ask questions or make comments. Justices, it seems, want to be the only ones to use humor.

Justice Scalia certainly employed humor during oral argument and laced his utterances with wit, such as in a 2010 free speech case when he probed the difference between "normal" violent videogames and "deviant" violent games whose sale had been restricted in California. Violence has long been part of children's entertainment, he suggested, citing Grimms' fairy tales (*Brown v. Entertainment Merchant Association* 2010). While at first blush such a reference may not seem particularly funny, the exchange between the attorney for California and Justice Scalia did draw laughter:[11]

Zackery P. Morazzini: California asks this Court to adopt a rule of law that permits States to restrict minors' ability to purchase deviant, violent video games that the legislature has determined can be harmful to the development—

Antonin Scalia: What's a deviant—a deviant, violent video game? As opposed to what? A normal violent video game?

Zackery P. Morazzini:—Yes, Your Honor. Deviant would be departing from established norms.

Antonin Scalia: There are established norms of violence?

Zackery P. Morazzini: Well, I think if we look back—

Antonin Scalia: Some of the Grimms' fairy tales are quite grim, to tell you the truth.

Zackery P. Morazzini: —Agreed, Your Honor. But the level of violence—

Antonin Scalia: Are they okay? Are you going to ban them, too?

Zackery P. Morazzini: —Not at all, Your Honor.

As part of his dry wit, Scalia was not averse to engaging in humor about bodily functions. *Glickman v. Wileman Brothers & Elliott Inc.* (1997) was a case focusing on whether a federal law mandating tree fruit growers to pay assessments to the department of agriculture each year violated their free speech rights. While the case focused on an important free speech debate, the oral arguments devolved at one point to a discussion of the different types of fruit grown by the respondents and Scalia was quick to crack a joke about a specific type of fruit—green plums:[12]

Antonin Scalia: And you object to that. You'd be here even if they weren't pushing the Red Jim or whatever this nectarine is.

Thomas E. Campagne: —Absolutely, because that's not truthful. I want to tell—

Antonin Scalia: Well, that . . . but isn't there another reason—

Thomas E. Campagne: —that you ought to buy green plums and give them to your wife, and you're thinking to yourself right now you don't want to give your wife diarrhea, but green plums—

Antonin Scalia: —Green plums? I would never give my wife a green plum.

Whatever the type of humor, it is inarguable that Scalia was the most humorous justice during his tenure on the bench. Figure 10.8 bears out this contention. We examined the proportion of cases where a justice elicited laughter according to the oral argument transcripts. Thus, while he was a serial interrupter, and spoke more often than his colleagues, he was also (in some sense) a serial comedian. His loquacious counterpart Justice Breyer, was a close second in terms of proportion of cases where a justice elicited laughter. From there, perhaps oddly, are the two chiefs under whom Scalia served—Roberts and Rehnquist. Chiefs are usually the ones to keep deco-

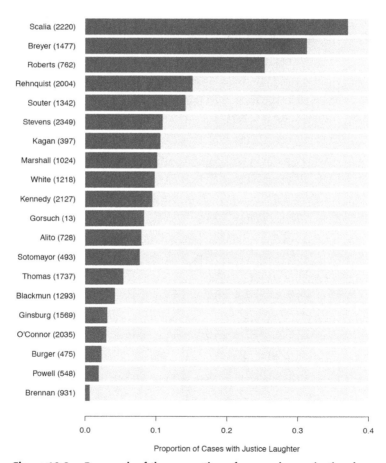

Figure 10.8. Bar graph of the proportion of cases where a justice drew laughter from the courtroom. The number in the parentheses next to a justice's name identifies the number of cases where a justice was at oral argument.

rum in the courtroom, so it is an interesting finding that they too exhibited a good deal of humor. The key finding for us, however, is that Scalia outperformed his colleagues when it came to chuckles from the gallery. While time will tell which justices takes the place as the class clown, readers should keep an eye on Kagan; her quips at oral argument are becoming legendary.

But did Scalia alter the overall tenor of humor in the courtroom during his thirty years on the bench? Figure 10.9 provides the data to answer the question. The proportion of cases with laughter *never* reached beyond 30 percent of the cases from 1982 to 1987. Then, in 1988, the proportion skyrocketed and only dropped a few terms in the early 2000s when the nation was reacting to a contentious presidential election and a devastating terrorist attack. From there, humor enriched more than 60 percent of cases in almost every term since 2004. In addition, as the bottom panel of figure 10.9 shows, there was much more laughter in a given case once Scalia joined the bench (with the caveat that the same dip exists in the early 2000s). Scalia's penchant for witticisms seems to have had a marked impact on the Court in the only public appearance it makes for a given case.

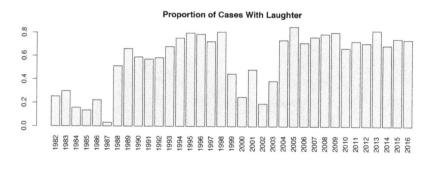

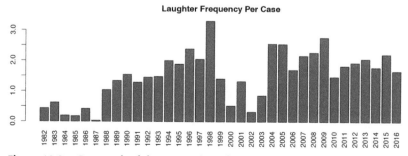

Figure 10.9.   Bar graph of the proportion of cases (top panel) and frequency of laughter per term (bottom panel) from 1982–2016.

Justice Scalia and Negative Tone

While Scalia influenced the number of questions justices asked, the number of words they spoke, and the amount of humor at oral argument, he also was known for asking hostile questions that could bring even the strongest attorneys to their knees. Court scholars and analysts agree that Scalia was known for the language he used during oral arguments. For instance, Little (2016) points out that he was known for his "colorful use of language in oral arguments." Rosen (2007) concurs when he suggests that Scalia was known to "dominate oral argument with aggressive questions and showy put-downs." Bryan et al. (2016) argue that Scalia utilized acerbic language when questioning attorneys with whom he disagreed.

A barb from Scalia could quickly turn an attorney's argument into "pure applesauce."[13] For instance, in *Marvin M. Brandt Revocable Trust v. U.S.* (2014), Steven J. Lechner began his oral argument seemingly reading from his prepared notes. Scalia jumped in and remarked: "Counsel, you are not reading this, are you?" After a moment of quiet, Breyer jumped in and said: "It's all right." An awkward oral argument ensued.

While Lechner was admonished for how he presented his arguments, David Friedman was vilified by Scalia for the substance of his arguments in *McCreary v. ACLU* (2005). Certainly Scalia disagreed with Friedman's argument that displaying the Ten Commandments in public schools and courthouses violated the Establishment Clause of the First Amendment and he pulled no punches in making this clear. At one point he quipped, "I don't think they're really saying that the particular commandments of the Ten Commandments are the basis of the Declaration of Independence. That's idiotic." Moments later he used the same harsh language: "If that's what it means, it's idiotic. I don't think anybody is going to interpret it that way. You can't get the Declaration of Independence out of the Ten Commandments."[14] In making these statements to Friedman, Scalia seemed to signal his clear belief that the First Amendment does not prohibit the public display of the Ten Commandments in either public schools or courthouses. He also made it clear that he is willing to dismiss arguments with harsh language.

To determine whether Scalia used harsher language than his colleagues at oral argument, we examine the number of "pleasant" and "unpleasant" words used by the justices during oral argument. To measure these words, we analyzed the transcripts using the two aforementioned dictionaries. As we describe in full detail above, this approach allows us to determine the tone of words people use. We show these data graphically in figure 10.10. Consider, first, the justices' use of positive and pleasant words. Scalia clearly used fewer positive and pleasant words during his tenure than did his colleagues. While the difference is not large, given that only a small percentage of words they use during

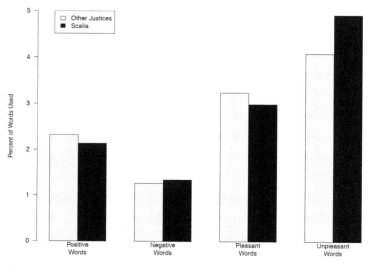

Figure 10.10. Bar graph of the percent of words used by justices that fall into various linguistic categories 1982–2016.

the arguments can be categorized in this manner, it is clear that Scalia's word choices were, to put it bluntly, not as pleasant as the words his colleagues chose to use.

On the other hand, it is even more evident that Scalia could use harsh language when speaking to the attorneys (or to his colleagues) during oral arguments. Although he showed only a slight penchant for using more negative words in his utterances, he used significantly more unpleasant words than his colleagues, including calling an argument idiotic in *McCreary*. This is consistent with the anecdotal accounts at the beginning of this section. Indeed, advocates and Court watchers perceived him as being aggressive and bombastic, the data bear out these claims!

Like our analysis of humor and interruptions, however, the question is whether Scalia's behavior was contagious. That is, did his colleagues use fewer good words when he joined the bench and more good words before and after his tenure? Figure 10.11 allows us to make this determination. The top panel shows the percentage of good words spoken by the justices, broken into positive and pleasant words. There was a slight dip in pleasant words as Scalia joined the bench but then the percentage stayed relatively stable (with some variation) throughout his time on the Court. Then, as his time came to a closer there was an uptick in this percentage. On the other hand, there was a much larger dip in the percentage of positive words once Scalia joined the Court and the downward trend continued throughout his thirty years. While we do not have enough data to make claims about the future of positive words, there has been a slight uptick in the percentage of them used since about 2007.

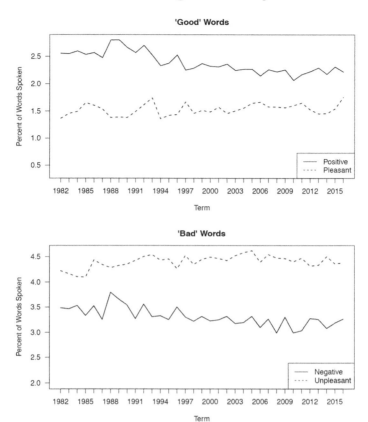

Figure 10.11. Percent of words spoken each term that use good words (top panel) and bad words (bottom panel).

The bottom panel of figure 10.11 demonstrates that the Court did indeed become slightly more negative when Scalia joined in 1986 but then the percent of negative words actually decreased throughout his tenure. The Court also seemed to increase its use of unpleasant words when Scalia ascended the bench but these percentages generally leveled off (with some variation) after that time. So while the Court became generally less negative with Scalia on the Court it also became less positive.

CONCLUSION

We end where we began—noting that the courtroom seems lonelier since Scalia's death in February 2016. His presence was sometimes larger than life and his biting questions and comments could cut off at the knees attorneys trying to make their case before the nation's high court. Despite his penchant for intimidation with his wit and intellect, lawyers will indeed miss him. As one advocate put it, "It's really hard to imagine standing at the podium without him there" (Kendall and Bravin 2016). Court watches and scholars agree with this sentiment and the data we presented here show just how strong an influence Scalia was as he sparred with counsel and colleagues alike.

Specifically, we showed that Scalia was one of the most active speakers and was quite verbose when he asked questions or made comments. While we do not show a direct correlation between his behavior and his colleagues' behavior, the data indicate individual justice's behavior was different when he joined the bench and after his death. In addition, Scalia had a penchant to interrupt his colleagues' questions and was sometimes admonished for doing so. Finally, his humor brought levity to the courtroom although his questions were often more negative than positive. While his negativity was not contagious his humor seemed to affect his colleagues' proclivity for eliciting chuckles from gallery. The bottom line is Scalia's presence had an effect on his colleagues' behavior which certainly changed the dynamics of oral arguments. Ultimately, he will be missed as he left his mark on arguments in a variety of ways.

The question is whether oral arguments have really changed since Scalia's death. Some signs indicate they have. For one, while he has not spoken since, just weeks into the new Court Era, Justice Clarence Thomas spoke for the first time in a decade. It is not hyperbole to say that everyone in the courtroom was shocked—to say the least (see Epps 2017). On the other hand, the Court has generally gone back to business as usual. Indeed, the justices have maintained a relatively steady level of questions and comments since his death. In the 38 arguments in which Scalia participated in the 2015 term, the court averaged 121 utterances for each oral argument. Since his death, the Court has averaged 109 utterances (Bishop and Parker 2016). On an individual level, Bishop and Parker (2016) suggest Sotomayor is the most prolific speaker. Specifically, in 31 oral arguments since Scalia's death, she averaged 22.3 questions or remarks per argument which is an increase from her prior average of 18.9 utterances per case. Thus, while things have changed, they, in many respects, have stayed the same since the Court lost one of the most prolific and verbose speakers in the history of its oral arguments.

NOTES

1. Certainly commentators have commented on the outsized influence Justice Scalia exerted on the law. For example, Linda Greenhouse remarked, much less charitably, that Justice Scalia's death "preserved democracy in North Carolina" because he would not be able to rule in the North Carolina redistricting cases (Greenhouse 2016).

2. To listen to an audio clip of this (and confirm for yourself how "Oyez" is pronounced!), navigate to www.oyez.org/about (last accessed October 6, 2017).

3. Sessions during the early part of the nineteenth century were so long (typically 11 a.m. to 5 p.m.) that rather than formally breaking for lunch, justices would take turns to go behind the curtain to take their lunch while oral argument continued in their absence (Cushman 2011, 122).

4. This can include a justice simply seeking to satisfy his or her curiosity about some tangential aspect of a case. For example, in *Rubin v. Coors Brewing Co.*, 514 U.S. 476 (1995), Justice Scalia, who some have identified as being more of a wine aficionado (Zona 2016), asked an attorney what the difference was between ale and beer.

5. We performed our text analysis using Benoit et al.'s (2017) "quanteda" package in R.

6. Data for the DAL were collected in the latter half of the 1990s. Over 200 volunteers rated words on each of the scales to generate the rating judgments that were used to create the DAL. We note that the types of words we use in this analysis—very unpleasant and very pleasant words—are only scored on the pleasantness continuum. Adding activation would allow us to measure "cheerful" or "nasty" words, but we believe pleasant and unpleasant words most directly tap into a speaker's emotions, which is our latent concept of interest.

7. Whissell (2001) suggests one main limitation to the DAL. Specifically, the scores are created in a context free manner. That is, words are scored individually and not within the passage where they are used. Thus, the DAL is insensitive to complexities in word choice like humor, irony, and sarcasm.

8. In order to invoke a federal court's power, the complainant must have suffered a concrete and particularized injury caused by the defendant that is redressable by the Court. This is the standing doctrine. See, e.g., *Lujan v. Defenders of Wildlife*, 504 U.S. 555 (1992).

9. Scalia's behavior was remarkable but clearly a double-edged sword. He asked so many questions his colleagues quickly became put out with him. Just two months after Scalia took his seat, Blackmun jotted exasperated comments in his private notes such as: "Too much questioning and arguing by Scalia again!" See *Pennsylvania v. Ritchie*, 480 U.S. 39 (1987) (Johnson 2009). Similarly, in *Freytag v. Commissioner*, 501 U.S. 868 (1991), Blackmun wrote: "Scalia always arguing with counsel!" In *Eastman Kodak Co. v. Image Technical Services, Inc.*, 504 U.S. 451 (1992), Blackmun wrote: "Scalia is insufferable here."

10. While the Chief did not use the exact phrase (shut up) as Blackmun wrote, his point is the same, especially given the tone of his voice. To hear the exchange navigate to http://www.oyez.org/cases/1990–1999/1991/1991_90_1577/argument and click on the clip titled "Chief tells Scalia to cool it."

11. To hear the audio navigate to http://www.scotusblog.com/wp-content/uploads/2016/02/Scalia-Brown-v-Entertainment-Merchants.mp3

12. To hear the audio navigate to https://www.press.umich.edu/special/goodquarrel/Mauro/Mauro-p091–4.mp3

13. *King v. Burwell*, 135 S.Ct. 2480 (2015) (Scalia, J. dissenting).

14. To hear this case navigate to http://oyez.org/cases/2000–2009/2004/2004_03_1693/argument.

REFERENCES

Adler, Stephen. 1987. "Scalia's Court." 9 *American Lawyer* 1, March, 18.

Alito, Samuel. 2017. "A Tribute to Justice Scalia." *The Yale Law Journal* 126: 1605–8.

Bennoit, Kenneth, Kohei Watanabe, Paul Nulty, Adam Obeng, Haiyan Wang, Benjamin Lauderdale, and Will Lowe. 2017. "quanteda: Quantitative Analysis of Textual Data." R package, version 0.99.12 (October 6, 2017). http://quanteda.io.

Bishop, Stewart and Stan Parker. 2016. "A New Justice Dominates Oral Arguments in Wake of Scalia's Death" Law360.com. June 10. Last accessed June 26, 2018. https://www.iadclaw.org/securedocument.aspx?file=1/7/A_New_Justice_Dominates_Law360_06_10_16_MCSungaila_MarkFleming1.pdf.

Black, Ryan C., Amanda C. Bryan, and Timothy R. Johnson. 2011. "An Actor- Based Measure of Salience: Information Acquisition and the Case of the United States Supreme Court" in *Issue Salience and Foreign Policy Analysis*, edited by Kai Oppermann and Henrike Viehrig, 240–57. New York: Routledge.

Black, Ryan C., Timothy R. Johnson, and Justin Wedeking. 2012. *Oral Arguments and Coalition Formation on the U.S. Supreme Court: A Deliberate Dialogue*. Ann Arbor: University of Michigan Press.

Black, Ryan C. and Ryan J. Owens. 2012. *The Solicitor General and the United States Supreme Court: Executive Branch Influence and Judicial Decisions*. New York: Cambridge University Press.

Black, Ryan C., Rachel A. Schutte, and Timothy R. Johnson. 2013. "Trying to Get What You Want: Heresthetical Maneuvering and U.S. Supreme Court Decision Making." *Political Research Quarterly* 66(4): 818–29.

Black, Ryan C., Maron W. Sorenson, and Timothy R. Johnson. 2013. "Towards an Actor-Based Measure of Supreme Court Case Salience: Information-Seeking and Engagement During Oral Arguments." *Political Research Quarterly* 66(4): 803–17.

Black, Ryan C., Sarah A. Treul, Timothy R. Johnson, and Jerry Goldman. 2011. "Emotions, Oral Arguments, and Supreme Court Decision Making." *Journal of Politics* 73(2): 572–81.

Bryan, Amanda C., Charles Gregory, and Timothy R. Johnson. 2016. "Loyalty and Deference at Oral Arguments: An Empirical Examination of How Supreme Court Justices Treat Solicitors General." *Loyola University Chicago Law Journal* 48: 439–74.

Clement, Paul. 2016. "Arguing Before Justice Scalia." *New York Times*. February 17, 2016.

Clerk of the Court. 2015. *Guide for Counsel in Cases to Be Argued Before the Supreme Court of the United States*. October Term 2015. https://www.supremecourt.gov/casehand/guideforcounsel.pdf (last accessed October 6, 2017).

Cushman, Clare. 2011. *Courtwatchers: Eyewitness Accounts of Supreme Court History*. Lanham, MD: Rowman & Littlefield.

Dubois, Stephanie L. 1997. "Gender Differences in the Emotional Tone of Written Sexual Fantasies." *Canadian Journal of Human Sexuality* 6: 307–15.

Frimer, Jeremy, Karl Aquino , Jochen E. Gebauer , Luke (Lei) Zhu, and Harrison Oakes. 2015. "A Decline in Prosocial Language Helps Explain Public Disapproval of the U.S. Congress." *Proceedings of the National Academy of Sciences* 12(21): 6591–94.

Fuchs, Erin. 2016. "Lawyer Who's Argued 73 Cases in Supreme Court Says Oral Arguments 'Changed Completely' after Scalia." *Business Insider*. February 13, 2016.

Greenhouse, Linda. 2016. "Pondering the Supreme Court's Future." *New York Times.* September 29, 2016.

Hasen, Richard L. 2015. "The Most Sarcastic Justice." *Green Bag* 18: 215–27.

Johnson, Timothy R. 2009. The Digital Archives of Justices Blackmun and Powell Oral Argument Notes, http://www.polisci.umn.edu/~tjohnson/oanotes.php.

———. 2004. *Oral Arguments and Decision Making on the United States Supreme Court*. Albany, NY: SUNY Press.

Johnson, Timothy R. and Ryan C. Black. N.d. "The Roberts Court and Oral Arguments: Has the Court Really Become More Collegial?" *Washington University Journal of Law and Policy* 54.

Johnson, Timothy R., Ryan C. Black, Jerry Goldman, and Sarah Treul. 2009. "Inquiring Minds Want to Know: Do Justices Tip Their Hands with Questions at Oral Argument in the U.S. Supreme Court?" *Washington University Journal of Law & Policy* 29(1): 241–61.

Johnson, Timothy R., Ryan C. Black, and Justin Wedeking. 2009. "Pardon the Interruption: An Empirical Analysis of Supreme Court Justices' Behavior during Oral Arguments." *Loyola Law Review* 55(2): 331–51.

Kendall, Brent and Jess Bravin. 2016. "Without Justice Scalia, Oral Arguments Will Lose a Bit of Their Bite," *Wall Street Journal*. https://www.wsj.com/articles/without-justice-scalia-oral-arguments-will-lose-a-bit-of-their-bite-1455666721. Last Accessed June 7, 2018.

Little, Laura. 2016. "Reflecting on Justice Scalia's Legacy." *Temple Now*, https://news.temple.edu/news/2016-02-20/reflecting-scalia-legacy. Last Accessed June 7, 2018.

O'Brien, David M. 2000. Storm Center: *The Supreme Court in American Politics*, 5th ed. New York: W. W. Norton & Company.

Owens, Ryan J. and Justin Wedeking. 2011. "Justices and Legal Clarity: Analyzing the Complexity of Supreme Court Opinions." *Law and Society Review* 45(4): 1027–61.

Pennebaker, James W. and Laura King. 1999. "Linguistic Styles: Language Use as An Individual Difference." *Journal of Personality and Social Psychology* 77(6): 1296–312.

Plutchik, Robert. 1994. *The Psychology and Biology of Emotion*. New York: Harper Collins.

Riback, Stuart M. 2003. "First Argument Impressions of the Supreme Court." *The Journal of Appellate Law and Practice* 5(1): 133–50.

Ringsmuth, Eve M. and Timothy R. Johnson. 2013. "Supreme Court Oral Arguments and Institutional Maintenance." *American Politics Research* 41(4): 651–73.

Russell, James A. 1978. "Evidence of Convergent Validity on the Dimensions of Affect." *Journal of Personality and Social Psychology* 36: 1152–68.

Rosen, Jeffrey. 2007. *The Supreme Court: The Personalities and Rivalries That Defined America* (199–200).

Sigelman, Lee and Cynthia Whissell. 2002a. "Projecting Presidential Personas on the Radio: Addendum on the Bushes." *Presidential Studies Quarterly* 32: 572–76.

Tausczik, Yla R. and James W. Pennebaker. 2009. "The Psychological Meaning of Words: LIWC and Computerized Text Analysis Methods. *Journal of Language and Social Psychology* 29(1): 24–54.

Totenberg, Nina. 2016. "Justice Antonin Scalia, Known for Biting Dissents, Dies At 79." *National Public Radio* (NPR). February 13, 2016. https://www.npr.org/2016/02/13/140647230/justice-antonin-scalia-known-for-biting-dissents-dies-at-79.

Warren, Charles. 1922. *The Supreme Court in United States Hitory.* Boston, MA: Little Brown and Company.

Wexler, Jay D. 2005. "Laugh Track." *Green Bag* (Autumn): 59–61.

Whissell, Cynthia, M. Fournier, R. Pelland, and K. Makarec. 1986. "The Dictionary of Affect in Language: Reliability, Validity, and Applications." *Perceptual and Motor Skills* 62: 875–88.

Whissell, Cynthia. 1989. "The Dictionary of Affect in Language." In *Theory, Research, and Experience*, Robert Plutchik and Henry Kellerman (eds). New York: Academic Press. 113–31.

Whissell, Cynthia. 1999. "Linguistic Complexity of Abstracts in Highly Cited Journals." *Perceptual and Motor Skills* 88: 76–86.

Zona, Hank. 2016. "Me and Antonin Scalia: A Wine Story." *The Grapes Unwrapped: Get to Know Wine.* http://thegrapesunwrapped.com/wp/2016/02/15/me-and-antonin-scalia-a-wine-story/ (last accessed October 6, 2017).

TABLE OF CASES

Brown v. Entertainment Merchant Association, 2 564 U.S. 786 (2010).

BP America v. Burton, 549 U.S. 84 (2006).

Bush v. Gore, 531 U.S. 98 (2000).

National Federation of Independent Business v. Sebelius, 567 U.S. 1 (2012).

City and County of San Francisco v. Sheehan, 135 S. Ct. 1765 (2015).

Eastman Kodak Co. v. Image Technical Services, Inc., 504 U.S. 451 (1992).

Elonis v. United States, 135 S.Ct. 2001 (2015).

FEC v. Wisconsin Right to Life (2006).

Freytag v. Commissioner, 501 U.S. 868 (1991).

Glickman v. Wileman Brothers & Elliott Inc., (1997).

Hernandez v. Mesa, 137 S.Ct. 2003 (2017).

Hodel v. Irving, 481 U.S. 704 (1987).

INS v. Chadha, 462 U.S. 919 (1983).

Lujan v. Defenders of Wildlife, 504 U.S. 555 (1992).

Marvin M. Brandt Revocable Trust v. United States, 134 S.Ct. 1257 (2014).

McCreary v. ACLU, (2005).

McCulloch v. Maryland, 17 U.S. 316 (1819).

McDonnell v. United States, 136 S.Ct. 2355 (2016).

Pennsylvania v. Ritchie, 480 U.S. 39 (1987).

Rubin v. Coors Brewing Co., 514 U.S. 476 (1995).

Stansbury v. California, 511 U.S. 318 (1994).

Tulsa Professional Collection Services, Inc. v. Pope, 485 U.S. 478 (1988).

United States v. R.L.C., 503 U.S. 291 (1992).

Chapter 11

Justice Scalia's
Concurring Opinion Writing

Ryan J. Owens and Christopher J. Krewson

In *Bond v. United States*, 131 S. Ct. 2355 (2014), the Supreme Court faced a monumental constitutional question: Is a federal statute passed to implement an international treaty under Article II constitutional when Congress otherwise would not possess the power to pass it under Article I? The facts of the case were salacious and tailor made for bad television. After Carol Anne Bond discovered her husband had impregnated their neighbor, Myrlinda Haynes, she opted for revenge. On over twenty-four occasions, Bond placed various chemicals on handles (doorknobs, car doors, and the mailbox) all over Haynes's property. The chemicals caused Haynes minor burns and were easily treated by simply washing her hands. But because Bond placed chemicals on Haynes's mailbox, her actions became a federal offense. Shockingly, the United States charged her with violating the Chemical Weapons Convention Implementation Act of 1998, which Congress passed to implement the "international Convention on the Prohibition of the Development, Production, Stockpiling, and Use of Chemical Weapons and on Their Destruction." What began as a run-of-the-mill state crime turned into a federal chemical weapons offense with constitutional implications.

Bond claimed that the Implementation Act was unconstitutional, as Congress lacked the authority under Article I's enumerated powers and the Tenth Amendment to pass such legislation. Crimes like those Bonds committed were state crimes and a province in which the federal government had no business. The United States claimed the constitution's Treaty Clause (Article II, § 2, clause 2) empowers it to pass all legislation that implements federal treaties—even though the legislation would otherwise be impermissible under the Constitution. In other words, the government argued that the Treaty Clause allowed it to accomplish what Article I and the Tenth Amendment precluded. The constitutional question was the stuff of law school exams.

But rather than deal with the constitutional issue in the case, the chief justice's majority opinion disposed of it on statutory interpretation grounds. The Chief wrote that the statutory language of the Implementation Act did not appear to reach non-warlike uses of chemicals. This refusal to deal with the real issue did not sit well with Justice Scalia.

In his concurring opinion, Justice Scalia chided the chief justice for ignoring the real issue in the case. He laid out precisely why he believed the Constitution could not support the government's broad power grab. Scalia's concurring opinion began with him accusing the Chief of ignoring the clear meaning of text to avoid confronting "a sweeping and unsettling Act of Congress." He railed that to justify the majority's decision, the Chief and his colleagues employed definitions of chemical weapons and toxic chemicals that directly contradicted definitions provided in the Act itself. Furthermore, he bluntly stated that the majority allowed their preference over outcomes to drive their legal analysis of the case; in other words, the "result-driven anti-textualism befogs what is evident." Having made his point, Justice Scalia then explained how he would have resolved "the *real* question" presented by the case.

Why did Scalia write a concurring opinion in *Bond*? How often did he write such opinions? How often, and under what conditions, did his colleagues write them? The answers to these questions have remained somewhat obscure. What is more, they are normatively important. After all, in some instances, a regular concurring opinion can take on a more legally persuasive status than the majority opinion, as happened in *Youngstown Sheet & Tube Co. v. Sawyer*, 343 U.S. 579 (1952). And for lawyers and judges charged with applying Supreme Court decisions, concurring opinions can obfuscate the law and make their tasks more difficult.

Despite the importance of concurring opinions—given their potential to weaken a majority opinion—scholars know little about the conditions under which justices write them and what opinion writers can do to prevent them. Indeed, even the best scholarship on concurring behavior laments our knowledge of these enigmatic opinions (Collins 2011; Corley 2010; Maveety, Turner, and Way 2010; Way and Turner 2006). For example, Corley, Collins, and Calvin (2011) note: "we still do not understand why an individual justice chooses to write or join a concurrence" (23). Maveety, Turner, and Way (2010) argue they have been "most difficult to understand" (628). And, West (2006) examines what he calls "concurring in part and concurring in the confusion."

This study is a modest attempt to explain Justice Scalia's concurring opinions and to compare his concurring behavior (in part) to his colleagues. Scalia's separate opinion writing has become the stuff of legends. We compare Scalia's regular concurrences to those of his colleagues over time. The results suggest that Scalia wrote concurring opinions when he became more distant ideologically with the majority coalition in the case, when he needed to rebut dissents, in salient cases, and when the Court altered precedent. Surprisingly, unlike his colleagues and contrary to expectations, Scalia was no more likely to write concurring opinions when the overall clarity of the majority's opinions decreased.

These results explain at least part of Justice Scalia's separate opinion writing. Moreover, they illuminate the conditions under which justices concur. As stated above, concurring behavior remains enigmatic. These results help further contextualize why and when justices concur.

This chapter unfolds as follows. In the first section, we briefly discuss existing knowledge of concurring behavior on the high court. We then theorize the conditions under which justices—and Justice Scalia in particular—would be likely to concur. We then present our data, methods, and results, and conclude with a broader discussion of those results.

WHAT WE KNOW ABOUT CONCURRING OPINIONS

Shortly after the Court hears oral argument in a case, the justices hold a conference to discuss how they believe the Court should decide it. Each justice states his or her views and then casts a preliminary vote to affirm or reverse the lower court. The most senior justice in the majority later assigns a justice to write the majority opinion. When the majority opinion writer circulates the draft opinion, each justice has a number of options. He or she can silently join the majority opinion, write or join a regular concurring opinion, write or join a special concurring opinion, or write or join a dissenting opinion (Wahlbeck, Spriggs, and Maltzmann 1999).

When a justice silently joins the majority, she signs on fully to the opinion. When a justice writes a regular concurrence, she agrees with the majority's disposition of the case as well as the majority's rationale, but wants to add something to what the majority opinion said, or stake out a slightly different position. That is, she "highlights a point, discusses a related topic, or expands on the majority's logic" (490). When a justice writes a special concurrence, she "offers an alternative legal rationale for the case outcome and, in so doing, parts company from the rest of the majority" (Wahlbeck, Spriggs, and Maltzmann 1999, 490). That is, she agrees with the disposition of the case but not with the majority's rationale for arriving at that conclusion (Spriggs and Stras 2011). So, for example, in *U.S. v. Little Lake Misere Land Co.*, 412 U.S. 580 (1973), Justice Stewart wrote to Chief Justice Burger, stating: "While I cannot agree with your opinion for the Court in this case, I do concur in the result you reach. In due course, I shall circulate a brief [special] concurring opinion" (Wahlbeck, Spriggs, and Maltzmann 2009). A justice who dissents, of course, disagrees both with the majority's holding and its rationale.

We focus here on regular concurring opinions. These concurrences are important for a number of reasons, not least of which is that they can take on precedentially binding status over time. Regular concurrences have persuasive power, and in some instances can overtake the majority opinion in terms of authoritativeness. For example, Justice Jackson's regular concurrence in *Youngstown* overtook Justice Black's majority opinion in the case. Justice O'Connor's concurrence in *Zelman v. Simmons-Harris*, 536 U.S. 639 (2002) has taken on importance as well. In a fairly extensive analysis, Kirman (1995) provides a number of examples of highly persuasive regular concurrences. In one example, he explains how Justice Blackmun's regular concurrence in *National League of Cities v. Usery*, 426 U.S. 833 (1976) blunted Justice Rehnquist's majority opinion. The majority held that any federal law that "directly displace[s] the States' freedom to structure integral operations in areas of traditional government functions" was unconstitutional. Blackmun's concurrence, however, framed the majority's opinion not as a strict rule but, rather, a balancing test. His concurrence allowed lower courts to circumvent the majority opinion in ways Rehnquist opposed.

Further underscoring the perceived importance of such concurring opinions, lawyers and justices regularly discuss them during oral argument. For example, in *Michigan v. EPA*, 135 S. Ct. 702 (2014), the solicitor general made clear reference to Justice Breyer's concurring opinion in *Whitman v. American Trucking Association*, 531 U.S. 457 (2001). In *Walker v. Texas Division, Sons of Confederate Veterans*, 135 S. Ct. 2239 (2015), the Texas Solicitor General made clear references to Justice Scalia's concurring opinion in *National Endowment for the Arts v. Finley*, 524 U.S. 569 (1998) and Justice Stevens's concurrence in *Pleasant Grove City v. Summum*, 555 U.S. 460 (2009). In the recently argued case *Gill v. Whitford*, (16–1161), all three attorneys at oral argument fell over themselves to discuss Justice Kennedy's concurring opinion in *Vieth v. Jubelirer*, 541 U.S. 267 (2004). Other examples abound, but what is clear is that lawyers and justices regularly discuss concurring opinions at oral argument.

Concurring opinions may also negatively influence how lower courts comply with high court opinions. For example, Benesh and Reddick (2002) find that lower courts comply more quickly with unanimous Supreme Court precedents. In their study of state supreme court treatment of U.S. Supreme Court precedent, Kassow, Songer, and Fix (2012) find that state supreme courts are more likely to treat positively Supreme Court precedents created by large coalitions. Corley (2009) finds that plurality opinions are more likely to be treated negatively by lower courts because of their inherent ambiguity. Because plurality decisions create confusion, they allow lower courts to shirk more easily. Lower courts are 42 percent more likely to treat a plurality versus a majority opinion negatively (Corley 2009).

Why Would Scalia Write Concurring Opinions?

So, why would a justice write a concurring opinion? Why would Justice Scalia have written them? Perhaps the most common explanation for justices' concurring behavior focuses on ideological differences between the concurring justice and the rest of the majority. Justices are increasingly likely to concur as they become more distant ideologically from the majority opinion writer (Spriggs and Stras 2011). Maltzmann, Spriggs, and Wahlbeck (2000) find that justices are more likely to circulate draft concurring opinions (either regular or special) versus joining the majority opinion when they are ideologically distant from the Court majority. A justice who is close ideologically to the majority coalition has a 0.06 probability of writing or joining a concurring opinion while a justice who is distant ideologically has a 0.10 probability of writing or joining a concurring opinion. Collins (2011) finds similar results.[1] In her book-length treatment on concurring opinions, Corley (2010) finds some evidence that ideological distance from the majority opinion author influences a justice's decision to write a concurrence. Segal and Spaeth (2002) sum up the ideological distance argument well when they state:

> Those who join the majority opinion are ideologically closer to the opinion writer than those who write regular concurrences; regular concurrers, in turn, are ideologically closer to the majority opinion writer than special concurrers; and to complete the picture, special concurrers are ideologically closer to the majority opinion writer than are justices who dissent. (386–87)

Ideology is likely to influence whether justices write concurring opinions for a number of reasons. First, as we explained above, a concurring opinion can help shape how others interpret and otherwise respond to the majority opinion. It can highlight areas of weakness with the majority opinion and, in so doing, influence how lower court judges and implementers apply the decision. A strong concurring opinion might offer alternative strategies for policy makers beyond the Court's majority opinion. Second, a concurring opinion might simply be a way to state one's relatively divergent views. A justice who sincerely wants some policy outcome or rule might feel more satisfied by spelling it out in a concurring opinion rather than simply joining the majority opinion silently (or writing it in a dissent, where it might carry less weight). Justice Scalia (1998) once stated that writing separate opinions "makes the practice of one's profession as a judge more satisfying . . . to address precisely the points of law that one considers important and no others . . . that is indeed an unparalleled pleasure" (22–23). Third, a concurring opinion can help explain why a justice who ordinarily might not be expected to agree ideologically with a Court decision nevertheless has done so in a case (Collins 2011). In this manner, a concurring opinion can reassure a justice's ideological constituencies. Given this scholarship, we expect that *Justice Scalia and his colleagues will be more likely to write regular concurring opinions when they are increasingly distant ideologically from the majority coalition.*

It is quite possible that justices write concurring opinions "to criticize a dissent," something called "riding shotgun" (Epstein, Landes, and Poser 2011, 285). Consider *Herrera v. Collins*, 506 U.S. 390 (1993) (Scalia, J., concurring), in which the Court held that a convicted defendant's claims of actual innocence based on newly discovered evidence did not create a ground for federal *habeas corpus* relief. Justice Scalia chided the dissent in his concurring opinion:

> There is no basis in text, tradition, or even in contemporary practice (if that were enough) for finding in the Constitution a right to demand judicial consideration of newly discovered evidence of innocence brought forward after conviction. In saying that such a right exists, the dissenters apply nothing but their personal opinions to invalidate the rules of more than two-thirds of the States, and a Federal Rule of Criminal Procedure for which this Court itself is responsible. If the system that has been in place for 200 years (and remains widely approved) "shock[s]" the dissenters' consciences, *post,* at 430, perhaps they should doubt the calibration of their consciences, or, better still, the usefulness of "conscience shocking" as a legal test. (506 U.S. at 427–28)

This desire to respond to the dissent likely is enhanced when there are multiple dissents. Consider *Cruzan v. Missouri Department of Health*, 497 U.S. 261 (1990; Scalia, J., concurring). In his concurring opinion, Justice Scalia stated: "The various opinions in this case portray quite clearly the difficult, indeed agonizing, questions that are presented by the constantly increasing power of science to keep the human body alive for longer than any reasonable person would want to inhabit it" (see 497 U.S. at 292). As such, we expect *Justice Scalia and his colleagues will be more likely to write regular concurring opinions as the number of dissenting opinions increases.*

The clarity of the majority opinion likely also leads justices to write concurring opinions. The clarity of the majority opinion—how it frames the law and facts—might influence whether justices write such opinions. This is particularly true for Scalia, who has (largely accurately) held himself out to be a paragon of clarity in writing (Scalia and Garner 2008; Scalia 1989). Again, in *Cruzan,* Justice Scalia stated: "I am concerned, from the tenor of today's opinions, that we are poised to confuse that enterprise as successfully as we have confused the enterprise of legislating concerning abortion—requiring it to be conducted against a background of federal constitutional imperatives that are unknown because they are being newly crafted from Term to Term. That would be a great misfortune" (see *Cruzan*, 497 U.S. at 292–3).

Recent studies show a relationship between the clarity of an opinion and judicial behavior. For example, Baum argues that lower court compliance with Supreme Court decisions is partly a function of the clarity with which the Court writes its opinion (Baum 1978; 1976). Corley and Wedeking (2014) discover lower courts are more likely to treat a Supreme Court precedent positively when the opinion that creates it expresses more certainty in its language. Black et al. (2017) find that lower courts are less likely to treat precedent positively when it is less clear, and that the Supreme Court adjusts the clarity of its opinions to suit the context of the cases it hears. Accordingly, we expect *Justice Scalia will be more likely to write a regular concurring opinion when the majority's opinion is unclear.*

We expect that contextual features influence whether justices write concurring opinions. Cooperation among justices seems likely to influence whether a justice writes a regular concurrence. Indeed, some evidence suggests that justices are less likely to concur in cases where the majority opinion writer cooperated with them in the past (Maltzmann, Spriggs, and Wahlbeck 2000). Thus, we expect that *the more a justice cooperated with the majority opinion author in the past, the less likely a justice will be to write a concurring opinion.*

Case salience likely matters. Maltzmann, Spriggs, and Wahlbeck (2000) find that justices are more likely to concur in salient cases. Their data showed a 34 percent change in the probability a justice concurs in legally salient versus non-salient cases (see also Collins and Martinek 2011; Corley 2010). If justices have policy goals, those goals are most likely effectuated in highly salient cases. Thus, we expect that *Justice Scalia and his colleagues will be more likely to write regular concurring opinions as the salience of the case increases.*

Finally, we know justices are influenced by workload considerations (Maltzmann, Spriggs, and Wahlbeck 2000). As their workload increases, they have less time to write separate opinions. This is particularly true as justices near the end of the Court term as big cases pile up. As such we expect that *Justice Scalia and his colleagues will be less likely to write regular concurring opinions as the end of the term nears.*

Data and Measures

We examine the behavior of justices with three different approaches. We analyze all justices from 1946–2011, the justices with whom Justice Scalia served from 1986–2011, and Justice Scalia's own behavior from 1986–2011. Our unit of analysis is the justice vote in a case.

Dependent Variable. Our dependent variable accounts for whether a justice *Wrote a Regular Concurrence* when he or she was in the majority coalition (but did not write the majority opinion). We obtained these data from the Supreme Court database.[2] The database describes a regular concurring opinion as one where the justice agrees with the Court's opinion as well as its disposition.

Ideological Distance From the Majority. To determine the ideological distance between the majority and the justice under analysis, we obtained each justice's Martin-Quinn score during the term in question (Martin and Quinn 2002). We then calculated the absolute value of the difference between the justice under consideration and the median justice in the majority coalition. Smaller values mean the justice and the majority coalition are ideologically close. Larger values mean the justice is ideologically distant from the majority coalition.

Number of Dissenting Opinions. To determine whether Scalia and his colleagues were more likely to write concurring opinions in the face of greater challenges to the majority, we counted the number of dissenting opinions in the case, as noted by the Supreme Court Database.

Majority Opinion Clarity. To measure the clarity of the Court's opinions, we employ two measures: textual readability and cognitive complexity.

Textual readability is generally defined as the ease with which a layperson can read and understand the language of the Court's opinions (Black et al. 2017). That is, it measures how easy a text is to read. Does the text require considerable education to read and understand? Or, is the text easily read and understood by someone with less education?[3] One can think of these scores as measuring the years of schooling (or grade level) one would attain in order to understand the text. The scores measure the difficulty a general reader is likely to encounter when reading a Court opinion. The two inputs for the Coleman-Liau Index, which is the readability metric we employ here, are word and sentence length. Texts with longer words and sentences will have higher values, which indicate lower readability. For ease of reference, we multiply the Coleman-Liau value by negative one so that larger values of readability represent more readable opinions.

Cognitive complexity represents how complex or simple an idea's framing is (Owens and Wedeking 2011, 1038–39). Stated more broadly, cognitive complexity examines the way in which people perceive and respond to events. Cognitive complexity contains two elements: differentiation and integration. Differentiation represents the degree to which an individual acknowledges multiple perspectives or dimensions associated with an issue. On the other hand, integration accounts for the ability to synthesize and connect different perspectives or dimensions of issues. These two features collapse into a unidimensional cognitive complexity score.

Less cognitive complexity looks like an "oh-this-again" frame. Language with less cognitive complexity tends to rely on "one-dimensional, evaluative rules in interpreting events in which actors make decisions "on the basis of only a few salient items of information" (Gruenfeld 1995, 5). Less complex language tends to be more stark, more absolute, and less nuanced. On the other hand, greater cognitive complexity is associated with subtle nuance and making distinctions. Language scored as cognitively complex "tends to interpret events in multidimensional terms and to integrate a variety of evidence in arriving at decisions" (Tetlock, Bernzweig, and Gallant 1985, 1228).[4] Increasingly complex language tends to address more perspectives than less complex language.

We measure the *Cognitive Complexity* of each majority opinion using the content analysis program Linguistic Inquiry and Word Count (LIWC) (Owens and Wedeking 2011). LIWC analyzes "attentional focus, emotionality, social relationships, thinking styles," and other features of language that measure its cognitive complexity (Tausclik and Pennebaker 2010, 24). More specifically, LIWC searches a text for over 2,300 words (or word stems) using specific dictionaries. LIWC assigns each word in a text to one of seventy predefined dimensions that have been categorized by independent examiners to measure the thinking styles of individuals. The software searches the text(s) to determine whether the words (or word stems) in its dictionary appear. It then provides a description of the percentage of words in the text that fall into each dimension. We employ ten LIWC dimensions that are directly connected with cognitive complexity: causation, insight, discrepancy, inhibition, tentativeness, certainty, inclusiveness, exclusiveness, negations, and percentage of words containing six or more letters. Following Owens and Wedeking (2011), we then standardized and collapsed the following ten indicators into one quantity of interest:[5]

Past Cooperation. We account for past cooperation between the justice and the majority opinion writer. We examine the percent of previous instances in which the justice and the majority writer joined together in some kind of separate opinion. To do so, we collected vote data from the Supreme Court Datbase.

Salience: Number of Amici. We count the number of amicus briefs filed in each case. To determine the number of amicus briefs filed from the 1946–2001 Supreme Court terms, we relied on Collins (2008). We collected amicus data from 2002–2011 using LexisNexis and the Court's docket sheets.

Salience: Alter Precedent. Justices may be more likely to write regular concurrences when they jolt the system by formally altering precedent. As Chief Justice Roberts stated in his confirmation testimony: "I do think that it is a jolt to the legal system when you overrule a precedent. Precedent plays an important role in promoting stability and evenhandedness. . . . It is not enough that you may think the prior decision was wrongly decided. That really doesn't answer the question. It just poses the question" (Roberts 2005). If the Supreme Court Database recorded a justice as having voted to alter precedent, we code the variable as 1–0 otherwise.

Salience: Strike Federal Statute. Just as the alteration of precedent is a "jolt to the legal system" the separation of power rocks when the Court strikes down an act of Congress. As such, we also coded for whether they invalidated the act of a coordinate branch. If the Supreme Court Database recorded a justice as having voted to strike an act of Congress, we code the variable as 1–0 otherwise.

Days Until Term Ends. Numerous studies have found that as the end of the Court's term nears, justices are less able to take on additional work (see, e.g., Maltzmann, Spriggs, and Wahlbeck 2000). As such, we control for the number of days until the term ends. Greater values reflect more time until the end of term.

Term. Because it is possible that justices, including Justice Scalia, filed more concurring opinions in recent terms, we control for the term of the Court. Larger values represent terms that are more recent.

Methods and Results

Before we present statistical results of Scalia's concurring behavior—and those of his colleagues—we first present some descriptive data showing how often justices wrote concurring opinions. Table 11.1 shows the proportion of instances in which each justice wrote regular concurring opinions from 1986–2015. To be sure, some justices served longer than others during that time period, but the data give us an indication of the concurring opinions of those with whom Scalia served.

The first thing to notice is that, consistent with conventional wisdom, Justice Scalia wrote concurring opinions more frequently than other justices, though Thomas comes very close. Whereas someone like Chief Justice Rehnquist rarely wrote regular concurrences—he wrote them in 0.5 percent of all majority opinions he joined—Scalia was less reticent, writing regular concurrences in 6.8 percent of the majority opinions he joined.

What is more, as figure 11.1 shows, Scalia seems to have been less active in writing concurrences at the tails of his career. Indeed, during the last few

Table 11.1. Proportion of Regular Concurring Opinions Written by Justices in the Majority, 1986–2015

Justice	Write Regular Concurrence 1986–2015
Marshall	.005
Rehnquist	.009
Kagan	.014
Roberts	.015
White	.027
Blackmun	.039
Souter	.042
Ginsburg	.044
Kennedy	.047
Powell	.048
Brennan	.049
O'Connor	.052
Breyer	.055
Sotomayor	.057
Alito	.058
Stevens	.063
Thomas	.068
Scalia	.068

terms of his career, the proportion of instances in which Scalia wrote regular concurring opinions declined. (He dissented slightly more then, though.) His high water mark came in the 2000 term, when he wrote regular concurring opinions in 12.1 percent of all majority opinions he joined. He was nearly as active—at least in terms of writing regular concurrences—in the 2001 and 1993 terms.

As figure 11.2 below shows, just as Scalia tapered off, Justice Thomas picked up. During the 2012 term, Justice Thomas wrote regular concurring opinions in 11 percent of the majority opinions he joined while Scalia wrote in 3.6 percent. In the 2013 term, Thomas wrote in 5.4 percent of cases he joined while Scalia wrote in 3.6 percent. And in the 2014 term, Thomas wrote in 13.5 percent of the cases he joined while Scalia wrote in 4.7 percent. The figure also shows that Justice Stevens was active in his concurring opinion writing.

So, the early indication is that Justice Scalia wrote a sizable amount of concurring opinions overall—but that in some terms his colleagues wrote more than him. Figures 11.1 and 11.2 show variation among the justices in how often they wrote concurring opinions, but we want to look deeper. We want to examine the conditions under which Justice Scalia, and his colleagues, wrote

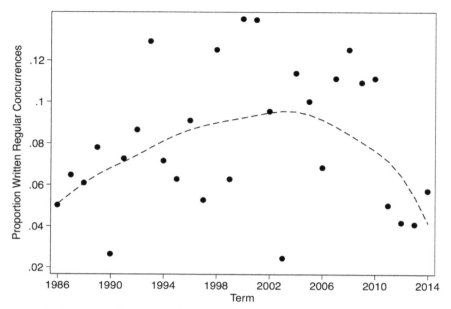

Figure 11.1.   Proportion Written Regular Concurrences

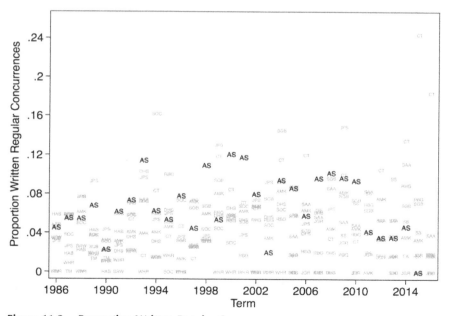

Figure 11.2.   Proportion Written Regular Concurrences

such opinions. To do so, we estimate a probit regression model. As stated above, the dependent variable is coded as 1 if, when in the majority coalition, a justice wrote a regular concurring opinion. (Thus, we exclude dissenters from the analyses.) Table 11.2 presents the results.

Model 1 estimates the probability that all justices from 1946–2011 wrote a regular concurring opinion. (We end in the 2011 term due to data limitations on our opinion content variables.) Model 2 estimates the probability that the justices with whom Justice Scalia served wrote a regular concurring opinion while in the majority. (These data run from the 1986–2011 terms.) Finally, Model 3 estimates the probability that Justice Scalia wrote a regular concurring opinion (during the 1986–2011 terms).

Three features stand out about Justice Scalia as compared to his colleagues. First, whereas the average justice across 1946–2011 was influenced by ideological concerns to write concurring opinions, Justice Scalia was perhaps more so. Making comparisons between coefficient sizes in different samples is not typically well advised, but it seems obvious that ideological distance between

Table 11.2.

	All Justices 1946–2011		Scalia Justices 1986–2011		Scalia Only 1986–2011	
	Coefficient	SE	Coefficient	SE	Coefficient	SE
Distance to Majority Coalition	0.05**	0.01	0.06**	0.01	0.14**	0.06
Number Dissents	0.20**	0.01	0.23**	0.24	0.16**	0.07
Readability	−0.04**	0.01	−0.05**	0.02	−0.02	0.05
Cognitive Complexity	−0.02**	0.00	−0.00	0.01	−0.02	0.02
Past Cooperation	−0.00	0.00	0.00	0.00	−0.00	0.00
Number Amici	0.02**	0.00	0.01**	0.00	0.01*	0.00
Alter Precedent	0.29**	0.06	0.14	0.10	0.49**	0.24
Strike Federal Statute	0.23**	0.09	0.22*	0.13	0.02	0.36
Days Until Term Ends	0.00**	0.00	−0.00	0.00	0.00	0.00
Term	0.01**	0.00	0.01**	0.00	0.00	0.00
Constant	−12.99**	1.53	−19.29**	5.54	−10.27	15.89
Observations	38,396		13,502		1,531	
Chi2 ·	505.27**		215.71**		26.83**	

** p>0.05 * p>0.10 two-tailed test. Dependent variable coded as 1 if the justice in the majority coalition wrote a regular concurring opinion.

Scalia and the median member of the majority coalition (and, thus, the policy position of the opinion) strongly influenced him. Indeed, the left panel of figure 11.3 shows the predicted probability any justice writes a concurring opinion as a function of his or her distance from the majority coalition. It seems clear that the greater the distance, the more likely a justice is to write a regular concurring opinion. This finding is strong for Scalia. Whereas Scalia had a roughly 5 percent probability of writing a regular concurring opinion when joining a majority opinion written by an ideological ally, that probability increased to 16 percent, a 220 percent change, when the opinion writer was ideologically distant.

Another feature stands out: the importance of dissenting opinions on concurring opinions. We cannot tell from these data which came first: the circulated dissent or the concurring opinion. But theory tells us that in many cases justices file regular concurring opinions to debunk a dissent, and the more dissents, the more opinions there are to debunk. As the number of dissenting opinions increases, we see a strong corresponding increase in the likelihood of writing a regular concurring opinion, even controlling for the salience of the case. If there were four dissents, we would predict the average justice to write a concurrence 13.7 percent of the time. For Justice Scalia, we would predict a concurrence 19.5 percent of the time.

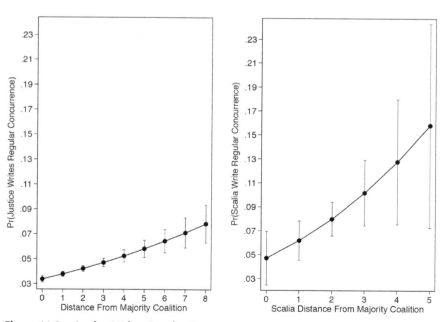

Figure 11.3. Justice Writes Regular Concurrence

Table 11.3. **Justice Writes Regular Concurrence**

Dissenting Opinions	All Justices	Scalia
0	.029 [.027–.031]	.062 [.047–.078]
1	.045 [.043–.048]	.086 [.070–.102]
2	.068 [.063–.073]	.116 [.078–.153]
3	.098 [.087–.110]	.152 [.078–.225]
4	.137 [.118–.157]	.195 [.074–.315]

The predicted probability of writing a regular concurring opinion when in the majority as a function of the number of dissents.

Surprisingly, the written content of the majority's opinion failed to influence Scalia's decision to write a concurrence. We theorized, based on Scalia's many non-judicial writings (e.g., Scalia and Garner 2008; Scalia 1989), that he would seek to "clarify" majority opinions that were not up to snuff. Yet this did not happen. Whereas other justices were less likely to write concurring opinions when, for example, the opinion was more readable, readability mattered not to Scalia—at least insofar as his decision to write concurring opinions. There is some evidence that some justices were less likely to write concurrences when the opinion was more cognitively complex (Model 1) the cognitive complexity seemed not to matter to Scalia. Again, this seems at odds with Scalia's stated desire for greater clarity in writing.

What is more, past cooperation with the majority opinion writer did not seem to influence whether Justice Scalia wrote a regular concurring. Nor did such cooperation seem to influence his colleagues.

Scalia and his colleagues were more likely to write regular concurring opinions in salient cases. All justices were more likely to write them when more interest groups participated in the case, a result that is not especially surprising. In such cases, justices go to greater lengths to influence the law and to state their views. In terms of altering precedent, most (majority) justices were more likely to write regular concurring opinions when they voted to overrule precedent versus when they upheld or otherwise applied it. Whereas Scalia's colleagues were more likely to write concurring opinions when they took the grave step of striking down federal legislation, Justice Scalia evidenced no qualms about striking it down. Unlike his colleagues, he did not appear to feel the need to explain why he, in particular, voted to strike down a federal law. Is this consistent with the claim that he was an "activist?" Perhaps. Or perhaps instead he agreed fully with the majority opinions as written and did not feel the need to reinvent the wheel.

There is some evidence that justices were more likely to write regular concurring opinions as the end of the term neared, but those results seem to be driven by justices prior to 1986 and, at any rate, the coefficient is so small as to be meaningless. Finally, the data suggest that justices were more likely to write regular concurring opinions in recent years than in the past, which accords with conventional wisdom.

Discussion

Why do justices write concurring opinions when they agree with the majority's disposition of the case? We theorized a number of possibilities and tested them empirically. The data illuminate the conditions under which justices, including Justice Scalia, concur. We learned, for example, that justices vary greatly in their proclivity to write regular concurring opinions. We also learned that justices as a whole consider ideology when deciding whether to concur. Those who are ideologically distant from the majority coalition are more likely to write regular concurrences than those ideologically close. Other common factors were the number of dissents and the salience of the case.

There are, of course, plenty of other reasons justices may write concurring opinions. Perhaps justices with certain kinds of personalities are more likely to concur. Perhaps justices concur more when they think they must explain their votes to preferred audiences. Perhaps they concur for the benefit of lower court judges or implementers. These and other questions should be examined more extensively. For now, though, the data suggest ideological concerns and a need to rebut the dissents strongly motivated concurring behavior.

What does this all tell us about Justice Scalia's legacy? Certainly, it tells us that Justice Scalia was one of the most prolific regular concurrers on the Court. Indeed, he wrote a regular concurrence about 12.1 percent of the time he joined the majority in 2000. Most of his career on the Court exhibited similarly active opinion writing. He outpaced all his colleagues in the majority. But why?

Some of his concurring behavior can certainly be chalked up to personality. He enjoyed writing; the ability to write for himself—without having to compromise—was something he relished. But surely just as important was his ideology. Justice Scalia's strong conservatism may be a key reason for his frequent concurrences. Every time he joined a majority opinion, he was to the right of the median justice in the majority. After all, only Justice Thomas flanked him on the right. So, his views, while sometimes reflected in majority opinions, were likely watered down by coalitional politics. Perhaps it is telling that the top five most active regular concurring opinion writers (according to table 11.1) sat on the flanks of the Court.

What else makes Scalia unique? The fact that textual clarity mattered little to him. We find no evidence of a systematic effect of these factors on Justice Scalia's decision to write a regular concurrence. Neither the textual readability nor the cognitive complexity of the majority opinion led Scalia to write regular concurrences.

Justices seem to write more concurring opinions these days. Whether that is normatively problematic or positive is a matter of subjective interpretation, though we tend to believe it is unhelpful. A chorus of separate opinions can confuse the state of the law and lead justices to resent one another. Who doesn't believe justices rolled their eyes every time Justice Kennedy authored a concurring opinion, hoping to place himself in the middle later? Whether we will return to an era of seriatim opinions seems unlikely, but the Court could certainly do more to speak with a stronger collective voice.

NOTES

1. Collins (2011) also finds limited evidence that justices concur to explain their counter-attitudinal voting.

2. See http://supremecourtdatabase.org/.

3. People use text readability scores to measure the degree of difficulty in reading a broad array of texts. For example, insurance companies and government agencies are often required by law to employ these measures to enhance the general readability of the documents they generate. See Stuart A. Grossman et al., *Are Informed Consent Forms that Describe Clinical Oncology Research Protocols Readable by Most Patients and Their Families?*, 12 J. *Clinical Oncology* 2211, 2211–15 (1994).

4. A number of studies have examined the role of cognitive complexity in judicial behavior. For example, Tetlock, Bernzweig, and Gallant (1985) discovered that liberals and moderates drafted more complex opinions than conservatives. Gruenfeld (1995) examined how majority coalition status influences the cognitive complexity of the opinion. Gruenfeld and Preston (2000) argued that justices upholding precedent interpreted the law with more complexity than justices overturning precedent. Owens and Wedeking (2012) found that justices who were cognitively stable were less likely to drift ideologically over time. Owens and Wedeking (2011) found that Justices Scalia and Breyer evinced the least cognitive complexity and that Justices Ginsburg, Marshall, and O'Connor evinced the most complexity.

5. The scholarship that employs LIWC argues strongly that it measures the underlying complexity of the ideas in the writing. For example, Tausczik and Pennebaker (2010) argue that examining language, as LIWC does, "provides important clues as to how people process . . . information and interpret it to make sense of their environment" (19). LIWC examines "how individuals are expressing themselves rather than what they are saying" (Pennebaker and Lay 2002, 273).

REFERENCES

Baum, Lawrence. 1976. "Implementation of Judicial Decisions: An Organizational Analysis." *American Politics Quarterly* 4(1): 86–114.

———. 1978. "Lower Court Response to Supreme Court Decisions: Reconsidering a Negative Picture." *Justice System Journal* 3: 208–19.

Benesh, Sara C. and Malia Reddick. 2002. "Overruled: An Event History Analysis of Lower Court Reaction to Supreme Court Alteration of Precedent." *Journal of Politics* 64(2): 534–50.

Black, Ryan C., Ryan J. Owens, Justin Wedeking, and Patrick C. Wohlfarth. 2017. *U.S. Supreme Court Opinions and Their Audiences*. New York: Cambridge University Press.

Carrubba, Clifford, Barry Friedman, Andrew D. Martin, and Georg Vanberg. 2012. "Who Controls the Content of Supreme Court Opinions?" *American Journal of Political Science* 56: 400–12.

Collins, Paul M., Jr., 2011. "Cognitive Dissonance on the U.S. Supreme Court." *Political Research Quarterly* 64(2): 362–76.

Collins, Paul M., Jr., and Wendy L. Martinek. 2011. "Judges and Friends: The Influence of Amici Curiae on U.S. Court of Appeals Judges." Paper Prepared for Delivery at the 69th Annual Meeting of the Midwest Political Science Association. Chicago, Illinois.

Corley, Pamela C. 2009. "Uncertain Precedent: Circuit Court Responses to Supreme Court Plurality Opinions." *American Politics Research* 37(1): 30–49.

———. 2010. *Concurring Opinion Writing on the U.S. Supreme Court*. New York: SUNY Press.

Corley, Pamela C., Paul M. Collins Jr., and Bryan Calvin. 2011. "Lower Court Influence on U.S. Supreme Court Opinion Content." *Journal of Politics* 73(1): 31–44.

Corley, Pamela C. and Justin Wedeking. 2014. "The (Dis)Advatnage of Certainty: The Importance of Certainty in Language." *Law and Society Review* 48(1): 35–62.

Gibson, James L., Gregory A. Caldeira, and Vanessa A. Baird. 1998. "On the Legitimacy of National High Courts." *American Political Science Review* 92(2): 343–58.

Gruenfeld, Deborah H. 1995. "Status, Ideology, and Integrative Complexity on the U.S. Supreme Court: Rethinking the Politics of Political Decision Making." *Journal of Personality and Social Psychology* 68: 5–20.

Gruenfeld, Deborah H. and Jared Preston. 2000. "Upending the Status Quo: Cognitive Complexity in U.S. Supreme Court Justices Who Overturn Legal Precedent." *Personality and Social Psychology Bulletin* 26: 1013–22.

Hamilton, Alexander. 1788. "Federalist Number 78."

Hettinger, Virginia A., Stefanie A. Lindquist, and Wendy L. Martinek. 2003. "Separate Opinion Writing on the United States Courts of Appeals." *American Politics Research* 31(3): 215–50.

Kassow, Benjamin J., Donald R. Songer, and Michael P. Fix. 2012. "The Influence of Precedent on State Supreme Courts." *Political Research Quarterly* 65(2): 372–84.

Kirman, Igor. 1995. "Standing Apart to Be a Part: The Precedential Value of Supreme Court Concurring Opinions." *Columbia Law Review* 95(8): 2083–2119.

Maltzman, Forrest, James F. Spriggs II, and Paul J. Wahlbeck. 2000. *Crafting Law on the Supreme Court: The Collegial Game*. New York: Cambridge University Press.

Martin, Andrew D. and Kevin M. Quinn. 2002. "Dynamic Ideal Point Estimation via Markov Chain Monte Carlo for the U.S. Supreme Court, 1953–1999." *Political Analysis* 10(2): 134–53.

Maveety, Nancy, Charles C. Turner, and Lori Beth Way. 2010. "The Rise of the Choral Court: Use of Concurrences in the Burger and Rehnquist Courts." *Political Research Quarterly* 63(3): 627–39.

Nelson, Michael J. N.d. "Elections and Explanations: Judicial Elections and the Readability of Judicial Opinions." Unpublished paper available at: http://mjnelson.org/papers/NelsonReadabilityAugust2013.pdf.

O'Brien, David M. 1999. Institutional Norms and Supreme Court Opinions: On Reconsidering the Rise of Individual Opinions. In *The Supreme Court in American Politics: New Institutionalist Interpretations*, ed. Howard Gillman and Cornell W. Clayton. Lawrence: University Press of Kansas, pp. 91–114.

Owens, Ryan J. and Justin P. Wedeking, 2011. "Justices and Legal Clarity: Analyzing the Complexity of Supreme Court Opinions." *Law and Society Review* 45(4): 1027–61.

Owens, Ryan J. and Justin Wedeking, 2012. "Predicting Drift on Politically Insulated Institutions: A Study of Ideological Drift on the U.S. Supreme Court." *Journal of Politics* 74: 487–500.

Owens, Ryan J., Justin P. Wedeking, and Patrick C. Wohlfarth. 2013. "How the Supreme Court Alters Opinion Language to Evade Congressional Review." *Journal of Law and Courts* 1(1): 35–59.

Pennebaker, James W. and Thomas C. Lay. 2002. "Linguistic Styles: Langauge Use As." *Journal of Research in Personality* 36: 271–82.

Scalia, Antonin. 1989. "The Rule of Law as a Law of Rules." *The University of Chicago Law Review* 56(4): 1175–88.

Scalia, Antonin and Bryan A. Garner. 2008. *Making Your Case: The Art of Persuading Judges*. St. Paul, MN: Thomson-West.

Segal, Jeffrey A. and Harold J. Spaeth. 2002. *The Supreme Court and the Attitudinal Model Revisited*. New York: Cambridge University Press.

Spriggs, James F. and David R. Stras. 2011. "Explaining Plurality Decisions." *The Georgetown Law Journal* 99: 515–70.

Tausczik, Yla R. and James W. Pennebaker. 2010. "The Psychological Meaning of Words: LIWC and Computerized Text Analysis Methods." *Journal of Language and Social Psychology* 29: 24–54.

Tetlock, Philip E., Jane Bernzweig, and Jack L. Gallant. 1985. "Supreme Court Decision Making: Cognitive Style as a Predictor of Ideological Consistency of Voting." *Journal of Personality and Social Psychology* 48: 1227–39.

Wahlbeck, Paul J., James F. Spriggs II, and Forrest Maltzman. 1999. "The Politics of Dissents and Concurrences on the U.S. Supreme Court." *American Politics Quarterly* 27(4): 488–514.

Wahlbeck, Paul J., James F. Spriggs and Forrest Maltzman. 2009. "The Burger Court Opinion Writing Database." http://supremecourtopinions.wustl.edu/

Way, Lori Beth and Charles C. Turner. 2006. "Disagreement on the Rehnquist Court: The Dynamics of Supreme Court Concurrence." *American Politics Research* 34(3): 293–318.

West, Sonja R. 2006. "Concurring in Part and Concurring in the Confusion." *Michigan Law Review* 104(8): 1951–60.

Zink, James R., James F. Spriggs II, and John T. Scott. 2009. "Courting the Public: The Influence of Decision Attributes on Individuals' Views of Court Opinions." *Journal of Politics* 71(3): 909–25.

TABLE OF CASES

Bond v. United States, 131 S.Ct. 2355 (2014).

Cruzan v. Missouri Department of Health, 497 U.S. 261 (1990).

Herrera v. Collins, 506 U.S. 390 (1993).

Michigan v. EPA, 135 S.Ct. 702 (2014).

National Endowment for the Arts v. Finley, 524 U.S. 569 (1998).

National League of Cities v. Usery, 426 U.S. 833 (1976).

Pleasant Grove City v. Summum, 555 U.S. 460 (2009).

United States v. Little Lake Misere Land Co., 412 U.S. 580 (1973).

Vieth v. Jubelirer, 541 U.S. 267 (2004).

Walker v. Texas Division, Sons of Confederate Veterans, 135 S. Ct. 2239 (2015).

Whitman v. American Trucking Association, 531 U.S. 457 (2001).

Youngstown Sheet & Tube Co. v. Sawyer, 343 U.S. 579 (1952).

Zelman v. Simmons-Harris, 536 U.S. 639 (2002).

Chapter 12

Justice Scalia's Confirmation Hearing Legacy

Alexander Denison and Justin Wedeking

On September 26, 1986, Chief Justice Warren Burger formally announced his retirement from the U.S. Supreme Court.[1] Despite immediate concerns that he was stepping down due to health issues, Burger told reporters he "never felt better," and insisted the retirement was to devote the entirety of his time to the organization of ceremonies for the two-hundredth anniversary of the Constitution to be held in 1987 (Weinraub 1986). Having disclosed his decision to President Reagan weeks prior, the White House simultaneously announced its plan for his replacement. Sitting Associate Justice William Rehnquist was nominated to assume the position of chief justice, and U.S. Court of Appeals judge for the District of Columbia, Antonin Scalia, was nominated to take Rehnquist's seat as associate justice.

Though the announcement of Burger's retirement came as a surprise to many, the president assured the American people that this newest nominee to the bench was "uniquely qualified" for the position. While he certainly had unique qualifications, with hindsight we can see that President Reagan's emphasis on "unique" was fitting in more ways than one. Whether people loved Scalia or hated him, he seemed exceptional in the amount of attention his Court writings or actions generated. This is somewhat ironic given the relatively inconspicuous nature of his confirmation hearings. In the announcement press conference that also included statements from Burger, Rehnquist, and Scalia, Reagan praised Scalia for his "intellectual power, the lucidity of his opinions and the respect he enjoys among his colleagues" (Weinraub 1986). While reporters were quick to pivot toward questions of the nominee's personal views on some recent controversial decisions, Scalia refused to answer, saying such investigation would be the responsibility of the Senate Judiciary Committee in coming weeks. Scalia was referring to the hearing that would eventually produce exactly *zero* votes against his confirmation.[2]

It was that lack of opposition, ironically, that we argue is crucial to what we call his confirmation legacy.

In this chapter we review and highlight aspects of Scalia's nomination and confirmation where the seeds of his confirmation legacy were sown. His calm and "routine" confirmation hearing, yet subsequent transformation into conservative icon, is one of the contributing reasons for why senators now pay so much attention to the proceedings. It is why confirmation hearings are now viewed as a vibrant and democratic forum for the discussion of constitutional change (Collins and Ringhand 2013). Indeed, as we point out later, Senator Joe Biden, reminiscing about his vote to support Scalia, called it his most regretted vote. To be sure, previous research has shown that televising the confirmation hearings has had an enormous impact on how the process is viewed and conducted (Farganis and Wedeking 2014) and that the Senator's party affiliation became a more important influence on the voting support as a result (Wedeking and Farganis 2010). But we think it is instructive to illuminate the legacy of Scalia's confirmation hearings because it connects the importance of the political environment and context of that time, an era that was both remarkably similar and different to the current era, to the recent politics leading up to Scalia's replacement, Neil Gorsuch. In many ways, despite the general lack of dispute over Scalia's confirmation at the time, his ascension to the Supreme Court stands as a point of caution for senators in more recent years, many of whom now recognize that the lack of scrutiny toward his nomination gave way to nearly three decades of what, at times, some might describe as stubborn and obstinate conservative leadership on the Court. Not only would Scalia come to embody an essential conservative element in the polarized political climate of recent memory, but we argue that his individual achievement in confirmation is itself a contribution to that heightened politicization.

To that end, we argue that while many scholars and pundits will undoubtedly emphasize and scrutinize the conservative legacy that Scalia left behind in his legal jurisprudence and the law, we think that one of his more unheralded legacies will be a modest contribution to our understanding of confirmation politics. Specifically, the legacy is rooted in an assorted combination of facts. It starts with his relatively inconspicuous acknowledgment and round of questioning by the senators on the Senate Judiciary Committee, followed by a lack of any substantive opposition in the Senate with respect to votes. And as we remark later in this chapter, there was very little persistent resistance in his questioning. Juxtapose those facts with Rehnquist's near-simultaneous nomination that seemed to mobilize a disproportionate amount of attention and opposition, which was, admittedly in hindsight, unusual for someone who was already on the Court. Notably, while the nominations yielded quite different outcomes in terms of Senate support, both Scalia and Rehnquist would enjoy strong reputations as conservative icons on the bench. Finally, this legacy is not fully cemented until it is considered in conjunction with the failed nomination of Robert Bork and the ensuing treatment of confirmation hearings.

We suggest that Scalia may be the last nominee of such ideological weight capable of avoiding a partisan battle for confirmation. After all, Bork's nomination was only one short year later, and like Scalia, Bork was a staunch conservative. Yet the Bork nomination and confirmation hearings produced a massive groundswell of opposition in terms of interest groups testifying while Scalia did not (Farganis and Wedeking 2014). While contentious confirmation politics are not new (Maltese 1998), conventional wisdom generally points to the Bork hearings as being the watershed moment of when the hearings changed. But we argue it is the collective contrast of the three hearings—Scalia's sandwiched between Rehnquist's and Bork's—along with the ensuing defeat of the Bork nomination, combined with the steady elevation of Scalia's iconic status amongst conservatives that serves as a crucial lens for how we view the current hearings. We view it as important not because we think they changed the structure of confirmation hearings in a monumental way, but because it contributed to our understanding of how senators and the public now behave such that no nominee will get a "free pass." That legacy left its imprint on the recent events surrounding the controversy over Scalia's replacement, with the refusal of Republicans to consider Obama nominee Merrick Garland and the subsequent Trump nomination of Neil Gorsuch that led to Senate's use of the so-called "nuclear option" to eliminate the filibuster for Supreme Court nominees. In other words, Scalia's considerable influence on the Court after his uncontested confirmation seemingly revitalized the examination of nominees in an era of heightened partisan discord that continues well into the twenty-first century.

To better understand how we arrived at this legacy, it is necessary to first look back at Scalia as an appointee, and second, how his confirmation hearings are situated within the larger context of the evolution of confirmation hearings (e.g., Farganis and Wedeking 2014). Along the way we examine parts of the hearings themselves and some data from Scalia's hearings. We close by arriving at the present day, connecting the legacy of Scalia to the forces that shaped the politics over who would be his successor.

Scalia as Appointee

As a former law professor at the University of Virginia School of Law and the University of Chicago, many pointed to Scalia's stints in academia as vital assets to his nomination, despite an identifiably conservative record on the bench. In his confirmation hearings, Scalia pointed out that this path to nomination was a unique, but distinguished one, as the first academic to be nominated since Felix Frankfurter in 1939, and one of the few to serve as a magazine editor (*Nomination of Judge Antonin Scalia to Be Associate Justice of the Supreme Court of the United States*). An expert in administrative law, Scalia spent time in various government roles in his early career, serving as general counsel for the Office of Telecommunications Policy under President Nixon and assistant attorney general for the Office of Legal Counsel under President Ford. Nominated and confirmed by President Reagan to the U.S. Court of Appeals for the District of Columbia in 1982, where he served alongside such notable figures as Ruth Bader Ginsburg and fellow Reagan Supreme Court nominee Robert Bork, Scalia served only four years before his nomination to the U.S. Supreme Court.

Though Scalia's ability to slide through his Supreme Court confirmation process relatively unscathed is the subject of much of our attention in this chapter, it is worth noting that Scalia's conservative bona fides were hardly in question. Upon entering office, President Reagan offered a number of promises regarding his approach to Court appointments, and Scalia certainly fits the mold for much of the fortieth president's judicial vision. After promising to appoint a woman to the bench, which Reagan successfully did in 1981 with the confirmation of Justice Sandra Day O'Connor, Reagan vowed to turn back the clock on the so-called "judicial activism" of the Warren and Burger Courts (O'Brien 2011).

Much of Reagan's commitment to a new era of "judicial restraint" can of course be traced back to the efforts of the Federalist Society, an organization dedicated to advancing more conservative ideals in the judiciary, including the judicial philosophy of "originalism" entwined so tightly in Scalia's judicial legacy. Alongside Reagan's attorney generals Edwin Meese, whose support for the organization would result in Justice Department positions for many Federalist Society leaders, Reagan and his successor George H. W. Bush would nominate many Federalist Society members for federal judgeships (Devins and Baum 2016). Scalia, an original faculty member for the organization, is among five members nominated to the Supreme Court since the society began in 1982, along with Robert Bork, Clarence Thomas, Samuel Alito, and Neil Gorsuch. As the first member to ascend to the Supreme Court, it is a testament to Scalia's commitment to the mission of the Federalist Society in its infancy that the organization remains an influential and passionate source of guidance for conservative appointers.

Reagan's attachment to a new conservative vision for the Supreme Court included particular attention to issue areas considered in need of remedy. As part of the effort to reverse the course established by the Warren and Burger

Courts, Reagan promised to nominate judges in favor of overturning *Roe v. Wade,* as well as those that would stand to protect prayer in schools (O'Brien 2011). Indeed, at least in these issue areas, Reagan would find a stable ally in Scalia. Ever the opponent to the *Roe* decision and the arguments regarding the legalization of abortion, Scalia insisted that no constitutional language protected the right to an abortion, nor did any framer intend for abortions to be a protected freedom (Fieldstadt 2016). In his dissent in the 1989 case of *Webster v. Reproductive Health Services* (which quite narrowly failed to overturn *Roe*), Scalia lamented that no matter the strident efforts of pro-life advocates and jurists alike, the "mansion of constitutional abortion law" would likely never be completely razed. Nevertheless, Scalia is remembered as one of the Court's most dedicated pro-life jurists.

Scalia's track record in the area of First Amendment protections for school prayer is similarly consistent. A devout Catholic for his entire life, Scalia, like Reagan, believed that prayer in school was constitutionally protected. True to his originalist stance, Scalia would go on to argue in *Lee v. Weisman* (1992) that prayer is in itself an American tradition evinced by the historical application of prayer in the public forum throughout the nation's foundational years. While this understanding would be applied in certain contexts, like that of prayer in a legislative body found to be constitutional in *Town of Greece v. Holloway* (2014), Scalia's stance on school prayer would never achieve the number of votes for a standing majority in his lifetime.[3]

Scalia's reportedly conservative track record on the D.C. Circuit would later be confirmed in his tenure on the Supreme Court, though he was by no means the only candidate drawing notice from the Reagan administration. Attention toward the possibility of a future promotion for Scalia ramped up in early 1986 due to a controversial decision that struck down the Gramm-Rudman-Hollings deficit-reduction law intended to balance the federal budget by the early 1990s. The D.C. Circuit found the delegation of executive authority to the comptroller general to be unconstitutional, as the officer tasked with administering expenditures was, in fact, an officer of the legislative branch (Brisbin 1998). The unsigned opinion was largely assumed to be the work of Scalia, whose adherence to the separation of powers and decision in deference to the executive branch greatly impressed members of the Reagan administration. The opinion, as it turns out, was just a glimpse of his legacy to come. But the opinion was also an important signal to the Reagan administration that Scalia would likely live up to his association with the Federalist Society as a conservative member of the highest court. It propelled Scalia to front-runner status for a Supreme Court opening, and also depicted him, along with colleague Robert Bork, as a champion of conservative values.[4] While Bork would of course be nominated later on in Reagan's time as president, Scalia was reportedly picked first due to his comparative youth and charisma (O'Brien 2011).

Scalia Confirmation Hearings

Of the two Supreme Court confirmation hearings of 1986, Scalia's proved to be the less contentious. The hearings would begin just four days after the Rehnquist hearings concluded, occurring on August 5 and 6, 1986, and remained relatively civil. To be sure, the Senate Judiciary Committee pointed to a number of issues of ideological concern, such as his expressed desires to loosen libel restrictions, his criticism of affirmative action policies handed down by the Supreme Court, and his personal views on abortion. However, the exchanges between he and the committee, both Republicans and Democrats, remained relatively free from divisiveness and antagonistic rhetoric that would come to typify some of the exchanges seen a short while later with Bork and then in more recent nominees, such as Gorsuch.

As an example, consider Scalia's exchanges with Senator Ted Kennedy (D-MA). Kennedy wasted no time with pleasantries as many of the committee's Republicans did. After a one sentence explanation of why he, and not Joe Biden, the ranking Democrat on the Committee, was the first Democrat to ask questions,[5] Kennedy asks, "Judge Scalia, if you were confirmed, do you expect to overrule the *Roe v. Wade*?" Scalia responded by saying, "Excuse me?" Kennedy immediately repeats the question and Scalia responds, "Senator, I do not think it would be proper for me to answer that question." The committee chairman, Republican Senator Strom Thurmond then interjects, "I agree with you. I do not think it is proper to ask any question that he has to act on or may have to act on." Scalia then tries to explain why. This results in a lengthy set of exchanges between Scalia and Kennedy with little bite to them on trying to determine how much weight Scalia gives precedent. It ultimately comes full circle with a relatively innocuous ending and Kennedy failing to "trip-up" Scalia and admitting defeat:

Judge Scalia: That is right, sir. And nobody arguing that case before me should think that he is arguing to somebody who has his mind made up either way.

Senator Kennedy: Well, then, what is the relevance of the previous decision? Does that have any weight in your mind?

Judge Scalia: Of course.

Senator Kennedy: Well, could you tell us how much?

Judge Scalia: That is the question you asked earlier, Senator. And that is precisely the question—

Senator Kennedy: I know it.

(*Nomination of Judge Antonin Scalia*)

While previous research shows that Scalia was forthcoming for the vast majority of his questions during the hearings, about 65 percent (Farganis and Wedeking 2014), this set of exchanges shows how Scalia would not answer that particular question. Yet, even after spending considerable time on it, Senator Kennedy more-or-less admits defeat and moves on after missing opportunities to press Scalia on his answers. This stands in stark contrast to the Gorsuch hearings where, for example, Democratic senator, Richard Blumenthal, kept pressing nominee Judge Gorsuch on why he wouldn't say his personal view of *Brown v. Board* of Education. After several attempts to get Judge Gorsuch to praise the decision, we get this exchange:

Senator Blumenthal: So, why will you not say that you agree with the result?

Judge Gorsuch: Senator, I don't know what it—I'm not sure what we're arguing about here.

Senator Blumenthal: We're not arguing. I'm just asking why you are so averse to saying "yes, it was the right result"?

(*Nomination of Judge Neil Gorsuch to Be Associate Justice of the Supreme Court 2017*)

It is the persistence in the Gorsuch hearings, without any retreat, that stands in marked contrast to the hearings of Scalia.

Another aspect of Scalia's hearing that were of particular note was increased attention on Judge Scalia's views on homosexual equality and sex discrimination. Despite numerous attempts from committee members to coax Scalia into a clear discussion of the differences in protections between those claiming racial discrimination and those claiming sex discrimination, it appeared as if the nominee would not divulge his interpretation on the matter fully. Even when called out for participating in an organization that excluded participation from women, Scalia created the appearance of hedging on elucidating his opinions on the issue, again claiming the issue may come before the Court.

From the very announcement of his nomination, Scalia steadfastly refused to engage in a discussion of issues that may arrive before the Court, and his performance in the hearings was certainly similar. While Scalia answered about 65 percent of his questions in a forthcoming manner, it is important to note that Scalia's candor was much lower than other temporally similar nominees, with Rehnquist above 70 percent, O'Connor at almost 80 percent, and then Bork, Kennedy, Souter, and Thomas all around 80 percent. Not until Ginsburg, who was around 60 percent, do we see any other nominee as close (Farganis and Wedeking 2014).[6] As one legal scholar observed, "Scalia's confirmation hearing less than two years ago was the essence of 'trust me,'" as the nominee was able to avoid definitive answers on several policy specific questions with relatively little pushback from the committee through his explanation that the various issues may soon be on the Court's docket (Totenberg 1987). At one point of the hearings, Senator Biden, citing boredom with the proceedings, remarked in turn: "Everything may come before the Court. There is nothing in American life that may not come before the Court; nothing. Therefore, if you applied that across the board, you would not be able to speak to anything" (Scalia Confirmation Hearings, 48).

Going further, a brief look at a number of the exchanges confirms that Scalia avoided answering some of the thornier questions from the Judiciary Committee, regardless of the senator's party. For example, when asked by Republican Chairman Strom Thurmond whether the other branches of government should always adhere to the opinions of the Supreme Court in light of the decision of *Marbury v. Madison*, Scalia responded by stating he would not discuss Supreme Court opinions, "even one as fundamental as *Marbury v. Madison.*"

Along similar lines, non-answers were provided for questions on the balance of liberty and security, the constitutional right to privacy, and civil rights precedent. Unlike Bork, who felt enough of his personal writings were available to the committee to warrant explicit answers on some personal views, Senators Leahy and DeConcini could not manage to pin Scalia down on his position toward the Freedom of Information Act, which Scalia heavily criticized in the past. He merely stated that those articles represented his views at the time they were written, but his current stance should remain private (Totenberg 1987). He did, however, reject the assertion that he was in some way opposed to basic First Amendment protections, noting that as a former academic and magazine editor, his professional life had benefitted from those protections.

To illustrate how these qualitative assessments fit with our argument about how his hearings contributed to his confirmation legacy, we need to add a systematic element to the analysis. First, we think it is important to highlight the basic fact that only twelve of the eighteen Judiciary Committee members asked questions during Scalia's testimony portion of the hearing. That is remarkable for its lack of scrutiny, and not duplicated in more recent hearings. This lack of scrutiny combined with Scalia's rise to iconic status amongst conservatives suggests that senators will no longer fail to scrutinize nominees, especially after what their scrutiny was able to show within the

Bork hearings. Furthermore, this was not purely along partisan lines, with five Republicans (Laxalt, Simpson, Denton, McConnell, and Broyhill) and one Democrat (Byrd) among the non-participatory. It might be one thing to suggest that Scalia "got off easy" if he did not field questions from only one side, but it was indeed both parties, suggesting that his legacy has both *institutional* and *partisan* roots.

Next, we use data from Farganis and Wedeking (2014) to further examine whether there might be any support in the data for Scalia's legacy. Accordingly, we find that Democrats asked about 180 questions while Republicans asked about eighty-two. Most of those questions were focused on Scalia's views and not trying to ascertain facts. Figure 12.1 plots the twelve senators who asked questions to Scalia. Specifically, it arranges them according to the senator's ideological distance from Scalia (x-axis) by the percentage of forthcoming responses (y-axis). If we disregard one outlier (Senator Strom Thurmond), we see there is a very strong negative correlation between ideology and forthcomingness ($r = -.68$). Not surprising, Senator Kennedy had the fewest questions answered in a forthcoming way, with only about 40 percent of his questions answered. At the same time, Senator Hatch had 100 percent of his questions answered in a forthcoming manner.

These results are intriguing because they further contrast with the later oddity of the committee unanimously voting to send Scalia's nomination to the full senate with a favorable recommendation. This provides support for our argument about Scalia's confirmation legacy and the need to consider his

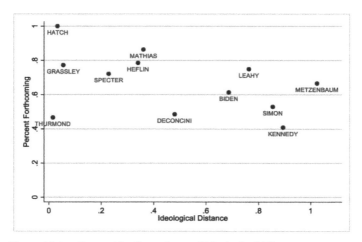

Figure 12.1.   Percent Forthcoming and Ideological Distance

hearing collectively with Bork's to better understand our current confirmation politics. In a sense, it is a feeling that at least the Democratic senators "missed" something during the hearings. Importantly, the figure 12.1 findings also suggest that something more is going on. To break down the questioning further, figure 12.2 arranges the senators from left to right in order of ideological proximity to Scalia. It shows the number of exchanges between Scalia and each senator, respectively, but also shows the distribution of the two types of questions: those seeking the *views* of the nominee and those ascertaining the *facts*.

Figure 12.2 shows an interesting pattern. Many of the ideologically close senators asked either no or very few factual based questions. If we combine this knowledge with the previous fact that those senators also had high forthcoming rates (with the exception of Thurmond), it suggests that the senators were able to ask Scalia questions about his views that were relatively straightforward in answering without needing him revealing too much. The lower number of questions also suggests that they were satisfied with the initial answers that Scalia gave, and perhaps had no intention of delving deeper into controversial territory.

In contrast, the right side of figure 12.2 shows that the Senate Democrats asked more factual based questions. This is consistent with the type of question-

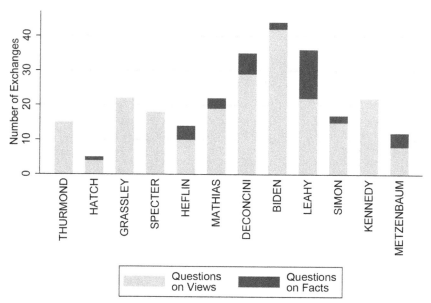

Figure 12.2. Number of Exchanges

ing one sees upon cross-examination, where an attorney tries to pin down a witness by asking a string of factual questions to walk them down a particular path where a trap is waiting to be sprung. And as we know from figure 12.1, those are the same group of senators where we observe lower levels of forthcomingness. This also supports the argument about Scalia's confirmation legacy, and the fact that so little effort was given by senators on the right side of the figure. While Scalia seemingly avoided the potential traps set by Democratic senators through a considerable amount of evasion, it stands to reason that Republicans saw little cause for alarm or need to step in on his behalf.

To be sure, it cannot be understated that Scalia's charm and oratory skills often shown through, as well as the wit he had been known for in opinions on the lower court. This charisma is said to have been one reason he was selected over Bork to fill Rehnquist's soon-to-be-vacant seat (O'Brien 2011). He at one point joked of his aversion to antitrust law, saying he would be happy to avoid the subject in the future since he never seemed to understand it.[7] Despite several attempts to push the nominee into uncomfortable territory by Democratic senators, the mood remained cordial and even light-hearted throughout the hearings, as Scalia and the committee joked about the flock of members with Italian heritage rushing to embrace him as a nominee, and the size of Scalia's family in attendance, leading Senator Paul Laxalt of Nevada to quip, "I can not think of one of my colleagues who would dare arouse the ire of the Scalia clan" (*Nomination of Judge Antonin Scalia*, 13). Not everyone, however, was amused by Scalia's performance, as Joseph L. Rauh Jr., testifying against the confirmation of the nominee, said, "He makes jokes. . . . He makes jokes about things we believe in deeply. He laughs at affirmative action. That has been quoted here. I can not understand putting someone on the Supreme Court who laughs at affirmative action" (*Nomination of Judge Antonin Scalia*, 212). This particular stance of extreme distaste was largely non-existent, however, in the committee's hearing.

Responses from the Senate Judiciary Committee regarding Scalia's performance were largely split along partisan lines. While many were disappointed in the nominee's refusal to answer many questions on personal views—to the point of Senator Arlen Specter speculating about changing the rules of confirmation hearings to better evaluate the candidates—all eighteen voted to recommend confirmation for Scalia. Senator Kennedy said Scalia was "a conservative, not an extremist," clarifying his personal distinction between Scalia and Rehnquist (Greenhouse 1986). Senator Biden acknowledged the ideological distance between he and the nominee, but remarked that Scalia's positions were "within the legitimate parameters of debate" (Greenhouse 1986).[8]

These rather muted interpretations of Scalia's ideological clout would be redacted by some Democrats in years to come. At the confirmation hearing of Ruth Bader Ginsburg, then-Chairman Biden would say, "The vote that I most regret of all 15,000 votes as a senator" was "to confirm Judge Scalia," adding that he had little idea of how "effective" he would be as a conservative force on the U.S. Supreme Court (Liptak 2016). Considering that following the relatively docile confirmation process of Anthony Kennedy no nominee would again achieve a unanimous vote on the Senate floor, it is quite possible that senators learned their lesson regarding a wide-open door for ideological nominees. It would not take long to witness Scalia's mode of decision making and reconsider the nonchalant approach to his vetting.

Rehnquist's Complementary Fight for Chief Justice

It is certainly worth emphasizing the ease by which Scalia was able to achieve confirmation in comparison to the battle waged against then Associate Justice William Rehnquist's promotion to Chief Justice. With the retirement of fellow Nixon appointee Warren Burger, Reagan intended to position Rehnquist as the leader of a new, more conservative era on the Court. Importantly, had Rehnquist failed to secure the position of Chief Justice, the vote on Scalia's nomination for Associate Justice would have been valueless. While Scalia achieved unanimous votes from both the Judiciary Committee and the Senate as a whole, the thirty-three floor votes against Rehnquist was at the time the highest ever garnered for a confirmed nominee. The issues surrounding Rehnquist's promotion were similar to that of his initial nomination from President Nixon in 1971, a nomination that had yielded the second highest number of "nays" for a confirmed nominee at the time ("Rehnquist, Scalia Win Senate Confirmation").

Judiciary Committee Democrats, and even some Republicans, hounded Rehnquist over allegations of racial bias, questioned his dedication to a number of precedents in the area of civil rights, and even returned to a matter of Rehnquist's alleged role in the intimidation of Phoenix voters in the 1960s. Massachusetts Democrat Edward Kennedy called Rehnquist "too extreme" to assume the role of Chief, while Democrat Paul Simon of Illinois said Rehnquist's conceptualization of the law "clearly alienates large numbers of American citizens" (Greenhouse 1986). Five committee Democrats ultimately voted against Rehnquist's nomination, and with the backing of a number of civil rights groups, several Senate Democrats threatened to filibuster the confirmation vote. Alternatively, many Senate Republicans were outspoken in their distaste for their Democratic colleagues' objections, with Senator Alan Simpson of Wyoming calling the hearings "a puerile exercise in justice bashing" (Kurtz 1986).

Despite the contentiousness of the Rehnquist confirmation hearings, the nominee was confirmed by a vote of 65–33. In line with the ideological missions of the Reagan administration, Rehnquist's ascension to chief justice and

Scalia's new role on the bench looked to be a boon for conservatives. While Rehnquist had proven to be the Court's most reliably conservative member since his initial confirmation in 1971, Reagan had now provided him with the leadership of the Court and what he hoped would be a like-minded ally. The two would serve as the anchors of the Court's conservative wing for almost twenty years, until Rehnquist's death in 2005. It is possible that Scalia was able to avoid much of the ideological wrangling due to the Senate's fatigue of the subject matter with Rehnquist. Members of the Judiciary Committee were undoubtedly familiar with Rehnquist's record on the Supreme Court and his position as a conservative stalwart, and Democratic senators were quick to point out their issues with promoting such an ideological justice. The positions of Scalia, comparatively cloaked and fewer in number via the DC. Circuit Court's opinions in his time, yielded far less scrutiny, despite general acknowledgement that his record was decidedly conservative.

The End of an Era in Confirmation Hearings?

The unanimous confirmation of nominees so evidently ideological as Antonin Scalia appears to be an event confined to the past. In many ways, Scalia represents an ideologue that managed to evade the heightened scrutiny others faced, including the ideologically similar Robert Bork in 1987 and Rehnquist who immediately preceded him. Indeed, some lessons may have been gleaned from the ease of the Scalia confirmation in terms of the fastidiousness of the Judiciary Committee. Not only have the number of questions asked of nominees increased since his confirmation hearings, but only one nominee (Ruth Bader Ginsburg) has been able to dodge as many questions as the late jurist (Farganis and Wedeking 2014). If senators looked back to see the performance of the Senate Judiciary Committee presiding over Scalia's confirmation hearings, many would undoubtedly notice a group largely incapable of drilling past the façade presented by the nominee and a lack of foresight that would come to haunt Democratic lawmakers for years afterward. The unfettered confirmation of what would become one of conservative America's true icons has likely contributed to a greater scrutiny of nominees on both sides, particularly as the partisan efforts showcased by individuals like Scalia continued to divide political institutions.

Despite Scalia's qualifications and performance in his confirmation hearings, there are reasons to believe the nature of confirmation hearings have changed since his time before the committee. First, it is likely that Scalia's ability to achieve unanimous consent from the Senate, even in light of what was an observably ideological voting record on the lower court and his past association with Republican administrations is the last of its kind. It has become more unlikely that senators of either party will allow a "free pass" to ideological nominees of an opposing administration. Second, the demeanor of judicial nominees when up against the Senate may be more contentious following Scalia, as many senators later realized they failed to press the nominee on key issues. Finally, increased elite polarization has made the confirmation process a more contentious battle than previous seen, as members of each party are more reluctant to work with and approve of the missions of the opposing party. All of these factors work to suggest that the ease by which Scalia was able to take the bench is likely the end of its kind.

Ideology, Demeanor, and the Comparative Failure of Bork

The confirmation record of Reagan Supreme Court nominees is certainly a "mixed bag" when considering the tremendous successes achieved by three of the nominees, and the struggles incurred among the three others. Scalia, Sandra Day O'Connor, and Anthony Kennedy all yielded unanimous confirmation votes from the Senate. As mentioned, Rehnquist's nomination to the chief justice position elicited a great deal of pushback, particularly among Democratic senators who felt his role as the most conservative justice of the Burger Court was not appropriate for ascension to the chief's position. Importantly, much of this pushback was because of the promotion to chief, not necessarily a rebuke to Rehnquist's ability to serve adequately as a justice. Finally, the first two nominees for the vacated position of Associate Justice Lewis Powell, D.C. Circuit judges Robert Bork and Douglas Ginsburg, both failed to find their way onto the Court. After admitting to smoking marijuana as a law professor at Harvard University, Reagan officials urged Ginsburg to withdraw his nomination from consideration (Roberts 1987). He did so on November 7, 1987, prior to going before the Senate Judiciary Committee. It is, however, the confirmation hearings of Robert Bork, now notorious for his performance before the Judiciary Committee and his subsequent failure to be confirmed, that lend to the most interesting comparison to the confirmation of Scalia.

With the retirement of Chief Justice Burger, Reagan administration officials mulled over several names to take the associate justice seat of William Rehnquist. Of course, Scalia would be nominated and take the position, but his colleague on the D.C. Circuit, Robert Bork, was also on the short list. A brief look at their credentials clearly illuminates why. Both had positioned themselves as conservative figures on the D.C. Circuit, arguably shifting what had been one of the most liberal institutions in American law toward a more conservative record. Both were involved with the conservative Federalist Society so influential within the Reagan administration. Both brought academic credentials to the position that differentiated them from many other federal judges. Finally, both took a similar approach to legal interpretation, advocating for a strict reading of the Constitution that puts great consideration into the original intent of the framers.

Additionally, as Bork would later recount following his failure at confirmation, their voting records on the D.C. Circuit were nearly identical. Citing the language of several supportive senators baffled at the opposition to his confirmation in 1987, Bork asserts that if he is an extremist, as many opponents claimed, then such a similar voting record would make Scalia, by any definition, similarly extreme (Bork 1990, 299). Based on Scalia's record on the Supreme Court, some detractors may now concede to Bork's point. Nonetheless, Scalia faced a miniscule fraction of the pushback levied against Bork, garnering a unanimous confirmation against Bork's 42–58 defeat.

Much has been debated of Bork's behavior before the Judiciary Committee, as his testimony was viewed by many to be combative. In some ways, it appeared that Bork took the confirmation hearings as a sort of intellectual debate between he and the committee, providing long, candid answers that trod through tedious explanations of his views on constitutional interpretation. Some have argued his answers failed to conform to what had, by that point, been widely considered to be part of America's adopted constitutional fabric. Indeed, Bork's answers differ greatly from that of the subsequent, successful Reagan nominee, Anthony Kennedy (Collins and Ringhand 2013), as well as the tight-lipped testimony of Scalia. As opposed to suggesting Bork answered too many questions, it is easy to see Scalia was asked far fewer questions and managed to avoid answering many of the contentious ones (Farganis and Wedeking 2014; Totenberg 1987).

By Bork's (1990) account, he did not appear to be able to avoid answering substantive legal questions as other nominees, including Scalia, had been able to, as he had already discussed many of these issues at length in print. Additionally, the midterm elections of 1986 flipped control of the Senate back to the Democrats, making the confirmation of a staunch conservative decidedly more difficult. Where Scalia's testimony was moderated by the supportive Senator Strom Thurmond, Bork faced Judiciary Committee chair, Joe Biden. Thus, despite the similarities between the two nominees, the differences in atmosphere account for a great deal in the disparity of the outcomes.[9]

Elite Polarization and Confirmation

Another explanation for Scalia's success depends on the increase in elite polarization, and in particular, the divergence between Democrats and Republicans in the Senate and the importance of ideological congruence demanded by the Reagan administration. While Reagan's tenure as president marked the beginning of a steady increase in polarization between Republicans and

Democrats, one of the consequences of the "Reagan Revolution," it was not until just after Scalia's confirmation that the slope of said trend began to increase exponentially. While the polarization among members of the Senate Judiciary Committee (Farganis and Wedeking 2014) as well as the House and Senate (McCarty, Poole, and Rosenthal 2007) truly began to diverge in the 1970s, the mid-1980s saw a notable uptick in elite polarization that has carried into the twenty-first century. While this does not necessarily account for Bork's demise, as discussed earlier, it certainly appears prevalent in the confirmation processes of more recent nominees. Following Anthony Kennedy's confirmation, no Supreme Court nominee has achieved unanimous consent from the Senate, and the divisiveness in voting appears to be on the rise. Excluding the confirmation vote of Clarence Thomas, whose nomination was marred by controversy over his allegedly inappropriate relationship with Anita Hill, partisan opposition to Supreme Court nominees gradually began to increase from the first Bush administration. Bush's nominee David Souter saw nine opposition votes, followed by three for Clinton's nomination of Ruth Bader Ginsburg, and nine again for Clinton appointee Stephen Breyer.

It is of course worth noting that the increased partisan division witnessed after Scalia is also a consequence of the intentions of the Reagan administration. Perhaps even more than Nixon before him, members of Reagan's administration understood the potential influence a truly conservative Supreme Court could provide, perhaps even serving to overturn disliked precedent. Thus, while O'Connor's confirmation was relatively uneventful, and Scalia's was all but ushered through, there has been a subsequent realization that a president's ability to continually fill vacancies on the Supreme Court with truly ideological candidates is of paramount importance to party politics. And as Republicans have continued to nominate justices affiliated with the strongly conservative Federalist Society first founded in the Reagan era, increased scrutiny is likely paid to these nominees considering the record of their first member to the high court, Scalia.

Partisan opposition to Supreme Court candidates increased from the early 1990s onward. Under George W. Bush's administration, many Democrats began publically calling for greater scrutiny toward judicial nominees, fearing that the Republican would work to appoint the most conservative nominees possible—nominees, Bush promised, that would practice in the mold of Antonin Scalia (Barnes 1999). With the retirement of Reagan appointee Sandra Day O'Connor and the death of Chief Justice Rehnquist, W. Bush was given two openings in a short amount of time. Originally picked to replace O'Connor, Bush nominated Roberts for the newly vacant chief justice position. The Senate floor vote was 78–22 in favor of the nominee, a notable departure from prior votes of confirmation, despite Roberts's considerable qualifications. After a controversial nomination and withdrawal of White House counsel, Harriet Miers, Bush nominated Samuel Alito. Democrats threatened a filibuster of the nominee, but failed to amass enough votes to avoid Republican cloture, and Alito was narrowly confirmed in a floor vote of 58–42. While slightly less heated, the Obama administration's first two nominations of Sonia Sotomayor and Elena Kagan continued this trend of polarized voting, with votes of 68–31 and 63–37, respectively.

Interestingly enough, one would think that the failure of the Bork nomination and the distaste levied by Democrats toward Scalia's eventual work on the Court would encourage the nomination of moderates to the institution. After all, as Congress has become more polarized and increasingly less capable of consensus (McCarty, Poole, and Rosenthal 2007; Binder 2003), the confirmation of Supreme Court nominees would surely be one of the more difficult battles. Despite these limitations, since 1990, appointments to the Supreme Court have only become *more* ideologically polarized, with Democratic presidents nominating more liberal judges and Republicans more conservative (Devins and Baum 2016). Essentially, the Court is more explicitly divided in liberal and conservative blocs than ever before, and while the battle for confirmation is undoubtedly more contentious, the promise of ideological congruence between the president, the nominee and like-minded members of Congress is preciously scarce. Despite his unanimous vote for confirmation, Scalia, perhaps better than any ideological nominee, exhibited the value of having strong ideologues on the Court in an era of ideological polarization in government.

To take this point one step further, it is likely that Scalia's own work on the Court helped encourage the ensuing rise in polarization seen throughout the federal government. As much a part of the "Reagan Revolution" as any member of Congress, Scalia, along with Rehnquist and Thomas, would go on to position himself as one of the conservative moment's most central figures. To remove Scalia, and Reagan's view of the Supreme Court more broadly, from the discussion of increased polarization in government would be to ignore an essential piece of its continual traction. While his confirmation occurs at a point of modest increase in congressional polarization, Scalia's time on the bench is not merely coincidentally linked to increases in both congressional and Supreme Court polarization. Alternatively, it is fair to suggest he is a major component of the snowball effect that led to increasing polarization among political elites, and more directly, increasing polarization in the process of Supreme Court nominations (Devins and Baum 2016).

Perhaps no event better shows Scalia's confirmation legacy in how the confirmation process has changed than the subsequent events after his death. As the Obama administration neared its end, many conservatives lamented the death of the conservative icon with the election approaching and their candidate, future-elect Donald Trump, trailing badly in most national polls. President Obama nominated a fairly moderate candidate in D.C. Court of Appeals judge, Merrick Garland, appointed to his circuit court position by President Clinton in 1997. Despite Republican praise of Garland in his D.C. Court of Appeals nomination, Senate Republicans refused to consider the nomination of Garland to the Supreme Court, arguing that with a new president to take office in a matter of months, the responsibility of filling the position should go to the newly elected executive. Despite protests from Democrats, and the unprecedented nature of the Republican blockade, Garland was never called before the committee for hearings, nor was he brought to the floor for a Senate vote.

Surprising many election observers, Republican Donald Trump defeated Democrat Hillary Clinton in the 2016 election. Trump, who many conservatives vowed to vote for exclusively because of the Supreme Court vacancy, had offered a list of prospective nominees during the campaign. Like Bush, Trump promised to nominate a strict constructionist (Mason 2017). On January 31, 2017, Trump announced the nomination of Judge Neil Gorsuch of the U.S. Court of Appeals for the Tenth Circuit. A well-educated and experienced jurist, many noted his ideological similarities to Scalia, with some scholars suggesting his position on the Court would be nearly identical to that of Scalia's (Epstein, Martin, and Quinn 2016), though others suggested he could be far more conservative (Black and Owens 2017).

With Democrats still fuming over the snub of Garland, the nominee narrowly escaped committee with an 11–9 vote before Democratic senators mounted a filibuster against his nomination. With Senate rules dictating nominees need to meet a sixty-vote threshold for confirmation, Republicans invoked the "nuclear option" in response, changing the rules of the Senate and dropping the threshold to a simple majority vote. The confirmation hearings were marred by the same polarized elements of the political climate that led to the nomination in the first place, and some commentators accused Gorsuch of being evasive during his testimony, if not outright dishonest (Epps 2017). Ultimately, Gorsuch was narrowly confirmed by a vote of 54–45, the smallest margin of confirmation since Clarence Thomas's disputed nomination twenty-five years earlier. It is only fitting to see Scalia's seat, attained in unanimity three decades earlier, become the subject of such party-driven dispute in an era marked by his influence.

CONCLUSION

When Gorsuch was sworn in for Scalia's spot, the partisan fighting was, for the time being, over. Scalia's confirmation hearing legacy led us down the path to a spot where the fight for the presidency seemingly hinged on people's preferences over who should sit on the Supreme Court. To be sure, in past presidential elections it was fairly common for voters or elites to talk about the importance of the next president picking a member of the Supreme Court. But the confluence of several factors led us to that peculiar environment where it seemed more crucial and salient than ever before (Devins and Baum 2016). It was a hearing that proved to be a microcosm for much of American politics.

Perhaps the most ironic curiosity of the Gorsuch hearings that went unexplored by most observers was what the late Justice Scalia might have thought of the fight over his replacement. While we cannot know his thoughts at this stage of the game, we think it is intellectually stimulating to consider his recent thoughts on the questioning that takes place at the confirmation process. While he benefitted tremendously from successfully avoiding many of the senators' thornier questions, one can possibly push that aside and attribute that to the nature of the times. But in a 2012 interview, Charlie Rose asked Justice Scalia what should the questions be to a current supreme court nominee. Scalia responds: "Much as I dislike the spectacle of confirmation hearings now, I prefer them to the alternative. As long as the court is revising the constitution, by god the people oughta have some say and they oughta be able to ask the nominee what kind of a constitution are you gonna give us. That's the most important question. Why shouldn't they be able to ask that?" (CBS—Rose 2012). Senators would undoubtedly agree.

We know that the fight to replace Scalia was crucial for legal policy and that it was going to be a hard-fought battle because it was a "critical" nomination that would potentially swing the balance of power on the Court (Ruckman 1993). However, we think the contentiousness and divisiveness of the nomination were felt precisely more so because of Scalia's own confirmation legacy.

NOTES

1. We thank David Schultz and Howard Schweber for helpful comments and suggestions.

2. It is not surprising that Republicans supported Scalia. For example, Republicans generally supported the Reagan administration's choice of nominees, with Judiciary Committee chair, Strom Thurmond, remarking that he expected "no problem in having either of the President's nominees confirmed" and promised to begin confirmation hearings for both nominees in short order (Weinraub 1986). But the amount of support that Scalia would mount from Democrats, even in hindsight, is truly surprising.

3. The Court would later deny certiorari in the school prayer case of *Elmbrook School District v. Doe* (*Doe v. Elmbrook School District* 687 F.3d 840 [7th Cir. 2012]), Scalia's dissent from the denial made the notable argument that the "First Amendment explicitly favors religion."

4. Regarding Scalia's newfound front-runner status, Nemacheck (2007) provides the "short lists" that presidents compiled for each vacancy from Hoover through H. W. Bush. Scalia was not on the short list for the vacancy that O'Connor would eventually fill in 1981 but was on the very short list after the Burger vacancy. In fact, only three names are listed for both short lists for the Burger and Rehnquist spots—Bork, Rehnquist, and Scalia.

5. Biden was introducing a drug regulation bill on the floor of the Senate.

6. The nominees following Ginsburg, which consists of Breyer, Roberts, Alito, Sotomayor, and Kagan were all above Scalia's level of nominee candor (Farganis and Wedeking 2014). Unfortunately, no data is available yet for Gorsuch.

7. If one counts the occurrences of the term "[Laughter]" in the transcript, which probably undercounts the instances of laughter, there are more than a handful during these serious proceedings.

8. Other senators seemed to be preoccupied by other stranger things. Senator Heflin wanted more privacy rights for smokers. He said, "I only have one or two questions Judge Scalia, I noticed you smoke a pipe. It may well be that someday you may have to rule in the right of privacy as to whether or not an individual can smoke a pipe in his study or in his bedroom, so I hope you take care of us smokers one of these days. I have no further questions" (*Nomination of Judge Antonin Scalia*). There is no indication of what the question was, as no question was asked and Scalia did not speak in response.

9. Another possible factor that explains some of the differences between Bork and Scalia's treatment before the Senate lies in how they were vetted and selected. Nemacheck (2007) shows that Scalia's nomination was a result of decision making involving the president, White House staff, and Justice Department staff. In contrast, Bork's nomination was narrower in scope, consisting only of the president and White House staff.

REFERENCES

Barnes, Fred. 1999. "Bush Scalia." *The Weekly Standard.*
Binder, Sarah. 2003. *Causes and Consequences of Legislative Gridlock.* Washington, DC: Brookings Institution Press.
Black, Ryan and Ryan Owens. 2017. "Neil Gorsuch Could Be the Most Conservative Justice on the Supreme Court." *Washington Post*—Monkey Cage, March 20. https://www.washingtonpost.com/news/monkey-cage/wp/2017/02/15/neil-gorsuch-could-be-the-most-conservative-justice-on-the-supreme-court/?utm_term=.86167c0ee26f.
Bork, Robert. 1990. *The Tempting of America.* New York: Free Press.
Brisbin, Richard A. 1998. *Justice Antonin Scalia and the Conservative Revival.* Baltimore: Johns Hopkins University Press.
CBS/PBS. 2012. Charlie Rose. *CBS This Morning: The View From the Bench.* "Justice Scalia on his Impact and Passion for the Law." Interview with Justice Scalia (November). https://www.youtube.com/watch?v=CNPuKv_pNks.
Collins, Paul M. and Lori A. Ringhand. 2013. *Supreme Court Confirmation Hearings and Constitutional Change.* Cambridge: Cambridge University Press.

Devins, Neal and Lawrence Baum. 2016. "Split Definitive: How Party Polarization Turned the Supreme Court into a Partisan Court." *The Supreme Court Review* 2016: 301–65.

Epps, Garret. 2017. "The Fundamental Dishonesty of the Gorsuch Hearings." *The Atlantic.* Accessed September 24, 2017. https://www.theatlantic.com/politics/archive/2017/03/the-fundamental-dishonesty-of-the-gorsuch-hearings/521097/.

Epstein, Lee, Andrew D. Martin, and Kevin Quinn. 2016. "President-Elect Trump and His Possible Justices." Unpublished manuscript.

Farganis, Dion, and Justin Wedeking. 2014. *Supreme Court Confirmation Hearings in the U.S. Senate: Reconsidering the Charade.* Ann Arbor: University of Michigan Press.

Fieldstadt, Elisha. 2016. "Supreme Court Justice Antonin Scalia's Most Controversial Remarks and Opinions." *NBCNews.com.* Last accessed January 19, 2018.

Greenhouse, Linda. 1986. "Senate Unit Backs Rehnquist, 13–5." *New York Times* (August 10, 1986).

Kurtz, Howard. 1986. "Senate Panel Approves Rehnquist, 13 to 5." *Washington Post* (August 15, 1986).

Liptak, Adam. 2016. "Antonin Scalia, Justice on the Supreme Court, Dies at 79." *The New York Times* (February 13, 2016).

Maltese, John Anthony. 1998. *The Selling of Supreme Court Nominees.* Baltimore: Johns Hopkins University Press.

Mason, Jeff. 2017. "Trump to Nominate 'Strict Constructionist' to Supreme Court: Pence." *Reuters.*

McCarty, Nolan, Keith T. Poole, and Howard Rosenthal. 2007. *Polarized America: The Dance of Ideology and Unequal Riches.* Cambridge, MA: The MIT Press.

Nemacheck, Christine L. 2007. *Strategic Selection: Presidential Nomination of Supreme Court Justices from Herbert Hoover through George W. Bush.* Charlottesville: University of Virginia Press.

Nomination of Judge Antonin Scalia to Be Associate Justice of the Supreme Court of the United States: Hearings Before the Senate Comm. on the Judiciary. 1986. 99th Cong., 2d, Sess. 33.

Nomination of Judge Neil Gorsuch to Be Associate Justice of the Supreme Court of the United States: Hearings Before the Senate Comm. on the Judiciary. 2017.

O'Brien, David. M. 2011. *Eye of the Storm: The Supreme Court in American Politics.* 9th ed,. New York: W.W. Norton & Company.

"Rehnquist, Scalia Win Senate Confirmation." 1987. In *CQ Almanac 1986*, 42nd ed., 67–72. Washington, DC: Congressional Quarterly.

Roberts, Steven V. 1987. "Ginsburg Withdraws Name as Supreme Court Nominee, Citing Marijuana 'Clamor.'" *New York Times.* November 8, 1987.

Ruckman, P. S. Jr., 1993. "The Supreme Court, Critical Nominations, and the Senate Confirmation Process." *Journal of Politics* 55(3): 793–805.

Totenberg, Nina. 1987. "The Confirmation Process and the Public: To Know or Not to Know." *Harvard Law Review* 101: 1213.

Wedeking, Justin and Dion Farganis. 2010. "The Candor Factor: Does Nominee Evasiveness Affect Judiciary Committee Support for Supreme Court Nominees?" *Hofstra Law Review* 39(2): 329–68.

Weinraub, Bernard. 1986. "Burger Retiring, Rehnquist Named Chief; Scalia, Appeals Judge, Chosen for Court." *New York Times.* June 18, 1986.

TABLE OF CASES

Lee v. Weisman, 505 U.S. 577 (1992).
Marbury v. Madison, 5 U.S. 137 (1803).
Roe v. Wade, 410 U.S. 113 (1973).
Town of Greece v. Holloway, 572 U.S. ___ (2014).
Webster v. Reproductive Health Services, 492 U.S. 490 (1989).

Chapter 13

Was Antonin Scalia a "Great" Supreme Court Justice?

James Staab

After the unexpected death of Antonin Scalia, legal scholars have been attempting to assess his judicial legacy. Scalia, who served on the Supreme Court from 1986–2016, made his name as a textualist. In statutory cases, he argued that judges should give primacy to the words of statutes and ignore legislative history. In constitutional cases, Scalia was a strenuous advocate of "original meaning"—or the idea that the words of the Constitution should be interpreted based on how they were understood by the society that adopted them. When judges strayed from the original meaning of the Constitution, Scalia was quick to point out how, in his view, their opinions were illegitimate and represented a threat to the U.S. democratic system of government. Scalia certainly had his critics, but he also had his admirers. Steven Calabresi, cofounder of the Federalist Society and a law clerk for Scalia during the Court's 1987–1988 term, claimed that Scalia was "the greatest Justice ever to sit on the Supreme Court" (Calabresi 2016, 575). Because of his unique contributions to originalism, two other legal scholars referred to Scalia as the "patron saint" of original meaning (Kesavan and Paulsen 2003, 1139). Even those who did not share Scalia's originalist approach to constitutional interpretation acknowledged his profound influence. In her remarks for the dedication of the Antonin Scalia Law School at George Mason University, Justice Elena Kagan described her former colleague as "one of the most important Supreme Court justices ever, and also one of the greatest" (Anderson 2016).

Although Scalia had a tremendous impact on how laws should be interpreted in the United States, it will be argued here that he should not be rated as one of the "great" Supreme Court justices. Admittedly, there is an element of subjectivity in determining what constitutes "greatness," and any assessment of Justice Scalia's legacy runs the risk of being premature since he died only two years ago. Nonetheless, there is some consensus among legal scholars over who have been the nation's truly great Supreme Court justices: John Marshall, Joseph Story, John Marshall Harlan I, Oliver Wendell Holmes Jr, Louis Brandeis, Charles Evans Hughes, Hugo Black, Earl Warren, and William J. Brennan[1]—and political scientists have put together useful lists of criteria that should be considered when making such assessments.[2] My examination of Justice Scalia borrows from these lists and emphasizes seven factors in particular: (1) length of service, including the production of a large body of respected judicial work; (2) judicial craftsmanship, or the ability to communicate clearly and memorably in writing; (3) influence, or whether the judge left an indelible mark on the law; (4) judicial temperament, or the qualities of being dispassionate and even-tempered; (5) impartiality, or the qualities of disinterestedness and maintaining a strict detachment from partisan activities; (6) vision of the judicial function, or the proper role of judges in a constitutional democracy; and (7) game changers, or whether the judge foreshadowed the future direction of the law and was on the right side of history. In my estimation, Scalia gets very high marks for (1), (2) and (3); low marks for (4) and (5); an average mark for (6); and a low score for (7). Accordingly, I would place Scalia in the category of a "near great" justice.[3]

Length of Service, including the Production of a Large Body of Respected Judicial Work

It goes without saying that in order for a person to be considered a "great" Supreme Court justice they must have served on the Court for an extended period of time. The nine "great" Supreme Court justices mentioned above served an average of 28.3 years. Benjamin Cardozo is sometimes listed as a "great" Supreme Court justice, but he served on the nation's highest court for only five-and-a-half years. In my view, Cardozo was a "great" judge, but he earned that distinction mostly from the time he served as a judge on the New York Court of Appeals.[4] Justice Scalia clearly satisfies the first criterion of greatness. He served as a Supreme Court justice for thirty years and on the D.C. Court of Appeals for another four years. He also was remarkably industrious. During his tenure on the nation's highest Court, Scalia wrote 867 opinions, 279 of which were majority opinions, 326 were concurring opinions, 224 were dissents, and 38 were opinions concurring in part and dissenting in part. He also wrote 135 opinions as a judge on the D. C. Court of Appeals.

During his legal career, Scalia also managed to write a large number of extrajudicial publications, including approximately fifty articles and three books. The quality of Scalia's scholarship was exceptional. In the area of constitutional interpretation, one of Scalia's first important articles was "Originalism: the

Lesser of Two Evils" (Scalia 1989). In that article, Scalia defended originalism both in principle and pragmatically. In principle, he argued that originalism better comported with the Court's decision in *Marbury v. Madison* (1803), which established the federal judiciary's power of judicial review. In order for *Marbury* to continue to be regarded as legitimate, Scalia maintained that judges must interpret the Constitution like a contract, with a fixed and unchanging meaning. Failure to do so, in his view, would result in judges making decisions better suited to the political branches of government. Scalia also argued that originalism was better than non-originalism because, as he put it, "You can't beat somebody with nobody" (Scalia 1989, 855). Scalia maintained that there was no consensus among non-originalists for what could be relied upon in making judicial decisions. "Are 'the fundamental values' that replace original meaning to be derived from the philosophy of Plato, or of Locke, or Mills, or Rawls, or perhaps from the latest Gallup poll?" (855). Scalia did acknowledge that in tough cases he might prove to be a "faint-hearted" originalist, but he defended originalism as the best way to curb judicial discretion.

In 1995, Scalia gave the Tanner Lecture at Princeton University, which culminated into the provocative book, *A Matter of Interpretation* (1997a). In this book, which included commentaries by Gordon Wood, Laurence Tribe, Mary Ann Glendon, and Ronald Dworkin, Scalia defended a textualist approach to interpreting both statutes and constitutions. Prior to his appointment to the Court, Scalia gave a canned speech at various law schools in which he challenged the use of legislative history in discerning the meaning of statutes (Scalia 1985–1986). Scalia drew upon that speech in his Tanner Lecture, contending that the use of legislative history was illegitimate for several reasons. First, and most fundamentally, he argued that reliance on legislative intent was inconsistent with democratic theory. According to Scalia, the guiding principle of the U.S. republic is that we have "[a] government of laws, not of men" (Scalia 1997a, 17). Lawmakers may intend what they will, but the only laws that bind people are the ones that are passed by a majority of both houses of Congress and approved by the president. Scalia also argued that there were several practical problems with using legislative intent as a substitute for the language of the law. First, in his view, it is next to impossible to find *the* sole intent of a law. Second, the sources relied on to assess legislative intent— floor debates, committee testimony, and committee reports—are not reliable indicators of the will of Congress. Third, reliance upon legislative history allows judges to reach whatever results they want. Based on these concerns, Scalia argued "that legislative history should not be considered as an authoritative indication of a statute's meaning" (Scalia 1997a, 29–30).

Scalia applied the same formalistic logic to constitutional interpretation— although, in this area, he did not reject the use of legislative history entirely.

Unlike in statutory cases, Scalia was willing to consult the debating history of the Constitution in order to construe ambiguous constitutional provisions. Scalia defended this apparent inconsistency by claiming that while he consulted the framers' intent in constitutional cases, he did so not to glean the subjective intentions of individual framers but to understand how the text of the Constitution was originally understood (Scalia 1997a, 38).

In 2012, Scalia coauthored what might be considered his *opus magnum*, a 567 page book containing fifty-seven canons of legal interpretation as well as thirteen falsehoods about how legal texts should be interpreted (Scalia and Garner 2012). The scope of the book makes it impossible to summarize briefly, but among the canons supported by the authors are: the "Supremacy-of-Text Principle," the "Ordinary–Meaning Canon," the "Fixed-Meaning Canon," the "Omitted-Case Canon," the "Whole-Text Canon," and the "Absurdity Doctrine." Among the false canons of legal interpretation are "the spirit of the statute should prevail over its letter," "the words [of legal texts] should be strictly construed," "remedial statutes should be liberally construed," "committee reports and floor speeches are worthwhile aids in statutory construction," "the purpose of interpretation is to discover intent," and "the Living Constitution is an exception to the rule that legal texts must be given the meaning they bore when adopted." In the book's foreword, Frank H. Easterbrook, chief judge of the Seventh Circuit, compared the book to Joseph Story's "magisterial" *Commentaries on the Constitution of the United States* (1833) (Scalia and Garner, xxvi).

During his long legal career, Scalia also wrote important articles on subjects ranging from legal standing to administrative law,[5] the president's removal power, federalism, freedom of speech, the Establishment Clause, affirmative action, and natural law. In sum, the body of judicial work produced by Scalia is truly impressive. It is safe to say that he easily satisfies the first criteria of what constitutes a great judge: longevity, including the authorship of a large body of respected judicial work.

Judicial Craftsmanship

Scalia also was one of the Supreme Court's "great" stylists. He had a remarkable command of the English language and his judicial opinions were authored with a rare combination of clarity, incisiveness, and flair. There are several things that made a Scalia opinion distinctive. First, they were incredibly well written. Scalia painstakingly labored over each word of his opinions. A self-described "greasy grind," Scalia constantly reminded his law clerks that "nothing is easy." Scalia's desire to "get it right" was likely taxing on everyone in his chambers. When an opinion was near completion, he would call the law clerk assigned the opinion into his chambers and they would go over it line-by-line. Library carts containing all of the sources cited in the opinion were made available, so the justice and his law clerk could laboriously check each one to make sure it was accurate—a process known as "booking" (Shanmugam 2016). Not only did Scalia demonstrate remarkable diligence in the craftsmanship of his judicial opinions, but his penchant for detail likely improved the work product of the entire Court. Scalia was known for lengthy "Ninograms" in which he would challenge a colleague's line of argument. Several of Scalia's colleagues acknowledged that his incisive feedback improved the quality of their own opinions. Justice Ginsburg, for example, has mentioned that her colleague's sharp dissent in *United States v. Virginia* (1996)—where the Court struck down single-sex public universities—improved the substance of her majority opinion (Ginsburg 2016). Scalia's judicial opinions set a high bar and are a lasting testament to his hard work ethic and attention to detail.

The second aspect of Scalia's opinions worth noting is that he wrote for a larger audience. Like all great authors of judicial opinions, Scalia used vivid metaphors to capture a particular legal point. One of Scalia's favorite metaphors came in *Morrison v. Olson* (1988), where the Court (7–1) upheld the independent counsel law. In lone dissent, Scalia criticized the majority for failing to appreciate James Madison's warning that in a republican form of government the legislature is the institution to be feared the most. Usually separation of powers questions "come before the Court clad, so to speak, in sheep's clothing," wrote Scalia, "[b]ut this wolf comes as a wolf" (699). In another separation of powers case, Scalia referred to the U.S. Sentencing Commission as "a sort of junior-varsity Congress" (*Mistretta v. United States* 1989, 427). In *Lee v. Weisman* (1992), he criticized the Court's ruling striking down nonsectarian prayers at graduation ceremonies as "psychology practiced by amateurs" (636). And who will ever forget Scalia's memorable description of the *Lemon* test used in Establishment Clause cases. Never able to convince a majority of the Court to inter *Lemon* once and for all, Scalia comically described the Court's flirtation with that test as follows: "Like some ghoul in a late-night horror movie that repeatedly sits up in its grave and shuffles abroad, after being repeatedly killed and buried, *Lemon* stalks our Establishment Clause jurisprudence once again, frightening the little children and school attorneys of Center Moriches Union Free School District" (*Lamb's Chapel v. Center Moriches Union Free School District* 1993, 398). Evidently, Scalia liked that metaphor so much that he would recite it to his colleague, Clarence Thomas, while making scary noises (Thomas 2016). On the second criterion of "greatness"—the ability to write clearly and memorably—Scalia again receives the highest of marks. The quality of his legal opinions has sometimes been compared to those of Holmes, Cardozo, and Robert Jackson—a comparison I would agree with.

Influential Judge

For a person who exhibited no lack of confidence, Scalia assessed his own judicial legacy rather modestly. In a March 2008 speech at the University of Central Missouri, Scalia was asked what he considered to be his most important opinion. He cited *Crawford v. Washington* (2004), a case that strengthened the requirements for the admissibility of hearsay evidence under the Confrontation Clause. He then added: "It's not much of legacy" (Scalia 2008). Similarly, when Scalia was asked in a 2013 interview how he thought he would be remembered fifty years from now, he responded: "Oh, my goodness. I have no idea. You know, for all I know, 50 years from now I may be the Justice Sutherland of the late-twentieth and early-twenty-first century, who's regarded as: 'He was on the losing side of everything, an old fogey, the old view.'" He then stated: "And I don't care" (Senior 2013, 15). Scalia was much too hard on himself! Three months after his address at the University of Central Missouri, Scalia authored the landmark decision in *District of Columbia v. Heller* (2008), which (for the first time in U. S. history!) recognized an individual right to bear arms under the Second Amendment. As we shall see in a moment, Scalia's view that the government could not regulate corporations from using their own treasury funds to engage in electioneering communications was eventually accepted by the Court. And, in other areas of the law, the Roberts Court moved closer to Scalia's views toward the end of his career.

Oral Argument

One area in which Scalia made an immediate impact was in how the Supreme Court conducts oral argument. Prior to Scalia's arrival, the justices asked very few questions during oral argument. Almost single-handedly, Scalia changed that. From his first days on the Court, Scalia asked sharp and incisive questions of counsel in an effort to get to the case's underlying issue and to steer the argument in a certain direction. He transformed what used to be dull affairs into engaging discussions about legal issues. Moreover, Scalia could be counted on to provide comic relief during these typically tense sessions. Several studies have shown that he got the most laughs during oral argument (Wexler 2005; Malphurs 2010). Scalia's approach to oral argument proved to be contagious. Almost all of the justices now pepper counsel with questions to get to the issue they care about and to make points with each other. As Justice Samuel Alito aptly put it, oral argument is now a "contact sport" (Alito 2017).

Textualist Approach

Scalia's forceful defense of textualism also left an indelible mark on the law. As Justice Kagan remarked, "we are all textualists now" (Kagan 2015). Prior to

Scalia's appointment to the Court, attorneys did not always include the actual language of statutes in their briefs. That certainly is not true anymore. Attorneys are now meticulous about including statutory language in their briefs, probably because they do not want to be criticized by a judge for not doing so. Moreover, law schools are more commonly offering courses on statutory interpretation. While most judges do not accept Scalia's extreme position of rejecting legislative history entirely, there probably is greater reluctance to rely upon such sources if they plainly contradict the words of the statute. When she was dean of Harvard Law School, Kagan credited Scalia with "transform[ing] the very terms of legal debate in this country" and for having "the most important impact over the years on how we think and talk about law, whether we agree or disagree with his positions" (Agule 2006). Since early iterations of originalism predated Scalia's judicial tenure, his textualist approach to statutory interpretation might be his most unique contribution to legal interpretation.

Scalia's originalist approach to constitutional interpretation also impacted the legal profession. While still a minority perspective, there are more originalists teaching at law schools and serving on state and federal courts. As Scalia comically put it: "I used to be able to say, with only mild hyperbole, that one could fire a cannon loaded with grapeshot in the faculty lounge of any major law school in the country and not strike an originalist. That is no longer possible" (Calabresi 2007, 44). The extent to which Scalia garnered support for originalism is reflected by the development of a progressive brand of originalism, which seems highly unlikely in the absence of Scalia's forceful defense of originalism (Amar 2005; Balkin 2011). One of Scalia's lasting legacies will be the extent to which he popularized originalism and provided it with a certain degree of respectability.

Within the camp of originalists, Scalia is credited with shifting the focus from one of "original intent" to that of "original meaning" (Kesavan and Paulsen 2003). In a speech he gave at the Justice Department just days before he was officially nominated to the Supreme Court, Scalia argued that the framers themselves did not believe that their subjective views were an authoritative guide to interpreting the Constitution (Scalia 1986a). Scalia instead maintained that the goal of originalists should be to determine how a particular provision was understood by the society at the time it was adopted. In fact, the landmark decision in *Heller* contained both variations of originalism. Scalia, the author of the majority opinion, relied primarily on an original meaning approach; meanwhile Justice Stevens, the author of the principal dissent, relied on an original intent approach.

Areas of Particular Influence

Justice Scalia's originalist approach to constitutional interpretation left a lasting mark on particular areas of the Court's jurisprudence. As already mentioned, Scalia's most important opinion was *Heller*. In that decision, the Court held that the Second Amendment guaranteed an individual right to keep and bear arms for self-defense. It is hard to overstate the importance of that ruling. Prior to 2008, it was the near-universal opinion of every federal court (including the U.S. Supreme Court!) that the right to bear arms had to be connected to a state militia. Scalia's opinion transformed what used to be regarded as a federalism provision into one that guaranteed an individual right to keep and bear arms for personal safety.

Another important area of law in which Scalia exercised considerable influence involved the Court's interpretation of the Confrontation Clause. Scalia interpreted that provision quite literally to require face-to-face confrontation. Despite an early loss in a case involving the use of one-way closed circuit televisions in courtrooms (*Maryland v. Craig* 1990), Scalia experienced a major victory in *Crawford v. Washington* (2004). In that decision, the Court ruled that out-of-court testimonial statements by an unavailable witness were inadmissible unless they were subject to cross examination. "Where testimonial statements are at issue," wrote Scalia, "the only indicium of reliability sufficient to satisfy constitutional demands is the one the Constitution actually prescribes: confrontation" (68–89). Scalia also influenced the Court's interpretation of the Sixth Amendment's right to a jury. Federal and state sentencing laws allowed judges to increase penalties in certain circumstances by a preponderance of the evidence. Beginning with two dissents in 1998, Scalia argued that such judicial discretion violated the defendant's right to have all facts that could enhance a punishment decided by a jury by proof beyond a reasonable doubt—a viewpoint that ultimately garnered majority support (*Almendares-Torres v. United States* 1998; *Monge v. California* 1998).

Scalia also wrote two important Court decisions in regulatory takings cases. In *Nollan v. California Coastal Commission* (1987), the Court held that property owners must be compensated for being required to provide a public easement along their beachfront property as a condition of receiving a building permit. Five years later, Scalia authored the Court's decision in *Lucas v. South Carolina Coastal Commission* (1992), which held that "when the owner of real property has been called upon to sacrifice all economically beneficial uses in the name of the common good, that is, to leave his property economically idle, he has suffered a taking" (1019).

Another jurisprudential area where Scalia played a significant role involved regulations of corporate speech. Scalia maintained that laws restricting corporations from using their own treasury funds for electioneering communications constituted viewpoint discrimination. One of his early opinions on the subject came in *Austin v. Michigan Chamber of Commerce* (1990), where the Court upheld a state ban on the use of corporate funds for independent expenditures in support of, or in opposition to, any candidate in state elections. Scalia filed a vigorous dissent, calling the Court's decision "Orwellian," "illiberal," and "incompatible with the absolutely central truth of the First Amendment: that government cannot be trusted to assure, through censorship, the 'fairness' of political debate" (680). Scalia's viewpoint would ultimately prevail in *Citizens United v. Federal Election Commission* (2010), where the Court overturned *Austin* and a portion of *McConnell v. Federal Election Commission* (2003), on the grounds that government restrictions on electioneering communications by corporations and unions were unconstitutional.

In other areas of constitutional law, Scalia shaped the Court's doctrine—although perhaps not to the extent he wanted. The Court's standing doctrine provides a good example. Prior to Scalia's appointment, he authored an important article arguing that legal standing was a crucial element of separation of powers, which if interpreted correctly prevents "an overjudicialization of the processes of self-governance" (Scalia 1983). As a federal judge, Scalia maintained that the three-part test used in standing cases must be strictly enforced so that traditional suits brought by aggrieved individuals are not turned into citizen lawsuits. In *Lujan v. Defenders of Wildlife* (1992), Scalia wrote the Court's decision holding that the "someday" intentions of members of a wildlife conservation group to return to places around the world where animals were endangered did not "support a finding of the 'actual or imminent' injury" required by prior case law. In subsequent cases, Scalia suffered some minor defeats (e.g., *Friends of the Earth v. Laidlaw Environmental Services* 2000), but the stricter gatekeeping role performed by today's federal judiciary bears an unmistakable Scalia stamp. Scalia also wrote notable opinions in the areas of political speech[6] and the Fourth Amendment[7]—although he did not dramatically change Court doctrine in those two areas. Despite Scalia's claim that he had "damn few" victories (Biskupic 2016), he did have some very important ones! In addition to the areas mentioned above, the Roberts Court's decisions on the subjects of affirmative action, desegregation, and voting rights moved closer to Scalia's views. For all of these reasons, Scalia should certainly be regarded as a very influential Supreme Court justice.

Judicial Temperament

Even though Justice Scalia amassed a large body of respected judicial work, was a gifted writer, and influenced a generation of lawyers about how to interpret the law, he gets a lower mark for his judicial temperament. In comparison to other justices who have served on the Supreme Court, Scalia's criticism of his colleagues' opinions was unprecedented. Scalia often said that he had no personal stake in a particular controversy, but the tone of his judicial opinions strongly suggested otherwise. Scalia regularly described his colleagues' legal analysis with words like "absurd," "ludicrous," "irrational," and "patently false." His sharp pen was applied to everyone on the Court. For example, during his last years on the Court, Scalia believed the Court was backtracking from his opinion in *Crawford v. Washington*. In a 2011 ruling, the Court held that a dying man's identification and description of the alleged shooter were non-testimonial, because the primary purpose of the evidence was to enable police assistance in an ongoing emergency (*Michigan v. Bryant* 2011). Scalia filed a blistering dissent in which he claimed that the Court's "opinion distorts our Confrontation Clause jurisprudence and leaves it in a shambles" (380). He also criticized Justice Sotomayor's statement of facts as follows: "Today's tale—a story of five officers conducting successive examinations of a dying man with the primary purpose, not of obtaining and preserving his testimony regarding his killer, but of protecting him, them, and others from a murderer somewhere on the loose—is so transparently false that professing to believe it demeans this institution" (379). In an unusual concurring opinion in *Ohio v. Clark* (2015), Scalia accused Justice Alito, the author of the Court's opinion, of wanting to overturn *Crawford*. "The author [Alito] unabashedly displays his hostility to *Crawford* and its progeny, perhaps aggravated by inability to muster the votes to overrule them." Scalia then added: "But snide detractions do no harm; they are just indications of motive" (2184). Even his judicial ally on the Court, Clarence Thomas, was not immune from Scalia's barbs. In a Fourth Amendment case, Scalia criticized Thomas's opinion as "serv[ing] up a freedom-destroying cocktail of two parts patent falsity" (*Navarette v. California* 2014, 1697).

Scalia, however, saved some of his sharpest criticisms for the moderate conservatives with whom he served. In *Webster v. Reproductive Health Services* (1989), the Court upheld four different state regulations affecting a woman's right to have an abortion, but it declined the government's request to overturn *Roe v. Wade* (1973). Scalia filed a concurring opinion in which he criticized the Court's "abstemiousness" and its "indecisive decision." "It thus appears," Scalia lamented, "that the mansion of constitutionalized abortion law, constructed overnight in *Roe v. Wade*, must be disassembled doorjamb by doorjamb, and never entirely brought down, no matter how wrong it may be" (537). However, Scalia singled out Justice O'Connor's concurring opinion for special treatment. O'Connor filed a separate concurrence in which she invoked the longstanding principle that "[t]he Court will not 'anticipate a question of constitutional law in advance of the necessity of deciding it'" (525–26). Scalia claimed that particular rule of judicial restraint did not apply in this case and O'Connor's assertion to the contrary "cannot be taken seriously" (532). He concluded his concurrence as follows: "Of the four courses we might have chosen today—to reaffirm *Roe*, to overrule it explicitly, to overrule it *sub silentio*, or to avoid the question—the last is the least responsible" (537).

Scalia also wrote stinging critiques of Chief Justice Rehnquist's opinions. Rehnquist was regarded as a strident conservative in the 1970s—earning him the nickname "the Lone Ranger"— but many scholars believe he moderated his views after he became chief justice. For example, in *Dickerson v. United States* (2000), Rehnquist surprisingly wrote the majority opinion upholding *Miranda v. Arizona* (1966), a decision he had previously strongly criticized. Scalia filed a bitter dissent. He argued that the Court's decision in *Miranda* was "preposterous," but that the Court's current opinion was even worse. "Today's judgment converts *Miranda* from a milestone of judicial over-reaching into the very Cheops' Pyramid (or perhaps the Sphinx would be a better analogue) of judicial arrogance. In imposing its Court-made code upon the States, the original opinion at least *asserted* that it was demanded by the Constitution. Today's decision does not pretend that it is—and yet *still* asserts the right to impose it against the will of the people's representatives in Congress" (465).

In *United States v. Virginia* (1996), the Court ruled that the Virginia Military Institute's all-male admissions policy violated the Equal Protection Clause. In solo dissent, Scalia called the Court's decision "illiberal" and its reasoning "not law, but politics-smuggled-into-the-law" (567, 569). Once again, however, Scalia saved some of his toughest jabs for Rehnquist. In his concurring opinion, Rehnquist argued that if Virginia had made a genuine effort to create a comparable institution for women it might have avoided an equal protection violation. "Any lawyer who gave that advice to the Commonwealth," retorted Scalia, "ought to have been either disbarred or committed" (594–95).

Justice Kennedy was the focus of many of Scalia's acerbic opinions. Scalia described Kennedy's analysis in one case as "terminal silliness" (*Romer v. Evans* 1996, 639). In another, he claimed that Kennedy's handling of precedent was "manipulative" (*Lawrence v. Texas* 2003, 587). He often criticized Kennedy for his "reasoned analysis" and for what Scalia thought was his use of flowery or poetic language. In one case, Scalia lambasted Kennedy's definition of "liberty" as the "sweet-mystery-of-life passage" (588). Even though Scalia said he did not believe in the *ad hominem*, he crossed that line on several occasions. In the gay marriage case, Scalia described Kennedy's opinion as "couched in a style that is as pretentious as its content is egotistical" (*Obergefell v. Hodges* 2015, 2630). He also wrote: "If, even as the price to be paid for a fifth vote, I ever join an opinion for the Court that began: 'The

Constitution promises liberty to all within its reach, a liberty that includes certain specific rights that allow persons, within a lawful realm, to define and express their identity,' I would hide my head in a bag." "The Supreme Court of the United States," Scalia continued, "has descended from the disciplined legal reasoning of John Marshall and Joseph Story to the mystical aphorisms of the fortune cookie" (2630n22).

Even though Scalia was a brilliant craftsman of judicial opinions, his criticism of his colleagues' opinions went too far. What distinguished Scalia's opinions is that he questioned his colleagues' intelligence, motives, and character. In a 1994 lecture to the Supreme Court Historical Society, Scalia defended the importance of dissenting opinions. Aside from the usual reasons one gives for authoring dissents, Scalia observed that the most important was the personal satisfaction they give their author: "To be able to write an opinion solely for oneself, without the need to accommodate, to any degree whatever, the more-or-less-differing views of one's colleagues; to address precisely the points of law that one considers important and *no others*; to express precisely the degree of quibble, or foreboding, or disbelief, or indignation that one believes the majority's disposition should engender—that is indeed an unparalleled pleasure" (Scalia 1994, 42).

It is clear that Scalia enjoyed writing strident dissenting opinions, but did they come at a cost? It is not likely that Scalia's no-holds-barred opinions harmed his ability to build coalitions in significant cases. That would put too much of the responsibility on Scalia and give insufficient credit to those justices who simply disagreed with him. For example, Scalia was not likely to persuade Justice O'Connor on the issue of abortion no matter how much he tried. The same can be said of Justice Kennedy on the issue of gay rights. However, Scalia's intemperate opinions damaged his reputation in two other ways. First, Scalia's take-no-prisoners approach to deciding cases was not the model of civility—a trait that is particularly important for judges! Scalia often said that good people have bad ideas, but he did not always limit his criticism to ideas. In a revealing 2013 interview, Scalia was asked if it was easier to be close to a colleague who is ideologically different, to which Scalia responded: "There may be something to that. If you have low expectations, you're not disappointed. When it's somebody who you think is basically on your side on these ideological controversies, and then that person goes over to the dark side, it does make you feel bad" (Senior 2013, 12). In an era of acute political polarization, Scalia's heated rhetoric did nothing to reduce it; in fact, it probably exacerbated it. Some legal scholars have observed that Scalia's fiery opinions are being modeled by law students and practicing attorneys (Chemerinsky 2015; Newman 2006/2007). Scalia is deservedly praised for maintaining close friendships with the justices with whom he ideologically disagreed (Brennan, Ginsburg, Breyer, and Kagan), but his relations with the moderate conservatives he served with must have been strained. Unfortunately, one of Scalia's legacies is that he was *the* most sarcastic Supreme Court justice in the nation's history (Hasen 2015).

More fundamentally, Scalia's willingness to write "foreboding" dissents could have jeopardized the independence of the federal judiciary. This is ironic because Scalia was a strong defender of an independent judiciary. During his confirmation hearings, Scalia extolled the virtues of life tenure for judges (Scalia 1986b, 99–100). In a 2010 interview, Scalia said that he could not fathom why the American people would want to impose term limits on federal judges, referring to the idea as "a solution in search of a problem" (Massey 2010). Nonetheless, another one of Scalia's legacies is that he left the framers' "least dangerous" branch of government more vulnerable to judicial reform proposals. It is no coincidence that as Scalia railed against the "Nine headed Caesar," the "Imperial Judiciary," and "the unelected committee of nine," proposals to limit the Court's jurisdiction and the tenure of federal judges began to appear (Constitution Restoration Act of 2004; Cramton and Carrington 2006). In his dissent in *Obergefell v. Hodges* (2015), the case in which the Court struck down state laws banning gay marriage, Scalia explained that he wrote his separate dissent to announce "that my Ruler, and the Ruler of 320 million Americans coast-to-coast, is a majority of the nine lawyers on the Supreme Court." He then ominously predicted that the Court's decision could lead to its own downfall. "Hubris is sometimes defined as 'o'erweening pride; and pride, we know, goeth before the fall. . . . With each decision of ours that takes from the People a question properly left to them—with each decision that is unabashedly based not on law, but on the 'reasoned judgment' of a bare majority of this Court—we move one step closer to being reminded of our impotence" (2631).

Impartiality

Justice Scalia's off-the-bench behavior also diminished his judicial legacy. His long association with the Federalist Society, which is the most powerful *conservative* legal organization in the United States, compromised his impartiality in some of the cases that came before the Supreme Court. Founded in 1982, the Federalist Society serves as an important network for connecting its members to public interest firms, government employment (particularly in the Justice Department), and judicial appointments. Even though the Federalist Society professes not to be directly involved in public policy (i.e., it does not lobby members of Congress or file cases as *amici*), it can hardly be described as politically neutral. Its mission statement defines its founding principles as "the state exists to preserve freedom, that the separation of governmental powers is central to our Constitution, and that is emphatically the province and duty of the judiciary to say what the law is, not what it should be." Its purpose is to bring together conservatives and libertarians "both to promote an awareness of these principles and to further their application through its activities."[8] In fact, in the mid-1990s, the Federalist Society pivoted in a more political direction when it established fifteen practice groups (modeled after the American Bar Association's), partly because of the unfavorable rating the ABA gave to Judge Bork during his confirmation hearings (Teles 2008, 167–73). And, while the Federalist Society made a conscious decision not to establish its own litigation center back in the 1980s, it provides a Pro Bono Center that connects its members to ideologically sympathetic public interest groups, several of which have been involved in major litigation in the federal courts (Teles 2008, 155; Hollis-Brusky 2015).

Justice Scalia maintained a thirty-four year relationship with the Federalist Society. As a law professor, he served as the first faculty advisor for the student chapter established at the University of Chicago. After he became a judge, Scalia gave keynote addresses at the society's National Lawyers Conventions in 1988, 2006, 2008, and 2014—an annual event that is now named in Scalia's honor. Scalia delivered the Barbara K. Olson Memorial Lecture in 2004 and was interviewed by Jan Crawford, the chief legal correspondent for CBS News, at the national convention in 2010. Over the years, Scalia also gave numerous talks at regional luncheons and dinners. Many of Scalia's law clerks were Federalist Society members, including two of its founding members.[9] In 2003 and 2005, Scalia co-taught a ten-hour course on separation of powers, which was made available only to members of the Federalist Society. In 2007, Scalia wrote the forward for the book celebrating the twenty-fifth anniversary of the Federalist Society (Calabresi 2007). The various forms of networking offered by the Federalist Society have clearly paid off. As Amanda Hollis-Brusky (2015) points out, the Federalist Society provided the "intellectual capital" to bring about a rightward shift in the Supreme Court's jurisprudence in the areas of gun rights, federalism, and corporate speech. Scalia's continued relationship with the Federalist Society, particularly after the mid-1990s when it established fifteen practice groups and a Pro Bono Center, was not the model of impartiality. In fact, it appears that Justice Scalia himself was not immune from the persuasive legal scholarship of the Federalist Society members.[10]

Recusal Requests

During his judicial tenure, Justice Scalia faced several recusal requests for off-the-cuff remarks he made during speeches. In a 2003 speech to the Knights of Columbus, Scalia criticized the Ninth Circuit Court's recent decision striking down the recitation of the pledge in public schools as a violation of the Establishment Clause. When the case was subsequently appealed to the Supreme Court, Michael Newdow, the atheist father who objected to the daily recitation in his daughter's public school, requested that Scalia recuse himself from participating in the case (Greenhouse 2003; *Elk Grove Unified School District v. Newdow* 2004). He did.

In a 2006 speech at Fribourg University in Geneva, Switzerland, Scalia was asked several questions about the rights of the foreign "enemy combatants" held in detention at Guantanamo Bay. One student asked if they had any rights under the U.S. Constitution, to which Scalia confidently said "no." "The United States Constitution gives its protection to American citizens everywhere in the world and to all persons in the United States. Foreigners in foreign countries have no rights under the American Constitution," explained Scalia. A few questions later, another student commented that Scalia's remarks, specifically related to Guantanamo, "scared" her. When she began to provide her own interpretation of U.S. foreign policy toward the Gitmo detainees, Scalia interrupted her: "I had a son [Matthew] on that battlefield. And they were shooting at my son. And I am not about to give this man who was captured in a war, a full jury trial. I mean it's crazy" (Scalia 2006; Murphy 2014, 340–48).

Only three weeks after Scalia's speech in Switzerland, the Court heard oral arguments in *Hamdan v. Rumsfeld* (2006), which raised the question of whether the Bush administration's proposed use of military commissions to try foreign enemy combatants violated domestic or international law. Because of Scalia's remarks at Fribourg University, a group of retired U.S. generals and admirals formally requested that he recuse himself from the case (Lane 2006). This time Scalia refused. In fact, when the Court handed down its decision that the proposed military commissions *did* violate domestic and international law, Scalia dissented. He argued that the Detention Treatment Act of 2005 stripped the federal courts of habeas jurisdiction over the detainees held at Guantanamo Bay, *and* that "an enemy alien detained abroad, has no rights under the [Constitution's] Suspension Clause" (670).

Probably Scalia's most publicized recusal controversy resulted from his duck hunting trip with Vice President Dick Cheney. On January 5, 2004, three weeks after the Court agreed to hear *Cheney v. United States District Court*, Scalia was caught by the media on the front-end of a several day duck-hunting trip with his long-time friend, Dick Cheney, a named party in the case. The two men were guests of Wallace Carline, a friend of Scalia's, who owned Diamond Services Corporation in Amelia, Louisiana. On behalf of Carline, Scalia invited the vice president to take part in the annual duck hunt in the spring of 2003, and the vice president accepted. Cheney then offered to fly Scalia, his son, and son-in-law, down to Louisiana on a government plane, which they accepted. Because Scalia and the vice president went on the duck hunting trip *after* the Court agreed to hear *Cheney*, Sierra Club, one of the parties in the case, formally requested Scalia to recuse himself. He refused (Staab 2006, 315–17).

Under Supreme Court rules, the decision to recuse lies with the individual justice and the standard is whether a justice's impartiality in a case might reasonably be questioned. In Scalia's view, his impartiality could not reasonably be questioned since there was no court precedent stating that a judge could not sit in a case involving a friend when that person is being sued in his official (as opposed to private) capacity. In a sixteen-page memorandum, Scalia blasted the press for inaccurately covering the controversy and maintained that recusal in this instance would hurt the integrity of the courts by allowing "elements of the press a veto over participation of any Justices who had social contacts with, or were even known to be friends of, a named official" (*Cheney v. United States District Court*, Memorandum of Justice Scalia 2004, 927). "If it is reasonable to think that a Supreme Court Justice can be bought so cheap," wrote Scalia, "the Nation is in deeper trouble than I had imagined" (929). Scalia did not write an opinion in *Cheney*, but he did join Justice Thomas's concurrence, which strongly defended the private deliberations and proceedings of the energy policy group chaired by Vice President Cheney.[11] Scalia regarded his decision not to recuse in *Cheney* as one of his greatest acts of political courage (Senior 2013, 15).

Partisan Opinions

There were also instances when Justice Scalia's opinions struck a partisan tone. Probably the most notable example came in *Bush v. Gore* (2000). In the Court's brief order granting review, Scalia signaled how he would ultimately vote on the merits. "The counting of votes that are of questionable legality," maintained Scalia, "does in my view threaten irreparable harm to petitioner, and to the country, by casting a cloud upon what he claims to be the legitimacy of his election. Count first, and rule upon legality afterwards, is not a recipe for producing election results that have the public acceptance democratic stability requires" (*Bush v. Gore* 2000, 1047). Three days later, the Supreme Court reversed the Florida Supreme Court, effectively giving the presidential election to George W. Bush.

On the lecture circuit, Scalia received substantial criticism for his role in the case. His typical response was: "Get over it" (Morgan 2012). At Fribourg University, Scalia was specifically asked what legal reasoning the Court used in reaching its decision? He initially responded that some court had to decide the case "because Mr. Gore had brought it into Court. It was the Democrats who wanted the courts to decide the question. . . . So, the question ultimately was whether the election of the president of the United States was going to be decided by the Florida Supreme Court or by the Supreme Court of the United States. That seems to be not a very hard question. There was no way in which we could have turned that case down." Scalia then turned to the legal rationale for the Supreme Court's decision. Seven of the nine justices, observed Scalia, agreed that a hand recount would violate the Equal Protection Clause because there was no way to guarantee that the counting of under-votes (e.g., dimples and chads) would be treated equally from county to county. "The only point on which we were in disagreement," he noted, "was whether having waited something like three weeks and looking like idiots—the greatest democracy in the world can't run an election, and we couldn't have a transition team in Washington to take over—should we give the Florida court another two weeks to straighten it all out? That was the only point on which we disagreed, and five of us said no. Enough is enough." Then taking a dig at the Florida Supreme Court, Scalia sarcastically said: "To fully appreciate the Florida case you need to read the opinion of the Florida Supreme Court. There was indeed a politically motivated court involved in this, but it wasn't mine" (Scalia 2006).

Immigration

Another instance of Scalia striking a partisan tone in a Court decision came in *Arizona v. United States* (2012). In 2010, Arizona passed a statute to strengthen immigration enforcement within its borders. The Supreme Court struck down three of the four challenged provisions under the Court's pre-emption doctrine. Scalia concurred in part and dissented in part. He would have upheld all of the provisions as part of a state's sovereign authority "to exclude . . . people who have no right to be there" (417). However, Scalia went beyond the legal issues presented in the case to comment on the Obama administration's enforcement of illegal immigration, which he described as "lax." "The Government complains that state officials might not heed 'federal priorities,'" wrote Scalia. "Indeed they might not, particularly if those priorities include willful blindness or deliberate inattention to the presence of removable aliens in Arizona" (428). Scalia also expressed sympathy for the apparent frustration by the citizens of Arizona. "Are the sovereign States at the mercy of the Federal Executive's refusal to enforce the Nation's immigration laws," asked Scalia? "Arizona bears the brunt of the country's illegal immigration problem. Its citizens feel themselves under siege by large numbers of illegal immigrants who invade their property, strain their social services, and even place their lives in jeopardy. Federal officials have been unable to remedy the problem" (436).

In an unusual move, Scalia then criticized an aspect of the Obama administration's immigration policy that had not even been briefed or argued by counsel. Two months after oral argument in the case, the Obama administration announced a policy that exempted illegal immigrants under the age of thirty from deportation for two years. Scalia used this new policy as a way to counter the government's argument that federal enforcement of illegal immigration was limited by scarce resources. "The President said at a news conference that the new program is 'the right thing to do' in light of Congress's failure to pass the Administration's proposed revision of the Immigration Act. Perhaps it is, though Arizona may not think so. But to say, as the Court does, that Arizona *contradicts federal law* by enforcing applications of the Immigration Act that the President declines to enforce boggles the mind" (435). The partisan tone of Scalia's dissent received substantial criticism from liberals and conservatives alike. E. J. Dionne, a liberal op-ed columnist for the *Washington Post*, called for Scalia to resign (Dionne 2012). Richard Posner, a conservative judge on the Seventh Circuit Court, described Scalia's dissent as having "the air of a campaign speech" (Totenberg 2012).[12]

Vision of the Judicial Function

Justice Scalia had a well-defined conception of the judicial role in a democratic system of government. Because of his criticism of the Living Constitution, one could easily overlook the important role Scalia believed judges perform in a constitutional democracy. Scalia relished telling audiences that his most important job as a judge was to say no to the people. In one speech, Scalia explained that the reason judges have life tenure is so they "can tell the people to go take a walk." "The most important thing I do in my job is to tell the majority that it can't do what it wants to do, because the Constitution forbids it. I stand between you and the majority, with the Constitution in my hand. And essentially, I tell the people, you know, 'people be damned, you cannot do this. The Constitution forbids you'" (Scalia 1997b). During his tenure on the Court, Scalia never shied away from voting to overturn laws he believed violated a clear constitutional command or encroached upon the powers of the federal judiciary (*Coy v. Iowa* 1988; *Plaut v. Spendthrift Farm, Inc.* 1995).

At the same time, Scalia believed the Living Constitution allowed the federal judiciary to get involved in political controversies it did not previously. "Every era raises its own peculiar threat to constitutional democracy," Scalia once remarked, and judicial activism "represents the distinctive threat of our times" (Scalia 1985, 706). In many areas of law, Scalia's jurisprudence can certainly be regarded as principled (Dorsen 2017). He reached "liberal" results in free speech and Fourth Amendment cases (see, e.g., *Texas v. Johnson* 1989; *Arizona v. Hicks* 1987; *Kyllo v. United States* 2001; *Maryland v. King* 2013). As noted earlier, Scalia's literal interpretations of the Confrontation Clause and the right to jury provision led to results he likely disagreed with. Scalia also was a principled critic of substantive due process, which he believed was an oxymoron and allowed for the greatest amount of "freewheeling lawmaking" by judges (Scalia, 1997a, 24). For example, he rejected what might be considered "liberal" substantive due process rights, such a right of abortion, a right to die, and a right of sexual preference. He also rejected invitations by libertarian conservatives to resurrect "the liberty of contract" doctrine (Scalia 1985), and he dissented in cases in which the Court held that corporations were protected against excessive damage awards under the Due Process Clause (*BMW of North America v. Gore* 1996).

Scalia's opinions in other areas of the law, however, were not so principled. For example, in interpreting Article I's Presentment Clause, Scalia argued that the legislative veto was unconstitutional, but the line item veto was not (Scalia 1979; *Clinton v. City of New York* 1998). When he was assistant attorney general of the United States, Scalia testified before Congress that the president's recognition power was exclusive, but in *Zivotofsky v. Kerry* (2015) he strongly suggested it was not (Scalia 1975, 176–77; *Zivotofsky* 2118). Scalia joined Court opinions that broadly expanded the scope of state sovereign immunity, even though the text of the Eleventh Amendment did not support such an expansive interpretation (e.g., *Board of Trustees of the University of Alabama v. Garrett* 2001). In *Boyle v. United Technologies Corp.* (1988), Scalia wrote the majority opinion *creating* a government contractor defense under federal common law, despite the fact that Congress declined to do so. In *McDonald v. City of Chicago* (2010), Scalia cast the decisive fifth vote to incorporate the Second Amendment to apply against the states, even though he previously maintained that "properly understood" the Second Amendment "is no limitation upon arms control by the states" (Scalia 1997a, 136–137n13). Scalia argued that *Miranda* was not constitutionally supported under the Fifth Amendment, but he voted in favor of the stop-and-frisk exception to the Fourth Amendment.[13] Scalia did not defend his regulatory takings opinions based on the original understanding of the Constitution, and, in one case, he admitted that the original meaning of the Takings Clause was to prohibit physical deprivations of property (*Lucas v. South Carolina Coastal Commission* 1992, 1028n15). Scalia's view that affirmative action violated the Equal Protection Clause never confronted the fact that race-conscious federal laws were enacted concurrently with the passage of the Fourteenth Amendment (Schnapper 1985; Rubenfeld 1997). And, while Scalia had some support for his view that corporations have a right to speak on matters of general public interest (*First National Bank of Boston v. Bellotti* 1978), his contention that the government could not regulate corporations from using treasury funds for electioneering communications was inconsistent with Court precedent and federal laws dating back to 1947.

However, the most breathtaking example of "freewheeling lawmaking" by Justice Scalia was his majority opinion in *Heller*. In arriving at the conclusion that the Second Amendment secures an individual right to bear arms, Scalia relied mostly on a textual argument. He maintained that while the primary purpose of the Second Amendment was to support state militias as a check on federal power (i.e., the creation of a large standing army), the language of the Second Amendment had a broader meaning. Scalia decoupled the prefatory clause—"A well-regulated Militia, being necessary to the security of a free state"—from the operative clause—"the right of the people to keep and bear Arms, shall not be infringed"—and argued that the latter clause was more encompassing. In the process, Scalia sidestepped the drafting history of the Second Amendment (i.e., Madison's original proposal contained a military exemption for religious purposes), and *sixty-nine* years of near-unanimous precedent finding that the right to keep and bear arms had to be connected to a state militia (e.g., *United States v. Miller* 1939; *Burton v. Sills* 1969; *Lewis v. United States* 1980, 65n8; but also see *United States v. Emerson* 2001).

Scalia's opinion in *Heller* received strong praise from the National Rifle Association and gun rights advocates, but it also received extensive criticism from legal scholars. Judge Posner argued that a true originalist method "would have yielded the opposite result," and that *Heller* provides evidence that the Supreme Court "exercises freewheeling discretion strongly flavored with ideology" (Posner 2008). He also characterized Scalia's opinion as a bad example of "law-office history." Judge J. Harvie Wilkinson III, also a conservative, contended that *Heller* was no different than *Roe v. Wade* (1973), where the Court upheld a woman's right to obtain an abortion (Wilkinson 2009). Both Posner and Wilkinson also faulted the *Heller* Court for giving "short shrift" to questions of federalism and the democratic process.

Game Changers

Most of the "great" Supreme Court justices have brought about major changes to the law. John Marshall (the "great" chief) is celebrated because his judicial opinions strengthened the union through a broad interpretation of national power. John Marshall Harlan I's dissent in *Plessy v. Ferguson* (1896) paved the way for *Brown v. Board of Education* (1954). Oliver Wendell Holmes and Louis Brandeis laid the groundwork for greater protection of freedom of speech. Hugo Black was a transformative figure because his total incorporation theory has been virtually accepted by the Supreme Court in practice. As Jack Balkin reminds us, great Supreme Court justices have in some ways been prophets, that is, they have been able to anticipate the future direction of the law (Balkin 2002).

A major problem for Justice Scalia's legacy is that his originalist jurisprudence was on the wrong side of history. As noted earlier, Scalia had major victories in the areas of gun rights, corporate speech, the Confrontation Clause, the right to a jury, property rights, and legal standing—the full ramifications of which cannot be underestimated. But Scalia was in dissent in many of the other constitutional controversies he faced. For example, he dissented in cases involving: (1) whether foreign "enemy combatants" have the right to habeas corpus when indefinitely detained at Guantanamo Bay (*Boumediene v. Bush* 2008); (2) whether the individual mandate requirement of the Patient Protection and Affordable Care Act was constitutional (*National Federation of Independent Business v. Sebelius* 2012); (3) whether the states can impose term limits on members of Congress (*U.S. Term Limits, Inc. v. Thornton* 1995); (4) whether government employers can make hiring and promotion decisions based on political patronage (*Rutan v. Republican Party of Illinois* 1990); (5) whether anonymous speech is protected under the First Amendment (*McIntyre v. Ohio Elections Commission* 1995); (6) whether states can impose contribution limits on candidates running for state offices (*Nixon v. Shrink Missouri Government PAC* 2000);[14] (7) whether a state law creating an eight-foot buffer zone around abortion clinics violates the Free Speech Clause (*Hill v. Colorado* 2000); (8) whether the teaching of creationism must be balanced with evolution in public schools (*Edwards v. Aguillard* 1987); (9) whether prayers at graduation ceremonies violate the Establishment Clause (*Lee v. Weisman* 1992); (10) whether the *Miranda* warnings must be applied in federal cases (*Dickerson v. United States* 2000); (11) whether individuals have a right to an attorney at the plea bargaining stage of a criminal case (*Missouri v. Frye* 2012; *Lafler v. Cooper* 2012); (12) whether the mentally retarded and minors can be sentenced to death (*Atkins v. Virginia* 2002; *Roper v. Simmons* 2005); (13) whether the Eighth Amendment's cruel and unusual provision applies to overcrowded prisons (*Brown v. Plata* 2011); (14) whether *Roe v. Wade* should be overturned (*Planned Parenthood v. Casey* 1992); (15) whether individuals have the right to remove life support under the Due Process Clause (*Cruzan v. Director, Missouri Department of Health* 1990); (16) whether parents have the right to reject expansive visitation privileges from grandparents (*Troxel v. Granville* 2000); (17) whether a male-only admissions policy at Virginia Military Institute violates the Equal Protection Clause (*United States v. Virginia* 1996); (18) whether peremptory challenges based solely on a prospective juror's sex violate the Equal

Protection Clause (*J.E.B. v. Alabama* 1994); (19) whether a state referendum removing gays and lesbians from the protection of anti-discrimination laws violates the Equal Protection Clause (*Romer v. Evans* 1996); (20) whether same-sex sodomy laws violate the Constitution (*Lawrence v. Texas* 2003); and (21) whether gays and lesbians have the right to marry in the United States (*Obergefell v. Hodges* 2015). That is quite an extensive list of dissents, and it is by no means exhaustive! During his first term on the Court, Scalia attended the eightieth birthday celebration for Justice Brennan. For the occasion, Brennan's law clerks gathered together all of the justice's most important opinions and set them on a table. Not missing a beat, Scalia looked at all of the opinions and quipped: "So little time, so much to overrule!" Reportedly, Brennan "roared with laughter" (Liberman Otis 2016). During his thirty years on the bench, Scalia did limit many Warren and Burger Court precedents, but he probably did not accomplish all of what he wanted to do.

If we look back in time, it is also important to note that Scalia's originalist jurisprudence was on the wrong side of landmark decisions. For example, Scalia would have been the lone dissenter in *Humphrey's Executor v. United States* (1935), where the Court unanimously limited the president's authority to remove the heads of independent regulatory agencies. "It has . . . always been difficult," Scalia wrote in a court of appeals decision, "to reconcile *Humphrey's Executor's* 'headless fourth branch' with a constitutional text and tradition establishing three branches of government" (*Synar v. United States* 1986, 1398). Scalia is on record for believing that the incorporation doctrine was an inaccurate interpretation of the Fourteenth Amendment. In *A Matter of Interpretation*, Scalia wrote: "If the *text* of the Fourteenth Amendment said that 'the Bill of Rights, which has hitherto been a restriction only upon the federal government, shall henceforth be a restriction also upon the states,' there might be room for an argument. . . . But it does not say that" (1997a, 142).

Even though Scalia was a strong supporter of government neutrality when it came to private political speech, he did not apply the same scope of protection to obscenity and libel. During his first term on the Court, Scalia called into question the *Miller* test, which is used to determine whether a publication is obscene (*Miller v. California* 1973). "[I]n my view," wrote Scalia, "it is quite impossible to come to an objective assessment of (at least) literary or artistic value, there being many accomplished people who have found literature in Dada, and art in the replication of a soup can" (*Pope v. Illinois* 1987, 504). Likewise, Scalia was a strong critic of *New York Times v. Sullivan* (1964), which held that public officials must prove actual malice in order to win libel damages. In judicial opinions, Scalia took strong exception to the "public bumping" and heavy burden placed on public officials as a result of *Sullivan*

(*Ollman v. Evans* 1984), and in speeches he argued that *Sullivan* was inconsistent with the original meaning of the First Amendment (Scalia 2010; Scalia and Whelan 2017, 202–4). In Establishment Clause cases, Scalia was a sharp critic of the *Lemon* test and, for that matter, every other test developed by the Supreme Court, including Justice Kennedy's "coercion" test. His approach to the Establishment Clause—that is, the Court should defer to American traditions and practices—would have cast him in a dissenting role in *Engel v. Vitale* (1962), where the Court struck down non-denominational prayers in public schools. In religious freedom cases, Scalia criticized the strict scrutiny test established in *Sherbert v. Verner* (1963). In one of his most important opinions on the subject, Scalia wrote the Court's decision holding that incidental infringements on religious practices do not have to be supported by a "compelling state interest" (*Employment Division, Department of Human Resources of Oregon v. Smith* 1990). Both liberals and conservatives criticized Scalia's opinion in *Smith*, which resulted in a congressional effort to repeal it.[15]

In the area of criminal procedure, Scalia would have dissented in *Mapp v. Ohio* (1961), the case that nationalized the exclusionary rule to apply against the states (Scalia and Whelan 2017, 191). Scalia voted to overturn *Miranda* and, as an original matter, he believed the Sixth Amendment "meant only that a defendant had a right to employ counsel, or to use volunteered services of counsel" (*Padilla v. Kentucky* 2010, 389)—a viewpoint that would have placed him in dissent in *Gideon v. Wainwright* (1963). Scalia also did not believe that the Constitution protected a general right of privacy. "The right to be left alone," Scalia once remarked, "good God, this is anarchy" (Scalia 2008). He also argued that the Equal Protection Clause was not meant to apply to women, nor to discrimination on the basis of sexual orientation (Massey 2010). Finally, it is paradoxical that the Court relied upon the "one-person, one-vote" principle in *Bush v. Gore*. In a 1980 speech, Scalia criticized the Court's holding in *Reynolds v. Sims* (1964), which rejected the idea that state legislatures could be "structured like the federal Congress, with one house selected on the basis that it is not proportional to population" (Scalia 1980).

Brown v. Board of Education (1954) presents a major problem for a positivist-originalist like Scalia. Many defenders of originalism concede that if their theory cannot support *Brown*, which struck down segregation in public schools, then the theory loses all of its credibility. On the few occasions when Scalia was asked about the challenge *Brown* poses for the originalist, he claimed that he would have joined the Court's decision. However, he never gave a thorough explanation for why he believed this. In a footnote in one case, Scalia maintained that the language of Thirteenth and Fourteenth Amendments, taken together, prohibited racial segregation (*Rutan v. Republican Party of Illinois* 1990, 95n1).[16] However, it is hard to see how a judge following Scalia's originalist philosophy could have sided with the petitioners in *Brown* (Turner 2014). The language of the Equal Protection Clause is not self-defining and Scalia strenuously argued that judges must follow tradition when constitutional language was uncertain. In his article defending an originalist approach to the Constitution, Scalia described the role of the judge as "sometimes better suited to the historian than the lawyer." It requires, in his words, "immersing oneself in the political and intellectual atmosphere of the time—somehow placing out of mind knowledge that we have which an earlier age did not, and putting on beliefs, attitudes, philosophies, prejudices and loyalties that are not those of our day" (Scalia 1989, 856–57). How could a judge following that particular methodology come to a favorable ruling for the *Brown* petitioners?

As Alexander Bickel convincingly demonstrated, the original intent of the Fourteenth Amendment was *not* to outlaw segregation in public schools (Bickel 1955). In fact, by 1954, when *Brown* was decided, the District of Columbia and twenty-one states either required or permitted segregation in public schools (Dickson 2001, 646n35). Scalia seemed to admit that his theory of originalism did not support *Brown*. When asked at the University of Central Missouri whether *Brown* was correctly decided based on the original meaning of the Fourteenth Amendment, Scalia replied: "We originalists refer to this [question] as waving the bloody red shirt of *Brown v. Board of Education*." He then claimed that he "would have been with the majority in *Brown*, because I think I would have joined Harlan's dissent in *Plessy*." But, he insisted, "That is the less important answer." "I will stipulate that you can do some good things . . . with the Living Constitution. . . . A stopped clock is right twice a day" (Scalia 2008).[17]

Finally, Scalia's originalist approach to the Constitution was deeply insensitive to how law impacted people, which was particularly noticeable in gay rights cases. In *Romer v. Evans* (1996), the Court struck down a state constitutional amendment that not only denied gays, lesbians, and bisexuals of any claim of preferential treatment but it removed them from the protection of anti-discrimination laws. In dissent, Scalia accused the majority of "mistaken a Kulturkampf for a fit of spite" (636). He characterized the amendment as "a modest attempt by seemingly tolerant Coloradans to preserve traditional sexual mores against the efforts of a politically powerful minority to revise those mores through use of the laws" (636). Scalia also suggested that even if Coloradans were motivated by "animus," it was not necessarily "un-American." In *Lawrence v. Texas* (2003), the Court struck down a state law banning same-sex sodomy. Once again, Scalia dissented. He argued that the law should have been upheld based on the state's legitimate interest in outlawing certain forms of "immoral" sexual behavior—"the same interest furthered by criminal laws against fornication, bigamy, adultery, adult incest, bestiality, and obscenity" (599). He also made the following observation: "Many

Americans do not want persons who openly engage in homosexual conduct as partners in their business, as scoutmasters for their children, as teachers in their children's schools, or as boarders in their home. They view this as protecting themselves and their families from a lifestyle that they believe to be immoral and destructive" (602).

CONCLUSION

In several respects, Justice Scalia was a "great" judge. Based on the afore-mentioned seven criteria for assessing greatness, Scalia deserves the highest marks in the areas of length of service (including the production of a large body of respected judicial work), judicial craftsmanship, and influence. Scalia served as a federal judge for thirty-four years and left behind an impressive body of judicial work. Scalia also was a master craftsman of judicial opinions who wrote with a rare combination of precision and flair. If you happened to be on the other side of a Scalia opinion, you had better have brought your "A" game. Gifted with a razor-sharp mind, he could find the smallest weakness in any good argument. Like all great authors of judicial opinions, Scalia in-vented vivid metaphors to make his opinions more memorable and to ensure that his legal opinions would be read well into the future.

Scalia also was an extremely influential judge. He single-handedly trans-formed oral argument from a passive event to a sparring competition. Scalia's defense of a textualist approach to interpreting laws left an indelible mark on the law. In statutory cases, attorneys are more careful to include the actual language of statutes in their briefs, and there is probably greater reluctance by judges to rely upon legislative intent if the language of the statute is clear. Even though still a minority point of view, Scalia's original meaning approach to constitutional interpretation was also influential. There are more original-ists in the legal profession and Scalia's tireless defense of originalism now requires that judges and legal scholars pay more attention to the Constitution's text and history. Scalia also had an impact on particular areas of the Court's jurisprudence, including the Second Amendment, the Confrontation Clause, the right to a jury, property rights, corporate speech, and legal standing.

However, Scalia receives lower scores in the four other areas for assessing greatness. In the area of "judicial temperament," Scalia receives a low score. His criticism of his colleagues' opinions went beyond what is customary in judicial opinions. His penchant for sarcasm (or the "zinger") frequently came at the expense of his colleagues. What made Scalia's opinions unique is that he often criticized his colleagues' intelligence, character, and motivations. While his strident opinions did not likely lose majorities in major cases, they were not the model of civility. What is more, Scalia's "foreboding" opinions about a "Nine-headed Caesar" brought unnecessary attention to the independence of the federal judiciary.

When examining the criterion of "impartiality," Scalia also gets a low mark. By maintaining a long and uninterrupted relationship with the Federalist Society, Scalia did not adequately disassociate himself from politics and the litigation that was sponsored by either its members or the conservative interest groups it indirectly supported. Always the professor, Scalia spoke on subjects he should not have, which resulted in three formal recusal requests. Some of Scalia's opinions also had an unmistakable partisan tone, particularly his opinions in *Bush v. Gore* and *Arizona v. United States*. Scalia acted as though his theory of originalism immunized him from criticism, but that would only apply if originalism itself was politically neutral—which, of course, it is not. Scalia was the "gladiator" for the cause of originalism, but we do not expect judges to be leaders of causes!

On the sixth criterion for assessing greatness—"vision of the judicial function"—Scalia gets an average mark. It is true that Scalia had a clear understanding of the judicial role and that he reached liberal results in particular areas of his jurisprudence, but he did not always practice the hallmarks of judicial restraint. His views that the government could not regulate electioneering communications by corporations, and that the Second Amendment protected an individual right to keep and bear arms for self-defense, overturned longstanding judicial precedent and legislative practices, both at the federal and state levels of government.

On the seventh criterion of greatness—"game changers"—Scalia once again receives a low mark. The difficulty of making the case that Scalia was a "great" justice is that he was on the losing side of so many decisions handed down during his tenure. In most of the major constitutional battles he faced—church-state, *Miranda*, the right to an attorney, capital punishment, abortion, gender discrimination, and gay rights—Scalia played the role of dissenter. And, unlike some of the Court's previous great dissenters—Harlan I, Holmes, and Black—it is not likely that Scalia's dissents will be vindicated by future generations. As a result, I believe the substance of Scalia's opinions will lose some of their relevancy over time, particularly in the areas of liberty and equality. For these reasons, I would rank Justice Scalia as a "near great" justice.

NOTES

1. See, e.g., Jonathan Turley, "The Supremes: Picking the Top Nine Justices of All Time," Jonathan Turley Blog, *Res Ipsa Loquitur* ("The Thing Speaks for Itself"), September 3, 2009. I recognize that scholars have compiled other lists of "great" Supreme Court justices, some of which include Roger Brooke Taney, Stephen Field,

Harlan Fiske Stone, Benjamin Cardozo, Felix Frankfurter, William O. Douglas, Robert Jackson, John Marshall Harlan II, and William H. Rehnquist. See, e.g., Schwartz (1995); Bradley (2003); Abraham (2008), 373–76; Sunstein (2014). While I cannot get into all of the specifics here, I would not include these other justices among my top nine. Cardozo, while a "great" judge, served on the Supreme Court for too short a period of time (Staab 2003). Meanwhile, I would not place Taney among the "great" Supreme Court justices because of his disastrous opinion in *Dred Scott v. Sandford* (1857). Field, Stone, Frankfurter, Douglas, Jackson, Harlan II, and Rehnquist were, in my view, "near great" judges (Abraham 2008, 373–76). I would also put Sandra Day O'Connor and John Paul Stevens on the list of "near greats." Current justices are not under consideration, including Justice Kennedy, who recently announced his retirement from the Supreme Court.

2. In 1982, political scientist Sheldon Goldman provided a list of eight characteristics that constituted a "good" judge, both at the trial and appellate levels: (1) neutrality as to the parties in litigation, (2) fair-mindedness, (3) being well versed in the law, (4) ability to think and write logically and lucidly, (5) personal integrity, (6) good physical and mental health, (7) judicial temperament, (8) ability to handle judicial power sensibly (Goldman 1982, 113–14). In his classic work on the history of Supreme Court appointments, Dr. Henry J. Abraham identified eleven basic criteria: (1) demonstrated judicial temperament; (2) professional expertise and competence, including intellectual analytical powers; (3) absolute personal, moral, and professional integrity; (4) an able, agile, lucid mind; (5) appropriate professional educational background or training; (6) the ability to communicate clearly, both orally and in writing, especially the latter; (7) resolute fair-mindedness and impartiality; (8) a solid understanding of the parameters of the proper judicial role of judges under our Constitution, including the seminal lines between judicial activism and judicial restraint; (9) diligence and industry; (10) ascertainable good health; and (11) leadership ability and collegial sensitivity (Abraham, 326). Jonathan Turley, professor of law at George Washington Law School, grouped his list of nine great Supreme Court justices into three categories: (1) game changers, (2) unyielding contrarians, and (3) towering visionaries (Turley 2009).

3. This ranking is based on the categories used by Henry Abraham: "Great," "Near Great," "Average," "Below Average," and "Failure" (Abraham, 373–76).

4. Cardozo served on the New York Court of Appeals for eighteen years, the last six of which as its chief judge. Moreover, Cardozo's widely read extra-judicial publications, including his influential *The Nature of the Judicial Process* (1921), were authored during his time as a New York Court of Appeals judge (Staab 2003).

5. Scalia was a strenuous champion of the *Chevron* doctrine.

6. See, e.g., *R.A.V. v. City of St. Paul* (1992) (ruling that a hate speech ordinance was underbroad); *Brown v. Entertainment Merchants Association* (2011) (striking down a state law banning violent video games aimed at children.).

7. See, e.g., *Arizona v. Hicks* (1987) (the "cursory inspection" of stereo equipment constituted a search); *Kyllo v. United States* (2001) (the use of a thermal imaging device to detect heat emanating from a home constituted a search); *United States v. Jones* (2012) (the use of a global-positioning-system (GPS) device on cars without

a warrant violated the Fourth Amendment); *Florida v. Jardines* (2013) (the use of drug-sniffing dog on a homeowner's front porch violated the Fourth Amendment).

8. http://www.fed-soc.org/aboutus/.

9. Those two founding members were Lee Liberman (Otis) (1986–1987) and Steven Calabresi (1987–1988), both of whom have continued to assume major leadership roles with the organization.

10. To bolster his majority opinion in *Printz v. United States* (1997), Scalia cited a law review article coauthored by David Lawson, a former law clerk and Federalist Society member, which argued that in order for a federal law to be upheld under the Necessary and Proper Clause, it must not only be "necessary" but it must be "proper." The authors also argued that the word "proper" should be narrowly construed to mean "peculiar," not simply "appropriate" (Lawson, et al. 1993). In the Court's decision in *District of Columbia v. Heller* (2008), Scalia cited several articles by Federalist Society scholars to strengthen his argument that the Second Amendment guaranteed an individual right to bear arms for self-defense (Volokh 1998; Volokh 2007; Barnett 2004). And while Scalia previously maintained that the Second Amendment was "no limitation upon arms control by the states," (Scalia 1997a, 136–37n13), he joined the Court's decision in *McDonald v. City of Chicago* (2010), which incorporated the Second Amendment to apply against state power. Prior to that decision, many Federalist Society members argued that the Second Amendment should be incorporated under the Fourteenth Amendment's Privileges or Immunities Clause—a point of view Scalia rejected. Nonetheless, he did conclude that the Second Amendment was a fundamental right under the Due Process Clause. In fact, Justice Alito, the author of the Court's opinion, cited a coauthored article by Steven Calabresi that contended that the right to bear arms was "fundamental" because a majority of states at the time of the Fourteenth Amendment's ratification had constitutional provisions protecting such a right (Calabresi and Agudo 2008).

11. The case involved discovery requests by two interest groups concerned that a Bush administration energy policy group, chaired by Vice President Cheney, did not comply with federal open-meeting and disclosure requirements. The administration objected to the discovery requests on both statutory and constitutional grounds. The Court ruled in favor of the administration, but remanded the case back to the district court.

12. Scalia also spoke on controversial topics that were not decided by the Court—although they could have been. The most notable example was Scalia's claim that torture was not covered by the Eighth Amendment (Stahl 2008). Scalia also expressed the view that the Supreme Court's decision in *Katz v. United States* (1967) unreasonably jeopardized the National Security Agency's secret wiretapping program during the War on Terror (Scalia 2008; Scalia and Whelan, 246–47). Interestingly, in 2013 the Court ruled, with Scalia joining the majority opinion, that the parties challenging the 2008 amendments to the Foreign Intelligence Surveillance Act lacked standing to sue (*Clapper v. Amnesty International USA* 2013).

13. In a concurring opinion in *Minnesota v. Dickerson* (1993), Scalia questioned whether the Court's decision in *Terry v. Ohio* (1968) was consistent with the original meaning of the Constitution. "I frankly doubt," observed Scalia, "whether the fiercely

proud men who adopted our Fourth Amendment would have allowed themselves to be subjected, on mere suspicion of being armed and dangerous, to such indignity" (381). Nevertheless, Scalia concluded that "though I do not favor the mode of analysis in *Terry*, I cannot say that its result was wrong" (382).

14. Scalia believed that *Buckley v. Valeo* (1976) "was wrongly decided" because, in his view, there was no constitutional distinction between campaign expenditures and contributions (*McConnell v. Federal Election Commission* 2003).

15. In 1993, Congress passed the Religious Freedom Restoration Act, which restored strict scrutiny analysis in religious freedom cases. In a subsequent case, the Court ruled that the RFRA went beyond Congress's enforcement power under section 5 of the Fourteenth Amendment, thereby limiting its scope to federal laws (*City of Boerne v. Flores* 1997).

16. See also Antonin Scalia and Bryan A. Garner, *Reading Law: The Interpretation of Legal Texts* (2012), 87–88 (making the same argument).

17. For similar reasons, a strong case can be made that Scalia's originalist philosophy would have placed him in a dissenting role in *Loving v. Virginia* (1967), which struck down bans on interracial marriage. There is virtually no evidence that the original intent or original meaning of the Fourteenth Amendment was meant to prohibit bans against interracial marriages (Bickel 1955, 56; Klarman 1995, 1919–1920).

REFERENCES

Abraham, Henry J. 2008. *Justices, Presidents, and Senators: A History of U.S. Supreme Court Appointments from Washington to Bush II* 5th New and Revised ed. Lanham, MD: Rowman & Littlefield.

Agule, Kelly. 2006. "Scalia Speaks in Ames, Scolds Aggressive Student." *The Record*, December 7, 2006.

Alito, Samuel. 2017. "A Tribute to Justice Scalia." *Yale Law Journal* 126:1605.

Amar, Akhil Reed. 2005. "Rethinking Originalism: Original Intent for Liberals (and for Conservatives and Moderates, Too)." *Slate* September 21, 2005. http://www .slate.com/articles/news_and_politics/jurisprudence/2005/09/rethinking_original ism.html.

Anderson, Nick. 2016. "'One of the Most Important Supreme Court Justices Ever': Justices, Academics Dedicate Scalia Law School." *Washington Post*, October 6, 2016.

Balkin, Jack M. 2002. "The Use That the Future Makes of the Past: John Marshall's Greatness and Its Lessons for Today's Supreme Court Justices." *William and Mary Law Review* 43(4): 1321–38.

———. 2011. *Living Originalism*. Cambridge, MA: Harvard University Press.

Barnett, Randy E. 2004. "Was the Right to Keep and Bear Arms Conditioned on Service in an Organized Militia?" *Texas Law Review* 83:237.

Bickel, Alexander M. 1955. "The Original Understanding of the Segregation Decision." *Harvard Law Review* 69(1): 1–65.

Biskupic, Joan. 2009. *American Original: The Life and Constitution of Supreme Court Justice Antonin Scalia*. New York: Sarah Crichton Books.

———. 2016. "You Get One Shot: How Justice Antonin Scalia Viewed the World," *Reuters* February 16, 2016.

Bradley, Robert C. 2003. "Selecting and Ranking Great Justices: Polls Results." In *Leaders of the Pack: Polls & Case Studies of Great Supreme Court Justices*, eds. William D. Pederson and Norman W. Provizer. New York: Peter Lang.

Calabresi, Steven G. 2007. *Originalism: A Quarter-Century of Debate*. Washington, D, Regnery Publishing.

———. 2016. "The Unknown Achievements of Justice Scalia" *Harvard Journal of Law and Public Policy* 39: 575.

Calabresi, Steven G. and Sarah E. Agudo. 2008. "Individual Rights under State Constitutions When the Fourteenth Amendment Was Ratified in 1868: What Rights Are Deeply Rooted in American History and Tradition?" *Texas Law Review* 87:7.

Cardozo, Benjamin N. 1921. *The Nature of the Judicial Process*. New Haven, CT: Yale University Press.

Chemerinsky, Erwin. 2015. "Justice Scalia: Why He's a Bad Influence." *Los Angeles Times*, July 14, 2015.

Constitutional Restoration Act of 2004. https://www.congress.gov/bill/108th-con gress/house-bill/3799/text.

Cramton, Roger C. and Paul D. Carrington, ed. 2006. *Reforming the Court: Term Limits for Supreme Court Justices*. Durham, NC: Carolina Academic Press.

Dickson, Del, ed. 2001. *The Supreme Court in Conference (1940–1985): The Private Discussions behind Nearly 300 Supreme Court Decisions*. New York: Oxford University Press.

Dionne, E. J., Jr. 2012. "Justice Scalia Must Resign." *Washington Post*, June 27, 2012.

Dorsen, David M. 2017. *The Unexpected Scalia: A Conservative Justice's Liberal Opinions*. Cambridge, UK: Cambridge University Press.

Ginsburg, Ruth Bader. 2016. "In Memoriam: Justice Antonin Scalia." *Harvard Law Review* 130: 1.

Goldman, Sheldon. 1982. "Judicial Selection and the Qualities that Make a 'Good' Judge" *The Annals of the American Academy of Political and Social Science* 462: 112–24.

Greenhouse, Linda. 2003. "Supreme Court to Consider Case on 'Under God' in Pledge to Flag," *New York Times*, October 15, 2003.

Hasen, Richard L. 2015. "The Most Sarcastic Justice," *Green Bag 2d* 18: 215.

Hollis-Brusky, Amanda. 2015. *Ideas with Consequences: The Federalist Society and the Conservative Counterrevolution.* New York: Oxford University Press.

Kagan, Elena. 2015. "The Scalia Lecture: A Dialogue with Elena Kagan on the Reading of Statutes." *Harvard Law School*, November 17, 2015. https://www.youtube .com/watch?v=dpEtszFT0Tg.

Kesavan, Vasan and Michael Stokes Paulsen. 2003. "The Interpretive Force of the Constitution's Secret Drafting History." *Georgetown Law Journal* 91: 1113.

Klarman, Michael J. 1995. "*Brown*, Originalism, and Constitutional Theory: A Response to Professor McConnell." *Virginia Law Review* 81: 1881.

Lane, Charles. 2006. "Scalia's Recusal Sought in Key Detainee Case." *Washington Post*, March 28, 2006.

Lawson, Gary and Patricia B. Granger. 1993. "The 'Proper' Scope of Federal Power: A Jurisdictional Interpretation of the Sweeping Clause." *Duke Law Journal* 43: 267.

Liberman Otis, Lee. 2016. "Antonin Scalia—A Justice in Full." *National Review*, February 21, 2016.

Malphurs, Ryan A. 2010. "'People Did Sometimes Stick Things in my Underwear': The Function of Laughter at the U.S. Supreme Court." *Communication Law Review* 10(2): 48–75.

Massey, Calvin. 2010. "Legally Speaking: A Conversation with Antonin Scalia." Hastings College of Law, September 26, 2010. https://www.youtube.com/watch?v=KvttIukZEtM.

Morgan, Piers. Interview of Justice Scalia and Bryan Garner regarding their new book, *Reading Law: The Interpretation of Legal Texts*. Aired July 18, 2012. https://www.youtube.com/watch?v=aOqiH-bTXIc   http://transcripts.cnn.com/TRANSCRIPTS/1207/18/pmt.01.html.

Murphy, Bruce Allen. 2014. *Scalia: A Court of One*. New York: Simon & Schuster.

Newman, Stephen A. 2006/2007. "Political Advocacy on the Supreme Court: The Damaging Rhetoric of Antonin Scalia." *New York Law School Law Review* 51: 906.

Posner, Richard A. 2008. "In Defense of Looseness: The Supreme Court and Gun Control." *The New Republic*, August 27, 2008.

———. 2012. "Scalia's Screed on Immigrants Needs Sourcing." *Arizona Daily Star*, June 28, 2012.

Rubenfeld, Jed. 1997. "Affirmative Action." *Yale Law Journal* 107: 427.

Scalia, Antonin. 1975. Assistant Attorney General, Office of Legal Counsel. *Congressional Oversight of Executive Agreements—1975*. Hearings before the Subcommittee on Separation of Powers of the Committee on the Judiciary, United States Senate, 94th Cong., 1st Sess., 15 May 1975.

———. 1979. "The Legislative Veto: A False Remedy for System Overload." *Regulation* November/December: 19–25.

———. 1980. "The Judges Are Coming." *Panhandle*, Spring 1980, reprinted at 126 *Congressional Record* 18920–22 (July 21, 1980).

———. 1983. "The Doctrine of Standing as an Essential Element of the Separation of Powers." *Suffolk University Law Review* 17: 881–99.

———. 1985. "Economic Affairs as Human Affairs," *Cato Journal* 4(3): 703–9.

———. 1985–1986. "Use of Legislative History: Judicial Abdication to Fictitious Legislative Intent." Unpublished Speech Delivered to Various Law Schools in 1985–1986 (on file with the author).

———. 1986a. Address before the Justice Department, Washington, D.C. In *Original Meaning Jurisprudence: A Sourcebook*, Appendix C (Office of Legal Policy, U.S. Department of Justice, 1987), 1–6.

———. 1986b. *Nomination of Judge Antonin Scalia, to Be Associate Justice of the Supreme Court of the United States.* Hearings before the Committee on the Judiciary, United States Senate, 99th Cong. 2nd Sess. (August 5 and 6, 1986).

———. 1989. "Originalism: The Lesser of Two Evils." *University of Cincinnati Law Review* 57: 849.

———. 1994. "The Dissenting Opinion." *Journal of Supreme Court History.* 1994 Yearbook: 33–44.

———. 1997a. *A Matter of Interpretation: Federal Courts and the Law.* New Jersey: Princeton University Press.

———. 1997b. Address delivered at Thomas Aquinas College, Santa Paula, CA. January 24, 1997. (On file with author).

———. 2006. Remarks at Fribourg University, Conference of Justice Antonin Scalia. Geneva, Switzerland. March 8, 2006. http://www.bafweb.com/?s=scalia+

———. 2008. "Constitutional Interpretation," Julius J. Oppenheimer Lecture, University of Central Missouri, Warrensburg, MO. March 4, 2008. (Video recording on file with author).

———. 2010. "Methodology of Originalism." 12th Annual Henry J. Abraham Distinguished Lecture, University of Virginia School of Law, April 16, 2010.

Scalia, Antonin and Bryan A. Garner. 2012. *Reading Law: The Interpretation of Legal Texts.* St. Paul, MN: Thomson/West.

Scalia, Christopher J. and Edward Whelan, eds., 2017. *Scalia Speaks: Reflections on Law, Faith, and Life Well Lived.* New York: Crown Forum.

Schnapper, Eric. 1985. "Affirmative Action and the Legislative History of the Fourteenth Amendment." *Virginia Law Review* 71: 753.

Schwartz, Bernard. 1995. "Supreme Court Superstars: The Ten Greatest Justices." *Tulsa Law Review* 31(1): 93–159.

Senior, Jennifer. 2013. "In Conversation: Antonin Scalia." *New York Magazine*, October 6, 2013, pp. 1–16. http://nymag.com/news/features/antonin-scalia-2013-10/.

Shanmugam, Kannnon K. 2016. "Justice Scalia: A Personal Remembrance." *Journal of Supreme Court History*, 41(3): 255.

Shultz, David. 2003. "Why No More Giants on the Supreme Court: The Personalities and the Times." In *Leaders of the Pack: Polls & Case Studies of Great Supreme Court Justices*, eds. William D. Pederson and Norman W. Provizer. New York: Peter Lang.

Staab, James B. 2003. "Benjamin Nathan Cardozo: Striking a Balance between Stability and Progress." In *Leaders of the Pack: Polls & Case Studies of Great Supreme Court Justices*, eds. William D. Pederson and Norman W. Provizer. New York: Peter Lang.

———. 2006. *The Political Thought of Justice Antonin Scalia: A Hamiltonian on the Supreme Court.* Lanham, MD: Rowman & Littlefield..

Stahl, Leslie. 2008. "Antonin Scalia: The *60 Minutes* Interview." April 27, 2008. http://www.cbsnews.com/videos/antonin-scalia-the-60-minutes-interview/.

Story, Joseph. 1833/1905. *Commentaries on the Constitution of the United States*, ed. Melville M. Bigelow, 5th ed., 2 vols. Boston: MA, Little, Brown, and Co.

Sunstein, Cass R. 2014. "Who Would Make the List of Supreme Court Greats." *Kansas City Star* April 2, 2014.

Teles, Steven M. 2008. *The Rise of the Conservative Legal Movement: The Battle for Control of the Law*. Princeton, NJ: Princeton University Press.

Thomas, Clarence. 2016. Keynote Address at the National Lawyers Convention Annual Dinner. Washington, DC, November 17, 2016. http://www.fed-soc.org /multimedia/detail/keynote-address-by-justice-clarence-thomas-event-audiovideo.

Totenberg, Nina. 2012. "Even Scalia's Dissenting Opinions Get Major Scrutiny." *All Things Considered*, NPR News, July 16, 2012.

Turley, Jonathan. "The Supremes: Picking the Top Nine Justices of All Time." Jonathan Turley Blog. *Res Ipsa Loquitur* ("The Thing Speaks for Itself"), September 3, 2009.

Turner, Ronald. 2014. "A Critique of Justice Antonin Scalia's Originalist Defense of *Brown v. Board of Education*." *UCLA Law Review Discourse* 62:170–84.

Volokh, Eugene. 1998. "The Commonplace Second Amendment." *New York University Law Review* 73: 793.

———. 2007. "Necessary to the Security of A Free State." *Notre Dame Law Review* 83:1.

Wexler, Jay D. 2005. "Laugh Track." *The Green Bag* 2d 9 (Autumn): 59–61.

Wilkinson, J. Harvie, III. 2009. "Of Guns, Abortions, and the Unraveling of the Rule of Law." *Virginia Law Review* 95:253–323.

TABLE OF CASES

Almendares-Torres v. United States, 523 U.S. 224 (1998).

Arizona v. Hicks, 480 U.S. 321 (1987).

Arizona v. United States, 567 U.S. 387 (2012).

Atkins v. Virginia, 536 U.S. 304 (2002).

Austin v. Michigan Chamber of Commerce, 494 U.S. 652 (1990).

BMW of North America v. Gore, 517 U.S. 559 (1996).

Board of County Commissions v. Umbehr, 518 U.S. 668 (1996).

Board of Trustees of the University of Alabama v. Garrett, 531 U.S. 356 (2001).

Boumediene v. Bush, 553 U.S. 723 (2008).

Boyle v. United Technologies Corp., 487 U.S. 500 (1988).

Brown v. Board of Education, 347 U.S. 483 (1954).

Brown v. Entertainment Merchants Association, 564 U.S. 786 (2011).

Brown v. Plata, 563 U.S. 493 (2011).

Buckley v. Valeo, 424 U.S. 1 (1976).

Burton v. Sills, 394 U.S. 812 (1969).

Bush v. Gore, 531 U.S. 98 (2000).

Bush v. Gore, 531 U.S. 1046 (2000).

Cheney v. United States District Court, 542 U.S. 367 (2004).

Cheney v. United States District Court, Memorandum of Justice Scalia, 541 U.S. 913 (2004).

Citizens United v. Federal Election Commission, 558 U.S. 310 (2010).

City of Boerne v. Flores, 521 U.S. 507 (1997).

Clapper v. Amnesty International USA, 568 U.S. 398 (2013).

Clinton v. City of New York, 524 U.S. 417 (1998).

Coy v. Iowa, 487 U.S. 1012 (1988).

Crawford v. Washington, 541 U.S. 36 (2004).

Cruzan v. Director, Missouri Department of Health, 497 U.S. 261 (1990).

Dickerson v. United States, 530 U.S. 428 (2000).

District of Columbia v. Heller, 554 U.S. 570 (2008).

Edwards v. Aguillard, 482 U.S. 578 (1987).

Elk Grove Unified School District v. Newdow, 542 U.S. 1 (2004).

Employment Division, Department of Human Resources of Oregon v. Smith, 494 U.S. 872 (1990).

Engel v. Vitale, 370 U.S. 421 (1962).

First National Bank of Boston v. Bellotti, 435 U.S. 765 (1978).

Florida v. Jardines, 569 U.S. 1 (2013).

Friends of the Earth v. Laidlaw Environmental Services, 528 U.S. 167 (2000).

Gideon v. Wainwright, 372 U.S. 335 (1963).

Hamdan v. Rumsfeld, 548 U.S. 557 (2006).

Hill v. Colorado, 530 U.S. 703 (2000).

Humphrey's Executor v. United States, 295 U.S. 602 (1935).

J.E.B. v. Alabama, 511 U.S. 127 (1994).

Katz v. United States, 389 U.S. 347 (1967).

Kyllo v. United States, 533 U.S. 27 (2001).

Lafler v. Cooper, 566 U.S. 156 (2012).

Lamb's Chapel v. Center Moriches Union Free School District, 508 U.S. 384 (1993).

Lawrence v. Texas, 539 U.S. 558 (2003).

Lee v. Weisman, 505 U.S. 577 (1992).

Lewis v. United States, 445 U.S. 55 (1980).

Loving v. Virginia, 388 U.S. 1 (1967).

Lucas v. South Carolina Coastal Commission, 505 U.S. 1003 (1992).

Lujan v. Defenders of Wildlife, 504 U.S. 555 (1992).

Mapp v. Ohio, 367 U.S. 643 (1961).

Marbury v. Madison, 5 U.S. 137 (1803).

Maryland v. Craig, 497 U.S. 836 (1990).

Maryland v. King, 133 S.Ct. 1958 (2013).

McConnell v. Federal Election Commission, 540 U.S. 93 (2003).

McDonald v. City of Chicago, 561 U.S. 742 (2010).

McIntyre v. Ohio Elections Commission, 514 U.S. 334 (1995).
Michigan v. Bryant, 562 U.S. 344 (2011).
Miller v. *California*, 413 U.S. 15 (1973).
Minnesota v. Dickerson, 508 U.S. 366 (1993).
Miranda v. Arizona, 384 U.S. 436 (1966).
Missouri v. Frye, 566 U.S. 134 (2012).
Mistretta v. United States, 488 U.S. 361 (1989).
Monge v. California, 524 U.S. 721 (1998).
Morrison v. Olson, 487 U.S. 654 (1988).
National Federation of Independent Business v. Sebelius, 567 U.S. 519 (2012).
Navarette v. California, 134 S.Ct. 1683 (2014).
New York Times v. Sullivan, 376 U.S. 254 (1964).
Nixon v. Shrink Missouri Government PAC, 528 U.S. 377 (2000).
Nollan v. California Coastal Commission, 483 U.S. 825 (1987).
Obergefell v. Hodges, 135 S.Ct. 2584 (2015).
O'Hare Truck Service, Inc. v. City of Northlake, 518 U.S. 712 (1996).
Ohio v. Clark, 135 S. Ct. 2173 (2015).
Ollman v. Evans, 750 F.2d 970 (D.C. Cir. 1984).
Padilla v. Kentucky, 559 U.S. 356 (2010).
Planned Parenthood v. Casey, 505 U.S. 833 (1992).
Plaut v. Spendthrift Farm, Inc., 514 U.S. 211 (1995).
Pope v. Illinois, 481 U.S. 497 (1987).
R.A.V. v. City of St. Paul, 505 U.S. 377 (1992).
Reynolds v. Sims, 377 U.S. 533 (1964).
Roe v. Wade, 410 U.S. 113 (1973).
Romer v. Evans, 517 U.S. 620 (1996).
Roper v. Simmons, 543 U.S. 551 (2005).
Rutan v. Republican Party of Illinois, 497 U.S. 62 (1990).
Sherbert v. Verner, 374 U.S. 398 (1963).
Synar v. United States, 626 F. Supp. 1374 (D. D.C. 1986).
Terry v. Ohio, 392 U.S. 1 (1968).
Texas v. Johnson, 491 U.S. 397 (1989).
Troxel v. Granville, 530 U.S. 57 (2000).
United States v. Emerson, 270 F.3d 203 (2001).
United States v. Jones, 565 U.S. 400 (2012).
United States v. Miller, 307 U.S. 174 (1939).
United States v. Virginia, 518 U.S. 515 (1996).
U.S. Term Limits, Inc. v. Thornton, 514 U.S. 779 (1995).
Webster v. Reproductive Health Services, 492 U.S. 490 (1989).
Zivotofsky v. Kerry, 135 S.Ct. 2076 (2015).

Index

abortion clinics, 335
abortion rights, 229, 297, 326, 333–34
ACA. *See* Affordable Care Act
accrual of claims, 31
ADA. *See* Americans with Disabilities
  Act
Adams, John, 72
Adarand Constructors, Inc. v. Pena, 52,
  198
ADEA. *See* Age Discrimination in
  Employment Act
administrative agencies, 4–5, 14–15
administrative law: *Chevron* test in,
  5, 12; Scalia's contributions to, 2,
  296
Administrative Procedures Act, 12
AEI. *See* American Enterprise Institute
affirmative action: in *Adarand
  Constructors, Inc. v. Pena*, 52;
  conservatives invalidating, 198;
  discrimination and, 51; Equal
  Protection Clause violated by,
  333; ethnic background and,
  175–76; in higher education, 53;
  neoconservatives opposition to, 174–
  75; race-based, 137; racial injustice
  and, 54; Scalia argument against,
  175, 198; sex factor in, 34
Affordable Care Act (ACA), 13, 333

African Americans, 176
age discrimination, 21–22
Age Discrimination in Employment Act
  (ADEA), 21
agency construction, 10
age of case, 113
aggregate citations, 112
Alexander v. Gardner-Denver Co.,
  43n31
Alien Tort Statute, 97, 99
Alito, Samuel, 67, 105, 107–8, 307
alter precedence, 280
ambiguous decisions, 110–11, 113
Amendments, conceptualization of,
  241n3
American Enterprise Institute (AEI),
  161
American exceptionalism, 163, 170
American law, 101–2
Americans with Disabilities Act (ADA),
  21
amicus briefs, 281
Amnesty International, 107
anonymous speech, 335
anti-discrimination laws, 150–51, 336,
  338
Anti-Federalist, 127–28
anti-Madisonian theory, 127, 131–32,
  142–51

antimilitary animus, 30
antitrust law, 301
Apportionment Act (1842), 145
arbitration: agreements, 38; of class
    claims, 43n34; decisions, 37–39
Arizona v. Hicks, 74
Arizona v. United States, 329, 338
Arizona v. Youngblood, 87–88
*Arlington v. Federal Communications
    Commission*, 11–12
AT&T Corp. v. Portland, 10
attorney's fees, 32–33, 42n22
*Austin v. Michigan Chamber of
    Commerce*, 320

background checks, 196
bad words, *265*
Baer, Lauren E., 13
Bailey v. United States, 78–79
Baker v. Carr, 128
balancing test, 79
Balkin, Jack, 335
Barbara K. Olson Memorial Lecture,
    328
bare animus, 133, 136–37
Barnett, Randy, 203, 206
Baroody, William Sr., 161–62
Bassham, Gregory, 49
Baum, Lawrence, 277
Bazelon, 15
BCRA. *See* Bipartisan Campaign
    Reform Act
behaviors, 256; interrupting, 259–60;
    off-the-bench, 327–28; sexual,
    338–39
Benefits Review Board, 41n17
Benesh, Sara C., 276
Berger, Raoul, 168, 189
Bernzweig, Jane, 289n4
bicameral national legislature, 125
Bickel, Alexander, 51, 338
Biden, Joe, 294, 300, 303
bidirectional decision making, 238–39
bigotry, 62
Bill of Rights, 72

biological evidence, 87–88
Bipartisan Campaign Reform Act
    (BCRA), 147
Biskupic, Joan, 53, 64
Black, Hugo, 314, 332
Black, Ryan C., 102, 112, 118n11, 258,
    279
Blackmun, Harry, 58; Harry Blackmun
    Papers, 69, 86; regular concurrence
    of, 276; Scalia's interruptions
    comment of, 258, 269n9
black-robed supremacy, 230
Blackstone, 116
*Blackstone's Commentary on the Laws
    of England*, 106
Blakely v. Washington, 3, 72
Blumenthal, Richard, 299
Bolick, Clint, 166
Bond, Carol Anne, 273
Bond v. United States, 269
Bork, Robert, 160, 168, 189, 306–7;
    conservative values of, 297–99;
    failed nomination of, 295; Scalia's
    differences with, 312n9
Boumediene v. Bush, 173
Bowers v. Hardwick, 58, 59
Boyle v. United Technologies Corp.,
    333
Bozell, L. Brent, 159, 168
BP America v. Burton, 253
Bradford, Mel, 163
Brandeis, Louis, 334
Bravin, 255
Brennan, William, 69, 129, 206, 316,
    336
Brest, Paul, 167
Breyer, Stephen, 248, 308; *Chevron* test
    approaches from, 6; English common
    law used by, 105–6; foreign courts
    considered by, 108; *Hernandez v.
    Mesa* comments by, 250; number of
    words spoken of, 253–55
bright-line rules, 79, 223–25, 240
British law, 98–99
Brown, 129

Brown v. Board of Education, 157–58, 169, 176, 192, 299, 334, 337–38
Brown v. Entertainment Merchants Association, 199, 225, 232–35
Bryan, Amanda C., 265
Buchanan, Pat, 160, 181
Buckley, William F., 155, 157
Buckley v. Valeo, 343n14
Burger, Warren, 173, 293, 304, 306
Bush, George H. W., 296
Bush, George W., 1, 197, 208, 308–9
Bush v. Gore, 197, 208, 330–31, 337; Scalia's partisan tone in, 340; Scalia's role in, 1

Calabresi, Steven, 315, 342n9
Calder v. Bull, 128
Calhoun, John, 246
California v. Green, 73
Calvin, Bryan, 272
campaign finance, 143–44, 200, 343n14
Canadian experience, 118n15
capitalism, 201
capital punishment, 85–86
Cardozo, Benjamin, 316, 340n1, 341n4
Carline, Wallace, 329
Carolene Products, 47–48, 148
Carpenter v. United States, 89
Carroll v. United States, 76
Carter, Jimmy, 161
Case importance, 113
Catholicism, 63, 157
cat's paw liability, 29–30, 39, 42n18
CBA. *See* collective bargaining agreement
charter corporations, 202
Chase, Samuel, 128
checks and balances, 125–26, 132
cheek-swab search, 77–78
chemical weapons, 272
Chemical Weapons Convention Implementation Act (1998), 273
Cheney, Dick, 329
Cheney v. United States District Court, 329–30

Chevron test, 173; in administrative law, 5, 12; application of, 7–14; Breyer's approaches to, 6; congressional delegation proof and, 8; Scalia's affinity for, 5–6; statutory ambiguity of, 6–14; Supreme Court refusing application of, 13; Thomas applying, 10
children, protection of, 199–200, 232–33
Chisholm v. Georgia, 128, 208–9
Christensen v. Harris County, 7
Christianity, 158
Church of Holy Trinity v. United States, 180
church-state doctrine, 177–81
Circuit court citations, 112
circuit court conflict, 111, 113
citation patterns, 110
citation rates, 114
Citizens United v. Federal Election Commission, 206, 321; campaign finance in, 200; corporate democracy in, 150; free expression in, 202–3; Kennedy, A., writing opinion on, 146–47
City and County of San Francisco v. Sheehan, 247
City of Richmond v. J.A. Croson Company, 176, 198
civility, 324
civil liability, 204–5
civil rights, 166, 171, 300
Civil Rights Act (1964), 159, 174
Civil Rights Act (1991), 31
class actions, 20, 35–37
class claims, arbitration of, 43n34
Clay, Henry, 248
Clean Air Act, 4, 12
Clement, Paul, 243
Clinton, Bill, 258
Clinton, Hillary, 159, 310
"The Code of a Gentleman" (booklet), 57
cognitive complexity, 280–81, 289, 289n4

Coleman-Liau Index, 280
colleagues: interruptions to, 259, *259*;
    Scalia criticizing, 63–64, 323–24
collective bargaining agreement (CBA),
    31
Collins, Paul M. Jr., 274, 277, 281
Colorado constitution, 133
color-blind justice, 174, 199
Commentaries on the Constitution of
    the United States (Story), 318
Commerce Clause, 171, 197
common law, 83, 241, 242
communities, homosexuality
    disapproval in, 136
comparator evidence, 22
concurring opinions, 274–75; criticizing
    dissent with, 278; dissenting opinions
    importance to, 286; empirical testing
    of, 288; end of term, 287–88; federal
    legislation struck down by, 287;
    ideological reasons for, 279–80, 287;
    of justices, *285*; majority opinions
    clarity from, 280–81, 289; of
    O'Connor, 324–25; oral arguments
    discussing, 276; regular concurrence
    and, 275–76; Scalia's frequency of,
    282–83; special concurrence and,
    275; of Thomas, 283; written regular,
    284–87
confirmation hearings, 293–94,
    298–303; change in, 305–6; elite
    polarization and, 307–9; Gorsuch,
    310; justices with unanimous,
    306; number of exchanges in, *302*;
    Rehnquist's battle in, 304–5
Confrontation Clause, 88–89, 322;
    Court's interpretation of, 324;
    Scalia's interpretations of, 335;
    violation of, 73
confrontations, 97, 324
Congress, 8–9, 195–97, 282, 309
Connick v. Thompson, 87
The Conscience of a Conservative
    (Bozell), 159

consensus, foreign law establishing,
    106–8
consequentialists, 96, 98
conservatism, 155–56; affirmative
    action invalidated by, 198; of
    Catholicism, 157; *National Review*
    reversal of, 172; originalism as
    political, 180; traditional, 162–64
conservatives: affirmative action
    invalidated by, 198; Bork and values
    of, 297–968; of Goldwater, 162;
    legal movement, 182; Reagan with
    power of, 165, 296–97; textualism
    approach of, 190
Constant, Benjamin, 140
Constitution: as color blind, 50; foreign
    courts interpreting, 96–97; foreigners
    in foreign countries and, 329;
    gerrymandering limits from, 149;
    government actions limited by, 129;
    homosexual sodomy in, 59; judicial
    review conceptualizing, 220–21; as
    law of land, 194; Living, 48, 105,
    193–94, 220–21, 332–33; Oklahoma,
    94; originalism uncovering meaning
    of, 205; weaker citizen protections
    of, 48
constitutional controversies, 335–36
constitutional doctrine, 130–31
constitutional interpretation: English
    common law in, 94–97; foreign law
    in, 93–94; framers intentions in, 189,
    317–18; natural law principles in,
    211; originalism method of, 207–8,
    221–22; original-meaning approach
    to, 209; Scalia's approach to, 321–
    22; texts original meaning for, 95
constitutional law, 96
constitutional politics, 125–26, 143,
    147–48; anti-Madisonian theory of,
    131–32; Ginsburg, R., using theory
    of, 127; in Supreme Court, 128–31
constitutional rights, 58–59, 138
Constitution Restoration Act, 117n5
content discrimination, 139

Contract Clause, 210–12
convictions, wrongful, 86
copyrights laws, 101
Corley, Pamela C., 274, 277, 279
corporate democracy, 150
corporations: campaign financing of, 200; charter, 202; electoral outcomes and expenditures of, 146–47; legislatures chartering, 201–2; Michigan, 145; speech regulations of, 322
corruption, 142–44, 147–50
court ideology, 119n19
Court of Appeals, 10
Coy v. Iowa, 73
Craig v. Boren, 56
Crawford, Jan, 326
Crawford v. Washington, 320, 322, 324
creationism, 335
crimes, unsolved, 78
criminal justice, 67–68, 89
criminal penalties, 107
cross-examination, 303
cruel and unusual punishments, 68–73, 99–101, 333
Cruzan v. Missouri Department of Health, 278–80
cultural insensitivity, 58
Curry, Brett, 110
Cushing, William, 209

Dahl, Robert, 141
DAL. *See Dictionary of Affect in Language*
days until term ends, 282
death penalty, 53, 85–86, 335; Eighth Amendment and, 106–7; foreigners views on, 99; foreign law and, 100; on juveniles, 100
decency, standards of, 99
decision making: bidirectional, 238–39; Model 2, 219, 238; originalism factor in, 238–39; SCP role in, 237; textualism setting boundaries for, 95

Declaration of Independence, 140–41, 176, 263
Defense of Marriage Act (DOMA), 60–61
democracy: abortion rights in, 229; corporate, 150; courts role in, 140; judge-made law not coexisting with, 224; majoritarian, 231–32, 234; in North Carolina, 268n1; representative, 127; same-sex marriage in, 141; Supreme Courts threat to, 231
Democracy and Distrust (Ely), 142
democratic bargain, 141
Democratic Party, 159, 162, 301–303
democratic politics, 135, 145
democratic process, 142–48
dependent variables, 278
destructive factions, 129–30
Detention Treatment Act, 329
Dickerson v. United States, 325
Dictionary of Affect in Language (DAL), 251–52, 269n6
Dionne, E. J., 332
Director, Office of Workers' Compensation Programs, Dep't of Labor (the Director) v. Newport News Shipbuilding and Dry Dock Company, 28–29
discrimination: affirmative action and, 51; age, 21–22; anti-discrimination laws and, 150–51, 336, 338; content, 139; Equal Protection Clause and minority, 34; Fourteenth Amendment protections of, 48–49; gender, 64; of race, 23, 41n9, 51, 53, 64, 85–86; religious, 25–26, 39; religious practice and, 138; reverse, 51; sex, 22, 27–28, 299; viewpoint, 139. *See also* employment discrimination; intentional discrimination
"Disease as a Cure" (Scalia), 175
dissenting opinions, 276; concurring opinions criticizing, 278; concurring opinions importance of, 286;

constitutional controversies with, 335–36; foreboding, 325; number of, 280; of Roberts, 61; Scalia enjoying, 326; of Stevens, 179

District court citations, 112

District of Columbia, 82

District of Columbia v. Heller, 191, 194, 225; Federalist Society articles cited in, 342; individual rights to bear arms in, 318; originalism in, 81–82, 241; prefatory and operative clauses in, 226

diversity, 53, 57

DNA evidence, 77

DOMA. *See* Defense of Marriage Act

domestic legislation, 97

double jeopardy clause, 97–98

Dred Scott v. Sandford, 341

drunk drivers, 81

due process, 87, 97, 333

Due Process Clause, 108, 335

due process liberty rights, 230

Duvall, Gabriel, 210

Dworkin, Ronald, 49

Eastern Airlines, Inc. v. Floyd, 96

education, 53, 57, 319

EEOC v. Abercrombie & Fitch, 25

Eighth Amendment: cruel and unusual punishments in, 68–73, 99–101; death penalty and, 106–7; law enforcement techniques and, 75; life-without-parole from, 107; originalism in, 70–73; torture not covered in, 342n12

Elauf, Samantha, 25–26

elections, 223

electoral outcomes, 146–47

electronic eavesdropping, 83–84

Eleventh Amendment, 202, 333

elite polarization, 307–9

elitists, 60

Elmbrook School District v. Doe, 311

Ely, John Hart, 142

emotional language, 251–52

empirical tests, 288

employer liability, 30

employment, 35–37, 41n12, 42n21

employment discrimination, 19, 40n5, 40n7; attorney's fees in, 32–33; class actions limited in, 20; *McDonnell Douglas* Test in, 20–21; *Oncale* opinion on, 27–28; rights, 38; statutory text adherence in, 39; in Title VII, 34

Employment Division v. Smith, 137

energy policy group, 342n11

Engel v. Vitale, 337

English common law: Alito citing, 105; Breyer using, 105–6; in constitutional interpretation, 94–97; false statements in, 98; foreign countries practicing, 113; foreign law and, 115; liberal justices relying on, 105–6; references to, *105*; Thomas citing, 104–5; for unreasonable search and seizures, 116

Entick v. Carrington, 76

Epps, Garrett, 49

Equal Justice Under Law, 84–85

equal protection cases, 197–99

Equal Protection Clause, 47–48, 325, 331, 335–38; affirmative action violating, 333; broad and expansive language of, 49; gender discrimination and, 64; homosexuality in, 58–59; intentional discrimination in, 55–56; minority discrimination and, 34

equal protections: of Fourteenth Amendment, 47; from O'Connor, 60; race and, 50; Scalia voice for regression of, 63; of women, 56–58

equal rights, for homosexuality, 140

Ervin, Sam, 168

Eskridge, William N., 13

Establishment Clause, 206, 319, 335, 337; destructive factions and, 129–30; *Lemon v. Kurtzman* test of, 177–80

Estelle v. Gamble, 70
ethnic background, 175–76
European Convention, 116
European Court of Human Rights, 100
euthanasia, 101
evidence, 22, 77, 87–88
evidentiary decision, 36–37
executive power, 173–74
external lived lives, 236–37
Ezell, Trevor W., 15

face-to-face confrontation, 322
faculty advisor, 166–67
faint-hearted originalist, 68, 192, 205–6, 222
Fair Housing Act (1968), 174
Fair Labor Standards Act (FLSA), 41n16
false statements, 98
Farganis, Dion, 301
FCC. *See* Federal Communications Commission
FEC v. Wisconsin Right to Life, 253
Feder, David, 15
federal authority, 163
Federal Communications Commission (FCC), 10
federal drug laws, 171
federal government, 128–29
federalism, 128, 170–73
Federalist Society, 155, 296, 308; articles cited from, 342; Calabresi founding of, 315; faculty advisor of, 166–67; legal scholarship in, 342n10; rule of law and, 169–70; Scalia's association with, 327–28, 340
federal judiciary, 327
Federal Labor Standards Act, 7
federal legislation, 287
Federal Rule of Civil Procedure 23, 35–36
fee-shifting provision, 33
Feldman, Stephen, 182
female employees, 34
female flight attendants, 33

Fifteenth Amendments, 145
Fifth Amendment, 60–61, 108, 333
fighting words, 139
firearms: background checks for, 196; *District of Columbia v. Heller* and rights to, 320; individuals right to bear, 81–82, 225, 334; militia, 82; musket-type, 83; regulation of, 81–84
firefighters, 31
First Amendment, 69; common law tradition toward, 240; free speech in, 130; originalist counterpoint to, 234–35; school prayer in, 297; speech to minors and, 200; Thomas's comments on understanding, 233–34; violent video games and, 232–33
Fix, Michael P., 276
flag desecration cases, 206–7
Florida Supreme Court, 197–98, 331
Florida v. Jardines, 76–77, 84
FLSA. *See* Fair Labor Standards Act
Food and Drug Admin. v. Brown & Williamson Tobacco Corp., 13
foreign countries, 113, 117n5
foreign courts, 96–97, 101, 104, 108–9
foreign enemy combatants, 327
foreign law: American law with embedded, 101–2; citation rates and impact of, *114*; consensus establishment and, 106–8; in constitutional interpretation, 93–94; in constitutional law, 96; death penalty and, 100; English common law and, 115; judicial hierarchies perceptions of, 109–11; justices referencing, 103; limiting use of, 98–99; references to, *102*, 117n1; Refugee Conventions meaning from, 117n6; Scalia's impact on citing, 115; Scalia's principles on, 94–101; sources of, 118n18; Supreme Court citing, 102–3, 110–12; from textualism, 95
foreign legal sources, 96

foreign practices, 107–8
formalism, 225
forthcoming responses, 301, 303
founding-era sources, 234
Fourteenth Amendment, 176;
    discrimination protections of, 48–49;
    equal protections of, 47; judicial
    overreach and, 234; majoritarian
    politics and, 136–37; moral
    principles from, 49; Privileges or
    Immunities Clause of, 191–92; racial
    discrimination and, 64; same-sex
    marriage and, 61–62, 105, 231;
    Scalia's comment on, 336; Scalia's
    mixed record on, 73–81; Scalia
    voice for regression and, 63; women
    protections in, 56
Fourth Amendment: cheek-swab search
    and, 77–78; individual rights in,
    88–89; original meaning in, 80;
    police authority in, 81; privacy
    preservation of, 75–76, 79; reckless
    driving in, 80; Scalia's opinions
    concerning, 89; stop-and-frisk in,
    333; technology reshaping, 75–76;
    trained police dogs under, 76–77;
    unsolved crimes and, 78
framers' intentions, 189, 211, 317–18
Francisco, Noel, 151
Frankfurter, Felix, 296
Freedmen's Bureau, 176
Freedom of Information Act, 300
freedom to govern themselves, 141
free-expression cases, 199–203
free-market economy, 201
free speech, 144–45, 232–35, 241n6;
    in First Amendment, 130; foreign
    courts in, 108; oral arguments on,
    301–62; rights, 104; viewpoint
    discrimination in, 139
Free Speech Clause, 140, 335
Friedman, David, 265

Gallagher, Maggie, 155
Gallant, Jack L., 289n4

Garland, Merrick, 295, 310
gay marriage. *See* single-sex marriage
gay rights, 59, 62, 326, 338
gender, 55–58
gender discrimination, 64
general civility code, 27
gerrymandering, 145–46, 149–50
Gill v. Whitford, 150, 276
Gilmer v. Interstate/Johnson Lane, 37
Ginsburg, Douglas, 306
Ginsburg, Ruth Bader, 308;
    constitutional political theory used
    by, 127; republican principles appeal
    of, 126–27; verbosity of, 255; VMI
    admitting women opinion of, 56
*Glickman v. Wileman Brothers & Elliott
    Inc.*, 262
Glossip v. Gross, 106
Goldman, Sheldon, 341
Goldwater, Barry, 155–56, 158–60, 162
Gonzales v. Raich, 171–72, 197
good words, 266, *267*
Gore, Al, 197
Gorsuch, Neil, 14, 89–90, *255*, 294–95;
    confirmation of, 310; justices
    behavior and, 256; as originalists,
    212; Scalia as model justice to, 212;
    straw man argument of, 150; as
    textualist, 116; Trump nominating,
    310
*Government by Judiciary: The
    Transformation of the Fourteenth
    Amendment* (Berger), 168
graduation ceremonies, 335
Graham v. Florida, 107
Gramm-Rudman-Hollings deficit-
    reduction law, 297
Great Society programs, 169
Greenburg, Jan Crawford, 71
Greene, Jamal, 53, 58, 62, 65
Greenhouse, Linda, 268n1
greenhouse gases, 12
Gressman, Eugene, 250
Grimms' fairy tales, 261–62
Gruenfeld, Deborah H., 289n4

Grutter v. Bollinger, 53
Guantanamo Bay, 329
Gutierrez-Brizuela v. Lynch, 15

Hague Convention on the Civil Aspects
    of International Child Abduction,
    103–4
Halbig v. Sebelius, 13
Halter v. Nebraska, 207
Hamdan v. Rumsfeld, 14, 173, 329
Hamilton, Alexander, 128, 143,
    171–72
Hansford, Thomas G., 119n19
Harlan, John, 73, 334
Harrington, Michael, 161
Harris v. Forklift Systems, Inc., 41n11
Harry Blackmun Papers, 69, 86
Haynes, Myrlinda, 273
*Heart of Atlanta Motel Inc. v. United
    States*, 171
Heller, Dick, 82
Herrera v. Collins, 86–87, 278
higher education, 53, 57
Hill, Anita, 308
Hitt, Mathew P., 112–13
Hobby Lobby case, 64
Hodel v. Irving, 253
Holland v. Illinois, 85
Hollis-Brusky, Amanda, 155–56, 328
Holmes, Oliver Wendell, 130, 333
homosexuality: anti-discrimination
    laws on, 150–51; community moral
    disapproval of, 136; equal rights
    for, 140; political power of, 134–35;
    religious objections to services for,
    150–51; Scalia's views on, 299;
    sexual behaviors and, 338–39;
    single-sex marriage and, 236;
    sodomy and, 58–59, 100. *See also*
    same-sex marriage
Horowitz, Michael, 165
Horowitz Report, 165–67
hostile questions, 265
hostile work environment (HWE), 26
Hudson v. McMillian, 71–72

human life, value of, 116
Human Rights Watch, 107
humor, in oral arguments, 261–63
Humphrey's Executor v. United States,
    336
HWE. *See* hostile work environment

Idaho law, 108
identity-based groups, 135
ideological reasons, 277–78, 280, 285,
    301
Illinois v. Cabelles, 76
Immigration Act, 332
immigration law, 97–98, 331–32
impartiality, 340
Imperial Judiciary, 229
incremental jurisprudence, 224
*Independent Federation of Flight
    Attendants v. Zipes*, 33, 39
individual rights, 67, 77; to bear
    firearms, 81–82, 225, 334; *District
    of Columbia v. Heller* and, 320; in
    Second Amendment, 82–83, 88,
    227–28, 334; in Sixth Amendment,
    88–89
In re Davis, 87
institutional-policy rationale, 223
INS v. Cardoza Fonseca, 6
INS v. Chadha, 250
intellectual entrepreneur, 156
intentional discrimination: cat's paw
    liability and, 29–30; employer
    liability in, 30; in Equal Protection
    Clause, 55–56; *McDonnell Douglas*
    Test determining, 23–24; seniority
    rules in, 32
internal legal principles, 236–37
International Child Abduction Remedies
    Act, 103
international treaty, 273
interracial marriage, 341n17
interruptions: behavior of, 259–60;
    Blackmun's comment on, 258,
    269n9; to colleagues, 259, *259*; by
    justices, 248–50, *260*; Rehnquist

rebuking, 258; Scalia and serial, 257–61

Jaffa, Harry, 170, 176
Jay, John, 209
J.E.B. v. Alabama, 55–56
Jefferson, Thomas, 72, 171, 177
Johnson, Lyndon B., 159
Johnson, Timothy R., 258
Johnson, William, 210–11
Johnson v. Transportation Agency, Santa Clara County, 34
Judeo-Christian tradition, 178–79
judge-made law, 224
judicial activism, 133–34, 294
judicial decisions, 117n5, 193
judicial hierarchies, 109–11
judicial magnum opus, 191
judicial opinions, 220, 223–24, 318–19, 339
judicial overreach, 234
judicial publications, 316–18
judicial restraint, 296
judicial review, 113, 220–21
judicial temperament, 323–27
jurisprudence, incremental, 224
jury selection, 107
jury trial, right to, 322
justices: bad and good words spoken by, *267*; characteristics of good, 341n2; common-law, 239; concurring opinions of, *283*; desire to influence of, 109–11; emotional language of, 251–52; English common law and reliance of, 105–6; foreign law referenced by, 103; Gorsuch and behavior of, 256; interruptions by, 248–50, *260*; liberal, 105–6; linguistic categories of, *266*; lower court decisions influence on, 109–10; number of turns of, *257*; number of words spoken of, *257*, *259*; oral argument breaks taken by, 269n3; oral arguments words spoken of, *256*, 256–57, *267*; Scalia as influential,

320; Scalia changing culture of, 259–60; serial interruptions of, 257–61; speaking turns of, 253; transcripts of, 251–52; unanimous confirmation hearings of, 306; utterances per case of, *255*; verbosity of, 252–57; workload considerations of, 279; written regular concurring opinions of, *284*. *See also* Supreme Court justices
juveniles, death penalty for, 100

Kagan, Elena, 264, 309, 315, 320–21
Kassow, Benjamin J., 276
Kasten v. Saint-Gobain Performance Plastics, Inc., 41n16
Katzenbach v. McClung, 171
Katz v. United States, 84, 342n12
Kemp, Jack, 166
Kendall, 255
Kennedy, Anthony, 58, 307–8; *Citizens United v. Federal Election Commission* opinion of, 146–47; criminal penalties evaluation of, 107; DOMA invalidated by, 60–61; electoral outcomes opinion of, 146–47; foreign courts referenced by, 104, 109; as Living Constitution proponent, 48; *McDonnell v. U.S.* comments of, 249–50; political speech suppression opinion of, 200; Scalia's acerbic opinions of, 325–26; unanimous confirmation of, 306; warrantless seizures opinion of, 78–79
Kennedy, Ted, 298–99, 304
Key, Francis Scott, 248
Kilpatrick, James, 168
King v. Burwell, 13
Kirk, Russell, 172
Kirkpatrick, Jeane, 165
Klein, Diane, 15
Korematsu v. United States, 129
Kristol, Irving, 161–63, 165
Kulturkampf, 132, 134–35, 137

Kyllo v. California, 75

Lafayette, Marquis de, 132
landmark decision, 336
Later reversed case, 113
laughter, during oral arguments, 263–64, *263–64*
law enforcement techniques, 75
law professors, 49, 295
Lawrence v. Texas, 59, 100, 225, 229, 338
laws: administrative, 2, 5, 12, 296; American, 101–2; anti-discrimination, 150–51, 336, 338; antitrust, 303; British, 98–99; common, 83, 241, 240; constitutional, 96; copyrights, 101; employment discrimination, 34; Equal Justice Under, 84–85; federal drug, 171; Gramm-Rudman-Hollings deficit-reduction, 297; Idaho, 108; immigration, 97–98, 331–32; judge-made, 224; rule of, 95, 169–70, 172–73, 193, 206, 223. *See also* English common law; foreign law
Lawson, David, 342n10
Laxalt, Paul, 303
Lazarus, 255
LCM. *See* legal conservative movement
Lechner, Steven J., 265
Lee v. Weisman, 178, 297, 319
legal concepts, 236
legal conservative movement (LCM), 155–57, 164, 165–67, 182–83
legal liberalism, 177
legal principles, 240
legal scholarship, 342n10
legislative intent, 317
legislatures, 125, 201–2, 221
legitimate, non-discriminatory reasons (LNRs), 21, 23
Lemon v. Kurtzman, 177–80
length of service, 316–18, 339
Lesbian, Gay, Bisexual, and Transgendered (LGBT), 58–62, 64–65

lethal injection, 106
Lewis v. City of Chicago, 31
LGBT. *See* Lesbian, Gay, Bisexual, and Transgendered
liberal agenda, 49
liberalism, 105–6
liberty of ancients, 140
liberty of contract doctrine, 331
life-without-parole, 107
Lincoln, Abraham, 170
linguistic categories, *266*
Linguistic Inquiry and Word Count (LIWC), 252, 281
Little, 265
Living Constitution, 105, 193–94, 220–21; Kennedy, A., proponent of, 48; Scalia's beliefs on, 332–33
LIWC. *See* Linguistic Inquiry and Word Count
LNRs. *See* legitimate, non-discriminatory reasons
Lochner v. New York, 129
Look Policy, 25–26
Lorance v. AT&T Technologies, Inc., 31
Loving v. Virginia, 176, 343n17
lower court decisions, 109–10
lowess smoothing line, 118n12
Lowi, Theodore, 142
Lucas v. South Carolina Coastal Commission, 322
Lujan v. Defenders of Wildlife, 323
Luther v. Borden, 126

Madison, James, 78, 131, 171, 319; bicameral national legislature needed by, 125; checks and balances principles of, 132; representative democracy and, 127
majoritarian democracy, 233–35, 236
majoritarian processes, 230–31
majority opinions: concurring opinions for clarity of, 278–80, 287; ideological distance from, 280; options after, 275; in Second Amendment, 239–40

Maltzmann, Forrest, 277, 279
Mandatory cases, 113
Marbury v. Madison, 300, 317
marijuana, 197
market metaphor, 130
marriage, 61, 108, 343n17
Marshall, John, 172, 173, 210, 334
Marshall, Lloyd, 15
Marshall, Thurgood, 53, 69; campaign
    contributions opinion of, 143; racial
    bias permitted assertion of, 85;
    Thomas replacing, 198
*Marvin M. Brandt Revocable Trust v.
    U.S.*, 265
Maryland v. King, 74, 77
*Masterpiece Cakeshop v. Colorado
    Civil Rights Commission*, 151
A Matter of Interpretation (Scalia), 317
Maveety, Nancy, 274
McCleskey v. Kemp, 53, 85
*McConnell v. Federal Election
    Commission*, 323
McCreary County v. ACLU of Kentucky,
    179–80
McCreary v. ACLU, 265
McCulloch v. Maryland, 220, 249
McDonald v. City of Chicago, 105, 191,
    206, 333, 342n10
McDonnell Douglas Test, 20–21, 23–24
McDonnell Douglas v. Green, 20, 40n3
McDonnell v. United States, 249–50
McIntyre v. Ohio Elections Commission,
    101
medical needs, 70–71
Meese, Ed, 168, 189, 296
mentally retarded, 100, 333
Michigan corporations, 145
Michigan v. EPA, 12, 276
Miers, Harriet, 309
military activities, 228
military government, 126
military service, 29–30
militia, well-regulated, 82, 208, 226–28
Miller, Banks, 110
Miller test, 336

Minnesota v. Dickerson, 342n13
minorities, unequal treatment of, 85
Miranda v. Arizona, 325, 335
Missouri v. McNeeley, 81
Mistretta v. United States, 3
Model 2 decision-making, 219, 238
moral decay, 147
moral disapproval, 136
moral principles, 49
Morrison v. Olson, 3, 319
Murphy, Bruce Allen, 1, 63
musket-type firearms, 83

*National Cable & Telecommunications
    Ass'n v. Brand X Internet Services*,
    10
*National Endowment for the Arts v.
    Finley*, 276
*National Federation of Independent
    Business v. Sebelius*, 247
National Firearms Act, 82
*National Labor Relations Board v.
    Jones and McLaughlin*, 3
National Lawyers Conventions, 328
National League of Cities v. Usery, 276
national powers, 196
*National Resources Defense Council v.
    Chevron*, 2
National Review, 157–60, 162–64, 172
*National Treasury Employees Union v.
    Von Raab*, 74
natural law principles, 211
natural rights, 241n3
Navarette v. California, 74, 79
negative tone, during oral arguments,
    265–67
Nemacheck, Christine L., 312n9
neoconservatives: affirmative action
    opposition of, 174–75; as Democrats,
    162; first generation of, 161; Great
    Society programs accepted by, 169;
    Kristol as, 163; new originalism and,
    169–70; Scalia assimilating views of,
    164; traditional conservatism from,
    162–64

"Neutral Principles and Some First
    Amendment Problems" (Bork), 168
New Deal legislation, 3–4, 15
Newdow, Michael, 329
New Jersey Plan, 196
new originalism, 169–70
New York Times v. Sullivan, 336–37
New York v. United States, 195, 197
Nine-headed Caesar, 340
Nixon, Richard, 160–61
*Nollan v. California Coastal
    Commission*, 322
non-originalism, 220–21
nonsectarian prayers, 319
North Carolina, 268n1
nuclear option, 295
number of exchanges, *302*
number of turns, 253–55, *257*
number of words spoken, 253–55, *254–
    57*, 256–57, *259*

Obama, Barack, 331
Obergefell v. Hodges, 105, 108, 140,
    228–31; religious disproportionality
    in, 181–82; same-sex marriage in,
    61; Scalia's dissent in, 225, 327
obscenity, 336
O'Connor, Sandra Day, 51; concurring
    opinion of, 324–25; confirmation
    of, 296; equal protections from, 60;
    originalist approach followed by,
    195–96; prisoner rights test of, 69;
    unanimous confirmation of, 306
*O'Connor v. Consolidated Coin
    Caterers Corp.*, 21–23
Office of Telecommunications Policy,
    161
Ogden v. Saunders, 210–11
Ohio v. Clark, 324
Oklahoma Constitution, 94
Olympic Airways v. Husain, 96
*Oncale v. Sundowner Offshore Services,
    Inc.*, 19, 26–27
O'Neill, Jonathan, 167, 194
one-person, one-vote, 337

operative clauses, 226
oppression, 52
optical-scan systems, 198
oral arguments: concurring opinions
    discussed during, 276; early days
    of, 248–49; on free speech, 260–62;
    justices interruptions in, 248–50,
    260; justice's linguistic categories in,
    266; justices taking breaks during,
    269n3; justices words spoken in,
    254, 256, 256–57; laughter during,
    263–64, *263–64*; negative tone
    during, 265–67; opinions generated
    by, 251; Oyez Project on, 251;
    purpose and strategy of, 249–51;
    questions asked in, 253; Scalia's
    humor during, 261–64; Scalia
    transforming, 243–44, 320; speaking
    patterns in, 255; Supreme Courts
    role of, 244–47; Supreme Court time
    allotment for, 247–48; of Thomas,
    268
original intent approach, 190
originalism, 19, 127; Brest coining term
    of, 167; constitutional interpretation
    by, 207–8, 221–22; Constitutions
    meaning uncovered by, 205;
    decision-making factor of, 238–39;
    in District of Columbia v. Heller,
    81–82, 239; in Eighth Amendment,
    70–73; faint-hearted, 68, 205–6,
    222; First Amendment counterpoint
    from, 234–35; founding-era sources
    in, 234; historical difficulties of,
    202–5; history reliance of, 194–95;
    institutional-policy rationale for,
    223; landmark decision and, 334;
    new originalism and, 169–70;
    non-originalism and, 220–21;
    O'Connor following approach
    of, 195–96; as original meaning
    approach, 190, 315; perfect opinion
    of, 241n1; personal viewpoints
    in, 225; as political conservatism,
    180; as politically neutral, 207;

politics of, 205–8; protection from
criticism of, 340; refinement of,
192; rule of law commitment to,
172–73, 206; Scalia's approach to,
321–22; Scalia's defense of, 339;
Scalia's first foray in, 168; Scalia's
justification for, 193–95; Scalia's
reference to, 80; Second Amendment
and Scalia's, 83; Supreme Court and,
192
"Originalism: the Lesser of Two Evils"
(Scalia), 317
original meaning, 209, 321; for
constitutional interpretation,
95; in Fourth Amendment, 80;
originalism and, 190, 313; Scalia
and discovering, 191; in textualism,
224–25
Otis, Lee Liberman, 167, 342n9
Overton v. Bazzetta, 71–72
Owens, Ryan J., 289n4
Oyez Project, 251

Paine, Thomas, 223
Panaro, Vince, 157
Parker, 268
parties, intent of, 103–4
partisan opinions, 330–31, 340
past cooperation, 281
payroll deduction, 108
Peckham, 129
Pennebaker, James W., 289n5
Perez v. Mortgage Bankers Association,
12
perjury prosecutions, 98
personal viewpoints, 225
PFC. *See* prima facie case
Phillips, Carter, 243
Pierce, Richard, 2
Pinkney, William, 248
Planned Parenthood v. Casey, 101, 225,
228–30
plea bargaining, 335
Pleasant Grove City v. Summum, 276
Plessy v. Ferguson, 129, 334

Podhoretz, Norman, 163, 174
police authority, 81
police dogs, 76–77
police investigations, 78
political power, of homosexuality,
134–35
politics: corruption in, 147, 149–50;
democratic, 135, 145; first
appointment in, 160–61; neutral
stance on, 207; of originalism,
205–8; speech on, 200. *See also*
constitutional politics
populist tone, 181
Positive foreign law reference, 112–13,
115
Posner, Richard, 15, 203, 332
post-conviction review, 86–87
Postratification Commentary, 227
Powell, Lewis, 50, 69, 304
power grab, 208
Precedent altering, 113
prefatory clauses, 226
Presentment Clause, 333
Presidential election, 2016, 310
Preston, Jared, 289n4
Prevention of Significant Deterioration
(PSD), 21
prima facie case (PFC), 21–22, 40n3
Printz v. United States, 101, 126, 195
prisoner rights, 69–71
prison populations, 109
privacy, 75–76, 79, 300, 312n8
private markets, 169
Privileges or Immunities Clause,
191–92
probit regression model, 285
proof of falsity, 24
protected speech, 233
provincialism, 93, 115
Pryor, William, 80
PSD. *See* Prevention of Significant
Deterioration
publications, judicial, 316–18
public easement, 322
The Public Interest (Kristol), 162

public meaning, 168–69
public nudity, 60
public schools, 178, 335, 338
punch-card ballots, 198

quid pro quo, 150

race, 151; affirmative action based
on, 137; bias based on, 85, 304;
classification by, 50; discrimination
of, 23, 41n9, 51, 53, 64, 85–86;
entitlement based on, 52; equal
protections and, 50; injustice, 54,
137; issues of, 85; preferences of,
54; Scalia's insensitivity to, 86;
segregation by, 140
rape, 77
Rauh, Joseph L., Jr., 301
R.A.V. v. St. Paul, 138
readability scores, 280, 289n3
Reagan, Ronald, 1, 155, 165, 293,
296–97
Reagan Revolution, 308–9
reasonable-person method, 192, 204
reckless driving, 80
Reconstruction Amendment, 151
recusal requests, 328–30, 340
Reddick, Malia, 276
*Reeves v. Sanderson Plumbing Products
Inc.*, 23–24
Refugee Conventions, 117n6
*Regents of University of California v.
Bakke*, 175
regression models, OLS, 113
regular concurrence, 275–76
Rehnquist, William, 69; confirmation
battle of, 304–5; interruptions rebuke
by, 258; nomination of, 293–94;
Scalia criticizing, 325
religion: discrimination by, 25–26,
39; disproportionality of, 181–82;
freedom of, 64, 104; homosexuality
objections from, 150–51;
nondiscriminatory practice of, 138;

repression of, 134; Title VII and
practices of, 25–26; traditions of, 180
Religious Freedom Restoration Act
(RFRA), 343n15
Rent-A-Center v. Jackson, 20, 38
representative democracy, 127
Republican Guaranty Clause, 126
Republican Party: civil rights of, 166;
confirmation questions by, 301–303;
nuclear option used by, 295; Scalia
supporting, 311n2; Virginia, 149;
white ethnic, 160
republican principles, 126–27
retaliation, 29, 41n13, 41n16
reverse discrimination, 51
Reynolds v. Sims, 128, 337
RFRA. *See* Religious Freedom
Restoration Act
Ricci v. DeStefano, 34
Richmond v. J.A. Croson Co., 51
right of confrontation, 97
rights-protecting opinions, 76, 78
right to jury trial, 322
right to privacy, 300
Ring, Kevin S., 47, 50
Roberts, John, 54; Bush, G. W.,
nominating, 308–9; dissent opinion
of, 61; gerrymandering case of,
149; political corruption opinion of,
149–50; same-sex marriage argument
of, 108; verbosity of, 253
Rockefeller, Nelson, 159
Roe v. Wade, 101, 229, 297–98, 324,
334–35
Romer v. Evans, 58, 133, 140, 148, 338
Roper v. Simmons, 100
Rose, Charlie, 311
Rosen, Jeffrey, 258, 265
Rossum, Ralph A., 48
rule of law, 95, 223; Federalist Society
and, 169–70; judicial decisions in,
193; originalism commitment to,
172–73, 206

same-sex marriage, 140, 325, 327, 336; in democracy, 141; Fifth Amendment and, 60–61; Fourteenth Amendment and, 61–62, 105, 231; homosexuality and, 236; *in Obergefell v. Hodges*, 61; proponents of, 61; Roberts argument against, 108; traditional marriage compared with, 61. *See also* marriage

same-sex sexual harassment, 19, 26–28

same-sex sodomy, 338

Samuel, Ian, 62

Scalia, Anthony. *See specific topics*

Scenic America, Inc., v. Department of Transportation, 15

Schechter Poultry v. United States, 3

school prayer, 297

Schuette v. Coalition to Defend Affirmative Action by Any Means Necessary, 64

Schultz, David A., 54, 63, 66

SCP. *See* social construction process

search and seizures, 74, 78–79, 116

Second Amendment: gun regulations in, 81–84; individual rights in, 82–83, 88, 227–28, 336; majority opinions on, 239–40; military activities in, 228; militia's firearms in, 82; pre-existing right of, 226; Scalia re-characterizing, 88; Scalia's originalists conclusions about, 83; state control in, 333; textualist interpretation of, 227

Securities Act, 99

Segal, Jeffrey A., 277

segregation, 140, 337–38

seizures. *See* search and seizures

self-defense, 82

Senate Judiciary Committee, 294, 298, 300, 305

seniority rules, 32

seniority system, 42n21

separation of powers, 125–26, 297, 319; administrative agencies and, 4–5; Brennan and, 128; congressional

ambiguity and, 9; Fifteenth Amendments and, 145; legal standing of, 323; Scalia's support of, 3, 6

serial interruptions, 257–61

sex, affirmative action factor of, 34

sex discrimination, 22, 27–28, 299

sexual behaviors, 338–39

sexual harassment, 19, 26–28

sexual orientation, 58–59, 62, 133

Shelby County v. Holder, 54, 64, 65n2

Shephard's Citations, 112

Sherbert v. Verner, 337

Silent Majority Strategy, 160

Simon, Paul, 303

single-sex education, 57, 319

single-sex marriage, 236, 325, 327, 336

Sixth Amendment: Confrontation Clause violation of, 73; individual rights in, 88–89; right to jury trial in, 322; trial by jury violation of, 72, 85, 97

Skidmore test, 9

Skidmore v. Swift & Company, 4

Skinner v. Oklahoma, 129

slavery, 50, 52, 54, 201

Smith, Christopher E., 54, 63, 66

social construction process (SCP), 235–39

social movement, 155

sodomy, 59, 100, 336

Songer, Donald R., 274

Sosa v. Alvarez-Machain, 99

Sotomayor, Sonia, 106, 255, 268, 309

Souter, David, 8–9, 308

Spaeth, Harold J., 277

speaking patterns, 255

special concurrence, 275

Specter, Arlen, 303

speech: anonymous, 335; corporate regulations of, 322; to minors analysis, 200; on politics, 200; protected, 233; unprotected, 138. *See also* free speech

speedy trial right, 106

Spriggs, James F., II, 119n19, 277, 279
Spyer, Thea, 60
Staab, James B., 54, 173
Stansbury v. California, 258
state crimes, 273
state sovereign immunity, 202
state supreme court, 276
statue of limitations, 31–32
statutory ambiguity, 6–14
statutory interpretation, 274
statutory language, 321
statutory text, 39
Staub v. Proctor Hospital, 29
Stevens, John Paul, 4, 14, 69; military
    activities reading of, 228; national
    powers and, 196; *Van Orden*
    dissenting opinion of, 179
St. Mary's Honor Center v. Hicks, 19,
    21, 23–24, 39
Stone, 141
stop-and-frisk, 333
Stop the Beach Renourishment,
    Inc. v. Florida Department of
    Environmental Protection, 105
Story, Joseph, 172, 180, 210, 226, 318
straw man argument, 150
Sullivan v. Everhart, 6
Sunstein, Cass, 2, 13
Supreme Court: argument time allotted
    in, 247–48; balance of power in,
    311; *Chevron* test application
    refused by, 13; Confrontation Clause
    interpretation of, 322; constitutional
    politics in, 128–31; democratic
    threat of, 231; external lived lives
    of, 236–37; Florida Supreme Court
    overruled by, 197–98, 329; foreign
    law cited by, 102–3, 110–12;
    gerrymandering cases of, 150;
    internal legal principles of, 236–37;
    legal concept application of, 236;
    oral arguments role in, 244–47;
    oral arguments time allotment of,
    247–48; originalism and, 192;
    recusal rules of, 330; retaliation

cases in, 41n13; Scalia nominated to,
    168; Scalia's appointment to, 160;
    Scalia's departure from, 256; Scalia's
    federalism on, 172; Scalia's impact
    on, 1–2; Scalia's Model 2 decision
    making in, 219; Scalia's verbosity in,
    252–57; SCP role in decision making
    of, 237; state, 276; Thomas ignoring
    precedent of, 241n6; transnational
    judicial dialogue used by, 116–17;
    unidirectional models of, 235
Supreme Court Historical Society, 326
Supreme Court justices: *Arlington*
    disagreements of, 11–12; great, 316;
    length of service, 316–18; major law
    changes by, 334–39; recusal requests
    by, 328–30
surveillance, 83
suspect classification, 137
Synar v. United States, 3

Taft, William Howard, 173
Takings Clause, 105, 333
Talbot, Mary, 64
Taney, Roger Brooke, 126, 340n1
Tarrien, David, 12
Tauscik, Yla R., 289n5
technology, 75–76, 84
Teles, Steven, 155
temperament, 63–64, 323–27, 339–40
Ten Commandments, 265
Tenth Amendment, 195–97
Terry v. Ohio, 340n13
Tetlock, Philip E., 289n4
Texas v. Johnson, 206
text readability scores, 280, 289n3
textual clarity, 289
textualism: conservative approach
    of, 190; criminal justice and, 89;
    decision-making boundaries in, 95;
    dictionary-centered, 203; foreign
    law from, 95; Gorsuch use of, 116;
    legislature intent and, 221; original
    meaning in, 224–25; prefatory and
    operative clauses and, 226; Scalia

advocate for, 47–48, 67–68, 320–21;
Second Amendment interpretation
by, 227; technological change in, 84
Thirteenth Amendment, 50
Thomas, Clarence, 67, 317; *Chevron*
test applied by, 10; concurring
opinions of, 283; diversity
questioned by, 53; English
common law cited by, 104–5; First
Amendment understanding comment
of, 233–34; Hill relationship with,
308; Marshall, T., replaced by, 198;
oral argument of, 268; as originalists,
212; Privileges or Immunities
Clause discussed by, 191–92; Scalia
criticizing, 324; speech to minors
analysis of, 200; Supreme Court
precedent ignored by, 241n6; traffic
stops opinion of, 79–80
Thompson, Smith, 210
Thompson v. North American Stainless,
28
Thurmond, Strom, 298, 300, 307
Title VII: in *Alexander v. Gardner-
Denver Co.*, 43n31; attorney's fees
authorized in, 32–33; employment
discrimination law in, 34; religious
practices in, 25–26; same-sex sexual
harassment under, 19, 26–28; statute
of limitations of, 31–32; UEP and,
28; zone of interests of, 28–29
Tonsor, Stephen, 163–64
torture, 342n12
Totenberg, Nina, 255
Town of Greece v. Holloway, 297
toxic chemicals, 274
traditional conservatism, 162–64
traditional marriage, 61
traffic stops, 79–80
transnational dialogue, 93
transnational judicial dialogue, 116–17
treaty, international, 273
Treaty Clause, 273
treaty interpretation, 103–4
trial, right to speedy, 106

trial by jury violation, 72, 85, 97
Trimble, Robert, 210–11
Truman, David, 142
Trump, Donald, 89–90, 159, 295, 310
*Tulsa Professional Collection Services,
Inc. v. Pope*, 258
Turner, Charles C., 274
Turner v. Safley, 69
Tushnet, Mark, 54, 63
The Two Faces of Federalism (Scalia),
171

UEP. *See* unlawful employment practice
Uniformed Services Employment
and Reemployment Rights Act
(USERRA), 29–30
United States, 117, 180. *See also*
American exceptionalism; American
law
United States v. Booker, 3
United States v. Eichman, 207
United States v. Gaudlin, 98
United States v. Jones, 76
United States v. Lopez, 197
United States v. Mead Corp, 8
United States v. Miller, 82
United States v. Virginia, 55–56, 58,
319, 325
United States v. Windsor, 60, 107–8,
225, 230
University of Chicago Law School, 165
unlawful employment practice (UEP),
28
unreasonable search and seizures, 116
*U.S.A., Inc. v. Natural Resources
Defense Council, Inc.*, 4
USERRA. *See* Uniformed Services
Employment and Reemployment
Rights Act
*United States v. Little Lake Misere Land
Co.*, 275
United States v. Seeger, 179
Utility Air Group v. the EPA, 12

Van Orden v. Perry, 179

verbosity, of justices, 252–57
video games, violent, 199–200, 232–33, 261–63
Vieth v. Jubelirer, 146, 276
viewpoint discrimination, 139
violent video games, 199–200, 232–33, 261–63
Virginia Military Institute (VMI), 56–58, 65n1, 335
Virginia Plan, 196
Virginia Republican Party, 149
virtue, 142–43, 147
VMI. *See* Virginia Military Institute
Voting Rights Act, 54, 65n2

Wahlbeck, Paul J., 277
Walker v. Texas Division, Sons of Confederate Veterans, 276
Wal-Mart, employment policies of, 35–36
Wal-Mart Stores, Inc. v. Dukes, 20, 35–37
War on Terror, 342n12
warrantless search and seizures, 74, 78–79
Warren, Earl, 316
Warsaw Convention, 96
Washington, Bushrod, 210–11
Washington v. Glucksberg, 101, 230
Waterhouse v. Hopkins, 27
Wattenberg, Ben, 162
Way, Lori Beth, 274
wealthy elites, 145
Weaver, Richard, 172
Webster, Daniel, 248–49
Webster v. Reproductive Health Services, 324

Wechsler, Herbert, 157–58
Wedeking, Justin, 258, 279, 301
Weidenbaum, Murray, 165
well-regulated militia, 82, 208, 226–28
Wesberry v. Sanders, 126
West, Sonja R., 274
West Virginia, et al. v. EPA, 1
Whissell, 251, 269n7
White, Byron, 69
Whitman v. American Trucking Association, 276
"Why I Am Not a Neoconservative" (Tonsor), 164
Wickard v. Filburn, 171
wildlife conservation group, 323
Wilkinson, J. Harvie, III, 334
Williams v. Illinois, 106
Wilson, James, 128
Wilson v. Seiter, 70
Windsor, Edith, 60
wiretapping program, 342n12
women, 56–58
words: bad, *267*; fighting, 139; good, 266, *267*; number of spoken, 253–55, *254–57*, 256–57, *259*; unpleasant, 266, *267*
workload considerations, 279
Wright v. Universal Maritime Service Corp., 37
written regular concurring opinions, *284–87*

Youngstown Sheet & Tube Co. v. Sawyer, 274

Zelman v. Simmons-Harris, 276
zone of interests, 28–29

About the Contributors

David Schultz is a Hamline University professor of political science who teaches across a wide range of American politics classes including public policy and administration, campaigns and elections, and government ethics. He is also a professor of law at the University of Minnesota, where he teaches election law, state constitutional law, and professional responsibility. A three-time Fulbright scholar who has taught extensively in Europe, and the winner of the national Leslie A. Whittington award for excellence in public affairs teaching, David is author/editor of over thirty books and one hudnred-plus articles on various aspects of law, government, ethics, and American politics, including coauthoring in 1996 the first published book—*The Jurisprudential Vision of Justice Antonin Scalia*—assessing Scalia's impact on the Supreme Court. Professor Schultz is regularly interviewed and quoted in the local, national, and international media on these subjects including the *New York Times, Wall Street Journal, Washington Post, The Economist*, National Public Radio, *La Nouvelle Observateur, L'Express, Der Spiegel, Verdens Gang*, and *To Vima*. His most recent books are *American Politics in the Age of Ignorance: Why Lawmakers Choose Belief over Research* (2013), *Election Law and Democratic Theory* (2014), and *Presidential Swing States: Why Only Ten Matter* (2015).

Howard Schweber joined the University of Wisconsin Political Science Department in 1999. Schweber teaches courses focusing on constitutional law and legal and political theory. He is the author of *Democracy and Authenticity* (2012); *The Language of Liberal Constitutionalism* (2007); *The Creation of American Common Law* (2004); and *Speech, Conduct, and the First Amendment* (2003); as well as articles, essays, and book chapters on a variety of related topics. His current areas of research include comparative constitutional law and democratic theories of representation. In addition to his position in the Political Science Department, Schweber is an affiliate faculty member of the Law School, the Legal Studies Program, and Integrated Liberal Studies. From 2011 to 2013 he was visiting professor and the first vice provost for academic affairs at Nazarbayev University in Kazakhstan, and in 2012 he was the Australian Fulbright Distinguished Chair in American Politics.

Mary Welek Atwell recently retired from Radford University where she was a professor of criminal justice. She has published four books dealing with legal subjects: *Equal Protection of the Law? Gender and Justice in the United States* (2002); *Evolving Standards of Decency: Popular Culture and Capital Punishment* (2004); *Wretched Sisters: Examining Gender and Capital Punishment* (2007; 2nd ed., 2014); *An American Dilemma: International Law, Capital Punishment, and Federalism* (2015); as well as numerous articles and reviews. She holds a PhD from Saint Louis University. She is currently at work on a book dealing with sexual harassment.

Ryan C. Black is associate professor of political science at Michigan State University and a faculty affiliate with the MSU College of Law. His research focuses on U.S. Supreme Court decision making. He has published two books with Cambridge University Press and one with the University of Michigan Press. He has also published over forty articles or chapters in a variety of peer-reviewed political science journals (e.g., *American Journal of Political Science, Journal of Politics*), peer-reviewed interdisciplinary journals (e.g., *Journal of Empirical Legal Studies*, Journal of Law and Courts), and law reviews (e.g., *Georgetown Law Journal*). His work has also been funded by the National Science Foundation.

Henry L. Chambers Jr. is a professor at the University of Richmond School of Law, has taught and written for over two decades in various areas of law, including employment discrimination, constitutional law, criminal law, white collar crime, and voting rights. His recent employment discrimination scholarship includes: "The Problems Inherent in Litigating Employer Free Exercise Rights," 86 *University of Colorado Law Review* 1141 (2015); "Reading Explicit Expansions of Title VII Narrowly," 95 *Boston University Law Review* 781 (2015); "The Cost of Non-Compensable Workplace Harm," 8 *FIU Law Review* 317 (2013); "The Wild West of Supreme Court Employment Discrimination Jurisprudence," 61 *South Carolina Law Review* 577 (2010). Chambers has been a member of the American Law Institute since 2002, and served as a part of the Members' Consultative Group for the ALI's Restatement of Employment Law.

Gerard Michael D'Emilio is a judicial term clerk in the United States District Court for the Western District of Oklahoma. He received his JD from the University of Oklahoma College of Law in 2018, his MM in Voice from Westminster Choir College in 2014, and his BA with highest honors in Politics and BM in Voice from Oberlin College in 2012. Prior to law school, he was a professional opera singer, working with such companies as Minnesota Opera, Gotham Chamber Opera, and the Glimmerglass Festival.

Alexander Denison is a PhD candidate and instructor at the University of Kentucky working in the areas of judicial politics, law, political behavior, and American institutions. A journalist by training, Alex worked in media for several years as a television reporter and anchor, news editor, radio host, and columnist. His research now focuses predominantly on the media's role in capturing Supreme Court activities and the subsequent effects these portrayals have on public perceptions of the Court. Recent research projects include coauthored studies (with UK professors Dr. Justin Wedeking and Dr. Michael Zilis) into how Supreme Court justices' negative rhetoric in opinion content shapes news coverage of decisions, and whether news content adequately emphasizes the content of opinions. His research can be found or is forthcoming in *Social Science Quarterly, Michigan State University Law Review,* and *Elon Law Review.*

Stephen M. Feldman is the Jerry W. Housel/Carl F. Arnold Distinguished Professor of Law and adjunct professor of political science at the University of Wyoming. He has published numerous articles and books, including *The New Roberts Court, Donald Trump, and Our Failing Constitution* (2017); *Neoconservative Politics and the Supreme Court: Law, Power, and Democracy* (2013); *Free Expression and Democracy in America: A History* (2008); *American Legal Thought from Premodernism to Postmodernism: An Intellectual Voyage* (2000). His writings have been translated into Japanese, Chinese, and Portuguese. He was a visiting scholar at Harvard Law School during the fall 2016 semester.

Charles F. Jacobs, PhD, is associate professor of political science at St. Norbert College. His research on law and the U.S. Supreme Court has appeared in such outlets as *Law and Human Behavior* and *Santa Clara Law Review.* His current research is a collaborative effort with St. Norbert professors of political science Dave Wegge and Wendy Scattergood that explores the public's preference and perception of the selection of judges to state courts. Additionally, Jacobs continues his work on the policy-making capacity of state courts in the arena of public school integration. He has also conducted research on the doctrinal perspectives of Justice Stephen Breyer of the U.S. Supreme Court regarding the rights of the criminally accused under the Constitution.

Timothy R. Johnson is Morse Alumni Distinguished Professor of political science and law at the University of Minnesota, past coeditor of the *Law and Society Review*, and a nationally recognized expert on U.S. Supreme Court oral arguments and decision making. He is the coauthor of *Oral Arguments and Coalition Formation on the U.S. Supreme Court*, coeditor of *A Good Quarrel*; and author of *Oral Arguments and Decision Making on the U.S. Supreme Court*. His research appears in a variety of academic journals including the *American Political Science Review*, *Journal of Politics*, *Law and Society Review*, *Political Analysis*, *Political Research Quarterly*, *American Politics Research*, *University of Illinois Law Review*, and *University of Minnesota Law Review*. In addition, his research and commentary have been covered by *The Economist*, *The Guardian*, *New York Times*, *Washington Post*, NPR, *MPR*, C-SPAN, *Slate*, *USA Today*, ABC, CNN, and the *National Journal*.

Ronald Kahn is the Erwin N. Griswold Professor of Politics emeritus at Oberlin College. He received his BA from Rutgers and his MA and PhD from the University of Chicago. He is a specialist on constitutional law, legal theory, and American political development. He has completed two books, *The Supreme Court and Constitutional Theory, 1953–1993* and *The Supreme Court and American Political Development* (with Ken I. Kersch). He is completing a book entitled *Constructing Individual Rights in a Conservative Age: The Supreme Court and Social Change in the Rehnquist and Roberts Court Eras* (forthcoming). Kahn has published numerous articles in political science journals and law reviews. He also has contributed chapters to books in various publications published by University of Chicago Press, Routledge, CQ Press, University Press of Kansas, and Little Brown. Kahn received the Distinguished Teaching and Mentoring Award from the Law and Courts Division of the American Political Science Association in 2006.

Christopher Krewson is a PhD candidate in the Department of Political Science at the University of Wisconsin-Madison. Starting in July 2018, he is thrilled to join Claremont Graduate University as an assistant professor in the Department of Politics and Government. Christopher's research is based in American politics, with a focus on judicial politics, political institutions, and political behavior. His dissertation examines how Supreme Court justices impact public perceptions on and off the bench.

Jesse Merriam is assistant professor of political science at Loyola University Maryland. He specializes in legal theory (focusing on the rule of law), constitutional law (focusing on church-state law), and the role of social movements in creating legal change (focusing on the legal conservative movement). Dr. Merriam received his JD from The George Washington University Law School in 2005, his MA in philosophy from Johns Hopkins University in 2012, and his PhD in political science from Johns Hopkins University in 2014. Merriam has published over ten articles in law-review and peer-reviewed journals. He is currently writing a book on the history and trajectory of legal conservatism.

Ryan J. Owens is professor of political science at the University of Wisconsin-Madison and is the director of the Tommy G. Thompson Center on Public Leadership. He also enjoys an affiliate status with the law school and is an Honorary Fellow in the Institute for Legal Studies. Owens studies judicial politics and American political institutions. Dr. Owens's work has appeared in the *American Journal of Political Science*; *Journal of Politics*; *Political Research Quarterly*; the *Georgetown Law Journal*; the *William & Mary Law Review*; the *University of Illinois Law Review*; *Law and Society Review*; and the *Journal of Law and Courts*. He has also published two books.

Christopher E. Smith, JD and PhD, is professor of criminal justice at Michigan State University. His primary research interests are judicial policymaking, the U.S. Supreme Court, court processes, and constitutional rights in criminal justice, especially prisoners' rights. He is the author or coauthor of over twenty books, including *The American System of Criminal Justice* (13th ed. 2013); *Constitutional Rights: Myths and Realities* (2004); *Law and Contemporary Corrections* (2000); and *Courts and the Poor* (1991). He is also the author of over one hundred scholarly articles that have been published in such journals as *Berkeley Journal of Criminal Law*, *Criminal Justice Studies*, *Criminal Justice Policy Review*, *Journal of Contemporary Criminal Justice*, *Justice System Journal*, and *Boston University Public Interest Law Journal*.

James Staab is a professor of political science at the University of Central Missouri. He received his BA from Roanoke College, his JD from the University of Richmond, and his PhD from the University of Virginia. His primary area of specialization is public law, broadly defined, including American constitutional law, civil rights and liberties, judicial politics, criminal procedure, comparative constitutional law, and jurisprudence. He has authored or co-authored articles or book chapters on various Supreme Court justices, including Levi Woodbury, Benjamin Cardozo, and Antonin Scalia. In 2006, he published a book on Justice Scalia titled *The Political Thought of Justice Antonin Scalia: A Hamiltonian on the Supreme Court* (Rowman & Littlefield). He is currently working on a book tentatively entitled *The Limits of Constraint: The Originalist Jurisprudence of Hugo Black, Antonin Scalia, and Clarence Thomas*. He received the Governor's Award for Excellence in Education in 2012 and the Byler Distinguished Faculty Award from the University of Central Missouri in 2014.

Maureen Stobb is an assistant professor of political science at Georgia Southern University. She researches and teaches in the area of public law. After receiving her Juris Doctorate from the University of Notre Dame Law School in 2002 and practicing immigration law for several years, she obtained her PhD in political science from the University of Texas at Dallas in 2015. Her research focuses on understanding the development of legal doctrine in U.S. appellate courts, focusing on the factors influencing judges in determining the applicable rules and standards to apply in each case, and how those rules and standards are interpreted by lower courts. Her primary areas of specialization are constitutional law, immigration law, and international law. Her published work focuses on the implementation and impact of international law. She is currently working on a study of immigration law on the U.S. Courts of Appeals.

Justin Wedeking is an associate professor of political science at the University of Kentucky. He researches and teaches in the areas of judicial behavior and decision making, Supreme Court confirmation hearings, oral arguments, and the role of courts in American society. He received his PhD from the University of Minnesota in 2007. His dissertation, titled, "Elite Framing and Supreme Court Decision Making," examines how legal actors frame arguments and make decisions. His research has been published in the *American Journal of Political Science*; *Journal of Politics*; *Law and Society Review*; *Journal of Law and Courts*; *American Politics Research*; *Justice System Journal*; *Judicature*; *Journal of Elections*; *Public Opinion, and Parties*; *Michigan State Law Review*; *Hofstra Law Review*; the *Loyola Law Review*, as well as multiple chapters in edited books. He has also coauthored three books: *Oral Arguments and Coalition on the U.S. Supreme Court: A Deliberate Dialogue* (2012); *Supreme Court Confirmation Hearings in the U.S. Senate: Reconsidering the Charade* (2014); and *U.S. Supreme Court Opinions and Their Audiences* (2016). His research has been covered by the *New York Times*, PBS, NPR, *SCOTUSBlog*, *McClatchy Newspapers, Miller-McCune*, and *CQ Weekly* among others.

CPSIA information can be obtained
at www.ICGtesting.com
Printed in the USA
BVHW04*0848260718
522423BV00003B/7/P